INCLUSIVE STATES

NEW FRONTIERS OF SOCIAL POLICY

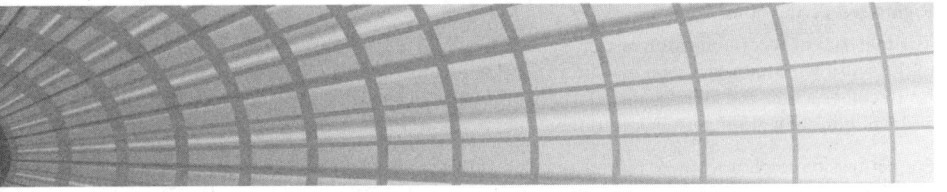

INCLUSIVE STATES

SOCIAL POLICY AND STRUCTURAL INEQUALITIES

Anis A. Dani and Arjan de Haan, Editors

THE WORLD BANK

© 2008 The International Bank for Reconstruction and Development / The World Bank

1818 H Street NW
Washington DC 20433
Telephone: 202-473-1000
Internet: www.worldbank.org
E-mail: feedback@worldbank.org

1 2 3 4 11 10 09 08

This volume is a product of the staffs of the International Bank for Reconstruction and Development / The World Bank and the Department for International Development of the U.K. The findings, interpretations, and conclusions expressed in this volume do not necessarily reflect the views of the Executive Directors of The World Bank or the governments they represent.

The World Bank does not guarantee the accuracy of the data included in this work. The boundaries, colors, denominations, and other information shown on any map in this work do not imply any judgement on the part of The World Bank concerning the legal status of any territory or the endorsement or acceptance of such boundaries.

Rights and Permissions

ISBN: 978-0-8213-6999-9
eISBN: 978-0-8213-7000-1
DOI: 10.1596/978-0-8213-6999-9

Cover photo: Women in Indonesia wait to vote on election day; Chris Stowers/Panos.

Cover design: Naylor Design, Washington, D.C.

Library of Congress Cataloging-in-Publication Data
Inclusive states : social policy and structural inequalities / edited by Anis A. Dani and Arjan de Haan.
     p. cm.—(New frontiers in social policy)
  Includes bibliographical references and index.
  ISBN 978-0-8213-6999-9—ISBN 978-0-8213-7000-1 (electronic)
  1. Social policy. 2. Developing countries—Social policy. 3. Structural adjustment (Economic policy)—Social aspects. I. Dani, Anis A. (Anis Ahmad) II. Haan, Arjan de.
  HN18.3.I545 2008
  320.60917'24—dc22

                                                                                    2008011425

In many developing countries, the mixed record of state effectiveness, market imperfections, and persistent structural inequities has undermined the effectiveness of social policy. To overcome these constraints, social policy needs to move beyond conventional social service approaches toward development's goals of equitable opportunity and social justice. This series has been created to promote debate among the development community, policy makers, and academia and to broaden understanding of social policy challenges in developing country contexts.

The books in the series are linked to the World Bank's Social Development Strategy. The strategy is aimed at empowering people by transforming institutions to make them more inclusive, responsive, and accountable. This involves the transformation of subjects and beneficiaries into citizens with rights and responsibilities. Themes in this series will include equity and development, assets and livelihoods, and citizenship and rights-based social policy, as well as the social dimensions of infrastructure and climate change.

Other titles in the series:

- *Assets, Livelihoods, and Social Policy*
- *Institutional Pathways to Equity: Addressing Inequality Traps*

Anis A. Dani
Series Editor
Adviser, Social Policy

CONTENTS

PART II. STRUCTURAL INEQUALITIES AND POLICY EXPERIENCE

PART III. INCLUSIVE INSTITUTIONS

BOXES

FIGURES

TABLES

This series—New Frontiers of Social Policy—aims to promote social development through systematic attention to the underlying social context and the social outcomes of development interventions and public policy. It compels the reader to think of social policy in terms of increasing access to productive assets, infrastructure, and goods and services; strengthening governance and accountability; enabling the rights and obligations of citizens to promote equitable access to development opportunities; and managing the social dimensions of conflict, natural disasters, and climate change. In doing so, it recognizes the central role of social policy in ensuring that development policies and programs are sustainable.

This book series has been conceived and produced for the broader development community, rather than for social policy specialists alone. This book places particular emphasis on, and attempts to overcome, the underlying causes of structural inequalities—whereby social groups based on ethnicity, race, tribe, gender, or cultural differences are systematically disadvantaged compared with other groups with which they coexist. These inequalities prevent many developing countries from realizing their full potential and may undermine the sustainability of development outcomes.

This book examines a variety of public interventions including affirmative action, targeted and tailored programs, and institutional reforms for more inclusive social policy with enhanced opportunities for indigenous peoples, women, cultural minorities, or other disadvantaged groups. The studies reveal the shortcomings of universal social policies in overcoming the barriers of structural inequality and draw attention to the enormous cost that these inequities place on society in terms of retarded development and increased risk of social instability and conflict. Overcoming structural inequality requires public policies, institutions, and programs that are inclusive, responsive, and accessible. Such policies should provide all citizens with the means to claim their rights, the opportunity for upward mobility, and the ability to participate in sustainable development.

This book points to the centrality of effective states as the proponent, administrator, and regulator of public policy, and by extension, social policy. In many developing countries this central role is undermined by weaknesses in state capacity, which in turn affects social development outcomes. Building implementation capacity of public institutions is therefore crucial. However, the analysis also indicates that deep-seated inequities cannot be overcome by state intervention alone. While public actions can create enabling conditions for upward mobility, these legal and institutional reforms and programs need to be reinforced by social movements and partnerships with the private sector and civil society for them to be sustainable.

Katherine Sierra
Vice President
Sustainable Development Network

Putting the "Social" Back in Public Policy—New Frontiers of Social Policy

The history of social development is as ancient as the history of human-kind. What sets *Homo sapiens* apart from other living organisms is their self-awareness, which allows them to evolve not just through natural selection but also through a process of social selection to develop more efficient and more acceptable ways of ordering and reorganizing their lives. Social selection allowed them to *accumulate knowledge* and become more efficient producers; *transfer knowledge* across time and space to enable reproduction and eventual dominance of the planet by the human species; *establish institutions* with predictable rules to govern their lives; *exercise choice* to explore new ideas, new places, and new modes of live-lihoods; and *reorder social relationships* between individuals and groups of individuals that constitute human societies. In doing so, these societies continuously go through a process of social development.

The Context

The discourse on "New Frontiers of Social Policy" was inspired by a pro-cess of dialogue and inquiry initiated at the Social Development Advisers Network (SDAN), held in Stockholm in January 2004. Participants at the SDAN meeting felt that with the 10th anniversary of the 1995 World Sum-mit for Social Development (WSSD) fast approaching, 2005 would be an opportune year to take stock and consider how to reinvigorate the global consensus on the set of social development commitments agreed to at the WSSD.[1] A second impetus came from the approval of the World Bank's (2005) social development implementation plan (Social Development Strategy), which seeks to mainstream social development across World Bank activities. These two strands were brought together at the follow-up SDAN meeting in Washington, DC, in February 2005, where agreement was reached to organize a conference to review the conceptual underpinnings of social policy and debate how to further the goals of the WSSD.[2]

The WSSD is a useful starting point for a discussion of social policy because it galvanized the attention of the world and succeeded in reaching consensus on a set of global commitments on social development. By 2000, however, the WSSD goals had morphed into the revamped global consensus on the Millennium Development Goals (MDGs). Through a well-developed theory of human development and immense resources, policy makers as well as multilateral and bilateral donors have supported the development of human capital assets at an unprecedented scale. A comparison of the MDGs with the WSSD commitments is therefore instructive (see table 1). The MDGs contain increased commitments for (a) eradicating poverty, (b) social sector provisioning (especially education and health), (c) promoting gender equality, and (d) ensuring environmental sustainability (providing clean drinking water and improving the lives of 100 million slum dwellers). What remains unexplained is why several key WSSD commitments, where performance was lagging, were discretely excluded from the MDGs without any discussion on the pros and cons of doing so.

Although there is more progress on goals such as education, primary health care, and, to a lesser extent, poverty reduction and gender equity, the report on the WSSD by the United Nations (UN) secretary general (United Nations 2005) recognizes significant gaps, particularly in employment (or livelihoods), social integration, and creation of an enabling environment— defined as improving the economic, legal, political, and institutional environment for sustained social development. A WSSD scorecard prepared for the 2005 SDAN meeting in Washington, DC (see table 1) mirrors the UN's findings and indicates that the only goals likely to be achieved, at least globally, are those in the sixth commitment on provision of primary education and primary health care, with some uneven progress across different countries on poverty reduction and gender equality.

Employment

There is growing recognition that without attention to employment, the MDGs will not be able to eradicate poverty. Having let the topic of

Table 1. Mapping of MDGs against WSSD Commitments

WSSD commitments	WSSD scorecard	MDGs
To create an economic, political, social, cultural, and legal environment that will enable people to achieve social development	– – –	
To eradicate absolute poverty by a target date to be set by each country	+/–	1. To eradicate extreme poverty and hunger
To support full employment as a basic policy goal*	– – –	
To promote social integration on the basis of the enhancement and protection of all human rights	– –	
To achieve equality and equity between women and men	+/–	2. To promote gender equality and empower women
To attain universal and equitable access to education and primary health care	+ +	3. To achieve universal primary education 4. To reduce child mortality 5. To improve maternal health 6. To combat HIV/AIDS, malaria, and other diseases
To accelerate the development of Africa and the least developed countries	–	
To ensure that structural adjustment programs include social development goals	– –	
To increase resources allocated to social development	–	
		7. To ensure environmental sustainability
To strengthen cooperation for social development through the United Nations	+	8. To develop a global partnership for development

Sources: World Summit for Social Development commitments: http://www.un.org/esa/socdev/wssd/agreements/index.html; WSSD Scorecard: adapted from Dani 2005; Millennium Development Goals: http://www.un.org/millenniumgoals/.

Note: WSSD scorecard indicates likelihood of achieving goals rated on a six-point scale (+ + + to – – –); a score of +/– indicates wide disparities among countries.

employment as a serious, monitorable goal drop during the discussion of the MDGs,[3] the UN's Department for Economic and Social Affairs has belatedly promoted expansion and improvement of opportunities for employment as a key component of social development. In 2006, the Economic and Social Council (ECOSOC) of the United Nations decided that the theme for the 2007–08 review and policy cycle by the Commission for Social Development[4] would be "Promoting Full Employment and Decent Work for All" (Ocampo and Jomo 2008). In parallel, employment has become an important topic of policy research at the World Bank, which has introduced a dedicated multicountry work program of analytical work on employment and shared growth. Employment was also a major part of the discourse on social policy at the "Experts Meeting on Social Policies for Development in a Globalizing World," held in Kellokoski, Finland, November 1–3, 2006 (Wiman, Voipio, and Ylönen 2007). In 2005, however, it was a well-recognized gap, and very little attention was paid to the informal livelihoods of the millions of poor households in developing countries.

Social Integration

The WSSD commitment to support social integration was inexplicably left out of the MDGs in spite of recent conflicts and ethnic cleansing in Southeastern Europe and Africa in the 1990s. The experiences of countries where underlying social tensions led to civil war—such as the Democratic Republic of Congo, Rwanda, and the former Republic of Yugoslavia—is evidence that without social integration, all the gains achieved by development processes remain at risk. The post-election ethnic violence in Kenya in 2008 suggests that other developing countries with weak social integration also remain at risk. Recent scholars have pointed to violence against market-dominant minorities (Chua 2003) or ethnic minorities (Appadurai 2006) to remind us that electoral democracy alone is not a solution. In many countries, there remains a significant unfinished agenda of nation building to accommodate ethnic, cultural, or religious diversity within the framework of a nation-state.

Clearly, social integration involves a different set of challenges from the remaining MDG targets because it infringes on issues of national sovereignty and because agreement has not been reached on the role of donor agencies and national policy makers in nation building. Social integration thus deserves a more detailed discussion than is possible in this preface, and as one of the priority themes discussed in Arusha, it will be the subject of a separate book in this series on social policy and citizenship.

Structural Adjustment Programs

Until 2004, macroeconomic and structural reforms were promoted by donor agencies to ensure fiscal discipline and introduce market-oriented reforms. These reforms are widely believed to have led to a reduction in social services (UNRISD 2006), including health and education. The attention to human development in the MDGs provided international financial institutions with an effective way to transcend the criticism levied against them during the era of structural adjustment, which emphasized macroeconomic stability and fiscal discipline. Drawing on country-driven poverty reduction strategies, the Poverty Reduction Grant Facility lending financed by the International Monetary Fund is more tolerant of social sector spending and more mindful of the distributional effects of macropolicy reforms (Harris and Kende-Robb, chapter 4). The development policy operations (DPOs)[5] financed by the World Bank place much greater emphasis on the quality of public expenditures and public services, increased allocations for poverty reduction expenditures (especially on health and education), and improved governance. To the extent that one subscribes to the human development concept of social policy, this new generation of instruments for budget support—which include poverty reduction support credits and development policy grants in low-income countries and development policy loans in middle-income countries—can rightly claim to be more responsive to social policy than the preceding generation of structural adjustment lending.

However, the human development goals of the MDGs are necessary but not sufficient to achieve inclusive and sustainable development. Recent evidence from cross-country studies of mobility in and out of poverty reveals that in the absence of universal health care, health shocks are the single biggest factor driving households below the poverty line (Krishna 2007; Narayan and Petesch 2007). Studies of pro-poor growth indicate that although human capital investments are important drivers of poverty reduction, the real benefits to the poor come from high school and college education. States that invested in both secondary and tertiary education saw the greatest reduction in inequality and the greatest increases in the growth elasticity of poverty (Besley and Cord 2007: 18). It is therefore important to acknowledge the limitations of the MDGs as adequate social policy responses to the likely effects of macroreforms. Social development outcomes are not just the outcomes of explicit social (sector) policies. Social effects can arise from the manner in which macroeconomic, structural, and sectoral policies are formulated and implemented, even when the policies themselves may not appear to be social policies.

DPOs are expected to draw on analysis of the poverty and social effects of policy and institutional reforms they support so as to maximize positive effects and minimize or mitigate adverse effects. Considerable evidence now shows that the effect of economic growth on poverty reduction is substantially influenced by initial inequality and changes in inequality, with the poverty reduction effect of growth being offset by rising inequality. The inequality effect is even more pronounced when the data are disaggregated into subnational groupings, because national averages mask significant variations in the regional pattern of growth (Besley and Cord 2007: 7–8). Relying on compensatory social sector services and support for the MDGs will not suffice. If the policy and institutional reforms they support are to be pro-poor, the new generation of DPOs will need to embrace a broader vision of social policy by designing reforms that fully internalize and address the distributional effects of those reforms and that pay attention to the quality and effectiveness of the institutions responsible for implementing them.

Why Were WSSD Commitments Left by the Wayside?

Despite the progress on human development, the sectoral focus of the MDGs has led to a relative neglect of the crosscutting social development commitments to create an enabling environment for social development and social integration and to support full employment. It is in these areas that significant gaps in achieving the WSSD commitments are still evident. Did the MDGs crowd out these goals? Was the replacement of the WSSD goals by the MDGs driven by the inability to articulate actionable social policies to address the crosscutting social development goals, or did this change in development priorities represent an implicit ideological shift in keeping with market-driven solutions toward greater individual responsibility for economic and social outcomes? Historically, the period after the fall of the Iron Curtain demonstrates a shift away from state-driven development, with both nation building and publicly owned economic activities going out of fashion. Even in the delivery of social services, countries increasingly moved away from universal public provisioning toward greater involvement of the private sector and an increasing introduction of citizen responsibility and user fees. The replacement of state-centered development by open polities and market-driven economics was paralleled by a loss of interest in the WSSD commitment to full employment and social integration, as well as weakened public commitments to universal social services. As a result, even in countries where the MDGs are expected to be fully achieved,[6] development policies will fall short of the more holistic social development goals of the WSSD.

Arguably, the weakness lies in social policy formulation. There has been relatively little progress in improving the overall environment for sustained social development, apart from the focused attention on improving public service delivery (see World Bank 2004). In hindsight, there appears to be a weakness in the lack of precision and conceptual articulation of the crosscutting WSSD goals themselves. Goals that are imprecise and that are not aligned with the sectoral divisions within government and donor agencies do not lend themselves easily to public action and to measurement to demonstrate progress against them.

Lack of employment or livelihood opportunities, weaknesses in the enabling environment, and lack of social integration pose high risks to social stability in developing and transitioning countries. These three themes therefore became the primary focus of the preparatory work for the Arusha conference and the empirical basis for subsequent analytical thinking and for operationalization of social development. But before considering the Arusha process, let us reflect a bit on the underlying assumptions and conceptual underpinnings of social development.

Conceptual Underpinnings of Social Development

Although there is a lack of consensus about the definition of *social development*, it is generally understood to comprise a set of objectives, including equity and social justice, which subsume objectives such as social inclusion, sustainable livelihoods, gender equity, and increased voice and participation. The principle of social justice articulated more eloquently in the *Report on the World Social Situation, 2001* (ECOSOC 2001), as the normative expression of the overarching concern with equity, most succinctly captures the essence of the WSSD and, as such, has tended to be accepted as the goal of social development. However, the acceptable standards of equity and its different manifestations in different social contexts are conditioned by the nature of the political economy and, in the 21st century, are substantially affected by transnational stakeholders in a globalized world. These processes need to be better understood before a theory of social development can be articulated.

The Search for Equity

Some see the concept of *equality* as problematic because they feel it implies equality of outcomes, whereas to others it is acceptable only as equality of opportunity and still others see it as equality of agency. With the fall of the Iron Curtain, most scholars and development practitioners have concurred that policies to achieve equitable economic outcomes, such as equality of income, are not feasible, although reducing severe inequalities, especially when they threaten social stability, remains a desirable goal. *World Development Report 2006: Equity and Development* (World Bank 2006) argues that policy makers and development agencies should focus on equality of opportunity, which has been the most common principle for public action to redress inequality and discrimination. The report recognizes the existence of inequality traps,[7] where interaction between various dimensions of inequality (wealth, power, social status) restricts economic and social mobility (Rao 2006: 11). In a similar vein, but with greater emphasis on the relational nature of inequities, Dani and de Haan (see chapter 1) argue that inequality merits deliberate policy action when it is structural (that is, when unequal status is perpetuated and reinforced by unequal relations in roles, functions, decision rights, and opportunities that are intricately bound in a web of interdependence). The existence of persistent inequality traps and structural inequality is among the most intractable challenges inhibiting social development.

For social development, the debate between equality of outcomes and equality of opportunity is a false one. The MDGs include clearly identified equitable outcomes for health and education, intermediary objectives such as gender equity, and longer-term outcomes such as environmental sustainability. Social development objectives tend to go even further in emphasizing processes of citizen voice and agency. Achieving these outcomes requires policy changes, institutional reforms, and public actions in the form of public expenditure allocations, implementation arrangements, and careful monitoring to ensure that basic social rights are accessible to all citizens, that minimum entitlements determined by the polity are achieved, and that social sustainability underpins economic and political processes. In the world of social development, there is thus much more of a continuum between the means and the ends, the processes and the outcomes. We therefore prefer *equity* as a more useful term because it helps to encapsulate equitable outcomes, when they are feasible and an agreed-upon part of the social contract; equitable opportunities, when outcomes depend partly on individual merit and effort; and equitable processes of voice and accountability. In social development discourse, these manifestations of equity are encapsulated in the term *social inclusion*.

Power Relations and Political Economy

Development processes do not occur in a vacuum. Policy choices, institutional reforms, public actions, and implementation are invariably affected by stakeholder interests and power relations. Any consideration of social development outcomes has to take account of power relations and the political economy at different levels.

The most common manifestations of political economy are poor targeting of benefits and elite capture. One of the main arguments against universal access to public services has been that public spending is badly targeted. Subsidies often tend to benefit the nonpoor rather than the poor. For example, when public education is free or heavily subsidized, as in many developing countries, children from better-off households benefit more than children of the poor. In most developing countries, when health care is free or heavily subsidized, coverage tends to be more limited and benefits urban dwellers more than rural populations. Similarly, a disproportionate amount of the subsidies for electricity and water lifeline tariffs for the lowest band of consumption, though intended for the poor, go to urban, nonpoor households. As evidence has mounted, donor agencies have pressed policy makers to improve targeting of free or subsidized services to primary education, primary health care, lower lifeline tariffs, and means-tested social assistance.

A more blatant form of political economy is elite capture. In recent years, governments have tried to overcome urban bias and spatial disparities by decentralizing public services to local governments and, in some countries, by providing resources to community groups for community-driven development. This principle of subsidiarity has been adopted on the premise that bringing services and decision making closer to beneficiaries will increase responsiveness and quality. Its success depends on the extent to which local government and community-driven development institutions are equitable or captured by local elites. The widely varying results again bring home the necessity of understanding political economy.

At the mesolevel, political economy is manifested through the persistence of group-based inequalities, such as those based on ethnicity, race, gender, or caste. Under unequal terms of engagement (that is, when power relations are unequal), equality of opportunity is insufficient and needs to be supplanted by a second principle of equality of agency (Rao and Walton 2004: 28–30) to overcome the disadvantages of group-based inequities. Kaushik Basu (2005) illustrates how community identity of individuals impedes their economic progress and argues for investing in participatory equity among disadvantaged groups to sustain economic development more effectively.

There is a growing, albeit somewhat grudging, acceptance of understanding and transforming power relations as an essential ingredient of development and poverty reduction. The renewed focus on poverty reduction as the central goal of the development community was explored in detail in the *World Development Report 2000/2001: Attacking Poverty* (World Bank 2000).[8] This report launched what would become the World Bank Group's corporate strategy based on the twin pillars of investment climate and empowerment. Later *World Development Reports* (specifically World Bank 2004, 2006) would lay out more detailed ideas on how to implement these two pillars. Similarly, the report of the UN's Commission on Human Security (2003) emphasizes two key strategies—protection and empowerment—for achieving its objective of complementing human development. Subsequent analytical work on empowerment is even more explicit about the connection between power, rights, and poverty (Alsop 2004; see also Alsop, Bertelsen, and Holland 2006).

For a variety of reasons, until recently, analysis of power relations was largely confined to the local level, as if the institutions of state were devoid of political economy. The interest in country-level sociopolitical analysis among several development agencies[9] gave rise to a new genre of studies focused more explicitly on the power relations inherent in social structures and on the ways these power relations affect governance as well as economic and social outcomes. Within the World Bank, this discussion has led to the formulation of a crosscutting strategy on Governance and Anticorruption (GAC) aimed at improving the quality of public institutions and services. Nonetheless, these efforts still view development from a state-centric perspective.

Social Policy in a Polycentric World

While historically social policy has been the purview of the state, the dynamics of stakeholder interests and the actors who can influence outcomes have changed in a manner that has made envisaging social policy solely from a state-centric perspective anachronistic. Stakeholders whose interests require a response from the state include citizens in general and organized interest groups within the country, as well as international stakeholders—donors, multinational corporations, international nongovernmental organizations, and transnational networks. These stakeholders place demands on but also contribute to—or at least influence—social policy outcomes in myriad ways. The service providers of social policy can be public or private, community or household, formal or informal. In parallel, the role of those governed by the state is also evolving from subjects governed by the state to citizens claiming their rights, fulfilling their obligations, engaging in policy debate, and holding public institutions to account. And for millions of households, it has also evolved from people beholden to a single state to migrant households operating in a transnational space, or from households confined within a physical space to households connected globally through virtual electronic networks. Social policy now operates in a truly polycentric world.[10]

A polycentric world is a logical extension of the concept of a globalized world. The principal underlying logic of globalization is the progressive integration of economies and societies. Globalization is driven by new technologies and economic relationships and by the national and international policies of a wide range of actors, including governments, international organizations, business, labor, and civil society (World Commission on the Social Dimension of Globalization 2004). The term *globalization* refers both to flows of information, commodities, people, and finance, which increasingly bring people and societies closer together, and to the policies and institutional arrangements arising out of policy choices that determine the nature of those flows. In the short run, the social effects of globalization may not be positive. Scholars and politicians alike have found it convenient to blame globalization for many of the weaknesses inherent in their societies and economies. However, if social behaviors are to be given any credence, millions of people see globalization as an opportunity rather than a constraint.

The existence of multiple stakeholder interests, multiple nodes of knowledge and influence, and an ever-increasing range of alternatives means that to be effective, social policy needs to transcend its defensive posture toward globalization. The state needs to reach out and imagine new possibilities and configurations for social policy in a polycentric world. Such an agreement would preserve the centrality of the state as the enabler, arbiter, and regulator of public action with a legitimate right to collect revenue and redistribute resources in accordance with the social contract. In a polycentric world, the state has a central role but needs to operate within a double compact (Ghani and Lockhart 2008: 193) of rights and obligations between citizens and their government, as well as between a government and the international community.[11]

Social Policy and Social Development

The divisions between (a) public and private domains and goods and between (b) public and private actions have given rise to public policy that consists of deliberative decision making and public actions to mediate the relationship between public and private spaces, rights, and responsibilities. Although the scope of public policy and the institutional choices for implementation vary across countries, at a minimum they include ensuring physical security for all citizens and noncitizens within their jurisdiction, providing public goods and services, creating an enabling environment for people to establish viable livelihoods, governing internal and external relations, raising taxes to administer society, and managing risks. Insofar as these public policies depend on structuring organizations and framing rules in ways that have distributional consequences and that influence social relationships and the rights and responsibilities of members of society, they constitute social policy.

Conventionally, social policy has been considered synonymous with government intervention to provide social services (Hall and Midgley 2004). A second generation of social policies emerged as residual social welfare in the form of safety nets, particularly to address the adverse impacts of adjustment and to help those not benefiting from market reforms. Like de Haan (2007), this book supports the extension of the traditional boundaries of social policy beyond social sectors and residual social protection toward a more holistic, developmental concept of social policy. However, because of the weaknesses of the state in many developing countries and the continued reliance of people on a multitude of nonstate institutions, this book recognizes the need to take a multicentric approach to social policy. Building on Gough and Wood's definition (2004: 22), the book defines *social policy* as a series of public policies designed to promote social development through a wide range of policy instruments, formulated and implemented by a variety of actors in a polycentric world.

In this book series, social development is envisioned as a natural complement to economic development with both intrinsic and instrumental value. Social development involves multiple levels of engagement among individuals, social groups, and society. It is achieved by strengthening the processes of (a) *inclusion* (the assets and capabilities of individuals to improve their well-being); (b) *accountability* (the capacity of social groups to exercise agency, transform their relationships with other groups, and participate in development processes); and (c) *cohesion* (the ability of society to reconcile the interests of its constituent elements, govern itself peacefully, and manage change). Social policies, then, are public policies aimed at promoting equality of opportunity to benefit individuals, equality of agency to benefit groups, and social integration to benefit entire societies and nations (adapted from Dani 2005).

The process of social policy formulation is a continuous process of self-reflection, contestation, and renewal of the policies and institutions that govern public actions and public goods. And because these policies and institutions affect them directly, members of a society have an inalienable right to exercise voice and influence over those policies, regardless of whether they choose to exercise that right or accept the prevalent social and political order as a better tradeoff than the instability arising out of policy contestations and uncertain futures. By definition, therefore, social policy consists of negotiated policy spaces that have efficacy when they are accepted as legitimate by members of a society and when they are part of an acceptable social contract. Any consideration of social policy, therefore, has to examine both the content and the process through which the social contract has emerged and is reconsidered, renewed, or refined.

The social, institutional, and political contexts in many developing countries pose dual challenges of integration. Many are still coping with difficulties of horizontal integration across sociocultural boundaries as diverse groups brought together in postcolonial nation-states struggle to coexist, while the vertical integration between state and citizens that presumes legitimacy based on an agreed-on relationship of mutual rights and responsibilities continues to be questioned. The visible manifestation of this situation is weak state institutions and poor governance, leading to a call for strengthening states through more systematic attention to a coherent framework of critical state functions (Fukuyama 2004; Ghani and Lockhart 2008). Social policies are likely to be redefined through the contestations taking place in the social, institutional, and political arenas as societies navigate the processes of horizontal and vertical integration. These changes are likely to lead to the formulation of new social contracts (a) between citizens and the state and (b) between the states and transnational actors.

The Arusha Conference

The Arusha Conference led to a reconsideration of the scope of social policy beyond the social provisioning for education, health care, and social safety nets to the formulation of social policy priorities that take account of the contexts of developing and transitioning countries. The conference focused on three WSSD commitments—employment, the institutional environment, and social integration—which had received inadequate attention in the WSSD decade and needed to be brought to the center of the social policy discourse to achieve meaningful social development. Given the predominance of the informal economy in developing countries, the theme of employment was recast to focus on assets and livelihoods. And given the enormous scope of the enabling environment, it was further disaggregated into a focus on inclusive institutions to address inequalities and institutions to address the social dimensions of infrastructure. The theme of social integration was also broadened beyond horizontal integration across social divisions to include (a) vertical integration between the state and citizens and (b) questions of legitimacy of public institutions. The contributions toward these themes are being synthesized and made publicly available through separate books in this series.

Perhaps even more important was the creative energy generated by the lateral thinking at the Arusha conference. This thinking is summarized most aptly in a statement that was drafted, debated, and issued at the concluding session. This joint conference statement lays out an agenda for action on social policy (page xxxv).

Social Policy in the Context of Developing Countries

In most developing countries, the mixed record of state effectiveness, market imperfections, and persistent structural inequities has undermined the effectiveness of social policy. The New Frontiers of Social Policy Series extends the discourse on social policy beyond conventional social service approaches, toward developmental policies and institutions for improving equality of opportunity and social justice.

Social policies are a subset of public policies that emerged originally in European nation-states. They were premised on *effective governance*: that is, a legitimated state, rule of law, well-functioning social and infrastructure services, and labor and financial markets (Gough and Wood 2004: 3). Social policy was synonymous with government intervention to provide essential social services and safety nets as instruments of social justice to sustain industrialization and the market economy.

Relatively little thought has been given to the suitability of this model of social policy for developing countries. The current focus of social policy is on social sectors and safety nets to help those left behind by market reforms. This approach has given rise to a widespread perception that social welfare measures are designed largely as palliatives to mitigate the adverse social impacts of structural reforms, rather than for developmental aims. Moreover, those social policies have been promoted while the preconditions for their efficacy—good governance and a well-functioning market economy—are themselves nonexistent.

Voices in developing countries have argued that social policy needs to promote broader developmental goals of equity and social justice, rather than be limited to social services. For that to happen, social policy needs to address two major challenges. First, initial inequities in asset endowments and power structures are often reinforced by unequal access to public institutions—a situation that perpetuates inequities unless social actors can exercise voice and agency to ensure that institutions are accountable and responsive. Second, globalization creates further inequities across countries, but it also empowers new social actors (from the private sector and civil society) and opens up new transnational and subnational spaces for policy contestation and dialogue. The challenge for social policy is to increase (a) the assets and capabilities of individuals and (b) the capacity of social actors to participate in development processes to achieve equity and social justice. For this challenge to be met, a social policy framework needs to emerge through the creation of a policy space for social action and the negotiation of a new social contract as part of a multistakeholder agreement in a polycentric world.

As stated at the outset, the social policy work program was inspired by the World Bank's Social Development Strategy, which espouses the three principles of inclusion, accountability, and cohesion. The social policy debate allows us to refine this strategy further and restate the objectives of social development as (a) the transformation of household welfare by investments in human capital and assets of the poor to promote social inclusion; (b) the transformation of institutions to make them more accessible, responsive, and accountable; and (c) the transformation of subjects into citizens capable of claiming their rights and fulfilling their responsibilities to foster social integration within society and an acceptable social contract with the state.

The social policy work program and the resulting book series has been created to encourage policy research and promote debate among the development community, policy makers, and academia and to broaden understanding of social policy challenges in developing countries. The aim of this series has been to broaden understanding of the scope of social policy and to highlight its intrinsic value as an essential, crosscutting ingredient of development that is distinct from but integrally linked to economic policy. To the extent that the books succeed in encouraging research and program innovation on the multiple dimensions or new frontiers of social policy and to the extent that they lead to a better understanding of the social dimensions of infrastructure, of climate change, and of development writ large, they will have achieved their purpose.

Anis Dani
Adviser, Social Policy
The World Bank

Notes

1. The WSSD was held in Copenhagen on March 5–12, 1995.
2. The conference on "New Frontiers of Social Policy," which convened in Arusha, Tanzania, December 12–15, 2005, was cosponsored by the World Bank, the U.K. Department for International Development, the Swedish International Development Cooperation Agency, and the governments of Finland and Norway.
3. There is a vague, unmonitorable target on youth employment under MDG 8: Develop a Global Partnership for Development. The targets under this goal read more like statements of intent to encourage a partnership and lack specific outcome indicators. The target on youth employment is equally vague: "In cooperation with developing countries, develop and implement strategies for decent and productive work for youth."
4. The Commission for Social Development is a functional commission of ECOSOC. It consists of 46 members elected by ECOSOC. Since the convening of the World Summit for Social Development in Copenhagen in 1995, the commission has been the key UN body in charge of the follow-up and

implementation of the Copenhagen Declaration and Programme of Action. The commission has taken up key social development themes as part of its follow-up to the outcome of the Copenhagen summit.

5. DPOs include loans, credits, and grants offered as budget support for policy and institutional reforms.

6. Although on aggregate there is considerable progress in achieving the MDGs, driven largely by China and India, many countries, particularly those in South Asia and Sub-Saharan Africa, are lagging and will be unable to achieve the MDGs.

7. See Bebbington and others (2008) for a discussion of different trajectories toward equitable societies.

8. The report recognizes that poverty is multidimensional and provides a framework stressing the importance of opportunity, empowerment, and security to address the nonincome dimensions of poverty.

9. See, for example, the country analytical work on power analysis by the Swedish International Development Cooperation Agency, on drivers of change by the Department for International Development of the U.K., and on country social analysis and governance assessments by the World Bank.

10. See Dani and Moser (2008) for further discussion about the implications of a polycentric world on assets and livelihoods of the poor.

11. I am grateful to Ashraf Ghani for introducing me to the concept of the double compact through his work on citizenship.

References

Alsop, R., ed. 2004. *Power, Rights, and Poverty: Concepts and Connections*. Washington, DC: World Bank.

Alsop, R., M. Bertelsen, and J. Holland. 2006. *Empowerment in Practice: From Analysis to Implementation*. Washington, DC: World Bank.

Appadurai, A. 2006. *Fear of Small Numbers: An Essay on the Geography of Anger*. Durham, NC: Duke University Press.

Basu, K. 2005. "Participatory Equity and Economic Development: Policy Implications for a Globalized World." Paper presented at the conference on "New Frontiers of Social Policy," Arusha, Tanzania, December 12–15. http://siteresources.worldbank.org/INTRANETSOCIALDEVELOPMENT/Resources/participatoryequity.pdf.

Bebbington, A. J., A. A. Dani, A. de Haan, and M. Walton. 2008. *Institutional Pathways to Equity: Addressing Inequality Traps*. Washington DC: World Bank.

Besley, T., and L. J. Cord, eds. 2007. *Delivering on the Promise of Pro-Poor Growth: Insights and Lessons from Country Experiences*. Washington, DC: World Bank and Palgrave Macmillan.

Chua, A. 2003. *World on Fire: How Exporting Free Market Democracy Breeds Ethnic Hatred and Global Instability.* New York: Anchor Books.

Commission on Human Security. 2003. *Human Security Now.* New York: United Nations.

Dani. A. 2005. "Policies for Social Development in a Globalizing World: New Frontiers for Social Policy." Discussion paper for the Technical Consultation on Social Policy, Meeting of the Social Development Advisers Network, Washington, DC, February 14, 2005.

Dani, A., and A. de Haan. 2008. "Social Policy in a Development Context: Structural Inequalities and Inclusive Institutions." In *Inclusive States: Social Policy and Structural Inequalities*, eds. Anis A. Dani and A. de Haan, 3–38. Washington, DC: World Bank.

Dani, A. and C. Moser. 2008. "Asset-Based Social Policy and Public Action in a Polycentric World." In *Assets, Livelihoods and Social Policy*, eds. C. O. N. Moser and A. Dani, 3–42. Washington, DC: World Bank.

de Haan, A. 2007. *Reclaiming Social Policy Globalization, Social Exclusion, and New Poverty Reduction Strategies.* Basingstoke, U.K.: Palgrave Macmillan.

ECOSOC (Economic and Social Council). 2001. *Report on the World Social Situation, 2001.* New York: United Nations.

Fukuyama, F. 2004. *State-Building: Governance and World Order in the 21st Century.* Ithaca, NY: Cornell University Press.

Ghani, A., and C. Lockhart. 2008. *Fixing Failed States: A Framework for Rebuilding a Fractured World.* Oxford, U.K.: Oxford University Press.

Gough, I., and G. Wood. 2004. *Insecurity and Welfare Regimes in Asia, Africa, and Latin America.* Cambridge, U.K.: Cambridge University Press.

Hall, A., and J. Midgley. 2004. *Social Policy for Development.* London: Sage Publications Ltd.

Harris, E., and C. Kende-Robb. 2008. "Integrating Macroeconomic Policies and Social Objectives: Choosing the Right Policy Mix for Poverty Reduction." In *Inclusive States: Social Policy and Structural Inequalities*, eds. A. A. Dani and A. de Haan, 97–120. Washington, DC: World Bank.

Krishna, A. 2007. "The Stages of Progress Methodology and Results from Five Countries." In *Reducing Global Poverty: The Case for Asset Accumulation*, ed. C. O. N. Moser, 62–79. Washington, DC: Brookings Institution.

Narayan, D., and P. Petesch, eds. 2007. *Moving Out of Poverty: Cross-Disciplinary Perspectives on Mobility.* Washington, DC: Palgrave Macmillan and World Bank.

Ocampo, J. A., and Jomo K. S., eds. 2008. *Towards Full and Decent Employment.* London: Zed Books.

Rao, V. 2006. "On 'Inequality Traps' and Development Policy." *Development Outreach* 8 (1): 10–13.

Rao, V., and M. Walton, eds. 2004. *Culture and Public Action.* Stanford, CA: Stanford University Press.

United Nations. 2005. "Report of the Secretary General on the World Summit of Social Development." United Nations, New York.

UNRISD (United Nations Research Institute for Social Development). 2006. "Transformative Social Policy: Lessons from UNRISD Research." Research and Policy Brief 5, UNRISD, Geneva.

Wiman, R., T. Voipio, and M. Ylönen, eds. 2007. *Comprehensive Social Policies for Development in a Globalizing World*. Helsinki: Ministry of Foreign Affairs.

World Bank. 2000. *World Development Report 2000/2001: Attacking Poverty*. Washington, DC: World Bank.

———. 2004. *World Development Report 2004: Making Services Work for the Poor*. Washington, DC: World Bank.

———. 2005. *Empowering People by Transforming Institutions: Social Development in World Bank Operations*. Washington, DC: World Bank.

———. 2006. *World Development Report 2006: Equity and Development*. Washington, DC: World Bank.

World Commission on the Social Dimension of Globalization. 2004. *A Fair Globalization: Creating Opportunities for All*. Geneva: World Commission on the Social Dimension of Globalization.

This statement was drafted by a committee of 25 participants. It was presented and debated at the closing session of the Arusha Conference (December 12–15, 2005), was subsequently revised to incorporate feedback received, and then was issued as a joint conference statement laying out an agenda for action on social policy:

In February of 2005, a large group of stakeholders—governments, donors, civil society organizations—met in New York to review progress on the commitments made at the World Summit for Social Development (WSSD) in 1995 in Copenhagen. The WSSD was an important historical moment, when the citizens and governments of the world agreed on the principles of equity and social justice as the objectives of development.

Since the WSSD, there has been a growing international consensus about the complementarity between social and economic development. We must therefore recognize that development policy is always simultaneously economic and social policy. Mainstreaming social policy involves recognizing and drawing on the social dimensions of all policies and programs.

Leading thinkers on social policy—including academics, policy analysts, practitioners, and policy makers from developing and developed countries—gathered in Arusha to discuss and debate how to foster these principles and augment existing social policies by greater attention to employment (livelihoods), social integration, and institutions.

We recognize that we have before us an enormous challenge of research, analysis, and implementation to achieve the objectives of social policy. We need to be modest about what we know, and what we do not know. And we need to remind ourselves that if we are to achieve social policy that is responsive to citizens, they need to be involved in the generation of knowledge, the debate on policy formulation, and the implementation of programs. We believe that these principles are necessary but not sufficient to achieve equitable development. There are many paths to socially desirable outcomes, and social policy should not fall into the trap of one-size-fits-all prescriptions. The manifestation of social policy principles within countries will be the result of contestations among citizens and will invariably be a compromise between what is desirable, feasible, and acceptable. This implies that policy formulation is, by definition, political.

With this in mind, we concluded that:

- The first new frontier of social policy is the transformation of subjects and beneficiaries into citizens. This implies policies that recognize and promote the universal rights and responsibilities of citizens, and strengthen the capacity of citizens to claim their rights.

  - Some of the most effective examples of progress on citizens' rights have come from alliances between the poor and other segments of society, suggesting that targeting public resources at the poor alone is not always the most effective way of empowering and building their capabilities.

- The second new frontier of social policy consists of fostering an enabling, accessible, responsive, and accountable state. This entails universal application of rule of law, and equal rights under the law for all citizens. Universal rights, however, need to be accompanied by legitimate, effective, and accountable institutions for policy formulation and implementation, with rigorous monitoring of outcomes. This implies recognizing and celebrating multiculturalism as a source of strength for societies, and supporting policies that accommodate diversity in the achievement of universal rights. And this also involves recognizing the role of power relations and creating institutional mechanisms that offer redress against power inequities.

- These two imply the third new frontier: strengthening the capacity of states to mobilize revenue from their citizens, and diminishing reliance on external aid. Domestic resource mobilization is the most effective means of enhancing citizen ownership and state accountability, and of ensuring sustainability. This presupposes a stronger enabling environment and resources for accelerated development. The international community—donors, governments, international organizations, and the private sector—will have to play their part to enable these processes.

- In the more familiar social policy terrain, such as education, health, and social protection, the implications of these new frontiers are a greater emphasis on equity outcomes, both in terms of access and quality of service.

- There are, however, new arenas that demand equal attention to social policy principles if development policy is to be responsive to citizens' needs. Concrete examples emerging from our discussions at this conference include

  - Strengthening assets and institutions to enhance market access for the poor.
  - Fostering more accessible and accountable institutions for providing infrastructure, utilities, and social services to all citizens.
  - Strengthening partnerships between public institutions and representative citizens' organizations to address the challenges of human settlements in the context of rapid urbanization and growth of urban slums.
  - Using the instrument of the law to empower the poor.

- But social policy might also be extended further, for example, to include

  - Attention to addressing the spatially induced challenges of rural areas.
  - Deploying fiscal policy to achieve economic and social development.
  - Considering the challenges of citizenship in an era of rapid globalization and international migration.

- The very rich discussions at the conference have highlighted

  - That we can learn more from analysis when cross-country comparisons are grounded in an understanding of the country context, including history, as well as social and institutional structures.
  - That the unit of analysis for social policy does not have to be the nation-state; some social policy concerns are better addressed at sub-national levels and others at trans-national levels.
  - That analysis and policy formulation can be enriched by drawing on the strengths of different disciplines and research methods, and local and global knowledge.

Participants of the Arusha Conference
December 15, 2005

Anis A. Dani is Adviser, Social Policy, in the Sustainable Development Network. An anthropologist by training, he worked on development research, on rural development projects, and in the nongovernmental organization sector in Asia prior to joining the World Bank in 1995. At the World Bank he has engaged in operational work in South Asia, East Asia, and Eastern Europe, conducting social research and managing projects. From 2000–05, he coordinated the Bank's work on social analysis, adapting it into an instrument for ex-ante, poverty, and social impact analysis of policy reforms leading to the production of *Poverty and Social Impact Analysis of Reforms: Lessons and Examples from Implementation* (with Aline Coudouel and Stefano Paternostro, World Bank 2006). He then led the Social Policy work program resulting in the book series, New Frontiers of Social Policy, and coedited *Institutional Pathways to Equity: Breaking Inequality Traps*. His research interests include social policy, social impacts of policy reforms, inequality, community-based natural resources management, and social dimensions of infrastructure. He is currently on secondment as Operations Adviser at the World Bank's Quality Assurance Group.

Arjan de Haan is Policy Analyst, Department for International Development (DFID), Beijing Office, where he manages rural development and knowledge programs and support to South-South learning. He has been Social Development Adviser at DFID since 1998, where he led the promotion of social science research, participation in Poverty Reduction Strategy Papers (PRSPs), and social protection. Subsequently, he advised on budget support and civil society programs in India, and led work on inequality in DFID's Policy Division. Since receiving his Ph.D. on labor migration in India, he has continued to publish on migration, including with Ben Rogaly, *Labour Mobility and Rural Society* (Frank Cass

2002). He worked at the Poverty Research Unit at the University of Sussex from 1996–98, where he led innovative analysis on social exclusion. During 2005–06 he was Visiting Professor at the University of Guelph. His recent books include *Reclaiming Social Policy* (Palgrave Macmillan 2007) and *How the Aid Industry Works* (Kumarian 2008).

Lynn Bennett has been Director, Social Development for the South Asia Region and Lead Anthropologist with the World Bank. She is now retired in Nepal, where she continues working as an anthropologist for the World Bank and the Department for International Development of the U.K. on issues of gender and social exclusion.

Anne-Marie Bonner previously worked in the Cabinet Office of Jamaica as Principal Director of the Policy Support Unit. She currently represents the government of Jamaica as the Consul General in Toronto, Canada.

Mayra Buvinić is Sector Director for Gender and Development at the World Bank. She was previously Division Chief for Social Development at the Inter-American Development Bank. She was a founding member and President of the International Center for Research on Women and is past President of the Association for Women's Rights in Development. She has published extensively on gender, poverty and development, health, violence, and social inclusion.

Catrine Christiansen is a Ph.D. research fellow in the Department of Anthropology, University of Copenhagen. She has conducted ethnographic fieldwork in Uganda since 1999 on religion, development, civil society, kinship, youth, and HIV/AIDS. She works toward bridging academic and applied work.

Siri Gloppen is Associate Professor of Comparative Politics at the University of Bergen and a Senior Researcher and Head of the Courts in Transition programme at the Chr. Michelsen Institute, Bergen, Norway.

Ian Gough is Professor of Social Policy at the University of Bath in the U.K. He is author, coauthor, or editor of nine books, the most recent being *Wellbeing in Developing Countries: From Theory to Research* (Cambridge

University Press 2007). He is a member of the Academy of Social Sciences and Chair of the College of Academicians.

Elliott Harris is Chief of the Development Policy Division in the Policy Development and Review Department at the International Monetary Fund. He has worked extensively on public expenditure policy issues and on African countries. He currently works on scaling up aid and donor collaboration; support for fragile states; the poverty reduction strategy approach; the Millennium Development Goals; and the Strategic Partnership with Africa.

Karin Hilmer Pedersen is Associate Professor in comparative politics at the Department of Political Science, Faculty of Social Science, University of Aarhus, Denmark.

Jeremy Holland has been a social development consultant with Oxford Policy Management since 2006. Previously he lectured in social development at the Centre for Development Studies, University of Swansea, U.K.

Martín Hopenhayn has been a Researcher since 1989 at the Economic Commission for Latin America and the Caribbean, Santiago, Chile. Previously he was professor at the Universidad de Chile (1980–98). He has published extensively on educational reforms, poverty-oriented policies, and ethnicity, among other social development issues.

Lars Johannsen is Associate Professor in comparative politics at the Department of Political Science, Faculty of Social Science, University of Aarhus, Denmark.

Caroline Kende-Robb is the Sector Manager of the Social Development Department at the World Bank. She previously worked for many years with community service organizations in Africa and was a manager in the private sector. She was the first Senior Social Development Specialist at the International Monetary Fund. She specializes in the poverty and social impacts of macroeconomic and structural policy reforms, including the poor in the policy making process, and community-driven development.

Alexandre Marc has served as Sector Manager, Social Development, for the Europe and Central Asia Region in the World Bank. In 2005 he was a visiting fellow at the Paris Centre d' Etudes et de Recherche Internationale where he undertook research on cultural identity and minorities. In 2006 and 2007 he was Director of the Roma Education Fund in Budapest, supporting the inclusion of Roma children in education.

Jacqueline Mazza is Senior Social Development Specialist at the Inter-American Development Bank and adjunct professor at Johns Hopkins University, School of International Studies. Her research interests lie in labor markets and social exclusion, and her most recent publication, co-authored with an IDB team, is *The Outsiders: The Changing Patterns of Exclusion in Latin America*.

Andrew Norton is a Lead Social Development Specialist in the Social Development Department of the World Bank. Previously, he was Head of Profession for Social Development in the U.K. Department for International Development, and a Research Fellow at the Overseas Development Institute, London.

David Recondo is Research Fellow at the Center for International Studies and Research of the National Foundation for Political Science and teaches at the Institute of Political Studies in Paris. He is working on political change and local participatory democracy in Latin America.

Dena Ringold is a Senior Economist at the World Bank. She leads operations in Argentina, Bolivia, and Chile in the areas of social policy and governance. Previously, she worked on economic and social transition in Central and Southeast Europe. In 2005 she was an Ian Axford Fellow in public policy based in Wellington, New Zealand.

Caroline Sage is a socio-legal researcher with degrees in law, anthropology, history, and film. She works in the Justice Sector Reform unit at the World Bank, focusing on integrating pro-poor justice concerns into broader development interventions.

Ken Sigrist has been working as a consultant on institutional development since he retired from the World Bank in 2000 and is now with Oxford Policy Management working on government reforms in Pakistan.

Susan Reynolds Whyte, Professor at the Department of Anthropology, University of Copenhagen, carries out fieldwork and research training in Uganda. Her work falls mainly in the areas of family, generation and gender, misfortune, health, disability, medicines, and international development.

Michael Woolcock is a Senior Social Scientist in the Poverty Team within the World Bank's Development Research Group. He is on external service leave at the University of Manchester in the U.K., where he is Research Director of the Brooks World Poverty Institute.

This book was inspired in part by discussions on inequality and equity during preparation of the *World Development Report 2006: Equity and Development*, and by discussions on transforming institutions to make them more inclusive and accountable during preparation of the World Bank's social development strategy. Those stimulating discussions brought home the importance of inclusive social policy as a key instrument to tackle inequality. For that inspiration we owe thanks to Michael Walton, Francisco Ferreira, Anthony Bebbington, Vijayendra Rao, and the rest of the *WDR2006* team; to Steen Lau Jorgensen and the strategy team; and to the Social Development Sector Board.

We also owe gratitude for the work on inequality at the Department for International Development of the U.K. (DFID), where we acknowledge the inspiration and support from Cindy Berman, Gerard Howe, Keith Mackiggan, Andy Norton, Christian Rogg, and Adrian Wood, among others. Rosalind Eyben, at IDS since leaving DFID, has continued to be a source of inspiration for thinking about poverty and inequality.

Many others have contributed intellectually to help us bring this book together. In addition to the authors, we would like in particular to acknowledge the contributions of, and exchanges of ideas with Lisa Anderson, Bob Deacon, Jean Luc Dubois, Ashraf Ghani, Ron Inglehart, Ravi Kanbur, Per Knutsson, Margaret Levi, Jomo Kwame Sundaram, Ashutosh Varshney, Timo Voipio, and Geof Wood. Nevertheless, the responsibility for the contents and any errors lies with the editors of this book and the authors of individual chapters.

We owe thanks to many who helped to organize the Arusha Conference. We would like in particular to mention the contributions of Kirsten Havemann, Liane Lohde, and the World Bank Country Office in Dar es Salaam. This book would never have seen the light of day but for the continual support provided by Joyce Chinsen, the meticulous editing of draft conference papers by Yvonne Byron-Smith, and the patience and persistence of Patricia Katayama and Mary Fisk in producing it.

Finally, we would like to acknowledge the generous contributions of the DFID, the Swedish International Development Agency, and the governments of Norway and Finland for the Arusha Conference, and the TFESSD donors for the production of this book.

AIDS	acquired immune deficiency syndrome
CONAPRED	Consejo Nacional para Prevenir la Discriminación (National Council to Prevent Discrimination) (Mexico)
CDSM	*consejo de desarrollo social municipal* (council for municipal social development)
CRC	Convention on the Rights of the Child
Demstar	Democracy, the State, and Administrative Reforms (program)
DFID	Department for International Development of the U.K.
DPO	development policy operation
ECOSOC	Economic and Social Council of the United Nations
ERO	Education Review Office (New Zealand)
EU	European Union
FDSM	Fondo de Desarrollo Social Municipal (Fund for Municipal Social Development) (Mexico)
FMS	Fondo Municipale de Desarrollo (Fund for Municipal Solidarity) (Mexico)
GAC	Governance and Anticorruption
GDP	gross domestic product
GSEA	Gender and Social Exclusion Assessment
HIV	human immunodeficiency virus
IDB	Inter-American Development Bank
ILO	International Labour Organization
IMF	International Monetary Fund
Jaspev	Jamaica Social Policy Evaluation
JAL	*juntas de acción local* (local action juntas)
LJR	legal and judicial reform
MDG	Millennium Development Goal

MTEF	medium-term expenditure framework
NGO	nongovernmental organization
NPC	National Planning Commission (Nepal)
NSPPI	National Strategic Programme Plan of Interventions for Orphans and Other Vulnerable Children, 2006–2010 (Uganda)
OBC	other backward caste
OECD	Organisation for Economic Co-operation and Development
PAHO	Pan American Health Organization
PMAS	Poverty Monitoring and Analysis System
PPA	participatory poverty assessment
PRGF	Poverty Reduction and Growth Facility
PRI	Partido Revolucionario Institucional (Institutional Revolutionary Party) (Mexico)
PRONASOL	Programa Nacional de Solidaridad (National Solidarity Program) (Mexico)
PRSP	Poverty Reduction Strategy Paper
PSIA	Poverty and Society Impact Analysis
SC	scheduled caste
SCP	Special Component Plan
SDN	Social Development Advisors Network
SPADA	Support to Poor and Disadvantaged Areas
ST	scheduled tribe
SEPPIR	Secretaria Especial de Políticas de Promoçao da Igualdade Racial (Ministry for the Promotion of Racial Equality) (Brazil)
SONEL	Société Nationale d'Electricité (National Electricity Company) (Cameroon)
UN	United Nations
UNDP	United Nations Development Programme
UNICEF	United Nations Children's Fund
UNPAC	Uganda National Programme of Actions for Children
UNRISD	United Nations Research Institute for Social Development
UPE	Universal Primary Education (program) (Uganda)
WHO	World Health Organization
WSSD	World Summit for Social Development

PART I

SOCIAL POLICY: LESSONS AND
NEW DIRECTIONS

Social Policy in a Development Context: Structural Inequalities and Inclusive Institutions

Anis A. Dani and Arjan de Haan

Achieving the Millennium Development Goals (MDGs) requires effective and inclusive states. Reducing income poverty, improving health and education indicators, and achieving gender equality—and indeed economic growth—all require effective institutions of governance. Achieving these goals in contexts of severe inequalities—those rooted in structural relationships reinforced by historical cultural norms and values—requires explicit policies to promote inclusion.

This book brings together a set of papers presented at the Arusha conference on New Frontiers in Social Policy.[1] It addresses several questions: Why are opportunities for advancement limited to some segments of society while other social groups are entrapped in a complex web of structural inequality? How do inclusive and accountable states emerge, and what role do social policies play in this? Under what conditions do various forms of state intervention become (more) inclusive? Or, put differently, what are the building blocks for such inclusive states? This volume addresses these questions in a wide variety of developing contexts, while the focus remains on understanding how inclusive policies have emerged and can emerge and how they can be supported.

In this book, *structural inequality* is defined as a condition that arises out of attributing an unequal status to a category of people in relation to one or more other categories of people, a relationship that is perpetuated and reinforced by a confluence of unequal relations in roles, functions, decision rights, and opportunities. *Inclusive states* are those whose policies are directed toward addressing the needs of all their citizens and creating equal opportunities for all. Citizens of such states have a say in the decisions about which services are provided, how those services are delivered, and where they can exercise democratic rights. The focus here is on *social policy*, as an umbrella term for policies and measures through which inclusive states seek to promote equity among their citizens.[2]

A concern for equity is—and indeed should remain—a central focus of social policy both as a means of leveling the playing field to encourage social mobility and as a means of ensuring equity in the distributional effects of policy reforms and development interventions. Such policy includes universal entitlements to strengthen the well-being of citizens through education and health services, targeted support for disadvantaged groups (social assistance for the poor and social services for the elderly or children), labor market policies, and affirmative action or other proactive measures to redress historical inequities. Social policy includes but is not limited to the traditional social sectors; such questions are equally relevant for broader development policy.[3] The contributions in this volume pay particular attention to policies that exist or that are needed so that states will include the groups that are most marginalized and that are often bound in relationships of structural inequality. The chapters also describe the various approaches and institutions of governance that help achieve this inclusion.

Although the analysis in this book is largely state centric, key to it is the relationship between states and citizens. Strong social contracts are thought to be central to the delivery of social policy, and conversely social policy plays a key role in the shaping of this social contract; the experience of Chile after the end of General Augusto Pinochet's dictatorship is an example. The social contract also defines the nature of citizenship and those who are regarded as full citizens.[4] For public goods and services to reach all segments of society, delivery mechanisms must be accessible, effective, and accountable, but where structural inequalities exist, the demands posed are even more challenging than otherwise. In an increasing number of countries, decentralization and community development approaches are being used to extend the outreach, accessibility, and effectiveness of public services. For those decentralized approaches to be effective and inclusive, the nation-state needs to create a policy and institutional framework that ensures constraints on arbitrary exercise of power and that includes mechanisms for citizens to claim their rights and hold public institutions to account.

This book is organized into three sections. The first looks at policy experiences at the macro-level, including lessons from Organisation for

Economic Co-operation and Development (OECD) and transitional countries. Those experiences show that the challenge to create inclusive institutions is an ongoing and context-dependent process. The second section focuses on structural inequalities and the particular challenges that they pose for policy making and for nation-state building in the South. The third looks at the building blocks of inclusive states. It focuses on how policy formulation and implementation can be effective and inclusive under specific conditions, including those with structural inequalities.

This introduction is structured as follows. After a general introduction to the relevance of social policy in the context of developing and transitional countries, the second section discusses the role of the macro-policy and institutional environment. The third section clarifies the concept and illustrates through empirical evidence the intractable challenges of structural inequality, while the fourth considers some of the policy and institutional responses to these challenges. The contributions of the individual chapters in this book are summarized separately in the fifth section of this introductory chapter. The concluding section synthesizes the materials presented in this book in the form of a social policy framework that can help address structural inequalities.

New Directions in Social Policy

In the OECD literature, the term *social policy* has a distinct place, but in the South its relevance and scope continue to be disputed. Much of the development literature has remained explicitly critical of the concept (for example, Kabeer and Cook 2000; Kanbur 2007[5]), with the notable exceptions of the United Nations Research Institute for Social Development (UNRISD) and University of Bath research programs. Similarly, in the practice of international development agencies, *social policy* as a concept has not found significant purchase. Instead, these agencies have found it more convenient to selectively address some elements of social policy aimed at developing human capital and mitigating risks. Donor assistance and public investments to expand human capital in developing countries since 1990 focused largely on primary education and primary health care, leading to contraction in the fiscal space for secondary and higher education. This shift broadened access to education, but it had an unintended negative effect on the quality of human capital.[6] Risk mitigation took the form of (a) social safeguards for involuntary resettlement and indigenous peoples and (b) social protection through social assistance, unemployment benefits, social funds, and cash transfers to help people adjust to a market economy. Both manifestations of risk mitigation were defensive measures conceived initially to help people cope with adverse impacts—social safeguards for development projects and social protection for structural reforms.

These programs have received a major boost since the publication of *World Development Report 1990: Poverty* (World Bank 1990), which helped draw attention to poverty reduction as a development goal. This objective was further reinforced by the World Summit for Social Development (WSSD) in Copenhagen in 1995 and subsequently by the articulation of the MDGs in 2000. However, the international focus often targeted poverty reduction, and debates on social protection and cash transfers have tended to neglect the broader social policies that shape the well-being of citizens. The lukewarm reception of the notion of social policy in international development studies and in development practice has tended to diminish the scope and, hence, the efficacy of social policy.[7] This book—indeed, this series as a whole—argues that this reductionist approach has been a mistake.

Rather than viewing policies and programs dealing with social aspects as instruments for economic development, this book views social policy as the vehicle for more holistic social development, whose overarching goal in keeping with the agreements reached at the WSSD is to promote equity and social justice.

Social development involves multiple levels of engagement: individuals, social groups, and society. It is achieved by strengthening the processes of (a) *inclusion* (the assets and capabilities of individuals to improve their well-being); (b) *accountability* (the capacity of *social groups* to exercise agency, transform their relationships with other groups, and participate in development processes); and (c) *cohesion* (the ability of *society* to reconcile the interests of its constituent elements, govern itself peacefully, and manage change). Social policies, then, are public policies aimed at promoting equality of opportunity to benefit individuals, equality of agency to benefit groups, and social integration to benefit entire societies and nations.[8] Contrary to the rather narrow selection of social policies applied to developing countries, social policy needs to encompass a wide range of public policies undertaken by a variety of actors through a range of instruments designed to promote this broader vision of social development.

This book and the accompanying volumes in the series are intended to highlight the importance of this more rounded view of social policy in the shaping of well-being (African Union 2006; UNRISD 2006; Wood and Gough 2006).[9] They are motivated by an understanding of the importance of the nation-state and universalistic public policies for development, as described by the concept of "the developmental state" and highlighted in Nordic and East Asian experiences.[10] The notion of social policy is also informed by the evidence that specific public policies are needed to address the concerns of marginal groups, through, for example, affirmative action and recognition of multiculturalism. As has become increasingly evident, processes of globalization have enhanced, not diminished, the importance of national public policies. They do so not only by mitigating negative effects through provision of social protection, but also in the broader context by creating the preconditions for economic growth through health and education programs and through public interventions aimed at creating the opportunity for a broad spectrum of citizens to participate in that growth. Globalization is also a cultural process, and it implies intensified exchange of ideas and public policy debates. Such exchanges have tended to strengthen the demand for recognition of at least some of the marginalized groups.

It is important to clarify what is meant by *policy*. This volume does not stop at describing existing public policies; it also describes how de jure commitments relate to de facto processes and outcomes. Moreover, it focuses on the actual day-to-day actions by policy makers and implementers and describes how their work enables social actors to overcome or perpetuate structural inequalities. In operational terms, the book emphasizes the importance of policy design, commitment, and institutional capacity and considers the ways policies are embedded in wider societal structures and norms: simply put, good policy with bad implementation is bad policy. When considering new frontiers of social policy, policy makers also need to recognize that government policy shapes state-society relations. It constitutes building a social contract, in which states create the conditions for effective citizenship and citizens hold the state accountable for providing access to public goods and services.

Lessons from OECD Social Policy

While employing the language of social policy, which is a subset of public policy, this book considers its pitfalls as well as its strengths. In chapter 2, Gough reflects explicitly on what we can learn from the OECD social policy literature.[11] Emergence of social policies can be explained by a variety of factors, summarized as the "five *Is*"—industrialization, interests, institutions, ideas, and internationalization—each of which highlights the very different circumstances under which social policies can and have emerged. Although Gough describes these factors in detail, it is worth reflecting on them here.

First, *industrialization* in Europe was central to the origins of the social policy and welfare states that emerged—albeit with enormous variation there too—when the industrial class became aware of the need for some degree of regulation and welfare sharing to create a steady pool of reliable and increasingly skilled and specialized workers to sustain the largely urban industries. In contrast, much of the poverty and social development concerns in the South remain focused—with a few notable exceptions—on rural areas, where livelihoods are largely agrarian. The overall importance of the state in delivering services (*decommodification*, in the social policy language) has remained relatively limited in the South.[12] This situation does not make social policies irrelevant in that context, but they manifest themselves in different ways—because of the different forms of articulation of class interest, because of the effects of structural inequalities, and because of the different role globalization plays in the 21st century.

Second, social policy in the North has often been associated with the emergence of urban working class *interests*. Workers' awareness of common interests stimulated unionization and allowed the working class to act as an interest group. Not only are the demographic contexts in the South very different, but so are the histories of trade unions. Where unions have had a strong presence, they have largely been restricted to the workers in the "formal" sector of state enterprises and in the modern sector, which have typically employed only about 10 percent of the labor force. Many of the entitlements associated with labor rights in developing countries have been further eroded in recent decades by labor market reform, which has weakened protection and entitlement of workers, often to attract foreign direct investment. The voice of organized labor thus plays a lesser role in most developing countries compared with what it did among early industrializers. However, nongovernmental organizations (NGOs)—particularly international NGOs—have become central players in international development debates, for example, in relation to social sector spending. Nevertheless, this role is fundamentally different from that of membership-based trade unions. By and large, the NGOs have been less representative of, or rooted in, local constituencies in the South.

As reflected in a number of the chapters in this volume, the inequalities that drive social policy in the South are radically different from those in the North. Across the South, racial and ethnic inequalities impose enormous—and in many cases only fairly recently acknowledged (as chapters 5 through 7 on Latin America show)—challenges to the formation of public policies. Even where deep-rooted inequalities have become part of official policy, as in South Asia, it has proved enormously difficult, given the pervasiveness of discriminatory social norms and practices, to address these inequalities effectively, and unintended consequences are paramount.

Third, lessons from OECD social policy highlight the importance of *institutions*, including political systems that favored redistribution, as well as the basic institutions of law, regulation, administrative systems, and effective control over the entire territory governed by a state. Many of these "preconditions" for social policy did not exist in countries in the South when social policy was introduced, and they are still in various stages of development across different countries. Social policy analysts thus need to be keenly aware of these differences. Similarly, social policy formulation and advice need to be sensitive to institutional environments and need to strengthen the basic institutions of governance as an integral part of social policy provisions.

The work of Peter Lindert (2004) highlights that "growing public" happened under conditions of simultaneous economic growth, increased state involvement, *and* expansion of voice—the last contributing to forms of accountability that transformed the OECD welfare states into vast engines of redistribution, without necessarily compromising economic growth. For historical reasons, in most developing countries, social policy is grafted onto weak institutions that have lower levels of accountability. Its sustainability depends on strengthening the functions of governance institutions generally, as highlighted by chapters 14 and 15 on public interest litigation and judicial reform. Perhaps the most important characteristic of the OECD welfare states as they emerged after World War II was the association of delivery of services with the extension of citizenship and rights: in the South, as Graham (2002: 4) emphasizes, extension of social protection "ultimately requires the development of a politically sustainable social contract."

The representativeness of governments has been key to the way social policies have been formulated, as in South Africa, where social policy became an explicit part of the apartheid regime; as in Latin America, where racial differences were equally strong but less formalized; and as in

South Asia, where affirmative action emerged directly out of the compromises leading to the formulation of constitutions. In India, this process began with affirmative action and reservation of special quotas in education and in public sector jobs for scheduled tribes and scheduled castes—a policy that Nepal is now seeking to emulate (see chapter 8). In Pakistan, affirmative action initially took the form of quotas for government jobs to privilege the poorer, lagging provinces and the rural populations. Following the growing recognition of voice and authority as a means to provide empowerment and reduce poverty, the decentralization programs introduced in Bangladesh, India, and Pakistan have earmarked quotas for women and other disadvantaged groups in local government entities. Although it is too early to evaluate the long-term effects of the quotas, recent trends suggest that this form of political empowerment may prove to be a powerful institutional mechanism for overcoming deep-seated inequities (Chattopadhyay and Duflo 2004; Ban and Rao 2008).

The fourth *I* as driver of social policy refers to *ideas*, the role of culture, ideologies, and epistemic communities. Values, of course, greatly influence public policies, as in Catholic, Protestant, and Confucian cultures, and as the research on welfare regimes highlights. These ideas have a great deal of path dependency and, hence, have been a main driver behind respective social policy regimes. The histories of post-transition countries show the importance of elites, their norms and values, and the norms around justice that are extremely important for making institutions of law work, particularly for the poor. For a social policy agenda in the South, one key concern revolves around the power of ideas—and who formulates them. Particularly in aid-dependent countries—and notwithstanding emphasis on ownership during the past 10 years—policy makers are at risk of being swept along by ideas emerging out of the donor debate, limiting the space for national public policy traditions to emerge.[13] The weak capacity of national think tanks and universities in many African countries also undermines the ability to develop such traditions.

Recent developments in China highlight the importance of ideas and norms and the ways they are created in the battlefields of political economy. The Chinese government—which actively sought international partnerships to develop public policies but could always set its own agenda—over the past few years has started to promote the concept of a harmonious society, which articulates dialectics of building on or actively promoting "traditional" values, in response to emergent economic needs, public policy crises, and national integration and political control.

The last of the "Five *Is*" refers to *internationalization*, a concept that the previous paragraphs already touched on. Values often migrate across borders—for example, within Europe, through colonialism, and through the Europeanization of the former Soviet bloc. Elites play equally important and independent roles, as Johanssen and Pedersen show in chapter 3 in their discussion of transition countries.

A distinguishing feature of social policy formulation in the South has been its situation in a global social policy debate. Social policy regimes have been heavily influenced by colonial traditions and articulated through ambitious modernizing elites. Economic crises and structural adjustment brought a sudden end to these projects. Subsequent social policy formulation has been heavily influenced by international organizations—typically under continuing weak public institutions. As mentioned, in aid-dependent countries, the role of international financial institutions, as well as the international NGO community, is very significant. In other countries, too, ideas from abroad are incorporated in a more proactive manner (notably in East Asian countries and European Union accession countries). During the period of rapid structural adjustment and transition, these international financial institutions were criticized for neglecting social policy. Recent policy directions, as described by Harris and Kende-Robb in chapter 4, acknowledge the need to make social policy more central and to describe the space that exists within macroeconomic policy design for integration of social policy. In chapter 7, Recondo highlights how international organizations played a role in spreading ideas around participatory democracy, while warning against looking for silver bullets.

The chapters in this book suggest that the social policy lessons derived from the OECD context are important and can be helpful, but they need further adaptation and innovation to increase their relevance to developing countries. Each of these factors manifests itself in substantially different ways across the globe. The second set of chapters (chapters 5 through 9) spells out the particular challenges these factors impose for social policy formulation, while the third set (chapters 10 through 15) illustrates institutional responses that confront these challenges in different contexts. Those responses are partial solutions, and this book seeks to lay them out as a road map for strengthening social policy outcomes. The next section discusses the importance of structural inequalities, which of necessity must be central to the design of instruments of social policy and, more broadly, public policy, including underlying notions of individual rights. Such structural inequalities pose additional challenges for institutions of social policy, and they need to be acknowledged and addressed in accordance with their local manifestations, to make those institutions more inclusive.

Structural Inequalities

Unlike most developing countries in the South, the creation of nation-states in the North involved fairly long, drawn-out nation-building projects, which led to relatively homogeneous populations. For the most part, diverse ethnicities played a relatively unimportant role, and one national language and culture were accepted through a process of incorporation and assimilation of minorities.[14] Although in the late 20th century, with a strengthened articulation of interests by immigrant communities and the North, this homogeneity and success of "integration" were questioned, by and large the European welfare states existing after World War II were not hampered by significant structural inequalities.

One key difference between state formation in the North and South has been taxation. As the Arusha statement highlighted, strengthening the capacity of states to mobilize revenue from their citizens and diminishing reliance on external aid have yet to be accepted as essential elements of the new social policy agenda. Such changes are not just a question of reducing aid dependency. Domestic resource mobilization is the most effective means of enhancing citizen ownership, increasing state accountability and ensuring sustainability. As Herbst (2000) described, for European states increasing taxation formed part of the process of state formation itself and was integral to the building of alliances, or social contracts, with citizens, often during wars. Homogeneity within the nation-state also made a higher level of taxation more palatable as a quid pro quo for the social contract of the welfare state. In the South, these processes have been radically different, and a social policy agenda must take into account the need to galvanize links between the state and groups of citizens.

Many of the postcolonial countries in Africa and South Asia gained independence in the aftermath of World War II, with boundaries arising out of recent colonial history rather than ethnocultural distinctions. Social integration of different ethnic and tribal groups within newly independent states has often proved challenging. The most acute conflicts have arisen when one tribe or ethnic group dominated—or was perceived to dominate—state power to the exclusion of others. Latin America suffered similar exclusion arising out of racial history: Euro-descendants were at the top and indigenous populations at the bottom of the hierarchy. In South Asia, caste structures provided another layer of hierarchies to tribal and ethnic differences. And gender inequalities permeate almost all societies. The structural inequalities arising from those roots have been highly resistant to change.

Structural inequality is a condition that arises out of attribution of an inferior or unequal status to a category of people, in relation to one or more categories of people.[15] By its very nature, structural inequality is relational. Unequal status is perpetuated and reinforced by unequal relations in roles, functions, decision rights, and opportunities, which are bound in a web of interdependence. Such inequality can consist of gender-based division of labor within households or economic dependency between tenants who lack alternatives and landlords who monopolize landownership. Ethnic, tribal, or racial division, reinforced by specialized economic roles, relationships, or livelihood regimes, perpetuates such structural inequalities, which become particularly severe when one of the groups manages to dominate state institutions. Structural inequality is reproduced by culturally, institutionally, and sometimes even politically sanctioned rights regimes that allocate differential rights to those with different structural status. Structural inequalities based on gender and tribal, ethnic, or racial differences have been the most pervasive. Typically, such inequalities persist when they are not recognized as arising out of pervasive structural conditions. Lack of recognition breeds a vicious cycle that reinforces those unequal relations. Denial of the underlying structural causes leads to the absence of laws, institutions, and norms to combat them. Those who are disadvantaged also suffer from unequal power relations. They lack voice, leading to passive behavior and acceptance of the adverse terms of recognition ascribed to them (see figure 1.1).

Structural inequality, almost by definition, does not change easily or quickly, but change does occur (see Bebbington and others 2008). Such transformations can result from an external political shock or externally induced opportunities that have a sustained effect, such as the imposition of ideologically driven regimes or the collapse of such regimes, as occurred when communist rule disintegrated in Eastern and Central Europe.[16] They can also result from internal processes, such as sociopolitical movements or the desire by Central and Southeastern European countries to align their policies and institutions with those of the European Union (EU). In South Africa, years of resistance by discriminated groups, combined with global

Figure 1.1. The Vicious Cycle of Structural Inequality

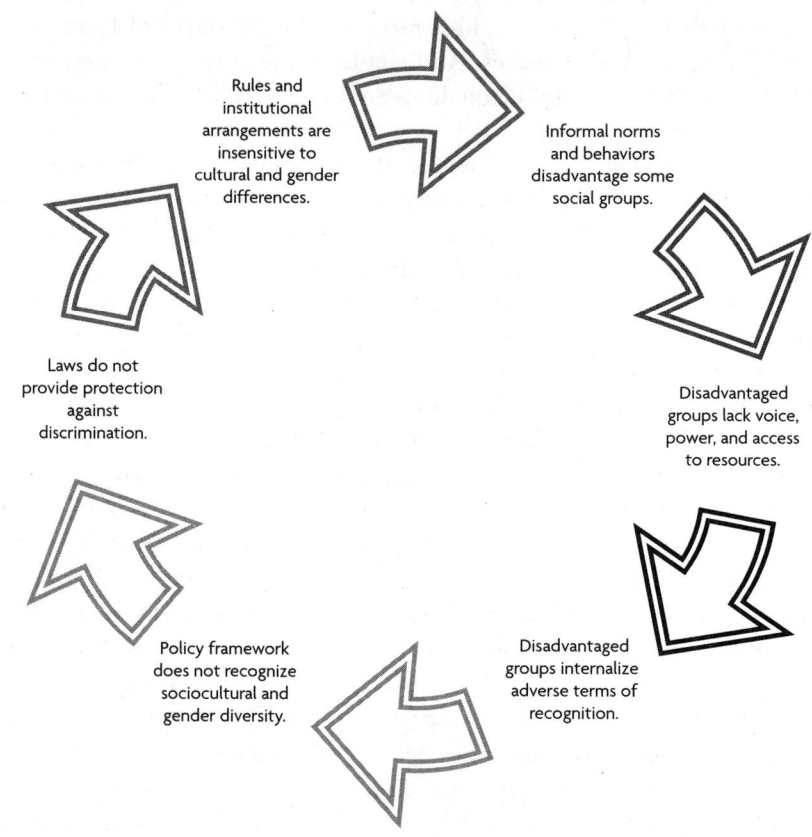

Rules and institutional arrangements are insensitive to cultural and gender differences.

Informal norms and behaviors disadvantage some social groups.

Laws do not provide protection against discrimination.

Disadvantaged groups lack voice, power, and access to resources.

Policy framework does not recognize sociocultural and gender diversity.

Disadvantaged groups internalize adverse terms of recognition.

Source: Author's construction.

sanctions and progressive support, led to the end of apartheid in 1994, 46 years after it was established. Structural inequality can also be transformed through fundamental changes in economic and social relations that, over time, lead to an erosion of culturally sanctioned inequality. For example, migration of millions of Indian and Pakistani workers to the Middle East has enabled large numbers of landless people to escape feudal bondage and unequal social relations in their home communities by operating under a completely different economic regime.

Finally, structural inequality can also be transformed by conflict and violence, when it triggers large-scale population displacement, which sometimes undermines traditional hierarchies. One of the most striking examples is the rise of the Taliban: young Muslim radicals usurped the leadership role of traditional tribal elders as they sought to assert themselves and their worldview within the institutional vacuum created by the Soviet Union's invasion and the internecine battles that followed the Soviet withdrawal from Afghanistan. Policy makers who misunderstand or ignore the significance of this structural transformation that enabled the rapid rise of the Taliban do so at their own peril. The withdrawal of Western support for the liberation of Afghanistan after the Soviet defeat created a vacuum allowing Al-Qaeda to take root and win the support of the Taliban. Understanding the underlying structural realities and the desire among the local youth for emancipation from tribal yoke, as is being attempted in Afghanistan, will be essential if the global threat of terrorism is to be checked.

In contrast to OECD countries, where conflicts arising out of social differentiation preceded industrialization and were part of the early years of nation-state formation, in many developing countries tribal, ethnic, religious, or other differentials remained unresolved when the countries emerged as postcolonial nations. Consequently, alongside less strongly developed state functions, postcolonial state formation and the services provided under the new social contract involved and continue to involve the shaping of nations out of diversity and deep structural inequalities. In postcolonial countries, particularly the settler economies of Latin America and southern Africa, inequalities are severe, and of a structural nature, unlikely to be reduced through the operation of markets, for example. The state and its institutions are deeply rooted in its social and economic structures, forming potential *inequality traps* (Rao 2006; World Bank 2006)—that is, situations where inequalities in economic, political, and social-cultural spheres reinforce one another (see Bebbington and others 2008). The state was never neutral to these inequalities, particularly where the colonial state had made these divisions central to the personnel of the state apparatus, electoral processes, and delivery of services (Mamdani 2005).

We observe a large diversity in the ways in which these inequalities are incorporated into public policy making. In South Africa (which, of course, was always exceptional in the extent to which racial inequalities were formalized), reducing inequalities has become a core part of public policies and the new social contract. But inequalities are very important elsewhere too: the extremely high income inequalities, particularly in the eastern and southern part of Africa, have only recently been highlighted. Little is known about the reasons behind those inequalities and possibilities for addressing them, or about the histories of nation building through which structural inequalities were addressed.[17] And even where income inequalities do not show in the indexes, underlying inequalities may persist—for example, regional inequalities in Ghana (Christiaensen, Demery, and Paternostro 2002; Shepherd and others 2004).

In Latin America, with its historical colonial settler economies, inequalities are severe, are of a structural nature, and are based on a combination of racial, geographic, and economic factors. After independence in the 19th century and after the abolition of slavery, it was a very long time before existing inequalities of race and ethnicity created under colonial rule were officially recognized by the state and began to be addressed. Over the past two decades or so, severe inequalities have come to the political center and are being explicitly addressed. For example, in Brazil, struggles for recognition, including group rather than individual rights (as discussed in chapter 6 by Hopenhayn), have become central to public policy, partly through experiences with participatory democracy (as discussed by Recondo in chapter 7). Gradually, lessons about the potentials and challenges are emerging, although the lessons are still limited compared with, for example, experiences with gender mainstreaming (see Buvinić and Mazza, chapter 5).

Some countries in Asia have made special efforts to strengthen the rights of disadvantaged citizens and address structural inequalities, either in response to civil unrest (as in Malaysia) or as part of the social contract that helped to unite disparate ethnic and caste groups within the national state structure (as in India). Nevertheless, the inequalities are deeply embedded and persistent, particularly in South Asia. In Nepal, as in Latin America, the inequalities have long been neglected by the state and by international actors; however, the crisis of the 1990s seems to have helped spark the formulation of policy responses (as Bennett argues in chapter 8). Policy responses appear to have had a limited effect in reducing socioeconomic inequalities, though the policy framework has radically reshaped the political arena, as de Haan shows with respect to India in chapter 9. Specific responses to deprived groups emerged in the public policy debate in the late colonial period and were repeatedly refined during the half century of independence, and the histories of these groups show that such policy responses can have unexpected and unintended consequences, as well as successes, thus bringing to the fore the limits of state intervention in changing social structures and norms.

The lessons about structural inequalities are by no means easy ones. They highlight the need for public policy to differentiate between poverty and inequality or social exclusion and to incorporate an understanding of power and discrimination. They also point to the need to address deprivation in economic, social, and cultural spheres simultaneously and to do so over a long period. Experience in this area is thus relatively limited and will be an important part of the policy dialogue for some time to come. The next section discusses possible building blocks of such social policies.

Inclusive Institutions

Given the challenges posed to social policy in the South with regard to basic institutions and the structural inequalities to which they respond and in which they are embedded, it is useful to look at examples of policy experiences that make states more effective as well as more inclusive.[18] The six chapters in the third part of this book look explicitly at how such institutions need to and can take account of diversity and inequalities, plus what instruments can contribute to making the state more inclusive: in and through legal and judicial institutions, education and health, affirmative action, labor markets, and policy monitoring. There is no single silver bullet, but the chapters in this book point to several measures that can help create inclusive institutions. These measures are summarized in figure 1.2. At the center lies recognition of structural inequality. Recognition of the fault lines of structural inequality is the simplest and yet often politically the most difficult pill to swallow as it challenges fundamental concepts of a nation-state or of a time-honored division of labor within households. Gender is an obvious example, as is acknowledgment of racial or caste-based inequalities. Recognition is also crucial because it generates a response in the form of policy tools to redress the condition, and data collection is often a powerful tool to that end. Macro-level elements can include global charters and national laws, rules, and regulations and creation of an enabling environment for broad public policy debates. Finally, tailored programs to increase access to public services and evaluation and participatory monitoring are key elements of creating inclusive institutions.

A first question is how institutions start to become more inclusive: what are the drivers of change? Elites can play an important role, as was highlighted for transition countries. Social unrest and violence—or, for

Figure 1.2. Elements of Inclusive Social Policy

Source: Author's construction.

example, health crises—often force policy makers to address public policy. Although India has a long history of affirmative action for disadvantaged sections of the population (scheduled castes, scheduled tribes, and later other backward castes), the government has since 2004 felt compelled to deliver more to the poorest sections of the population. It does so partly by introducing new schemes, but also—more significantly in the context of our discussion—by introducing rights-based approaches, which are prompted by sustained civil society advocacy. (Consider, for example, the new Employment Guarantee Scheme and the Right to Food and Right to Information campaigns and legislation.) Equally important are initiatives generated by the groups themselves, as Ringold highlights in chapter 11, which focuses on the Māori of New Zealand and the rich experience in services they have developed, owned, and provided. But sustaining such initiatives and making them have broad effect are challenging. In chapter 7, Recondo reinforces the finding that to be sustainable local initiatives must be accompanied by supportive national-level public policy.

This point brings us to the question of how public institutions can be adapted to become more inclusive. The case studies in this book suggest that typically countries enact laws against gender discrimination, establish rules for governance, and implement project grants within the framework of that law. Discussions on education and health highlight a number of practical areas: recognition of and possibilities for minorities to learn their mother tongue, adaptation of health services and recognition of traditional healing practices, sensitivity to different needs and norms in policies for child support (as Christiansen and Whyte describe for Uganda in chapter 12), and adaptation of processes of participation. Sometimes the choice of policies is relevant for the question of inclusion: for example, it may be the case that unconditional cash transfers are more empowering and inclusive than the provision of food. Equally important is the way in which any of these benefits are provided and the way they shape the relationship between state institutions and citizens. As Ringold argues in chapter 11, both targeted and universal approaches may be needed in practice. Sometimes an emphasis on accountability may lead to preference for one instrument over another: contribution and insurance principles, for example, may strengthen the possibility to claim rights rather than to have to ask for handouts (though such claims, too, have their disadvantages).

But there are also, in the language of women's empowerment, "strategic issues." The first is the recognition that emerges through social movements or other forms of group-based agency for asserting rights (Rao and Walton 2004) and for acceptance of diversity among citizens as equals (see Appadurai 2004). The concept of multicultural citizenship (Kymlicka 1995, 2006), which Marc builds on in chapter 10, helps highlight the challenges posed by diverse populations. But concepts of diversity and multiculturalism have been met with hostility because they are often seen as undermining nationalism by questioning the unity associated with the nation-state. Hence, it is important to understand the local contexts in which struggles for recognition are rooted and the recent histories of state formation through which diversity has been addressed.

The second strategic issue is the opportunity and commitment to address diversity across the range of public institutions. Typically, this strategy involves opening the space for broader forms of participation in policy formulation. For example, the Bonn Agreement on Afghanistan stipulated that a new Afghan constitution be adopted by a participatory forum—the *Loya Jirga*. As experience in the North (for example, at the London Metropolitan Policy) and in the global South shows, addressing deep-rooted sentiments of discrimination is extremely challenging. Recent work by Eyben and Moncrieffe (2007) highlights the importance of language and of the labels and categories used in policy frameworks. Such categories potentially reinforce cycles of inequality; hence, institutions may need to interrogate their own frames of reference. Legal institutions may need to become more inclusive. Mainstreaming diversity may involve lengthy processes of supporting capacity building. Monitoring policy processes and outcomes—as in chapter 13 on Jamaica by Bonner, Holland, Norton, and Sigrist—can help improve relationships between citizens and political leaders, as well as policy implementers.

The ways in which greater inclusiveness can be achieved are manifold and will be context specific. In chapter 11, Ringold highlights the diversification of service delivery in New Zealand and shows how a combination of universal and mainstreamed policies (based on recognition of distinctness) and policies targeted to specific populations was found to enhance inclusiveness. As the two chapters on legal instruments (chapter 14 by Gloppen and chapter 15 by Sage and Woolcock) show, technical design is only a small part of the picture. Such policy change needs to take into account broader norms and institutions and must be accompanied by articulation of voice and capacities to negotiate the legal system.

At present, inclusiveness is not part of the MDG framework. Neither is it common in much of the governance literature. But for at least three reasons, a notion of inclusiveness should occupy a central part of the international policy debate:

- Social integration is central to the WSSD declaration that underpins the MDG framework.
- Movements around the world demand that institutions become more inclusive.
- As with gender inequality, inclusiveness interacts positively with other development outcomes.

Stakeholder involvement takes on dual significance: (a) stakeholders can become agents of social monitoring and ensure that monitoring and evaluation promote greater accountability, and (b) stakeholders can play a stronger role in the dialogue on policy reforms.

An Overview of This Volume

The chapters in this volume are organized around three main themes. The first set looks at macrofactors that are important for institutions and states to be more inclusive. The second looks at cases of structural inequality and the ways such inequality has begun to be challenged. The third describes a number of specific policy instruments that engender more inclusiveness.

The matrix in table 1.1 summarizes the key elements of a framework for understanding the characteristics of inclusive states, derived from the case study chapters of this book. The matrix follows the structure of the book and classifies the elements within the macrostructure, structural inequality, and inclusive institutions into policy, legal, institutional, and normative domains. A final column maps out implementation processes along the same four domains.

Elements of the macrostructure in table 1.1 are derived largely from chapters 2 to 4. The policy domain, which is derived from chapter 4 by Harris and Kende-Robb, integrates macroeconomic policies with social policies, leading to pro-poor outcomes reflected in the normative domain. The elements of the legal and institutional domains emerge largely from Johanssen and Pedersen's analysis in chapter 3 of the responsive state but also, to some extent, from chapter 14, in which Gloppen explores public interest litigation and social rights, and chapter 6, in which Hopenhayn describes his notion of social citizenship.

The key elements of structural inequality in the policy domain are recognition of gender equality and multicultural rights as policy objectives to ensure inclusive citizenship (see chapter 5 by Buvinić and Mazza, chapter 6 by Hopenhayn, chapter 10 by Marc, and chapter 11 by Ringold). Those group-based inequalities have been resilient precisely because they were long not recognized as being significant or unjust. The invisibility of such social divides poses a major challenge for social policy. Changes in the policy domain can in the long run influence the normative domain. More often than not, however, challenges to the normative domain come from social movements, which then lead to policy changes. One benefit of globalization and the information technology revolution is the emergence of global networks and the internationalization of ideas, with enormous potential for accelerating normative changes through transnational social movements and policy changes, such as adoption of global conventions and charters. Actions within the legal domain include affirmative action, reservation of quotas (chapter 9 by de Haan), and rights-based social policy

Table 1.1. A Framework for Inclusive States

Domain	Macrostructure	Structural inequality	Inclusive institutions	Implementation processes
Policy	• Macroeconomic policies integrated with social policies	• Gender equality • Multiculturalism • Universal rights	• Law in policy	• Participatory policy dialogue and public debate
Legal	• Accountable democracy • Citizenship rights and responsibilities	• Affirmative action • Reservation • Rights-based social policy	• Rules and regulations for universal access to justice • Public interest litigation	• Freedom of information • Paralegals and legal awareness
Institutional	• Dense cooperation with civil society	• Decentralization • Targeted and tailored programs for access to assets and services	• Bridging of formal and informal systems	• Incentives • Mechanisms of accountability
Normative	• Improved pro-poor outcomes of macroeconomic policies through distributional analysis	• Identity politics • Terms of recognition	• Rules embedded in norms and values	• Transparency, voice, and accountability • Equality of agency

Source: Author's construction, on the basis of the contributions to this volume.

(chapter 8 by Bennett). In addition to the research included in this book, recent work in four Latin American countries (Chile, Guatemala, Peru, and Uruguay) and South Africa applies a human rights approach to social policy and documents the use of "social guarantees" to specify entitlements and obligations and to ensure the fulfillment of those obligations by the state (World Bank 2007).

Several important lessons on inclusive institutions arise from chapter 14 by Gloppen and from chapter 15 by Sage and Woolcock, as well as from chapter 7 by Recondo. For policies to be effective, they must be enshrined in law, but laws can be invoked only when rules and regulations have been formulated. In chapter 14, Gloppen illustrates how mechanisms such as public interest litigation can give voice to the voiceless and allow the uptake of collective issues where no individual claimant is likely to have claims large enough to justify the transaction costs of litigation. However, she reminds us that public interest litigation works only in environments where the legal system is responsive to social rights and where the litigation is reinforced by active social movements. As highlighted in chapter 7 by Recondo and chapter 15 by Sage and Woolcock, these rules and regulations work well if they are legitimized by existing norms. Bridging formal and informal systems is thus essential both for access to justice and for effective delivery of public services.

Last and arguably the most crucial part of the framework lies in the implementation processes that breathe life into structures and institutions. To be inclusive, structures must be based on the normative principles of transparency, voice, and accountability, as well as on equality of agency. Several chapters (chapter 3 by Johanssen and Pedersen, chapter 4 by Harris and Kende-Robb, chapter 6 by Hopenhayn, and chapter 7 by Recondo) highlight the importance of participatory policy dialogue or public debate, which can contribute to the formulation of pro-poor policies. In the legal domain, freedom of information laws, legal awareness, and paralegal services have shown good potential, whereas incentives and accountability have enabled the social policy evaluation process to achieve more inclusive social policy (see chapter 13 by Bonner, Holland, Norton, and Sigrist).

Macrocontext

The first set of chapters revolves around the larger question: how do inclusive (and accountable) states emerge? This set includes chapter 2, in which Gough describes the OECD welfare state experience, emphasizing the economic, social, and political conditions under which welfare states have grown historically. In chapter 3, Johanssen and Pedersen focus on more recent events in transition countries and under what conditions "responsive states" (which have stronger participatory values and denser state–civil society relations) emerge. In chapter 4, Harris and Kende-Robb represent the perspective of an important international actor whose primary focus is on the economic viability of states and discuss how the International Monetary Fund envisages the relationship between economic and social policy choices.

In chapter 2, Gough summarizes explanations advanced for the development of European welfare states in the 20th century and considers what lessons this history holds for developing countries in the 21st century. Gough defines what we mean by *social policy* and emphasizes the combined effect of socioeconomic environment, interest organizations, political institutions, and ideas on the shaping of social policy. He advocates a more contextual regime approach to policy learning and reviews a wide variety of factors behind welfare states, including a growing proletariat and unionization, democratization, social democracy, nation building, religion, cultural diversity, the role of ideas and policy networks, and the effect of globalization and supranational agencies.

In chapter 3, Johanssen and Pedersen focus on the radical transition of former communist countries to democratic governance and market system, describing how responsive states emerge. A *responsive state*, as defined by Johanssen and Pedersen, is one that is held accountable through competitive democracy, but also through cooperation with interest groups. A responsive state is, thus, a meeting place of a strong democratic state and strong civil society. Using surveys among elites, compared across countries, Johanssen and Pedersen show where values of participation, openness, and inclusiveness—accompanied by practices of participation—actively invite or welcome civil society participation. Although they warn that the number of observations is too small to draw firm conclusions, their analysis shows that values and practices of participation do not compromise wealth creation and that more responsive states tend to be associated with more equal societies. Economic growth can strengthen responsive states, but such states can also be fostered by international commitment and institutional pressure, as demonstrated by the EU enlargement process. In turn, state responsiveness affects policy outcomes, inequality, and poverty: responsive states are "kinder and gentler."

In chapter 4, Harris and Kende-Robb argue that macroeconomic frame-works, social objectives, and poverty reduction goals need to be explicitly integrated and that there is more scope for increasing the pro-poor bias of macroeconomic policy. This integration requires a full awareness of the tradeoffs and of the short- and long-term effects of macroeconomic policies on social outcomes, and vice versa. Integration requires an interdisciplinary approach that uses social, economic, institutional, and political analysis to identify the links and transmission mechanisms between macroeconomic policies, poverty, and livelihoods. This approach can contribute to enhanced public transparency and ownership and can identify the best policy combi-nation for equitable growth, poverty reduction, and social justice.

Structural Inequalities

The second set of chapters focuses on the challenges posed by forms of social exclusion that have historical and cultural roots, described here as *structural inequality*. The three Latin American examples of structural inequality represent exclusionary behavior that is deeply rooted in colonial history and colonial policies, like many of the structural inequalities in Africa analyzed by Mamdani (2005). These forms of inequality or exclu-sion have, in many cases, been recognized only recently and only partly transformed in postcolonial development. Three chapters on Latin America describe, respectively, the major fault lines of discrimination and recent policies that have started to address them, the ways ethnic diversity and different systems of rights challenge public policy, and the effects and chal-lenges of movements for participatory democracy. Two chapters focus on South Asia, with its long-standing processes of exclusion on the basis of caste, tribe, and or ethnicity.

In Latin America, as Buvinić and Mazza (chapter 5) describe, major fault lines of ethnic and racial discrimination have fairly recently come to the fore, and new policies have been formulated to address them. Buvinić and Mazza describe building blocks for social inclusion policies in Latin America, highlighting the need for both complementary actions in differ-ent sectors and participation of state and nonstate actors to advance in social inclusion. They emphasize the importance of constitutional and legal protections for group rights; international and national antidiscrimina-tion laws, including excluded groups in national statistics; and enactment of land and property rights. They describe experiences with government ministries or offices ("national machineries") created to promote women's empowerment, and they examine three sets of public policies in affirmative action, education, and labor markets to promote inclusion, with particular emphasis on gender inequality.

Hopenhayn (chapter 6) emphasizes the challenges posed by ethnic diversity for public policy and the judicial system, which is normally designed on the basis of individual rights. His chapter describes in more detail the challenges that group identities (based on ascribed categories). Groups pose to public policy and the justice system in the same Latin American context, marked by acute inequalities. Inequality and cultural difference, or *ascriptive conditions*, are linked: ethnic minorities, women, and young people suffer from vulnerability, poverty, and social exclusion. Indigenous groups pose particular challenges to juridical and political institutions, questioning the rationality of social distribution, the individual basis of law, and nation-state sovereignty. Addressing these inequalities requires differentiated policies in education and health, recognition of groups defined by ascription or cultural identity, self-government and holding of collective rights, and judicial reform.

Recondo (chapter 7) describes participatory democracy and decentralization in indigenous regions in Mexico and Colombia. He stresses that inclusion is enhanced by the interaction between (a) citizen action and local processes and (b) modes of public policy. He highlights the challenges that exclusion of different groups can pose to social policy in the context of decentralization efforts introduced in part to address that exclusion. Decentralization processes promoted through the 1990s in indigenous Mexico and Colombia saw participatory democracy as a prerequisite for sustainable development, with communitarian traditions given official recognition as legitimate forms of local governance. The participatory devices promoted by central governments and multilateral agencies had unintended consequences. Recondo concludes that promotion of sustainable development should emphasize context specificity rather than best practices and that such work should be long term and incorporate an understanding of politics and power. The cases he examines bring home the reality that decentralized and participatory development presupposes the existence of strong, stable, and legitimate states.

In Nepal, long-standing forms of discrimination have received more explicit attention by research analysts and policy makers. In chapter 8, Bennett maps out the nature of historical exclusion and describes the policy process that is seeking to address this problem. Her chapter is based on a collaborative World Bank and U.K. Department for International

Development policy research study that aims to influence the formal policy-making process and support its implementation. The chapter analyzes government and civil society responses to gender, caste, and ethnic discrimination, including legal issues, access to health and education, group-based approaches, and affirmative action. It argues that sustained policy reform inevitably involves culture change, particularly if such policies need to overcome persistent inequalities like those caused by caste, ethnic, and gender-based exclusion.

Like Bennett, de Haan (chapter 9) highlights the need for constitutional and legal systems favoring affirmative action to be accompanied by changes in beliefs and attitudes. His chapter focuses on the ways public institutions in India themselves include and exclude, with particular reference to affirmative action, and the ways in which many public policy programs reserve positions and allocate funds on the basis of groups characteristics (scheduled caste, scheduled tribe, and other backward castes) in ever more complicated frameworks. He argues that deep-rooted differences and inequalities continue to pervade progressive public policy practices and shows that inequalities have been reinforced by policy and political practices—including by donor engagement—through categories and classifications in use, official inaction or delays, attitudes of officials, and modes of representation, including through civil society organizations.

Inclusive Institutions

The third set of chapters looks at specific sectors and social policy instruments, including the challenges of addressing unintended consequences. The chapters discuss experiences with incorporating diversity and multiculturalism within public policy institutions; the implications of diversity for child support in Uganda, where the way state support is organized can clash with the way child support is embedded in family and social relations; and the potential and limitations of instruments of law to address deep-rooted inequalities.

In chapter 10, Marc addresses the challenges of addressing cultural diversity in service delivery, particularly in contexts where cultural minorities have been unrecognized and, hence, invisible or discriminated against. Drawing on analysis of "multicultural citizenship" and *Human Development Report 2004* (UNDP 2004), he notes the growing recognition of cultural and ethnic diversity—which often accompanies globalization—in the design and implementation of development programs, for national governments, as well as for local governments and providers of public services. These programs include ones in education (multilingual education, curriculum content) and health (respect for cultural background and traditional curative practices). Recognition of cultural differences is essential from an equality point of view, because cultural minorities are often among the poorest groups. It can also enhance individual and collective agency and will help reduce conflicts.

In chapter 11, Ringold develops the theme of diversity further, with a focus on Māori, the indigenous people of New Zealand. They have made impressive gains and contribute across education, economic, cultural, and social spectrums—though challenges remain because Māori are disproportionately unemployed or are in vulnerable jobs and are disproportionately represented among the poor. Māori development approaches provide a valuable record of experience and innovation in the services developed, owned, and provided by Māori. Initiatives have made mainstream programs more inclusive and responsive, as the result of the formulation of policy strategies, capacity building within government departments, and considerable diversification of service delivery. New Zealand has sought to calibrate the extent to which policies should be universal, mainstreamed, and applicable to the entire society and the extent to which they should be targeted to specific populations. The results suggest that both universal and targeted policies are needed in such contexts: inclusive policies that reach all New Zealanders and policies that recognize the cultural distinctness and particular needs of Māori.

Focusing on Uganda, Christiansen and Whyte (chapter 12) study the child support that emerges from the interaction between global social policy frameworks and the local reality of a relatively weak state apparatus. They examine practices of government institutions and NGOs in providing social security to children in conformity with the Convention on the Rights of the Child, and they analyze different approaches based on targeting and universalism. These practices interact with kinship networks and local patterns of child support. Welfare of children is shaped not only through inclusion in or exclusion from these formal institutions but also through family and personal networks—where children give and find support and the values, resources, and expectations that shape the domestic arena. The two spheres do not operate in isolation; the norms and categories in the formal arena influence those within the domestic arena. Children designated as orphans and recipients of help in official domains may not be recognized in similar terms within informal networks. Christiansen and Whyte question whether the way gender is incorporated into social policy or the focus on individual rights within the Convention on the Rights of the Child sufficiently recognizes local norms and practices.

In chapter 13, Bonner, Holland, Norton, and Sigrist discuss the Jamaican initiative to monitor and improve social policy. This initiative links technical innovation in the collection of information to a process of institutional change and inclusiveness at different levels of governance. It has promoted locally generated but nationally comparable benchmarks designed to encourage institutional change in the relationships among citizens, the political directorate, and technocrats. Such change, Bonner and colleagues argue, will improve social policy design and delivery. The emphasis on the interaction of local and national evidence-based policy discussions has helped create political space for institutional change and greater inclusiveness. But considerable institutional challenges remain because of the politicized nature of institutions, the role of hierarchy and patronage, and the prevalence of "turfism" within and between political parties.

In chapter 14, Gloppen investigates litigation as a strategy to advance the social rights of marginalized people, asking under what conditions it is likely to be effective. Conditions that are favorable to public interest litigation include effective voicing of social rights grievances, responsiveness of courts to social rights claims, competent public interest litigators. The ability of judges to find appropriate remedies, and authorities' compliance with judgments and implementation through social policies. However, litigation on its own has limited potential to achieve a real policy effect without organizations and social movements that use litigation as part of a broader strategy of social and political mobilization.

In chapter 15, Sage and Woolcock discuss legal and regulatory systems more broadly, focusing on the intersection of social development, policy, and judicial reform to reimagine justice reform processes. Effective legal systems are a precondition for development and poverty reduction, for example, in enforcement of property rights, equality before the law, and transaction reduction. But legal systems often, in fact, serve to perpetuate inequitable power relations and discrimination, producing legal inequality traps. Structures of inequality affect both the creation of institutions in the justice sector and the context within which they operate. Sage and Woolcock attribute the limited success of attempts at judicial reform to three factors: the missing law in policy, the missing rules in law, and the missing norms in rules. Like Gloppen in chapter 14, they highlight the embeddedness of law in broader societal institutions, organizations, and norms, and they warn against silver bullets to address deep-rooted problems of inequality. Difficulties arise when the normative understandings embedded in local-level systems are at odds with the rights and responsibilities articulated by state law. In those circumstances, focusing purely on state regimes and access to formal systems has severe limitations. Judicial reform is bound to fail if it focuses only on the formal, codified aspects of those mechanisms, thereby ignoring the broader system of rules that gives them legitimacy.

Conclusion and the Way Forward

Lessons from the emergence of OECD welfare states and postcommunist countries indicate that inclusive states can emerge under a diverse range of conditions. Levels of economic wealth are obviously important, but so are political interests, ideas, and international influence. Social policy design and implementation are highly context specific, with opportunities and inevitably choices for diverse forms of social policy design, institutions, and implementation. This book highlights two sets of key challenges in the debate on social policy in the international development literature. Each requires further policy analysis and operationalization.

First, policy design needs to take into account the potential weakness of basic state functions—including the macropolicy environment and rule of law—in many developing countries. The efficacy of social policy provisions, such as programs of cash transfers and human development investments, depends heavily on the quality of those basic state functions. Emphasis on strengthening public expenditure management is now widely accepted, not just for fiduciary reasons but also because the quality of public expenditure has important ramifications for social policy outcomes. But this emphasis on strengthening state functions needs to be extended to a perception of how such state policies create social contracts and, indeed, define citizenship.

Second, in most developing countries, such policies are grafted onto social structures that are marked by deep and historically rooted structural inequalities. Experience around the world indicates that such inequalities pose significant challenges to the provision of services and social policy and require long-term commitment to address deep-rooted questions and problems. The forms in which this commitment can occur are manifold and arise from different sources. This book describes some of the challenges found in different contexts and some of the ways in which these challenges can be—and are being—addressed.

The framework for inclusive states that emerges from this book envisages integration of macroeconomic policies with social policies and emphasizes the importance of paying attention to the legal and institutional domains, as well as to inclusive citizenship. This message is underscored by the consensus reached in the Arusha declaration on "the transformation of subjects and beneficiaries into citizens." Such a transformation "implies policies that recognize and promote the universal rights and responsibilities of citizens, and strengthen the capacity of citizens to claim their rights."

In the South, inclusive states must be created in a context of structural inequalities. These inequalities have been resilient precisely because inequalities based on gender, ethnicity, or other group characteristics were long not recognized as being significant or unjust. The invisibility of these social divides poses a major challenge for social policy. The first step to address this problem has to be to document and monitor how these inequalities produce differential social outcomes, which leave many mired in inequality traps. Actions within the legal domain to address such inequalities include affirmative action, reservation of quotas, and rights-based social policy or social guarantees that specify minimum entitlements for all citizens. Challenges to inequalities often come from various expressions of voice and agency, ranging from identity politics to social movements. The emergence of global networks and internationalization of ideas in recent years has strengthened such movements.

For policies to be effective, they must be enshrined in law. But laws can be invoked only when rules and regulations have been formulated, allowing for universal access to justice. Mechanisms such as public interest litigation can give voice to the voiceless, but only in environments where the legal system is responsive to social rights and where the litigation is reinforced by active social movements. These rules and regulations work well if they have been grafted onto deliberative traditions and are legitimized by existing norms. Bridging formal and informal systems is thus essential both for access to justice and for effective delivery of public services.

Arguably, the most crucial part of promoting inclusive states lies in the implementation processes that breathe life into structures and institutions. Such processes include participatory policy dialogue and public debate, which international donors, after many years of ignoring their significance, now actively encourage through poverty reduction strategies. This encouragement has, in turn, led governments to consult with their own constituencies rather than look upward to donors for help with policy formulation. When stakeholders have access to the evidence from distributional analysis, the inclusive policy dialogue can lead to formulation of pro-poor policies. In the legal domain, two important measures can be freedom of information laws and support for paralegals to create legal awareness and increase access to justice for the poor. Freedom of information is now an integral part of governance and anticorruption efforts. Pro-poor justice reform is in its infancy, but it can focus on the intersection of social development, policy, and judicial reform by linking policy to laws, laws to rules, and rules to the cultural norms and social relations from whence they arise. The social policy evaluation process in Jamaica (see chapter 13) highlights the importance of incentives and accountability to achieve more inclusive social policy. These implementation processes must be derived from the normative principles of transparency, voice, and accountability, as well as from equality of agency.

The recommendations for establishing inclusive states that emerge from this analysis are as follows:

- Systematic data collection on the relationship between diversity and inequality
- Endorsement of global charters, conventions, and declarations and enactment of national laws of nondiscrimination and affirmative action
- Formulation of rules and regulations to implement inclusive policies and laws, such as affirmative action
- Implementation of targeted and tailored programs to increase access to public services
- Careful monitoring and evaluation, including participatory monitoring, of program outcomes and effects
- Creation of an enabling environment to encourage stakeholder involvement in policy debates.

Understanding how inclusive institutions emerge and how they can be supported is crucial for many reasons. Citizens around the world are demanding more accountability from their governments: they demand better services, but also different ways of state-citizen interaction. Inclusiveness is key to the United Nations frameworks from which the MDGs are derived. This book indicates that there is no inherent tradeoff between (a) inclusiveness and (b) efficiency or economic growth. On the contrary, inclusive institutions can deliver better services to the entire population, build human and social capital, increase agency rather than dependency, and generate transparency and rule of law, thus leading, in the long run, to more sustainable and equitable development.

Notes

1. The Arusha conference was convened on December 12–15, 2005, by the World Bank in collaboration with the U.K. Department for International Development, the Swedish International Development Cooperation Agency, and the governments of Norway and Finland.
2. Different countries and communities have different valuations about the importance of equity, the levels of inequality that are acceptable, and the extent to which the focus of public policy should be on equality of opportunity or of outcomes.
3. Similar questions are being explored for assets and livelihoods through another set of papers from the Arusha conference, published under the title *Assets, Livelihoods, and Social Policy*, edited by Caroline Moser and Anis Dani (2008).
4. The Arusha conference issued a joint statement at its closing session that highlights as the overarching objective the transformation of subjects and beneficiaries into citizens, implying often the need to strengthen the capacity of citizens to claim their rights. See also Mamdani (2005).
5. A first draft of Kanbur (2007) was presented at the Arusha conference in December 2005.
6. The exceptions were countries like China and India, which continued to invest in higher education with their own resources, sometimes in defiance of contrary advice from international development agencies. Many countries in Africa, Latin America, and South Asia, however, were starved of public resources for higher education.
7. For a fuller exposition of this argument, see the preface of this book, which explains why social policy in the South needs to address an even wider range of issues than in OECD countries.
8. This definition is adapted from the issues paper first articulated in Dani (2005) and is discussed further in the preface of this book.
9. De Haan (2007) elaborates this point and discusses the social policy literature in detail.
10. For such experiences, see Fritz and Menocal (2007) and other contributions in the special issues of *Development Policy Review*, Kwon (2005), Mkandawire (2004), and UNRISD research on the late industrializers of Scandinavia and East Asia.
11. This volume, like other work on social policy, follows the idea that while lessons from OECD countries are not directly applicable, the method of social policy analysis can help inform the analysis in the South.
12. In the words of Gough and Wood (2004), the "welfare mix" is radically different in the South. The role of the state in the South in delivery of services is typically far less important (though social spending as a proportion of the

overall government budget or of gross domestic product is not necessarily low). Instead, informal networks and families play a greater role as providers of services. Although this situation makes notions of social policy problematic, it does not make them irrelevant. Rather, it implies that social policy design needs to be sensitive to and supportive of (not crowd out) informal and family- or household-based support networks.

13. See, for example, Paul Stubbs (2003: 333), who in discussing the role of inter-national nonstate actors on social development policy refers to the oligopoli-zation of the eight "super NGOs." By super NGOs, he means the families or federations of the largest international NGOs, which account for half the aid dispersed through NGOs and up to 80 percent of the financial assistance in complex emergencies. Also see Jeremy Gould's analysis (2003: 353) of the role of international NGOs in the policy process during the formulation of the first poverty reduction strategy in Tanzania. The international NGOs assumed the role of "surrogate civil society" in formulating and monitoring that strategy, leading to the unintended consequence of crowding out domestic NGOs from contributing constructively to social policy debates.

14. This summary is clearly an oversimplification of the complexities involved during the emergence of nation-states in the North. It ignores the treatment of minorities still residing across national boundaries and the discrimination against specific social groups considered culturally distinct (for example, the anti-Semitism or discrimination against the Roma that is found in many Cen-tral European countries). Ethnic tensions were particularly acute in the former Yugoslavia, which ultimately fragmented because of the absence of similar national integration.

15. The notion of structural inequality bears some resemblance to the concept of *inequality traps* (Bourguignon, Ferreira, and Walton 2007; Rao 2006), defined as "situations where the entire distribution is stable because the various dimen-sions of inequality (in wealth, power, and social status) interact to protect the rich from downward mobility, and to prevent the poor from being upwardly mobile" (Rao 2006: 11).

16. The communist ideology was inherently transformational, challenging existing power structures and propagating a more egalitarian ideology. Without deny-ing the social and economic costs of that process, communist states were able to provide more equitable social services to their citizens by overriding tradi-tional power structures. Similarly, the French Revolution and the American War of Independence provided platforms for more egalitarian and socially mobile societies.

17. One exception is the historical analysis of social integration in Tanzania by Samuel Wangwe (2005).

18. The Arusha conference called for fostering enabling, accessible, responsive, and accountable states. This effort entails providing equal rights under the law

for all citizens and requires legitimate, effective, and accountable institutions for policy formulation and implementation, with rigorous monitoring of outcomes. In many countries, mobilizing revenue and reducing aid dependence are key ingredients for accountable states.

References

African Union. 2006. "Meeting Social Development Challenges: Social Policy Framework in Africa." African Union, Addis Ababa.

Appadurai, A. 2004. "The Capacity to Aspire: Culture and the Terms of Recognition." In *Culture and Public Action*, eds. V. Rao and M. Walton, 59–84. Stanford, CA: Stanford University Press.

Ban, R., and V. Rao. 2008. "Tokenism or Agency? The Impact of Women's Reservations on Village Democracies in South India." *Economic Development and Cultural Change*, forthcoming.

Bebbington, A. J., A. Dani, A. de Haan, and M. Walton. 2008. *Institutional Pathways to Equity: Addressing Inequality Traps*. Washington, DC: World Bank.

Bourguignon, F., F. Ferreira, and M. Walton. 2007. "Equity, Efficiency, and Inequality Traps: A Research Agenda?" *Journal of Economic Inequality* 5 (2): 235–56.

Chattopadhyay, R., and E. Duflo. 2004. "Women as Policy Makers: Evidence From a Randomized Policy Experiment in India." *Econometrica* 72 (5): 1409–43.

Christiaensen, L., L. Demery, and S. Paternostro. 2002. "Growth, Distribution, and Poverty in Africa: Messages from the 1990s." Policy Research Working Paper 2810, World Bank, Washington, DC.

Dani, A. 2005. "Policies for Social Development in a Globalizing World: New Frontiers for Social Policy." Discussion paper for the Technical Consultation on Social Policy, Meeting of the Social Development Advisers Network, Washington, DC, February 14, 2005.

de Haan, A. 2007. *Reclaiming Social Policy: Globalization, Social Exclusion, and New Poverty Reduction Strategies*. Basingstoke, U.K.: Palgrave Macmillan.

Eyben, R., and J. Moncrieffe, eds. 2007. *The Power of Labelling: How People Are Categorized and Why It Matters*. London: Earthscan.

Fritz, V., and A. R. Menocal. 2007. "Development States in the New Millennium: Concepts and Challenges for a New Aid Agenda." *Development Policy Review* 25 (5): 531–52.

Gough, I., and G. Wood, with A. Barrientos, P. Bevan, P. Davis, and G. Room. 2004. *Insecurity and Welfare Regimes in Asia, Africa, and Latin America: Social Policy in Developmental Contexts*. Cambridge, U.K.: Cambridge University Press.

Gould, J. 2003. "Transnational Actors and the Politics of Poverty Reduction." *Global Social Policy* 3 (3): 349–53.

Graham, C. 2002. "Crafting Sustainable Social Contracts in Latin America: Political Economy, Public Attitudes, and Social Policy." Center on Social and Economic Dynamics Working Paper 29, Brookings Institution, Washington, DC. http://www.brookings.edu/es/dynamics/papers/socialcontracts/socialcontracts.pdf.

Herbst, J. 2000. *States and Power in Africa: Comparative Lessons in Authority and Control*. Princeton, NJ: Princeton University Press.

Kabeer, N., and S. Cook. 2000. "Re-visioning Social Policy in the South: Challenges and Concepts." *IDS Bulletin* 31 (4): 1–10.

Kanbur, R. 2007. "What's Social Policy Got to Do with Economic Growth." *Indian Journal of Human Development* 1 (1): 3–19.

Kwon, H.-J., ed. 2005. *Transforming the Developmental Welfare State in East Asia*. Basingstoke, U.K.: Palgrave Macmillan.

Kymlicka, W. 1995. *Multicultural Citizenship*. Oxford, U.K.: Oxford University Press.

———. 2006. "The Global Diffusion of Multiculturalism and Minority Rights." Paper presented at the Social Development Department and Development Research Group Social Science and Policy Seminar Series, World Bank, Washington, DC, March 9. http://siteresources.worldbank.org/INTRANETSOCIAL DEVELOPMENT/Resources/TheGlobalDiffusionofMulticulturalismand MinorityRights.pdf.

Lindert, P. H. 2004. *Growing Public: Social Spending and Economics Growth since the Eighteenth Century*. Cambridge, U.K.: Cambridge University Press.

Mamdani, M. 2005. "Political Identity, Citizenship, and Ethnicity in Post-colonial Africa." Keynote address, conference on New Frontiers of Social Policy: Development in a Globalizing World, Arusha, Tanzania, December 12–15. http://siteresources.worldbank.org/INTRANETSOCIALDEVELOPMENT/Resources/revisedMamdani.pdf.

Mkandawire, T., ed. 2004. *Social Policy in a Development Context*. London: Palgrave Macmillan.

Moser, C., and A. Dani, eds. 2008. *Assets, Livelihoods, and Social Policy*. Washington, DC: World Bank.

Rao, V. 2006. "On 'Inequality Traps' and Development Policy." *Development Outreach* 8 (1): 10–13.

Rao, V., and M. Walton, eds. 2004. *Culture and Public Action: Cross Disciplinary Dialogue on Development Policy*. Stanford, CA: Stanford University Press.

Shepherd, A., and E. Gyimah-Boadi, with S. Gariba, S. Plagerson, and A. Wahab Musa. 2004. "Bridging the North-South Divide in Ghana." Background paper for *World Development Report 2006: Equity and Development* Washington, DC: World Bank. http://siteresources.worldbank.org/INTRANETSOCIAL DEVELOPMENT/Resources/North_South_Divide_Ghana_Shepard_et_al.pdf.

Stubbs, P. 2003. "International Non-state Actors and Social Development Policy." *Global Social Policy* 3 (3): 319–47.

UNDP (United Nation Development Programme). 2004. *Human Development Report 2004: Cultural Liberty in Today's Diverse World.* New York: UNDP.

UNRISD (United Nations Research Institute for Social Development). 2006. "Transformative Social Policy: Lessons from UNRISD Research." Research and Policy Brief 5, UNRISD, Geneva.

Wangwe, S. 2005. "Culture, Identity, and Social Integration: The Tanzania Experience in Social Integration." Paper presented at the World Bank conference on New Frontiers of Social Policy: Development in a Globalizing World, Arusha, Tanzania, December 12–15. http://siteresources.worldbank.org/INTRANETSOCIAL DEVELOPMENT/Resources/244329-1133801177129/Wangwe.rev.1.pdf.

Wood G. D., and I. Gough. 2006. "A Comparative Welfare Regime Approach to Global Social Policy." *World Development* 34 (10): 1696–712.

World Bank. 1990. *World Development Report 1990: Poverty.* Washington, DC: World Bank.

———. 2006. *World Development Report 2006: Equity and Development.* Washington, DC: World Bank.

———. 2007. "Realizing Rights through Social Policy." Social Development Department, World Bank, Washington, DC.

CHAPTER 2

European Welfare States: Explanations and Lessons for Developing Countries

Ian Gough

Given the longevity and vast institutional presence of welfare states in Europe, examining whether they can offer any lessons to the developing world is worthwhile. Clearly, lessons can take the form of negative warnings, as well as positive role models. Because social policy can refer to both government actions and the study of those actions, however, two types of possible lessons exist: (a) models of social policy action to follow or avoid and (b) forms of social policy analysis that help address emerging social problems. In an earlier survey titled "Social Security in Developed Countries: Are There Lessons for Developing Countries?" Atkinson and Hills (1991) concluded that few lessons can be drawn concerning policy recommendations, but many arise on the methods of social policy analysis. This chapter adopts that general perspective.

The origins of European social policy are difficult to identify. In the United Kingdom, modern social policy can perhaps be dated from the New Poor Law Act of 1834 and the 1842 *Report on the Sanitary Condition of the Labouring Population of Great Britain* (Chadwick 1965 [1842]). State intervention in education and social security came much later. The Prussian state introduced compulsory education earlier, and in 1883, Otto von Bismarck introduced the world's first health insurance program, followed by old-age pensions in 1889. Before the onset of World War I, the United

The author is indebted to Dr. Emma Carmel, to Dr. Barbara Darimont, and especially to Prof. Stephan Leibfried for constructive comments on earlier drafts, and to my research student Dr. Young-jun Choi for comments plus work on the bibliography. None bears any responsibility for what follows.

Kingdom saw the introduction of old-age pensions, school meals, and the first social insurance scheme. By that time, a dense network of local and municipal services in health, housing, and social care had reached much of Europe also.

The terms *Sozialstaat* and *Sozialpolitik* first appeared in Germany in the mid-19th century, almost a century before the term *welfare state* emerged in Britain in the early 1940s. Post–World War II political settlements in several Western countries heralded extensive and comprehensive social policies. The emerging national welfare systems frequently replaced or displaced cooperative, enterprise, or workers' welfare provision, while extending territorial, socioeconomic, and occupational coverage in the process. Although the shape of social policy differs across countries and policy domains, it is a significant feature of Organisation for Economic Co-operation and Development (OECD) states[1] in the second half of the 20th century. Therborn (1983) defined welfare states as those states where more than one-half of all government expenditures are devoted to social policy, as opposed to the economy, the military, law and order, infrastructure, and other traditional state functions. On this basis, even the United States qualified as a welfare state in the last quarter of the 20th century.

Given that our focus is European social policy, we must first define *Europe*. Even if we confine ourselves to the pre-enlargement European Union (EU) of 15 members, we encounter the same problem that most researchers encounter: different "welfare state regimes" (Esping-Andersen 1990, 1999) or different "families of nations" (Castles 1993) within the EU. Four are generally identified (Ferrera and Rhodes 2000):

- Liberal: Ireland and the United Kingdom
- Social democratic: the Nordic countries
- Continental: Austria, the Benelux countries, France, and Germany
- Southern: Greece, Italy, Portugal, and Spain.

Thus, Europe is not homogeneous, and its lessons are plural. Indeed, Europe offers a natural and well-studied landscape of differing social policy responses to broadly similar social problems. Because one of its more pervasive lessons is that there are multiple routes to broadly similar goals, a major analytical task is to understand the reasons behind these differences. Many studies extend the field of comparison to the OECD world of industrial capitalist states, thus including Australasia, Canada,

Japan, and the United States. This extension compounds the issue of diversity but offers still more variability to enrich comparative analysis. This chapter demonstrates that comparative social policy analysis supplies a rich set of findings, theories, and hypotheses for the developing world.

Definitions, Measures, Problems of Method

Although much research has been done into the development of social policy in Europe and the OECD over the past century, for the purposes of this chapter one issue that must be determined from the outset is the meaning—and hence the measures—of social policy: the so-called dependent variable problem. Following Deacon (2003a), one can distinguish the "three Rs": regulation, redistribution, and rights. This approach immediately suggests three ways of assessing the extent and nature of social policies:

1. *Regulation* encompasses the major legislation and regulations that modify the behavior of private actors to achieve publicly recognized goals, justified by some reference to normative values. The private actors can be individuals in households, firms and collective economic actors, and groups and movements in civil society. This variable suggests a vast scope for social policy, although in practice it is restricted to policies designed to influence something directly—such as Beveridge's (1942) "Five Giants": (a) want (social protection, money transfers); (b) disease (health services, both preventive and curative); (c) squalor (housing and urban planning); (d) ignorance (education and training); and (e) idleness (employment policies).
2. *Redistribution* means the extent to which the state, through taxation and public expenditure, redistributes factor or primary incomes in a progressive direction. This variable entails measures of public spending and of taxation and other forms of revenue. Although easier to measure than rights, they pose questions of meaning; all else being equal, growing unemployment will result in growing public expenditure on benefits for the unemployed, and an aging population will result in higher pension and health spending. However, these expenditure trends may mask stagnation or even reversal in terms of benefits, rights, or redistribution. Also, as the definition of regulation suggests,

the state can influence welfare outcomes by regulating, mandating, taxing, or subsidizing private actors. Social needs can be met by a mix of institutions, something more often appreciated in developing countries' contexts.[2]

3. *Rights* refer to the extent to which substantive social and economic rights (as opposed to procedural civil and political rights) are guaranteed by the state to the entire population (although this guarantee can be qualified by residence, nationality, and citizenship). Following T. H. Marshall (1950), this variable identifies the defining characteristic of welfare states as the use of state-guaranteed rights to counter the power of money or political connections. After World War II, full employment was recognized as an equivalent economic right in several countries.

All three Rs have been used as dependent variables in Western social policy research; however, the dominant focus in all three has been the direct role of the state. Important exceptions to this general focus include studies of employment policies, where tripartite corporatist arrangements with business and unions often take center stage, and research on varieties of capitalism (Crouch and Streeck 1997; Hall and Soskice 2001).

Another way of conceptualizing the dependent variable is to distinguish inputs, outputs, and outcomes in social policy.

- *Inputs* refer to legislative inputs, or the expenditure of resources, whether monetary or workforce (such as, spending on social protection).
- *Outputs* can refer to the implementation of legislation and the provision of specific services (such as, coverage rates of social insurance benefits for designated groups).
- *Outcomes* refer to the final effects on individuals (such as, poverty, mortality, or literacy rates) or on societal distributions (level of inequality).

In all these definitions, social policy can be studied as a whole or with a focus on different policy areas, such as health, education, social protection. Some analysts, such as Kasza (2002), argue that researching specific policy areas is less misleading and avoids aggregating very different entities into a spurious overall measure. In contrast, some examples of complementary or substitutive effects on welfare outcomes—see Castles's (1998a) cross-national study of owner-occupied housing as a functional alternative to pensions in providing security in old age—qualify the utility of studying policy areas in isolation.

There is also an understandable search for parsimony. Yet the wider the scope of the dependent variable, the greater the research problems, as Castles (1998b: 4) observes:

- Complex policy processes are rarely likely to have singular determinants.
- There is no guarantee that the factors influencing policy will be invariant over time.
- There is no reason to suppose that different kinds of policy outputs will have the same determinants.
- Different policy outputs impact on different welfare outcomes in complex ways.

Two methodologies have predominated in this research. The first comprises qualitative, often historical, research on a single country or small-scale comparisons of two or three countries. Examples include Heclo (1974) and Weir, Orloff, and Skocpol (1988). These works have provided valuable insights into the complex evolution of social responses to changing social structures and the emergence of new social problems. The second methodology comprises quantitative, cross-national analysis over time, across nations, or both. Typically, it involves about 18 nations that are industrialized and relatively affluent and that have been democratic since World War II; in recent years, the previously undemocratic Greece, Portugal, and Spain have been added (Castles 1998b). Multiple regression analysis has been a favored tool, despite criticisms (Janoski and Hicks 1994; Shalev 2007). The major issues with such techniques are overdetermination, with too many variables chasing too few cases, and, to a lesser extent, multicollinearity.[3]

Stiller and van Kersbergen (2005) provide a useful review of research findings. One problem they identify is the interdependence between independent variables and dependent variables. If such variables are interdependent, contrasting theoretical explanations can be validated simultaneously. Nevertheless, they and other reviewers appreciate that, over the past three decades, comparative cross-national research building on detailed single-country studies has yielded a cumulative growth in understanding of social policy. The following sections survey some of this research.[4]

Social Policies in Europe and the OECD: The "Five Is"

Figure 2.1 presents a modified form of a basic textbook model of policy making, based on Easton (1965) and Hill (2003). It first distinguishes three explanatory factors: industrialization, interests, and institutions.

Figure 2.1. A Simple Model of Social Policy Making

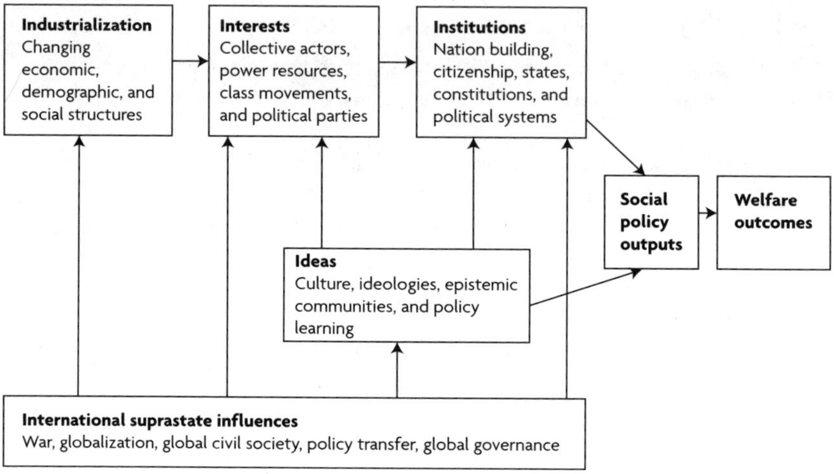

Source: Author's diagram, based on Easton 1965 and Hill 2003.

Interestingly, these factors were developed in roughly this historical order in the literature. Two more factors are also considered: (a) ideas and ideologies (which can operate both through interest groups in civil society and through governmental institutions) and (b) international influences (the original model focused entirely on internal explanatory factors). This section summarizes research findings on the effect of the "five Is" on European and OECD social policy.[5]

Industrialization and Other Macrosocial Changes

In the 1950s and 1960s, the dominant school identified social policy as a consequence or correlate of industrialization (Aaron 1967; Cutright 1965; Wilensky 1975; Wilensky and Lebeaux 1958). The dependent variable was public social expenditure as a share of gross domestic product (GDP), and the relationship was demonstrated in time-series and cross-sectional analysis. Researchers generally agreed that "economic growth and its demographic and bureaucratic outcomes are the root causes of the general emergence of the welfare state" (Wilensky 1975: xiii; see also Mishra 1977; Pampel and Williamson 1989). At an accounting level, it would not be surprising if the share of social expenditure rose faster than economic growth (if such services were superior economic goods) or in response to demographic change (if the number of school-age children or pension-age elderly rose as a proportion of population).

Nevertheless, several more fundamental explanations have been advanced to account for this relationship. The first was based on Talcott Parsons's theory of functional differentiation. As societies developed, new public bodies, such as sanitation agencies, health services, and income support, would take over the functions traditionally performed by families and communities. However, the new social policies did not displace other institutions; rather, the decline of traditional forms of provision under the pressures of industrialization and demographic change called forth new public bodies and responsibilities (Wilensky and Lebeaux 1958; see also Mishra 1977). This theory is similar to Karl Polanyi's (1944) account in *The Great Transformation* of the "societal responses" to the social upheavals brought about by the "disembedding" of labor markets from prior social relations. All these accounts, however, could be, and were, criticized as *functionalist*: that is, as assuming that a new social "need" would necessarily be identified and met—and would be met by new public institutions.

Gough (1979) attempted to avoid the charge of functionalism by explaining social policy innovation in the face of capitalist industrialization by the centralization of states fostered by rising class struggles. Rimlinger (1971) developed a more comparative and historically informed account of industrialization, while still recognizing the ultimate basis of welfare policy in Europe as the proletarianization of the workforce and the new insecurities faced by this growing class. Gerschenkron (1962) demonstrated the advantages of the latecomer in the West, whereby Germany could industrialize faster than the United Kingdom by benefiting from technological learning, thus providing a systemic argument for why industrialization is not a uniform process. These perspectives all qualify the simple industrialization thesis and are returned to later in this chapter.

Demographic transition has long been recognized as a concomitant of economic development and transformation. Demographic shifts include a fall in mortality and fertility rates, a decline in three-generational households, and a move to smaller households. Later trends have included increased divorce and remarriage and rising numbers of lone-parent households. Independently, these trends strongly influence new social policies, from social protection to care services. Yet research by the OECD reveals three important caveats to this demographic story. First, these trends occur at widely differing rates across countries. The family in southern Europe, for example, exhibits remarkably low rates of fertility, divorce, births outside marriage, and single parenthood, and it exhibits significantly high numbers of elderly individuals living with their children (Gough 2000: 131–52).

Second, in all countries, the family retains a central role in managing the articulation of labor markets and welfare states and in providing care work and managing security. The pressures for state-provided or regulated alternatives to the family will continue to build, but their form will differ according to the persistence of the household economy. Here, a study of Italy and southern Europe could provide useful lessons for the developing world. Third, and most important, national social policies are implicated in these different demographic outcomes. By enabling or stymieing the ability of women and men to combine paid work and child care, they can encourage, delay, or discourage fertility; fertility becomes an endogenous factor within different welfare systems (Castles 2002).

This discussion leads to the effects of other social structures that stress national diversity as opposed to sources of convergence. Two important factors here are religion and ethnicity. Since Max Weber and Stein Rokkan (see Flora 1999), the importance of religion within Europe has focused on the post-Reformation division between Catholicism and Protestantism and the subsequent independence from, or integration of, the church with the state. The relationship with social policy is not simple; strong links between the state and the Lutheran church led to extensive early social interventions in Sweden, and by the end of the 19th century, new Catholic doctrines of "social capitalism" and subsidiarity fostered different forms of state and societal responsibility. The differences between Protestant, Catholic, and mixed religious nations persist. For example, the proportion of the population baptized into the Catholic Church can explain several persistent social policy features, such as social transfers (positive) and women working (negative) (Castles 1998b). This finding suggests that the influence of other faiths and related values should feature when one is studying the development of social policies across the diverse nations of the world.

The effect of other horizontal differentiating factors, such as language, race, and ethnicity, on the development of state welfare has figured in historical studies of state building (Flora 1999; Flora and Heidenheimer 1981). It has also played an important role in explaining the rudimentary welfare statism of the United States in terms of its ethnic and racial diversity (compared with that of industrial European countries). According to Goodhart (2004), cultural diversity—the result of increased migration into Europe in recent years—threatens the social cohesion and willingness to pay high taxes on which European welfare states depend. A regression analysis by Taylor-Gooby (2005) finds that diversity does negatively affect social expenditure, but the existence of left-wing politics dramatically reduces this effect. This finding suggests interests and institutions mediate the effect of horizontal diversity on territorial social policy.

Interests: Collective Actors, Power Resources, Democracy, and Parties

Theoretical and empirical critiques of modernization theses were complemented by empirical findings, notably the exceptional trajectory of the United States. Those factors gave rise to a second set of explanations in the 1970s, which moved beyond macrosocial changes to prioritize the collective organization and powers of major social actors, notably social classes. Although this theory is sometimes referred to as the *social democratic model* (Castles 1978), the label *power resources* or *democratic class struggle model* (Korpi 1978, 1983) may be more helpful. All such models begin from a class-based clash of interests. In an original study of the cross-national policy perspectives of labor and business interests in 1881 and 1981, Therborn (1986) found (not surprisingly perhaps) labor advocating greater state economic interventions, full-employment policies, universal and extensive social policies, and greater fiscal redistribution and economic equality. Business organizations favored incentives to growth, private provision plus low coverage of social benefits, and low redistribution. The hypothesis was that the distribution of power resources between the main social classes of capitalist society determined the extent, range, and redistributive effects of economic and social policies. It is helpful here to distinguish the effects of (a) extraparliamentary class-based mobilization and (b) political party systems after democratic representation has been established.

The creation, self-activation, and mobilization of groups of workers that accompanied capitalist industrialization have been featured in many accounts of the origins of European welfare states. Proletarian and other struggles, trade unions, and socialist parties formed a backdrop to the emergence of national social policies throughout Europe (Gough 1979). In their account of the origins of the U.S. New Deal in the 1930s and President Johnson's Great Society program in the 1960s, Piven and Cloward (1972) describe how mobilization by poor and dispossessed groups in the United States forced social concessions from resistant elites. Following World War II, the dominant "political settlement" in Europe was an exchange of labor's acceptance of a capitalist economy in return for the acceptance by capital of collective representation and bargaining, social services, and social protection.[6]

Nonetheless, after universal suffrage was granted, the terrain of class and other social struggles was altered (Flora 1986–87; Flora and Heidenheimer

1981). Interestingly, democratization has rarely been studied as a causal factor in the development of welfare states. However, in a study of the introduction of social insurance programs before World War I, Flora and Alber (1981) demonstrated that absolutist states, such as Bismarck's Germany, pioneered social policies precisely to sidestep democratization.

One exception was Hewitt (1977), who demonstrated the importance of the "simple democratic hypothesis" in accounting for country differences in equality outcomes. When democracy was established, unions' rights were recognized in law, and parties representing working classes and other subordinate interests were permitted to organize, leading to a decisive shift in the class balance of power. Working-class organizations and parties had more leverage to counter the previously natural-seeming demands of business and traditional elites. Within this school, analysts placed different emphases on the role of unions and other collective organizations, on the voting share of leftist political parties, and on parties' shares of cabinet posts or their role in the executive. Castles (1978), stressed the weakness and dividedness of the Right, rather than the strength of the Left as the decisive factor. Baldwin (1990) argued strongly that class coalitions had been historically important in major social policy innovations; for example, urban–rural coalitions are likely to result in universalist welfare states. The link between strong trade unionism and centralized, neocorporatist industrial relations systems has spawned another strand of analysis and explanation.

Numerous studies have corroborated these two arguments centered on interests.[7] The upshot is that class struggles matter and politics matter. The industrialization and modernization of Europe and the West did not generate welfare states per se; rather, these trends were reflected in class cleavages, class organizations within civil society, their respective powers, their economic and social mobilization, and later, their parliamentary representation. A crucial factor has been the emergence of ideologically based parties pursuing a class-based program of reform in place of clientelist or personalized parties.

Nevertheless, the class-power resources approach could not explain the early introduction of social policies by non-class-based parties or the subsequent emergence of strong welfare systems in countries with relatively weak unions and social democratic parties, such as the Netherlands (Skocpol and Amenta 1986; Therborn 1989). Studies also revealed the importance of third-sector provision outside the state and the market— by religious organizations and other voluntary bodies. For example, in

Germany and the Netherlands, Protestant, Catholic, Jewish, and secular (and now Muslim) organizations provide parallel social services. The result is a "pillarized" social policy.

The important but differing influence of both Protestantism and Catholicism previously noted was amplified with the founding of Christian Democrat parties. Christian Democrat welfare states in Europe provide very generous transfer benefits, especially to male breadwinners, but with a low commitment to full-employment policies and the provision of social services (van Kersbergen 1995).

Esping-Andersen's (1990) influential work on welfare state regimes combined the analysis thus far, identifying not two, but three, worlds of welfare capitalism: liberal, social democratic, and conservative or Christian Democratic (see box 2.1).

BOX 2.1

The Welfare Regime Synthesis

Esping-Andersen (1990) elaborated three worlds of welfare capitalism in the democratic member states of the OECD, not just the two poles of liberal and social democratic identified in the power resources theory. He also argued strongly that social expenditure was not an acceptable measure of social policy: "It is difficult to imagine that anyone struggled for spending *per se*" (Esping-Andersen 1990: 21).

The welfare state regime approach instead developed three distinct criteria of welfare capitalism and three sets of measures to complement it. First came the mix of the role of states and markets in the production of welfare—to which was added the role of households in Esping-Andersen's later work (1999). Let us call this the *welfare mix*. Second, he posited a new measure of welfare outcomes, which tracked the reality of social rights in a country—*decommodification*. This measure assessed "the degree to which individuals, or families, can uphold a socially acceptable standard of living independently of market participation" (1990: 37). In the 1999 book, he complemented this measure with the parallel concept of *defamilialization*; "a de-familializing regime is one which seeks to unburden the household and diminish individuals' welfare dependence on kinship" (Esping-Andersen 1999: 51). The third criterion is the effect of these two factors on the dominant pattern of stratification in a country, measured by the degree of segmentation and inequality in different social security systems. These factors provide

(continued)

BOX 2.1

The Welfare Regime Synthesis (*continued*)

positive feedback, shaping class coalitions that tend to reproduce or intensify the original institutional matrix and welfare outcomes, resulting in strong path dependency.

Esping-Andersen identified three welfare state regimes in advanced capitalist countries with continual democratic histories since World War II: liberal, conservative-corporatist, and social democratic. He summarized their characteristics as shown in the accompanying table.

The Three Worlds of Welfare Capitalism

Role of	Liberal	Conservative-corporatist	Social democratic
Family	Marginal	Central	Marginal
Market	Central	Marginal	Marginal
State	Marginal	Subsidiary	Central
Welfare state:			
Dominant locus of solidarity	Market	Family	State
Dominant mode of solidarity	Individual	Kinship Corporatism Statism	Universal
Degree of decommodification	Minimal	High (for breadwinner)	Maximum
Modal examples	United States	Germany and Italy	Sweden

Source: Adapted from Esping-Andersen 1999, table 5.4.

Institutions: States, Constitutions, and Political Systems

In the post–World War II United Kingdom, T. H. Marshall (1950) famously interpreted growing state responsibility as the last stage in the extension of citizenship. Civil rights emerged in the 18th century, culminating in the 1832 Reform Act, followed by the spread of political rights, notably an extension of the suffrage, in the 19th and early 20th centuries. The crucial third stage for Marshall (1950: 11) was the emergence of social rights in the first half of the 20th century: "The right to a modicum of economic welfare and security, to share to the full in the social heritage, and to live the life of a civilized being according to the standards prevailing in society." The welfare state was the culmination of this third stage and could reasonably be dated in the United Kingdom from July 5, 1948, when the National Insurance Act and the National Health Service Act came into force. Continental scholars recognized, however, that this sequence varied across countries; Bismarck's Germany extended social rights to social security precisely as a foil to extending political rights.

Stein Rokkan, in turn, developed a much more extensive theorization of the welfare state as a final stage in nation building in Europe (Flora 1999). The role of social policy institutions in the building of nation-states and welfare states has long been acknowledged (Heclo 1974; Skocpol 1985). For one thing, a welfare state requires an effective tax state, as Schumpeter (1918/1991) long ago recognized. In several countries, an overarching drive toward welfare statism occurred, as in Bismarck's Germany, where social insurance in the 1880s provided a social motor to consolidate the unification of 1870 and 1871 (Rimlinger 1971). In several federal countries today, the welfare state can act as a force for unity (Obinger, Leibfried, and Castles 2005); when secession threatens, the welfare state can act as a lightning rod for articulation of interests and provide compensation for socio- and ethno-territorial divisions and inequalities.[8]

By the late 1980s to the early 1990s, a new institutionalism had entered comparative research into social policy development, notably to explain the nature and blocks to reforming and cutting back developed welfare systems, as seen in the work of Paul Pierson (1994). This school of thought places the nature of the state and political institutions and their patterns of development center stage. It largely explains the nature of and variations between national social policies in terms of the mediating role of institutions of the state and its policy-making processes.

Significant differences in state structures and political systems, however, have proved more difficult to operationalize and measure to assess their effect in facilitating or blocking significant social policy reforms. Two major strands of thought have emerged. First, following the work of Immergut (1992) and Maioni (1997), research has concentrated on the centralization of decision making at the summit of political systems and the extent to which the executive is insulated from parliamentary and electoral pressures. If power is dispersed and many veto points exist, then relatively small and well-organized groups can block the systemic changes required to radically reform health or social security programs (see Bonoli

2000). Thus, federal systems (see Obinger, Leibfried, and Castles 2005) or constitutional separation of powers hinder the development of welfare states—doubly so if both are present. Conversely, parliamentary systems of government encourage party discipline and minimize special-interest lobbying. The second strand emphasizes the bureaucratic legacies of past social programs—the way that public teachers and health workers, for example, or new clienteles, such as old-age pensioners, can mobilize to defend and extend social programs and benefits (Flora 1986–87; Pierson 2000).

A combination of these three factors—industrialization, interests, and institutions—might now be characterized as the orthodox model of social policy in the West (see box 2.2).

BOX 2.2

The Orthodox Model

In an early synthetic and cross-national analysis, Huber, Ragin, and Stephens (1993) tested the effects of state differences on social expenditure, generosity of benefits, extent of redistribution, and other measures of social rights. They concluded that constitutional structures played an important role in explaining the contrasts between Sweden, on the one side, and Switzerland and the United States, on the other. However, they also found that the first two factors—industrialization and interests—remained significant: all else being equal, aging populations and high-income levels led to higher social expenditure. More important, social democracy strongly influenced decommodification and redistribution, while Christian democracy fostered high transfer benefits but also high unemployment.

The model can be summarized as follows:

1. The development of social policy is determined by all three factors—industrialization, interests, and institutions.

2. However, the factors explain different aspects and measures of social policies—the dependent variable problem.

3. Thus, independent variables and dependent variables are interdependent. Stiller and van Kersbergen (2005) refer to this finding as the matching problem: that cause and effect tend to be specified at different levels of analysis. This problem will require stronger causal theorizing and more sophisticated methodologies in the next generation of welfare state research.

Source: Huber, Ragin, and Stephens 1993.

Ideas: Culture, Ideologies, and Epistemic Communities

The orthodox model however, omits one explanation once common in the 19th century—the role of ideas and their influence on reforming elites. Three levels, varying from more to less abstract, are distinguished: the role of (a) cultural systems, (b) ideas and dominant ideologies, and (c) epistemic communities and policy transfer.

The influence of cultural systems, including religious and other worldviews, on the formation of states and welfare states has been hinted at already. For example, Catholic social thinking provided a distinctive antisocialist and antiliberal rationale for public social policies. The principle of *subsidiarity*—that policies be enacted at the lowest effective social level—not only recognized the crucial role of family, community, workplace, and church, but also advocated a significant place for local, regional, and national public bodies (see also Castles 1993). The resurgence of cultural explanations in recent years has occurred partly to explain different family patterns and gender roles within Europe and the OECD. Pfau-Effinger (2005) recognizes the relative autonomy of cultural values, yet sees them as alterable in the face of basic contradictions, such as the clash between individualism and the gendered division of labor within families and marriage that create dependence. Nevertheless, it would be fair to conclude that cultural explanations of policy making are more sophisticated in development studies than social policy studies (for example, Rao and Walton 2004).

Culturalist explanations face particular problems explaining policy changes, a recurring theme of Hall's (1989) work on the power of ideas in policy change. Hall (1993) later distinguished three orders of policy learning: first order, influencing policy settings; second order, influencing policy instruments; and third order, where policy goals are questioned and revised. He applied these orders to explain the rise of neoliberal thinking in the 1970s, which had profound consequences for Western welfare states. The Golden Age of postwar Keynesian welfare states was founded on extensive employment opportunities and a complementarity between labor markets and welfare systems. This harmony between economy and social policy is commonly perceived to have broken down with the challenge of monetarism in the 1970s (Mishra 1984). Later, Jessop (1993) claimed that Keynesian welfare states were being replaced by the "Schumpeterian workfare state," although whether as a dominant discourse or as a reality was ambiguous. In the 1990s, the discourse of welfare state crisis fused with ideas of globalization. These crisis discourses have wide resonance today, although they are undermined by studies that demonstrate the quiet, incremental adjustments of European social policies to their changing economic environments.

One notable counteridea is the productive welfare state. Originating in Sweden in the 1930s, this concept recognizes the contribution to modernization and prosperity of good-quality and equitable education, health care, population, and family policies. The idea has recently been rediscovered with the shift to a postindustrial economy wherein human capital assumes central importance and in the new "Third Way" discourse (Giddens 1998). Thus, social policies were not and are not solely about redistribution. Some policies, such as early school meals in the United Kingdom, have always been perceived as performing a productive public-good role. In general in Europe, protective and productive welfare states have developed together—national schooling and national health systems accompanying the development of social insurance and national safety nets. Indeed, they are difficult to disentangle.

A third school has studied the role of ideas in policy innovation and learning through the concept of *epistemic communities,* defined as "a network of professionals with recognized expertise and competence and authoritative claims to policy-relevant knowledge within a domain or issue area" (Haas 1992: 3). Economists provided one powerful example of an epistemic community in the modern world, but social policy experts provide an important alternative epistemic community in most European countries. In some writings, this literature fused with previous work on policy communities, issue networks, and advocacy coalitions. All recognized that learning was an important driver of policy change. Both dominant discourses and epistemic communities can be harnessed to explain the influence of ideas on reform-minded elites and their role in framing the options for policy change—preemptive reforms from above (Gough 1979: chapter 4).

International: Suprastate Influences on Policy Making

The former accounts all share a focus on the individual nation-state and on internal factors explaining the emergence of social policy and national welfare states. Until two decades ago, few recognized that external, supranational factors and agencies played any role in this process, with one exception: the impact of war.

For the most part, World War II has been a taken-for-granted backdrop in postwar thinking on social policy in Europe, but analysts generally recognize that it marked a decisive turning point in the emergence of "big government," extensive welfare states, and citizenship rights to benefits and services (Parry 1986). "Total" war required the full mobilization of societies' resources, which enhanced both social demands and state capacities, as Titmuss (1950) demonstrated in his study of the impact of World War II on the postwar U.K. welfare state (see also Peacock and Wiseman 1961). This influence was prefigured in the impact of the American Civil War on U.S. veterans' and early federal programs, as Amenta and Skocpol (1988) illustrated. Although little comparative analysis exists, major differences occurred across nations, between victors and vanquished, and between those countries occupied or fought over and those not (see Castles 1998b).

Elsewhere, the external environment was the postwar settlement of the United Nations system and the Bretton Woods institutions. These posed significant constraints on economic and social policy making, as witnessed in the United Kingdom in 1977, when the government was required by the International Monetary Fund (IMF) to cut its budget deficit and social spending. Nevertheless, within this framework, social policies were assumed to be formulated by nation-states with significant autonomy. The importance of transnational and supranational factors in the making of social policy began to be recognized with the decoupling of the U.S. dollar and the move toward monetarist and neoliberal policies in the late 1970s. However, it was the emergence of Eastern Europe from behind the Iron Curtain and the discourse and partial reality of globalization that prompted significant research into the role of supranational factors on the development of national social policies.

It is possible to identify supranational equivalents of all four national factors previously described:

1. *Globalization* involves relatively unplanned, autonomous supranational and interconnected trends affecting the socioeconomic environment of national policy making. Much research in the OECD has focused on the effect of increasing economic openness on national social policies.
2. *Global civil society* means the organization of interests at a supranational level, including labor, international nongovernmental organizations, social movements, and pressure groups.
3. *Global governance* deals with the increasing role of international governmental organizations, including the United Nations, IMF, World Bank, International Labour Organization, World Trade Organization, and World Health Organization, as well as important

regional associations, notably the OECD and the EU, and powerful nation-states, notably the United States and its agencies.

4. *Global epistemic communities* are the increasingly interconnected policy networks and communities operating at the supranational level.

The chapter will now consider briefly the effect of the first and fourth factors on European welfare states, although the third is of great importance in much of the developing world.

Economic openness. The term *economic openness* refers to the growing openness of Western economies to trade and investment flows, the multinational siting of integrated production systems, and financial deregulation. The dominant hypothesized effect on the welfare states of the West was initially negative: the retrenchment of uncompetitive welfare states—a "race to the bottom" in taxation, regulation, state responsibilities, social rights, and redistribution (Mishra 1999). More specifically, greater trade competition was predicted to generate deindustrialization and loss of unskilled jobs; greater capital flows to lead to tax competition, "social dumping," and a reduced bargaining power of states and labor; and financial deregulation to produce a decline in states' macroeconomic policy autonomy.

Against this hypothesis, an empirical observation and a counterthesis can be made. Identified first by Cameron (1978), the empirical observation is that the share of social expenditure in GDP positively correlates with openness to trade across the OECD, and this link appears to be growing in strength (Rodrik 1998; see also Garrett 1998). The counterthesis, first advanced by Katzenstein (1985) and later more systematically by Rieger and Leibfried (2003), explains this fact in terms of reverse causation: modern Western welfare states formed the vital precondition for postwar international economic liberalization, because only social policy could assume the social protection functions previously provided by tariffs and quotas. In democracies, only when national individual rights to social benefits had been established could governments seriously entertain dismantling trade protection and open up domestic markets to foreign competition.

Scharpf and Schmidt (2000) and their colleagues did one of the most in-depth studies on the effect of these factors on Western welfare states. Despite their initial view that economic globalization would impose convergent and downward pressures, the results did not support this conclusion. Rather, Scharpf and Schmidt (2000) found that countries reacted differently to common international challenges according to their domestic institutions; countries were moving on different employment and welfare system trajectories between which there was little transition (see also Bowles and Wagman 1997). This finding supports Esping-Andersen's (1999: 165) conclusion that in the face of economic openness, "the inherent logic of our three welfare regimes seems to reproduce itself." Another study by Pierson (2001) and colleagues reinforced this finding, concluding that external globalization pressures are far less significant for contemporary welfare states than the internal pressures of postindustrialism, including aging and declining fertility, the switch to service jobs, and family instability.

As a result, the evidence supporting the negative impact of economic globalization on European welfare states is weak. The conclusion, rather, is that domestic and international institutions, interests, and ideas mediate economic globalization pressures. This argument has been developed in relation to the advanced capitalist countries of the North, notably in the work of Swank (2002). Now it is appearing in research into social policy reform in the transitional countries (Müller 2002, 2003; Orenstein 2000) and the developing world—for example, Mesa-Lago (2000) on Latin America and Gough (2001) on East Asia. However, others dispute that the weak impacts on powerful Northern states will be replicated, especially among small weak Southern states (Deacon 2003b).

Cross-national policy learning and transfer. Between 1907 and 1908, Lord Beveridge and David Lloyd George visited Germany to study the new system of state social insurance; this was a highly visible, but by no means the earliest, example of policy learning and policy transfer from abroad. Hennock (1987) documents the German precedents of U.K. social reform; Heclo (1974) develops the concept of political or policy learning and applies it to the spread of social policy ideas. Hall (1993), as we have seen, broadened this concept to social learning. These concepts have both informed and fostered a growing literature on policy transfer: the development of programs, policies, or institutions within one jurisdiction based on the ideas and practices of another (Dolowitz with others 2000; Rodgers 1998). Such transfers can vary from those imposed by fiat or threat of heavy penalties or conditionality, to, at the other extreme, voluntary lesson drawing. Others would emphasize the hegemonic role of dominant ideas in a world of unequal actors.[9]

One form of policy transfer of growing importance to developing countries is the influence of international organizations. Here, the West can provide a variety of lessons, including the influence of the OECD on European welfare states (Armingeon 2004); the influence of the EU on member states (see, among many studies, Pochet and Zeitlin 2005); and a comparison of the influence of the OECD and the EU on national employment policies (Noaksson and Jacobsson 2003). These studies may offer some lessons for developing countries, but a scholarly tradition already exists of studying policy transfer within development studies. In fact, emphasizing policy learning runs counter to the earlier stress on path dependency. Policy transfer is likely more important in the early construction of social policies but is marginalized when institutionalization sets in.

Lessons for Developing Countries

This chapter now briefly retraces the steps outlined and considers some of the immediate implications and lessons for social policy in the developing world. Like Atkinson and Hills (1991), it interprets lessons as methods of social policy analysis and certain proven findings likely to be of wide applicability. This chapter cannot do justice to the complex issues involved, but, in the context of this book, prioritizing social policy scholarship on welfare states in Europe seems more appropriate, allowing readers to draw their own conclusions on its applicability to the developing world.

Industrialization and Postindustrialism: Economic and Social Conditions and Change

The importance of societal conditions and structural change has been underplayed in recent thinking on welfare states and their transformation, but these issues are central to understanding social policy in the developing world.

National social policies developed in European societies that were rapidly industrializing and came to fruition in the mass deruralization in the decades following the World War II (Esping-Andersen 1999).[10] Later research has focused on the new demands placed on welfare states by the subsequent stage of deindustrialization, postindustrial capitalism, and the growth of the service economy. Today, developing countries can learn lessons from both phases. Industrialization explanations are likely to remain relevant in the newly emerging workshops of the world, particularly in Asia. However, the growing secondary sector is combined with larger tertiary and primary sectors than were found in European societies in the late 19th and early 20th centuries, with implications for growth, taxation, labor market security, and the applicability of the European social insurance model. Above all, the pervasive dualism of developing economies—the gulf between major cities and rural areas, as well as the extensive spatial inequalities—is beyond comparison with Europe now and Europe a century ago.

The demographic transition has accelerated dramatically at successive stages of world development. All projections of its effect on existing social provisions in the developing world—whether schools, pensions, or health services—are correspondingly dramatic. However, these projections assume all else is equal, which is precisely what is increasingly questioned, notably in the case of pensions, following a World Bank (1994) report. Here the lessons drawn from Europe to date have been predominantly negative—unsustainable social protection programs to avoid.

The role of families and households in attempting to mitigate risk and secure welfare is far more extensive in the developing than in the industrial world. However, two clear and rather unexpected lessons can be derived from comparative European research: countries vary considerably in their family and household structures and trends, and social policies plainly influence this variation. The positive lesson is that Scandinavian-style family programs can ease the combination of work and family life, thus enabling more women to work and, all else being equal, reducing child poverty rates. Evidence suggests that such productivist social policy can also contribute to sustainability by preventing dramatic falls in fertility—an important positive lesson, especially for fast-developing countries faced with rapidly aging populations.

Although a recurring theme in U.S. research and debates, the effect of heterogeneity and homogeneity within countries in facilitating or blocking systemic state policies has not been researched in any systematic cross-national way. The evidence from Europe echoes that found by Alesina, Glaeser, and Sacerdote (2001) when comparing 56 countries (including developing countries). They concluded that ethnolinguistic differences alone are not significant in restraining the share of social expenditure, but that racial fractionalization is the most significant single factor. This finding suggests that diversity per se is strongly moderated by interests and institutions.

Interests

In the zones of global accumulation, notably East Asia, proletarianization proceeds at breakneck speed and has fostered unofficial trade unions and militant class struggles in uneven ways. Some evidence indicates that class mobilization in the Republic of Korea has fueled pressures for a welfare state. In such countries, one observes the classic European social insurance dynamic (Hort and Kuhnle 2000, though see Rieger and Leibfried 2003: chapter 5): social insurance begins with groups of manual and factory workers in large industrial firms, gradually rippling outward to include medium and small enterprises; agricultural, white-collar, and service workers; the self-employed; and later, in some countries, even the unemployed and homemakers. Thus, the social insurance state proceeded from the strong to the weak. Social insurance offers a built-in transitional strategy—the very opposite of today's dominant target-the-poor approach. However, this lesson is less applicable where capitalist development is not accompanied by proletarianization and class conflict.

Moreover, research on the origins of social insurance and allied programs in Europe suggests that democracy was not a precondition—rather the opposite. The Bismarckian strategy has clear parallels, for example, in East Asia, where authoritarian leaders have introduced social policies to strengthen national solidarity, secure the loyalty of elites, and legitimize undemocratic regimes. However, the democratic class-struggle thesis convincingly shows the importance of democratic organization, though more so when allied to the mobilization of class organizations in civil society. This, in turn, explains why democratization in Korea may be leading to a more inclusive proto-welfare state (Gough 2004). Hence, two distinct lessons can be learned from Europe: specific state social policies are commonly initiated by authoritarian regimes, but democratization changes their form. Above all, consistent democratic pressure from below facilitates a move from favors, clientelism, and conditional help to meaningful social rights.

Institutions

The role of welfare systems in extending citizenship as a later phase of state and nation building in Europe has been emphasized previously—so, too, have national variations in the nature and timing of these processes. Of course, these historical institutionalist arguments have many parallels with the building of nation-states across the modern world: from the development of social protection policies in the face of the 1930s depression in the Southern Cone of Latin America, to the ambitious plans for welfare states in newly independent former colonies such as Ghana and Sri Lanka, to the concessionary social programs to stem revolutionary pressures such as those in the Philippines in the early 1950s. More comparative study of these antecedents and paths—and of the forms of social citizenship on offer—is needed. All these cases, however, presuppose state institutions with certain minimal capacities and legitimacy; a welfare state presupposes a reasonably well-functioning state. Where states are failed, "shadow," or collapsed, this cannot happen.

The effect of constitutional structures on social policy development is difficult to discern from research undertaken in the OECD. One strand of research in the new institutionalist tradition emphasizes the role of two groups created by social programs. First, there are providers: professionals, such as doctors and teachers, and other organized public sector workers, together with private sectors, such as insurance and construction. Another potential pressure group emerges when social programs appear: welfare "clienteles" such as pensioners, tenants of public housing, and so forth. One lesson from a comparative study of health care in Europe and the United States is that universal social programs and rights are blocked when providers and private interests organize ahead of consumers and civil organizations. This lesson is critical at a time when privatization policies encourage private providers, giving them an institutional head start over consumers and citizens.

Ideas

Being predominantly Christian, Europe provides few opportunities for comparative study of the effect of different world religions on social policy development. It is striking, therefore, that the differences between Protestant, Catholic, and mixed Protestant–Catholic countries, and the effect of Christian Democrat parties are so significant. This observation suggests that current research into the influence of faiths on policy in the developing world is not misplaced. The emergence of proto-welfare states in East Asia, for example, has prompted the study of Confucianism and the Confucian welfare state (Jones 1993). Rieger and Leibfried (2003: 261) argue that these countries exhibit a "fundamentally different orientation to social policy" from the West and claim that "Confucian culture can be identified as the fundamental cause of an independent path of welfare state evolution in East Asia." Drawing on Max Weber's studies of Confucianism and Protestantism, Rieger and Leibfried argue that the distinctive East Asian orientation to social policy is "framed" by Confucian values, although no inescapable iron law is at work.

In connection with ideologies, post–World War II European welfare states developed alongside Keynesian models of the macroeconomy and associated ideas of economic planning. Thus, the rise to domination of the neoliberal economic paradigm in the 1970s threatened the welfare state model, too, and various forms of retrenchment and restructuring of welfare systems were promulgated. In O'Connor's (1973) terminology, this phenomenon has called forth two counterreactions based on accumulation and legitimacy issues. The first is recognition of the productive contribution of social policies through investment in human capital and now in social capital. The second, as the resurgence of interest in Polanyi demonstrates, is recognition of the costs of economic "disembedding" in terms of immiseration, exclusion, social dislocation, threats of social unrest, and consequent delegitimation of regimes, all of which require and encourage new modes of social protection. Examples of both discourses can be found in the history of European and Western social policy making.

International Influences

The impact of different kinds of war and major civil strife in the developing world is likely to be as important as in the West. Big wars are major learning experiences; if such collective effort can be mobilized for destructive or defensive purposes, why can't the same happen for peaceful, constructive ends? Moreover, a plateau effect is likely to occur in state expenditures and competencies, which rarely contract to their prewar levels. In countries that have fought major wars, such as Vietnam, extensive veterans' programs and benefits exist that can form the basis for more generalized programs. In contrast, in territories that provide fighting zones for outside forces, such as Sierra Leone, almost all indigenous informal agencies and networks can be destroyed, resulting in acute insecurity and deprivation. Consequently, more research is needed on how different forms of conflict and wars affect social policy.

Europe offers a valuable lesson on economic openness and social protection. Its open economies (compared with the virtually self-sufficient United States) exhibit more universal and generous levels of social protection. The statistical association between openness to trade and spending on social protection in the West amounts almost to a law. The clearest explanation is that social protection is the only alternative to trade protection if social disintegration is to be avoided. Yet economic openness does not automatically support the emergence and spread of social protection systems. In parts of the developing world, the necessary state infrastructure has been destroyed by neoliberal reforms promulgated by international institutions and powerful states. The sequencing in the South is too often the opposite of that in the North: globalization has preceded welfare state formation and previous forms of national economic protectionism have been forcibly swept aside before even a rudimentary system of social protection has been put in place.

In terms of policy transfer and learning, Europe's experience offers ambivalent lessons. Studies of the influence of the World Bank and other external actors on pension reforms in the transitional countries of Eastern Europe have found that, even in such vulnerable states, domestic interests and institutions strongly mediate external policy advice and pressures. However, many highly indebted low-income countries in the South will lack the power and institutional capacities to adapt international policy models to their contexts. Policy transfer imposed by fiat or threat of heavy penalties or conditionality is very different from policy learning—indeed, they can be mutually exclusive. European countries, with a few time-limited exceptions (for example, Germany under the Versailles Treaty), have not experienced permanent dependent learning, which represents a novel barrier to the emergence of autonomous social policy in much of the South.

Conclusion

This brief survey aims to demonstrate the value of studying the lessons gained through research on the emergence of European welfare states over the past century. Two analytical lessons are clear: First, a combination of structural factors, interest-based mobilization, political institutions, and policy discourses has determined patterns of social policy development. This finding adds weight to Booth and Lucas's (2004) critique of much policy advice and practice in the developing world: that there is a "missing middle"—a clearly specified chain of causation between policy and intended outcome. Social policy must always be embedded in structural, political, and institutional contexts.

A second analytical lesson from European social policy is more contestable. It is the importance of path dependency: how, once established, patterns or constellations of social policies tend to reproduce and are rather impervious to radical change, short of encountering a major crisis or external intervention. Esping-Andersen (1990) argues this tendency most forcefully in his influential framework of welfare state regimes, which has received considerable empirical confirmation. In a recent collaboration with Geof Wood and others, I attempt to extend this framework to identify a wider range of "welfare" regimes across the developing world (Gough and Wood, with others 2004; Wood and Gough 2006). In brief, this work argues strongly that different institutionalized patterns across the South will also shape the nature and success of different social policy reforms. The implications are that social policy recommendations must adapt to dominant welfare regimes. It may be argued that developing countries today are more constrained by the global environment and face much greater intervention from supranational institutions—and thus exhibit much weaker path dependency in social policy. However, this conclusion should not be assumed, especially at policy implementation level: scholarship on Northern welfare states demonstrates the still overriding importance of internal factors.

Thus, social policy proposals must be contextualized. More specifically, they must take account of existing patterns of social provision, the distribution of institutional responsibility, the interests that these patterns express and perpetuate, and the resulting inequalities of power. This observation does not mean that policy learning, transfer, and change cannot occur. Nor does it necessarily reject applying universal principles to policy goals. But it does caution against recommending universal policy designs, instead favoring context-specific proposals that take account of culture, political economies, and inherited institutions. Fundamental social goals should be based on an agreed consensus on basic needs or capabilities, as are many contemporary human rights. But "need satisfiers," including social policies, are more likely to be successful if adapted to local environments (Gough 2004).

Notes

This chapter was written as part of the Wellbeing in Developing Countries (WeD) Economic and Social Research Council (ESRC) programme at the University of Bath. The support of the U.K. ESRC is gratefully acknowledged.

1. This statement excludes recent members and Turkey, a founder member.
2. Kim (2005) calculates that in the Republic of Korea, total "welfare" expenditure accounted for 22 percent of gross domestic product in 1997, a figure not far removed from the size of the social budget in the United States. However, only 9 percent was expenditure by the state; the remainder was mostly market spending (7 percent), enterprise welfare (4 percent), and family transfers (3 percent).

3. Considerably more work has been done on social protection and money transfers than on social services in kind. Studying services, such as health and social care, encounters still greater problems in identifying the dependent variable and greater intracountry variation attributable to local funding and provision. The biggest gap has been the serious study of education policy; for recent attempts to remedy this, see Allmendinger and Leibfried (2004) and Thelen (2006).

4. One qualification must be stated about the survey that follows: It does not give proper weight to the influence of gender issues on the emergence of social policies, at all stages of the model. Given their significance in both the North and the South, this weakness should be addressed in a subsequent version.

5. This classification is similar but not identical to the six schools of thought of comparative public policy developed by Schmidt (1996), though it was developed independently. For a fuller account see Schmidt (2000).

6. Paradoxically, the interests and influence of business have been little studied until recently (see Farnsworth 2004; Mares 2003).

7. See Stiller and van Kersbergen (2005) for a good recent survey.

8. Canada, however, has experienced a decentralization of social competencies over the past half century (Banting 2005).

9. The most systematic account is world society theory developed by Meyer and others (1997), in which global cultural and associational processes construct dominant worldwide models of reality, resulting in a strong isomorphism in institutional arrangements, including social policies.

10. The United Kingdom is the most notable exception to this generalization. As the pioneer of both industrialization and derularization, the country developed its social policies at a later stage of these processes.

References

Aaron, H. J. 1967. "Social Security: International Comparisons." In *Studies in the Economics of Income Maintenance*, ed. O. Eckstein, 13–48. Washington, DC: Brookings Institution.

Alesina, A., E. Glaeser, and B. Sacerdote. 2001. "Why Doesn't the U.S. Have a European Style Welfare State?" Discussion Paper 1933, Harvard Institute of Economic Research, Cambridge, MA.

Allmendinger, J., and S. Leibfried. 2004. "Education and the Welfare State: The Four Worlds of Competence Production." *Journal of European Social Policy* 23 (1): 63–81.

Amenta, E., and T. Skocpol. 1988. "Redefining the New Deal: World War II and the Development of Social Provision in the United States." In *The Politics of*

Social Policy in the United States, ed. M. Weir, A. S. Orloff, and T. Skocpol, 81–122. Princeton, NJ: Princeton University Press.

Armingeon, K. 2004. *The OECD and European Welfare States*. Cheltenham, U.K.: Edward Elgar.

Atkinson, A. B., and J. Hills. 1991. "Social Security in Developed Countries: Are There Lessons for Developing Countries?" In *Social Security in Developing Countries*, ed. E. Ahmad, J. Drèze, J. Hills, and A. Sen, 81–111. Oxford, U.K.: Oxford University Press.

Baldwin, P. 1990. *The Politics of Social Solidarity: Class Bases of the European Welfare State, 1875–1975*. Cambridge, U.K.: Cambridge University Press.

Banting, K. 2005. "Canada: Nation-Building in a Federal Welfare State." In *Federalism and the Welfare State: New World and European Experiences*, ed. H. Obinger, S. Leibfried, and F. G. Castles, 89–137. Cambridge, U.K.: Cambridge University Press.

Beveridge, W. 1942. *Social Insurance and Allied Services*. London: H. M. Stationery Office.

Bonoli, G. 2000. *The Politics of Pension Reform: Institutions and Policy Change in Western Europe*. Cambridge, U.K.: Cambridge University Press.

Booth, D., and H. Lucas. 2004. "Monitoring Progress towards the Millennium Development Goals at Country Level." In *Targeting Development: Critical Perspectives on the Millennium Development Goals*, ed. R. Black and H. White, 96–123. London: Routledge.

Bowles, P., and B. Wagman. 1997. "Globalization and the Welfare State: Four Hypotheses and Some Empirical Evidence." *Eastern Economic Journal* 23 (3): 317–36.

Cameron, D. R. 1978. "The Expansion of the Public Economy: A Comparative Analysis." *American Political Science Review* 72 (4): 1243–61.

Castles, F. G. 1978. "Scandinavia: The Politics of Stability." In *Modern Political Systems: Europe*, 4th ed., ed. R. C. Macridis. Englewood Cliffs, NJ: Prentice Hall.

———, ed. 1993. *Families of Nations*. Dartmouth, U.K.: Aldershot.

———. 1998a. "The Really Big Trade-Off: Home Ownership and the Welfare in the New World and the Old." *Acta Politica* 33: 5–19.

———. 1998b. *Comparative Public Policy: Patterns of Post-War Transformation*. Cheltenham, U.K.: Edward Elgar.

———. 2002. "The World Turned Upside Down: Below Replacement Fertility, Changing Preferences, and Family-Friendly Public Policy in 21 OECD Countries." *Journal of European Social Policy* 13 (3): 209–27.

Chadwick, E. 1965 [1842]. *Report on the Sanitary Condition of the Labouring Population of Great Britain*. Chicago: Aldine.

Crouch, C., and W. Streeck. 1997. *Political Economy of Modern Capitalism: Mapping Convergence and Diversity*. London: Sage.

Cutright, P. 1965. "Political Structure, Economic Development, and National Social Security Programs." *American Journal of Sociology* 70 (5): 537–50.

Deacon, B. 2003a. "Global Social Governance Reform." Globalism and Social Policy Programme Policy Brief 1, Stakes, Helsinki.

———. 2003b. "The Social Dimension of Regionalism: An Alternative to Globalization?" In *New Social Policy Agendas for Europe and Asia: Challenges, Experiences and Lessons,* ed. K. Marshall and O. Butzbach, 491–94. Washington, DC: World Bank.

Dolowitz, D. P., with R. Hulme, M. Nellis, and F. O'Neill. 2000. *Policy Transfer and British Social Policy: Learning from the USA?* Buckingham, U.K.: Open University Press.

Easton, D. 1965. *A Framework for Political Analysis.* Englewood Cliffs, NJ: Prentice-Hall.

Esping-Andersen, G. 1990. *The Three Worlds of Welfare Capitalism.* Cambridge, U.K.: Polity Press.

———. 1999. *Social Foundations of Postindustrial Economies.* Oxford, U.K.: Oxford University Press.

Farnsworth, K. 2004. *Corporate Power and Social Policy in a Global Economy.* Bristol, U.K.: Policy Press.

Ferrera, M., and M. Rhodes, eds. 2000. *Recasting European Welfare States.* London: Frank Cass.

Flora, P., ed. 1986–87. *Growth to Limits: The Western European Welfare States since World War II.* 4 vols. Berlin: de Gruyter.

———. 1999. "Introduction and Interpretation." In *State Formation, Nation-Building and Mass Politics in Europe: The Theory of Stein Rokkan,* ed. P. Flora, S. Kuhnle, and D. Urwin, 1–91. Oxford, U.K.: Clarendon Press.

Flora, P., and J. Alber. 1981. "Modernization, Democratization and the Development of Welfare States in Western Europe." In *The Development of Welfare States in Europe and America,* ed. P. Flora and A. J. Heidenheimer, 37–47. New Brunswick, NJ: Transaction Publishers.

Flora, P., and A. J. Heidenheimer. 1981. "The Historical Core and Changing Boundaries of the Welfare State." In *The Development of Welfare States in Europe and America,* ed. P. Flora and A. J. Heidenheimer, 17–34. New Brunswick, NJ: Transaction Publishers.

Garrett, G. 1998. *Partisan Politics in the Global Economy.* Cambridge, U.K.: Cambridge University Press.

Gerschenkron, A. 1962. *Economic Backwardness in Historical Perspective.* Cambridge, MA: Belknap Press.

Giddens, A. 1998. *The Third Way: Renewal of Social Democracy.* Oxford, U.K.: Polity Press.

Goodhart, D. 2004. "Too Diverse?" *Prospect,* February.

Gough, I. 1979. *The Political Economy of the Welfare State.* London: Macmillan.

————. 2000. *Global Capital, Human Needs, and Social Policies: Selected Essays 1994–1999*. Houndmills, U.K.: Palgrave Macmillan.

————. 2001. "Globalization and Regional Welfare Regimes: The East Asian Case." *Global Social Policy* 1 (2): 163–89.

————. 2004. "Human Well-Being and Social Structures: Relating the Universal and the Local." *Global Social Policy* 4 (3): 289–311.

Gough, I., and G. Wood, with A. Barrientos, P. Bevan, P. Davis, and G. Room. 2004. *Insecurity and Welfare Regimes in Asia, Africa, and Latin America: Social Policy in Developmental Contexts*. Cambridge, U.K.: Cambridge University Press.

Haas, P. M. 1992. "Introduction: Epistemic Communities and International Policy Coordination." *International Organization*, 46 (1): 1–35.

Hall, P. A., ed. 1989. *The Political Power of Economic Ideas: Keynesianism across Nations*. Princeton, NJ: Princeton University Press.

————. 1993. "Policy Paradigms, Social Learning, and the State: The Case of Economic Policymaking in Britain." *Comparative Politics* 25 (3): 275–96.

Hall, P. A., and D. Soskice. 2001. *Varieties of Capitalism: The Institutional Foundations of Comparative Advantage*. Oxford, U.K.: Oxford University Press.

Heclo, H. 1974. *Modern Social Politics in Britain and Sweden: From Relief to Income Maintenance*. New Haven, CT: Yale University Press.

Hennock, P. 1987. *British Social Reform and German Precedents: The Case of Social Insurance 1880–1914*. Oxford, U.K.: Clarendon.

Hewitt, C. 1977. "The Effect of Political Democracy and Social Democracy on Equality in Industrial Societies: A Cross-National Comparison." *American Sociological Review* 42 (3): 450–64.

Hill, M. 2003. *Understanding Social Policy*. 7th ed. Oxford, U.K.: Blackwell Publishing.

Hort, S. O., and S. Kuhnle. 2000. "The Coming of East and South-East Asian Welfare States." *Journal of European Social Policy* 10 (2): 163–84.

Huber, E., C. Ragin and J. D. Stephens. 1993. "Social Democracy, Christian Democracy, Constitutional Structure, and the Welfare State." *American Journal of Sociology* 99 (3): 711–49.

Immergut, E. 1992. *Health Politics: Interests and Institutions in Western Europe*. New York: Cambridge University Press.

Janoski, T., and A. Hicks. 1994. *The Comparative Political Economy of the Welfare State*. Cambridge, U.K.: Cambridge University Press.

Jessop, B. 1993. "Towards a Schumpeterian Workfare State? Preliminary Remarks on Post-Fordist Political Economy." *Studies in Political Economy* 40 (Spring): 7–39.

Jones, C. 1993. "The Pacific Challenge: Confucian Welfare States." In *New Perspectives on the Welfare State in Europe*, ed. Catherine Jones, 198–217. London: Routledge.

Kasza, J. G. 2002. "Illusion of Welfare 'Regime.'" *Journal of Social Policy* 31 (2): 271–87.

Katzenstein, P. J. 1985. *Small States in World Markets*. Ithaca, NY: Cornell University Press.

Kim, J. W. 2005. "Dynamics of the Welfare Mix in the Republic of Korea: An Expenditure Study between 1990 and 2001." *International Social Security Review* 58 (4): 3–26.

Korpi, W. 1978. *The Working Class in Welfare Capitalism: Work, Unions, and Politics in Sweden*. London: Routledge and Kegan Paul.

———. 1983. *The Democratic Class Struggle*. London: Routledge and Kegan Paul.

Maioni, A. 1997. "Parting at the Cross-Roads: The Development of Health Insurance in Canada and the United States." *Comparative Politics* 29 (4): 411–31.

Mares, I. 2003. *The Politics of Social Risk: Business and Welfare State Development*. Cambridge, U.K.: Cambridge University Press.

Marshall, T. H. 1950. *Citizenship and Social Class*. Cambridge, U.K.: Cambridge University Press.

Mesa-Lago, C. 2000. *Market, Socialist, and Mixed Economies: Comparative Policy and Performance—Chile, Cuba, and Costa Rica*. Baltimore. MD: Johns Hopkins University Press.

Meyer, J. W., J. Boli, G. M. Thomas, F. O. Ramirez. 1997. "World Society and Nation State." *American Journal of Sociology* 103 (1): 144–81.

Mishra, R. 1977. *Society and Social Policy: Theoretical Perspectives on Welfare*. London: Macmillan.

———. 1984. *The Welfare State in Crisis: Social Thought and Social Change*. Brighton, U.K.: Wheatsheaf.

———. 1999. *Globalization and the Welfare State*. Cheltenham, U.K.: Edward Elgar.

Müller, K. 2002. "Beyond Privatisation: Pension Reform in the Czech Republic and Slovenia." *Journal of European Social Policy* 12 (4): 293–306.

———. 2003. *Privatising Old-Age Security: Latin America and Eastern Europe Compared*. Cheltenham, U.K.: Edward Elgar.

Noaksson, N., and K. Jacobsson. 2003. *The Production of Ideas and Expert Knowledge in OECD: The OECD Jobs Strategy in Contrast with the EU-Employment Strategy*. Report 2003: 7. Stockholm: SCORE (Stockholm Centre for Organizational Research). http://www.score.su.se/pdfs/2003-7.pdf.

Obinger, H., S. Leibfried, and F. G. Castles, eds. 2005. *Federalism and the Welfare State: New World and European Experiences*. Cambridge, U.K.: Cambridge University Press.

O'Connor, J. 1973. *The Fiscal Crisis of the State*. New York: St. Martin's Press.

Orenstein, M. A. 2000. "How Politics and Institutions Affect Pension Reform in Three Postcommunist Countries." Policy Research Working Paper 2310, World Bank, Washington, DC.

Pampel, F. C., and J. B. Williamson. 1989. *Age, Class, Politics, and the Welfare State.* Cambridge, U.K.: Cambridge University Press.

Parry, R. 1986. "United Kingdom." In *Growth to Limits: The Western European Welfare States since World War II—Volume 2: Germany, United Kingdom, Ireland, Italy,* ed. P. Flora, 155–240. Berlin: de Gruyter.

Peacock, A. T., and J. Wiseman. 1961. *The Growth of Public Expenditure in the United Kingdom.* Princeton, NJ: Princeton University Press.

Pfau-Effinger, B. 2005. "Culture and Welfare State Policies: Reflections on a Complex Interaction." *Journal of Social Policy* 34 (1): 3–20.

Pierson, P. 1994. *Dismantling the Welfare State? Reagan, Thatcher, and the Politics of Retrenchment.* Cambridge, U.K.: Cambridge University Press.

———. 2000. "Increasing Returns, Path Dependence, and the Study of Politics." *American Political Science Review* 94 (2): 251–67.

———, ed. 2001. *The New Politics of the Welfare State.* Oxford, U.K.: Oxford University Press.

Piven, F., and R. Cloward. 1972. *Regulating the Poor: The Functions of Public Welfare.* Oxford, U.K.: Tavistock.

Pochet, P., and J. Zeitlin. 2005. *The Open Method of Co-ordination in Action.* Brussels: Peter Lang.

Polanyi, K. 1944. *The Great Transformation: The Political and Economic Origins of Our Time.* New York: Rinehart.

Rao, V., and M. Walton, eds. 2004. *Culture and Public Action: Cross Disciplinary Dialogue on Development Policy.* Stanford, CA: Stanford University Press.

Rieger, E., and S. Leibfried. 2003. *Limits to Globalization.* Cambridge, U.K.: Polity Press.

Rimlinger, G. 1971. *Welfare Policy and Industrialization in Europe, America, and Russia.* New York: John Wiley.

Rodgers, D. T. 1998. *Atlantic Crossings: Social Politics in a Progressive Age.* Cambridge, MA: Belknap Press.

Rodrik, D. 1998. "Globalization, Social Conflict, and Economic Growth." *World Economy* 21 (2): 143–58.

Scharpf, F. A., and V. A. Schmidt. 2000. "Conclusion." In *Welfare and Work in the Open Economy,* vol. 1, ed. F. A. Scharpf and V. A. Schmidt, 310–36. Oxford, U.K.: Oxford University Press.

Schmidt, M. G. 1996. "When Parties Matter: A Review of the Possibilities and Limits of Partisan Influence on Public Policy." *European Journal of Political Research* 30: 155–83.

———. 2000. "Die sozialpolitischen Nachzüglerstaaten und die Theorien der vergleichenden Staatstätigkeitsforschung." In *Der gezügelte Wohlfahrtsstaat:*

Sozialpoltik in reichen Industrienationen, ed. H. Obinger and U. Wagschal, 22–36. Frankfurt am Main: Campus.

Schumpeter, J. 1991. "The Crisis of the Tax State." In *The Economics and Sociology of Capitalism*, ed. R. Swedberg, 99–140. Princeton: Princeton University Press.

Shalev, M. 2007. "Limits and Alternatives to Multiple Regression." In *Capitalisms Compared*, ed. L. Mjøset and H. Clausen, 261–308. Oxford, U.K.: Elsevier.

Skocpol, T. 1985. "Bringing the State Back In: Strategies of Analysis in Current Research." In *Bringing the State Back*, ed. P. B. Evans, D. Rueschemeyer, and T. Skocpol, 3–37. Cambridge, U.K.: Cambridge University Press.

Skocpol, T., and E. Amenta. 1986. "States and Social Policies." *Annual Review of Sociology* 12: 131–57.

Stiller, S., and K. van Kersbergen. 2005. "Welfare State Research and the Independent Variable Problem: What to Explain and How to Explain?" Paper presented at the ESPANet conference, Fribourg, Switzerland, September 22–24.

Swank, D. 2002. *Global Capital, Political Institutions, and Policy Change in Developed Welfare States*. Cambridge, U.K.: Cambridge University Press.

Taylor-Gooby, P. 2005. "Is the Future American? Can Left Politics Preserve European Welfare States from Erosion through Growing 'Racial' Diversity?" *Journal of Social Policy* 34 (4): 661–72.

Thelen, K. A. 2006. *How Institutions Evolve: The Political Economy of Skills in Germany, Britain, the United States, and Japan*. Cambridge, U.K.: Cambridge University Press.

Therborn, G. 1983. "When, How, and Why Does a Welfare State Become a Welfare State?" Paper presented at European Consortium for Political Research Joint Workshops, Freiburg, Germany, March 20–25.

———. 1986. "Karl Marx Returning: The Welfare State and Neo-Marxist, Corporatist, and Statist Theories." *International Political Science Review* 7 (2): 131–64.

———. 1989. "'Pillarization' and 'Popular Movements.' Two Variants of Welfare State Capitalism: The Netherlands and Sweden." In *The Comparative History of Public Policy*, ed. F. G. Castles, 192–241. Cambridge, U.K.: Polity Press.

Titmuss, R. 1950. *Problems of Social Policy*. London: H.M. Stationery Office.

van Kersbergen, K. 1995. *Social Capitalism: A Study of Christian Democracy and the Welfare State*. London: Routledge.

Weir, M., A. S. Orloff, and T. Skocpol, eds. 1988. *The Politics of Social Policy in the United States*. Princeton, NJ: Princeton University Press.

Wilensky, H. L. 1975. *The Welfare State and Equality: Structural and Ideological Roots of Public Expenditures*. Berkeley: University of California Press.

Wilensky, H. L., and C. N. Lebeaux. 1958. *Industrial Society and Social Welfare: The Impact of Industrialization on the Supply and Organization of Social Welfare Services in the United States*. New York: Russell Sage Foundation.

Wood, G. D., and I. Gough. 2006. "A Comparative Welfare Regimes Approach to Global Social Policy." *World Development* 34 (10): 1696–712.

World Bank. 1994. *Averting the Old Age Crisis: Policies to Protect the Old and Promote Growth*. Oxford, U.K.: Oxford University Press.

CHAPTER 3

The Responsive State: Openness and Inclusion in the Policy Process

Lars Johannsen and Karin Hilmer Pedersen

The transitions of former communist countries to democracy and the market system were, indeed, revolutionary. The governing ideology changed; political systems altered—and with them the way in which leaders were selected, elected, and held accountable; and market reforms in each country redistributed wealth and life opportunities among citizens.

With regard to absolute poverty and equality, the differences between the countries are astonishing. As figure 3.1 illustrates, though some countries have succeeded in combining poverty reduction and equality, others are beset by both poverty and inequality. However, poverty may go hand in hand with equality (Mongolia), whereas poverty reduction can go hand in hand with inequality (Estonia, Georgia, Kazakhstan). The central puzzle here is that economic wealth alone cannot account for these differences. Equality in life chances and wealth are considered normative concepts and hence are often associated with specific political programs. The question this chapter will consider is whether the differences can be ascribed to characteristics of the state—in particular to the development of a responsive state.

A responsive state (Johannsen 2002) is one that is held accountable, not only through the normal procedures of competitive democracy, but also through cooperation with interest groups in the formulation and execution of political priorities. It also retains a degree of autonomy for political action. Therefore, the responsive state can emerge only where a strong civil society meets a strong democratic state (Bernhard 1996; Foley and Edwards 1996).

Figure 3.1. Absolute Poverty and Inequality

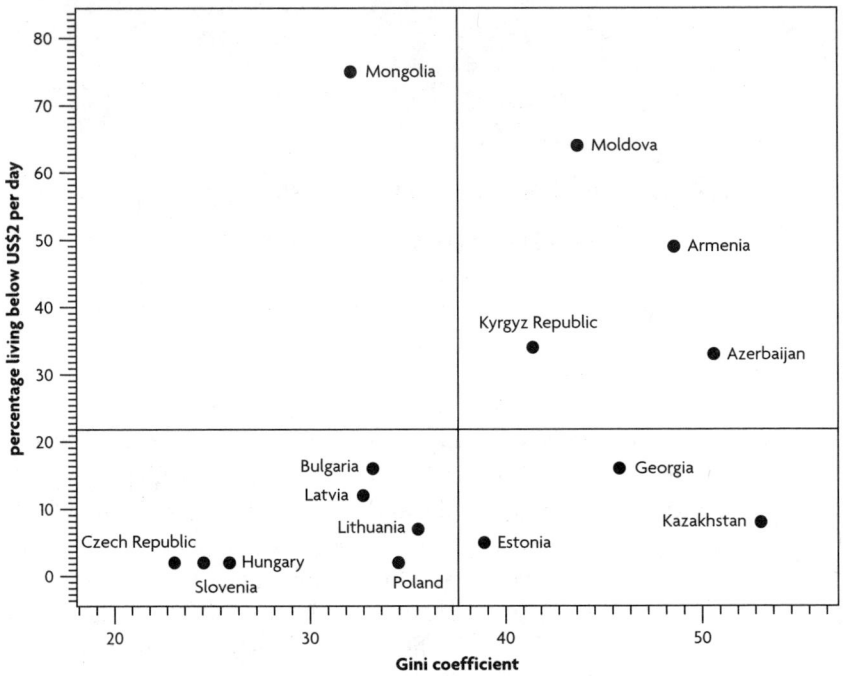

Source: Demstar survey.

The concept of the responsive state combines three trains of thought. First, in democratic discourse from Tocqueville on, it has been argued that civil society is the "infrastructure and organizational bedrock of democratic societies" (Zimmer 2005: 11), balancing the state and empowering the many by providing resources, experiences, and common identifications (Rueschemeyer 1998). Second, the concept of the responsive state draws on Putnam's concept of civic community, according to which civicness not only improves democracy qualitatively but also enhances the capacity of political institutions to solve political, social, and economic problems (Putnam with Leonardi and Nanetti 1993). Third, the concept builds on insights from diverse sources such as Evans (1995), Leftwich (1995), and Weiss (1998). Despite their differences, these theorists emphasize the importance of state–society links. They argue that the involvement of civil society increases the legitimacy of policy decisions and the ability of the state to make socially and economically viable decisions. Moreover, they are well aware of the flipsides to responsiveness and involvement: the risk that the state will be constrained by particularistic interests, paving the way for state capture and increased inequality. In accordance with Evans's (1995) concept of embeddedness, Weiss's (1998) discussion of state capacity, and Bernhard's (1996) discussion of consolidated democracy, the responsive state retains reformative autonomy. Furthermore, dense cooperation between public authorities and civil society supported by values of participatory democracy is the hallmark of the responsive state.

Paraphrasing Lijphart's (1999) research on consensus democracy, one might ask, do the ethics and organizational features of the responsive state also have distributional consequences, making it a kinder and gentler species? Critics will undoubtedly be quick to dismiss such research as normative. This claim has some obvious merit when only the branding as "a kinder and gentler species" is considered. However, although the democratization of the postcommunist countries called for a new balance between state and society, governance is more than the formal rules of election and the way in which government decisions are made. As the World Bank (1991) posits, governance also considers its ends when achieving levels of economic, human, and institutional development that benefit the population as a whole. With this background in mind, this chapter has three main aims: first, to track variations in the degree of openness and inclusion in 15 postcommunist countries; second, to contribute to the debate about Europeanization (that is, the discussion of whether the effect of European proactive policies pursued in the enlargement process results in the development of dense networks between the state and the civil society); and third, to test whether responsiveness reduces poverty and promotes equality. The chapter will analyze the results of a survey that was part of the Democracy, the State, and Administrative Reforms (Demstar) program. The Demstar survey involved semistructured interviews with ministers and high-ranking officials in government institutions in 15 postcommunist countries.[1] The chapter begins by outlining some of the theoretical points of departure related to openness and inclusion. It then charts the values assigned to participation and measures the density of state–society relations, before discussing the effect of a European model as an impetus for responsiveness and openness. Finally, it develops a number of explorative models that demonstrate the consequences of responsiveness for equality. In conclusion, the chapter outlines the policy implications.

The Point of Departure

Theories on openness and inclusion fall into two main categories—pluralism and corporatism—which differ with respect to how civil society actors gain access to decision making.

Pluralism underlines the politics of competition between the multitudes of freely organized interest groups vying for influence and makes the point that responsive governments listen to all voices before making decisions. It thus questions the importance of representation through election as the basic element in a democracy by positing that organized groups are capable of influencing policy (Dahl 1967) and that group pressure is a way to limit state power, thereby giving rise to a more democratic society. Critics of the pluralist model have maintained that, in reality, societies are not plural. They have pointed to unequal access to power caused by structurally related differences in political and economic resources (Schattschneider 1960). They also note that some groups have preferential (and undemocratic) access to decision making (Lindblom 1977). Moreover, corporate strategies of using money to win political support by establishing advocacy groups or orchestrating "AstroTurf" campaigns (Deal and Doroshow 2003; Lyon and Maxwell 2004) cannot be construed as evidence of an empowered civil society in the way pluralism traditionally conceives it.

By contrast, corporatism emphasizes a coordinated and centralized bargaining relation between the government and key interest groups representing business and labor. It also stresses facilitation of government decision making through political recognition of interest groups, while, in turn, the organizations in question become subject to more or less formalized obligations, for example, to behave responsibly and predictably and to refrain from making nonnegotiable demands and using unacceptable tactics (Offe 1981: 135). The problem exposed by the corporatist model is that granting preferential status to peak organizations representing the divide between capital and labor does not necessarily guarantee social consensus. Furthermore, if the consent of both sides of industry is required for all major state policies, corporatism can hinder policy innovation even where it is badly needed, as in the case of post-communist society. Two anonymous Slovenian ministers responding to the Demstar survey make this point. On the one hand, they note that "if you please trade unions, you achieve social peace. Still, this is expensive and causes budget deficit." On the other hand, they add, "They [business associations] wanted to implement their interests, exclude competition, and achieve a price level that would require no rationalization."

Pluralism and corporatism are often viewed as two extremes, each generating its own consequences for state–society relations. Criticisms of both the core of pluralism and that of corporatism correspond to the concept of state capture. That is, rather than public interests being aggregated and mediated through democratic processes, decisions are made to appease specific interests (Hellman and others 2000). Consequently, with the critique of both pluralism and corporatism as their point of departure, neopluralists defend the necessity for the state to play a proactive role in nurturing and supporting civil society organizations (other than peak organizations), thereby leveling the playing field of interest access to the political processes (Dunleavy and O'Leary 1987; Petracca 1994). Thus, the neopluralist's advocacy of an active state can be seen as a critique of both the corporatist and the pluralist models and as an attempt to achieve an open state that is sensitive to civil society at large, while avoiding state capture through institutional arrangements.

Beyond the traditional clustering of state–society relations, the degree of openness and inclusion of political and administrative systems incorporates two related aspects. The first stresses that the values guiding policy makers and administrators are important factors when it comes to practice (Blyth 2001). Two questions arise: Which kind of democracy do the elite prefer? Do the elite see gains from including interests groups in the policy process? These questions assess the willingness, receptiveness, and eagerness of the state elite to develop a responsive state by fostering openness and inclusion.

The second aspect involves the character of the contacts between policy makers and civil society with regard to frequency and institutionalization. First, while the number of access points is definitely increased by factors such as multilevel government, specialization, a growing public sector, and economic development, it is even more pronounced in countries facing transition to market and welfare society. Consequently, the number of possible contacts in state–society relations has multiplied during the past 10 to 15 years. Second, while pluralism stresses access to decision making by various pressure groups, hence ensuring that nobody dominates, corporatism implies that inclusion is institutionalized, at least to some extent. Without having considered pluralist or corporatist modes of governance, several respondents to the Demstar survey note that civil society access to decision making should be regulated and transparent to avoid irregularities. A Georgian minister said, "Forcing lobbyists to comply with the legislation would minimize hidden private interests that are incorporated into the lobbying." This observation implies that regular and open contacts between government and civil society decrease the risk of state capture, or, in other words, that ad hoc and personal contacts may undermine executive capacity to make transformative policies (see Pedersen and Zubek 2005). Preliminary results suggest that there are indeed differences between countries where inclusion is institutionalized and those that rely on ad hoc formation, with access dependent on policy issues (Johannsen and Pedersen 2005).

Two additional points should be highlighted regarding the character of the contacts. First, a distinction must be made between the constituent parts of the policy process. One part of the policy process focuses on decision making—that is, the co-optation of interests into bargaining and policy formulation. Another focuses on implementation. With respect to implementation, researchers since Pressman and Wildavsky (1973) have argued that configurations of interests and organizations have consequences for the efficiency and success of a policy program.[2] Second, in accordance with the more fragmented view of public authorities implicitly recognized by neopluralist accounts, not only may different sectors have different traditions and be more or less open; they may also vary in the density and character of their relations with different interest organizations, given the level of sector responsibility (see a five-sector comparison by Johannsen and Nørgaard 2005).

In a postcommunist context, openness and inclusion highlight the specific character of civil society organizations as another important issue. For many reasons, postcommunist states are dominated by weak and deformed civil societies (Bernhard 1996). This situation makes inclusiveness problematic from the outset. Not only, at least in theory, did communism do its best to stamp out socioeconomic differences, it also attempted to destroy civil society in practice. At the dawn of democracy in 1989, Linz and Stepan (1996: 352) found the number of independent movements to be discouragingly low. They were able to account for just 13, 21, and 60 organizations in Bulgaria, Hungary, and Poland, respectively. Fortunately, this situation has changed. However, while Ágh (2001) and Mansfeldová and others (2005) point to the massive growth in the number of associations, Howard (2000) argues that, measured by membership, organizations in postcommunist Europe remain weak.

As argued previously, to avoid capture, the responsive state combines substantial democracy, where citizens are encouraged to participate, organize, and seek influence, with a transparent, autonomic state. The next section maps and compares the values and practices in the surveyed countries.

Mapping Values on and Practices of Openness and Inclusion

The questions posed by the Demstar survey cannot tap all aspects of values and actions in an exhaustive manner. However, they do suffice for a substantial description and discussion. Thus, we will now focus, first, on the values of inclusion and, second, on the density of the contacts between civil society and policy makers and administrators.

The Value of Participation

The intrinsic values accorded by policy makers and administrators to citizens' participation and civil society inclusion in the policy process are tracked through a number of generalized questions. These questions focus, first, on the values of participatory democracy in contrast to elite democracy and, second, on attitudes to lobbying and the effect of incorporating concerted interests in policy formulation and implementation—that is, how civil society is appraised in its approaches to decision making and implementation.

The values ascribed to participatory democracy are traced by asking respondents to choose from among three alternative forms of democracy. These forms range from pure elite democracy to participatory democracy, where citizens are active and organized in various political and civil society organizations through which they gain influence. Figure 3.2 shows striking differences, at a general level, in the desired form of democracy. Overall, little more than 56 percent of the policy makers and administrators support participatory democracy, but there is notable variation between the countries. More than 80 percent of the respondents in the Czech Republic express support for participatory democracy, whereas slightly more than 10 percent do so in Azerbaijan. More important despite the apparent correlation between development and participatory democratic values,[3] the distribution also indicates that significant minorities among the more prosperous countries support elite democracy.

Figure 3.2. Support for Participatory Democracy

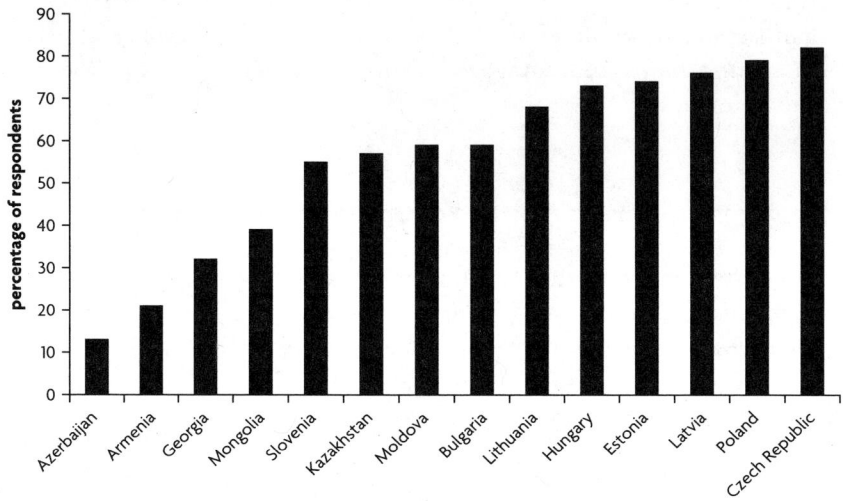

Source: Demstar survey.
Note: The survey question was not asked in the Kyrgyz Republic. Values express the percentage of respondents in each country who stated, "The public should become actively engaged in parties, associations, local government, and so forth, to gain greater influence on politics."

Values of participation are also depicted through attitudes to lobbying. *Lobbying* is a difficult term because it has both positive and negative connotations. Its negative aspects are closely related to the risk of state capture or the danger that, as one Slovenian minister who responded to the survey put it, "Lobbying leads to corruption."[4] However, in a less value-laden connotation, *lobbying* is connected to provision of information and policy support, in clear contrast to information bias and erosion of impartiality. Because of the duality of the concept, we include the respondents' evaluation of inclusion in addition to the questions on lobbying.

The results show that, in the eyes of policy makers and administrators, lobbying constitutes a discrete form of openness. Policy makers and administrators are aware of both aspects of lobbying, but they put different emphases on them. Although the Estonians and Poles place more value on lobbying because it can provide information and political support, the Azerbaijanis seem to be acutely aware that such information can be biased and that the impartiality of a ministry eroded (see table 3.1). Policy makers do distinguish between the political benefits and costs of lobbying. This distinction is corroborated by factor analysis that demonstrates the two aspects of lobbying. However, because none

Table 3.1. Attitudes toward Lobbying and the Value of Including Interests in Policy Formulation

| | Survey response | | | | Formulation: decisions improve when concerned interests are incorporated (1:4) |
| | Lobbying is positive because ... | | Lobbying is negative because ... | | |
Country	It provides the information needed (0:1)	You get support from the concerned groups (0:1)	The information is biased (0:1)	It erodes the impartiality of the ministry (0:1)	
Armenia	0.5	0.4	0.4	0.5	3.1
Azerbaijan	0.8	0.7	0.9	0.9	3.1
Bulgaria	0.8	0.8	0.3	0.4	3.9
Czech Republic	0.6	0.6	0.7	0.5	3.3
Estonia	0.9	0.7	0.2	0.2	3.8
Georgia	0.7	0.5	0.2	0.1	3.6
Hungary	0.6	0.6	0.3	0.1	3.9
Kazakhstan	0.5	0.3	0.5	0.6	3.7
Kyrgyz Rep.	0.7	0.4	0.4	0.6	3.7
Latvia	0.8	0.5	—	—	3.8
Lithuania	0.9	0.3	0.4	0.5	3.9
Moldova	0.5	0.4	0.6	0.5	3.5
Mongolia	0.3	0.6	0.5	0.5	3.5
Poland	0.9	0.7	0.7	0.7	3.9
Slovenia	0.8	0.7	0.4	0.1	3.8

Source: Demstar survey.

Note: — = not available. See annex for wording of survey questions.

of the four items assessing the value of lobbying are correlated with the generalized view of democracy or the view that policy decisions can be improved by incorporating concerned interests, we are led to believe that these views are currently unrelated to the question of civil society inclusion and have therefore excluded this question in further analysis.

In contrast to lobbyism, a fairly strong correlation exists between the generalized value of democracy and the perceived value of including various interests in the policy formulation process.[5] The participation dimension (see table 3.2) covers the fundamental perspective on how democracy should be and the potential for increasing efficiency by co-opting non-state-concerned interests in the process of policy formulation. The participation factor thus measures not only the extent to which participatory democracy, as a fundamental value, is shared by a country's policy makers, but also the extent to which they feel that inclusion is beneficial and improves decision making.

Density

The previous discussion sought to tap the value placed on openness and inclusion. Although the chapter will go on to focus on actual involvement, it is worth emphasizing that these two aspects need not be correlated. For example, policy makers can hold values of participatory democracy dear, but the actual level of involvement may remain low because of the weakness of civil society. If the state is to be embedded in civil society, civil society must evolve, as discussed previously. In trying to ascertain the density of state–civil society relations, we therefore included not only a number of questions concerning the use of external advisers in policy making, the reliance on nongovernmental organizations (NGOs) for information, and the extent of working relations, but also a question designed to learn whether policy makers and administrators feel pressured to initiate new legislation.

Table 3.2. Participation and Effectiveness

	Component
Are decisions improved when concerned interests are incorporated in formulation?	0.920
(Answers ranged from 1 = no, worse, to 4 = yes, mostly) Participatory view of democracy	0.920

Source: Demstar survey.
Note: Extraction method: principal component analysis. Initial eigenvalue: 1.691; 84.56 percent of variance explained.

Evidently, some feel the pressure more than others. The first question in table 3.3 demonstrates that Czech, Estonian, and Polish policy makers feel the heat compared with their Azerbaijani and Georgian counterparts. Because of the wording of the question, we cannot conclude that Czech civil society is more vibrant than Georgian civil society; it can be only a plausible hypothesis. The pressure felt by ministers and administrators could be due to the presence of strong economic actors, international organizations, or both trying to force issues onto the agenda. However, the likelihood that a strong civil society puts pressure on the government is great considering that pressure is strongly correlated with level of development, as shown by gross domestic product (GDP) per capita.[6]

The second question in table 3.3 shows that external advisers are used more frequently in Hungary, Poland, and Slovenia than in Armenia.

Table 3.3. Forms of Inclusion in 15 Postcommunist States

Country	Have you felt under pressure from outside actors to initiate new legislation? (0;2)	To what extent are external advisers used in the policy-making process? (1;4)	Have you relied on NGOs for information? (0;1)	Do civil servants have close working relationships with NGOs? (0;2)
Armenia	0.6	1.9	0.3	1.5
Azerbaijan	0.3	2.0	0.2	1.4
Bulgaria	0.8	2.4	0.6	1.5
Czech Republic	1.4	2.3	0.6	1.2
Estonia	1.4	2.5	0.4	1.0
Georgia	0.3	2.4	0.5	1.2
Hungary	1.3	2.7	0.5	1.6
Kazakhstan	0.8	2.3	0.1	1.2
Kyrgyz Rep.	0.7	2.3	0.4	1.5
Latvia	1.0	—	0.4	0.9
Lithuania	1.1	2.5	0.5	1.5
Moldova	0.5	2.4	0.5	1.1
Mongolia	0.5	2.2	0.3	1.6
Poland	1.3	2.9	0.3	1.4
Slovenia	1.2	2.7	0.4	1.2

Source: Demstar survey.
Note: — = not available. See annex for wording of survey questions.

Moreover, Bulgarian and Czech ministers tend to base their policies on information from NGOs more than Kazakhstani ministers (see the third question in table 3.3). Finally, Latvian civil servants work less closely with NGOs, whereas Hungarian and Mongolian civil servants are likely to have more permanent relations with NGOs (see the fourth question in table 3.3).

There are differences between the countries, but the number of differences within countries is truly noteworthy. A few examples may serve as illustration. First, Mongolian ministers feel little pressure but report close working relationships with NGOs. Second, the Moldovan political and administrative elite frequently rely on information from NGOs but have few working relations with them. Third, the Armenians rarely use external advisers, feel little pressure, and report close working relations. These differences led us to construct a simple additive index of the four questions, running from 0 to 9, measuring the density of state–society relations. It should be noted, however, that this additive index is explorative because the number of cases is too small for a full-scale test for robustness.[7] Consequently, the additive density index will be used only for explorative purposes to supplement the direct test of its constituent parts when we seek to measure the relationship between responsive states and equal societies.

The Map of Inclusion and Participation

The additive density index has a further advantage. In combination with the participation factor, it allows for a simple empirical map of openness and inclusion. A quick glance at figure 3.3 confirms the intuitively grasped differences and commonalties between the countries. The relationship between values and practices marked by the regression line is striking and unmistakable. All the new European Union (EU) member states are situated in the upper right-hand corner. They are characterized by shared support for participatory democracy and understanding of the value of including civil society in the policy-making process. They are also characterized by greater density in state–society relations. These countries are thus more responsive, in the terminology of this chapter, than those in the lower band, stretching from Armenia to Kazakhstan. The countries in the lower band are all characterized by a lower degree of density but are otherwise diverse in their participatory values, the Armenians being less likely to believe in participatory democracy and finding little added

Figure 3.3. Map of Inclusion and Participation

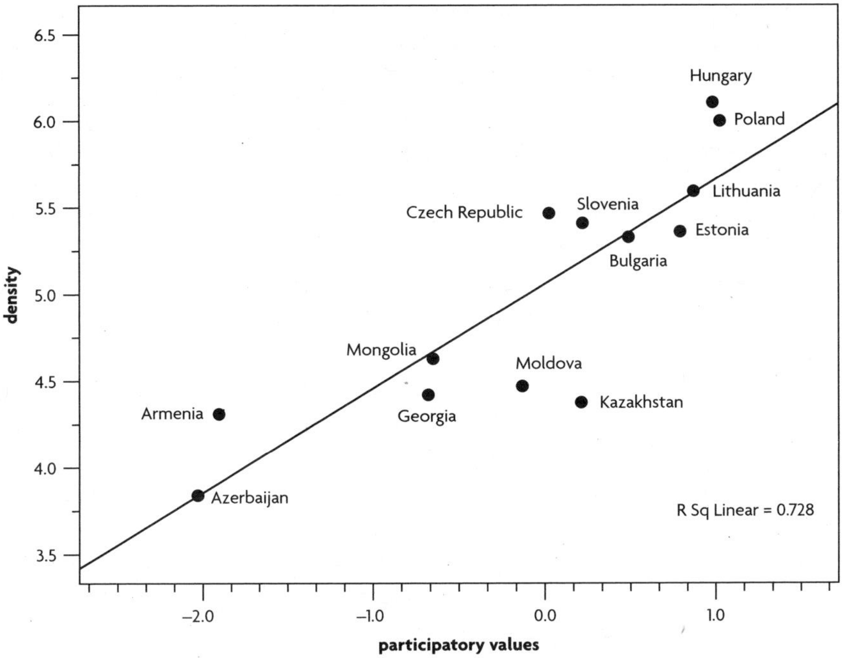

Source: Authors' calculation based on data from Demstar survey.
Note: R^2 linear = 0.728.

value associated with including interests in decision making. Last, we find Azerbaijan, which exhibits the fewest contacts and, like Armenia, sees little value in participation.

The introduction to this chapter hypothesized that responsiveness, as defined by values and density, would make for more equal societies. A quick comparison of figures 3.1 and 3.3 supports this hypothesis. The countries in the lower left quadrant of figure 3.1, which exhibit less absolute poverty and a more equal distribution of incomes, are all found in the upper right-hand corner of figure 3.3, with high participatory values and strong density. This position is shared by the new and coming EU member states, which could indicate that the very process of moving toward EU membership contributes to values and practices of participation. This possibility will be the subject of discussion in the next section. Later discussion will consider whether the intuitive proof of a relation between inclusiveness and outcome can be substantiated.

The European Model of Inclusion

Inclusion of civil society actors in the policy-making process requires, first, the willingness of politicians and administrators to include nonstate actors and, second, the existence of nonstate actors.

The first aspect touches directly on the value of participatory democracy as mapped in the previous section. The EU requirements for prospective member states, as set out in the Copenhagen criteria of 1993, include a functioning democratic government, in accordance with the European model of democratic inclusion of civil society interests. Reflecting the logic of both neopluralism and corporatism (Hix 2005), the European Commission required all relevant social groups to be included in the negotiations over the 31 chapters of the *acquis communautaire*. In this way, the EU put pressure on the applicants to engage in direct negotiations with civil society, whether or not the politicians held participatory values dear at an intrinsic level. Changing values is a difficult and often long-term matter. However, changing the institutional setup may affect the perceived value of participation.

The second aspect concerns the existence of groups that can be included. In the negotiation guidelines, the commission explicitly asked whether "social partners are sufficiently developed in order to discharge their responsibilities at the EU and national level" (European Commission 2004: 47). Thus, a country's readiness for EU membership is contingent on the development of participatory democracy. This process made the applicant countries aware of gaps they had to fill before becoming acceptable to the EU. Moreover, the EU has, in substantive ways, encouraged and provided financial support to civil society organizations, hence making it clear that civil society organizations should be regarded as essential parts of democratic societies.

The results of our survey show that influence from international actors relates to, first, the values of participation[8] and, second, the practice of including civil society actors as measured by the density variables, the use of advisers,[9] reliance on NGOs for information,[10] and perceived pressure to initiate new policies.[11] The negotiation process was dominated by an asymmetrical power relation between the EU and the applicant countries (Grabbe 2001). Consequently, as Szabó (2005: 95) points out, the EU, as the realm of modernity and democracy, has served as an inevitable "reference group" for all political camps in eastern and central European countries, thus forcing the governments and elites to keep up with the EU in their partnership with civil society. The new EU countries, to a greater extent than non-EU candidates, believe that foreign actors have attempted to influence their policies and regulation.[12] This fact suggests that the effect of the EU accession process is more important than the conditionality associated with aid donations. However, this argument is somewhat falsely conceived, because a number of the countries included in the analysis have never intended to apply for EU membership. For those countries, aid conditionality may be very relevant.

Reducing Poverty and Inequality

International pressure is another factor behind the development of dense state–society relations. However, turning to the consequences in the sense of the outcome of responsiveness, we developed several empirical models. An explorative design was necessary because (a) a restricted number of cases were available, (b) the survey was not ideally specified to contribute to this debate, and (c) there were divergent opinions on how to gauge poverty and equality. We decided, therefore, to use a full battery of three groups of explanatory variables: first, the value of participation; second, the four density variables, both independently and as conflated in the density index; and third, wealth used as a control.

We test our hypothesis by using four indicators as dependent variables. First, our model specifications include inequality, which is expressed in the Gini coefficient. However, in absolute terms, people may be better off in a rich country with a high degree of inequality than in a more equal but poorer one. Therefore, second, we use the "US$2-a-day" criterion as a measure of absolute poverty. These two variables were briefly touched on in the first section and in the variation in the sample depicted in figure 3.1. However, we were acutely aware that the US$2-a-day definition would strongly reflect wealth and so introduced a third variable, whereby *poverty* is defined as the percentage living below the national poverty line. This variable reveals the national context of poverty, but it cannot fully replace the $US2-a-day criterion as the absolute poverty measure.

Taking these three variables together, we constructed two indexes to measure inequality; Inequality (1) and Inequality (2), reflecting the Gini coefficient and either of the two poverty measures, respectively.[13] Finally, we added spending on health as a separate indicator to check whether the implicit causality argument would be validated. In other words, does responsiveness affect not only overall social measures such as poverty and equality, but also more concretely related policy issues? Thus, higher public expenditure on health could indicate a socially more concerned and caring state.

It is imperative to recall that the results are based on a limited number of cases. Therefore, so as not to throw away contributory variables, we decided to use relatively liberal criteria in our regression model. We chose to apply a probability level of 0.1 to enter and 0.2 to remove. Moreover, given the limited number of cases, robustness (consistency across the models) is more important than statistical significance. In the analyses, we use all the above-mentioned variables, leaving the 12 models reported in table 3.4. Models 1 to 6 report the results using the explanatory variables: pressure, advisers, information, and working relations. Models 1D to 6D report the results when swapping these with the density index.

The explanation that emerges is not just a story of a trinity of wealth, participatory values, and density, but also one of the importance of state responsiveness. A closer look at the nonstandardized coefficients in model 1 reveals that an increase in working relations on the three-point scale is expected to reduce the Gini coefficient by a dramatic 18 points. This finding should be compared with the expectation that a US$1,000-increase in wealth would reduce the Gini coefficient by about three points. In terms of eradicating absolute poverty, wealth appears to provide the strongest explanation (models 2 and 2D), but when the politically defined poverty criteria are included, participatory values become important (models 4 and 4D). The importance of density is revealed across the board, either with one or two of the items alone (models 1, 3, 3D, 4, 5, and 6) or in the form of the index (models 1D, 3D, 5D, and 6D). Thus, all 12 models produce consistent results. The variables carry the expected signs across the board, indicating that dense state–society relations do indeed reduce poverty and inequality when controlled for economic wealth. Furthermore, in the two spending models, dense relations increase the relative expenditures on health. These results indicate a rather robust explanation.

Thus, by associating responsiveness with political outcomes modeled on explaining between-country differences in poverty and equality, we have found that responsiveness reduces poverty and promotes equality. In other words, responsive states are, to paraphrase Lijphart (1999), kinder and gentler.

Table 3.4. Responsiveness Reduces Poverty and Inequality

	Dependent model	Gini (1)	Gini (1D)	Poverty (US$2) (2)	Poverty (US$2) (2D)	Inequality (1) (3)	Inequality (1) (3D)
Values	Participation						
Density	Pressure	−0.369*				−0.509**	
	Advisers						
	Information						
	Working relations		−0.794***				−0.538***
	Density index						
Control	GDP per capita	−0.812***		−0.669***	−0.661***	−0.452*	−0.482***
	Explained variance (adjusted R^2)	0.663	0.596	0.405	0.385	0.792	0.856
	N	15	14	15	14	15	14

	Dependent model	Poverty (national) (4)	Poverty (national) (4D)	Inequality (2) (5)	Inequality (2) (5D)	Expenditure (health) (6)	Expenditure (health) (6D)
Values	Participation	−0.525***	−0.729***				
Density	Pressure					0.800***	
	Advisers			−0.633***			
	Information	−0.529**		−0.500***			
	Working relations						
	Density index				−0.847***		0.467*
Control	GDP (per capita)						0.475*
	Explained variance (adjusted R^2)	0.703	0.472	0.875	0.682	0.608	0.475
	N	11	11	11	11	15	14

Source: Author's calculations based on data (see table 3.A.1) and the Demstar survey.

Note: *** = significant to the 0.01 level; ** = significant to the 0.05 level; * = significant to the 0.10 level; Inequality (1) = factor of Gini and poverty (US$2); Inequality (2) = factor of Gini and poverty (national definition). Models labeled with D following model number reflect that a density index is used instead of pressure, advisers, and information and working relations. Only significant results are reported in the final model. Standardized coefficients are reported except when otherwise noted.

Responsiveness: Some Policy Implications

Anyone making the journey from Budapest, Hungary, to Chişinau, Moldova, can be expected to return with a tale of stark differences in absolute poverty and relative equality. These differences are obvious between and within the former communist countries.

Although traditional modernization and development theories lay a strong claim to the correlations between wealth, poverty reduction, and increasing equality, theories that focus on the role of the state are only in their formative stages. As argued in this chapter, the concept of the responsive state (dense cooperation between public authorities and civil society supported by values of participatory democracy) is nurtured by increasing wealth, but an explanatory dimension is added by arguing that responsiveness has consequences for political outcomes. This added explanatory dimension suggests that much can be gained through a more systematic combination of state theories and insights from modernization and development theory.

The concept of the responsive state seeks to escape the determinism associated with modernization by combining values and organization. Moreover, in our discussion on the inclusion of civil society actors in the EU accession process, we contend that those applying for membership used the EU as a reference group, overruling conflicting political and organizational values. This discussion demonstrates that international society can enhance the conditions for the emergence of a civil society and its inclusion in the policy process, thereby paving the way for more equal societies.

Annex

The Survey

The survey was part of a research program, Democracy, the State, and Administrative Reforms (Demstar), conducted from 2000 to 2005. Demstar focused on the role of the state and state administrations in former communist countries (see the program's Web site at http://www.demstar.dk). The program was initiated and headed by the late Ole Nørgaard, a professor at the Department of Political Science, University of Aarhus. It was supported by the Danish Social Science Research Council and the University of Aarhus Research Fund.

The survey consisted of semistructured interviews with 955 ministers and high-ranking officials in government institutions in 15 postcommunist countries: Armenia, Azerbaijan, Bulgaria, the Czech Republic, Estonia, Georgia, Hungary, Kazakhstan, the Kyrgyz Republic, Latvia, Lithuania, Moldova, Mongolia, Poland, and Slovenia. It was carried out between 2001 and 2003.

Database Variables

The database variables are shown in table 3.A.1. When otherwise not noted, the variables are aggregated from the microdatabase (the Demstar survey), using country as the break variable.

Table 3.A.1. Database Variables

Variable	Description
Gdpcap00	GDP per capita = constant year 2000 US$ (units). Source: World Bank 2004. GDP per capita applied: 2000 for all countries.
Gini95–04	Gini coefficient, measured as difference in disposable income. Source: World Income Inequality database (http://www.wider.unu.edu/wiid/wiid.htm). Gini applied: 2000 for all countries, except Kazakhstan (1996) and Mongolia (1997).
Povert95–04	Poverty (percentage of population living on less than US$2 a day). Source: World Bank 2004. Poverty applied: 1998 for all countries, except Poland (1999); Georgia, Kyrgyz Republic, Lithuania, and Moldova (2000); and Azerbaijan, Bulgaria, and Kazakhstan (2001).
Poverty (national)	Poverty headcount ratio at national poverty line (percentage of population). Source: World Bank 2004. Poverty (national) applied: Poland (1994); Estonia (1996); Kazakhstan (1997); Bulgaria, Georgia, Hungary, and Moldova (1998); Mongolia (1999); Armenia (2000); Kyrgyz Republic (2001); and Azerbaijan (2002).
eu1997	EU candidate country in 1997.
eu2004	EU member country in 2004.
eu2007	EU candidate country for 2007.
Health00	Public expenditures on health as percentage of GDP for 2000 Source: World Bank 2004.
q4mean	Relied on NGOs for information (0 = no, 1 = yes).

(continued)

Table 3.A.1. Database Variables *(continued)*

Variable	Description
q4amean	Extent to which external advisers are used in policy-making process (ranges from 1 = rarely to 4 = always).
q7mean	Common practice in ministry to have close working relationships with NGOs (0 = no, 1 = yes).
q22mean	Did foreign actors try to influence policy and regulations? (0 = no, 1 = yes).
q24mean	Have you felt under pressure from outside actors to initiate new legislation? (ranges from 0 = never to 2 = often).
q26mean	Do civil servants have close working relationships with NGOs? (ranges from 0 = no to 2 = yes, most of the time).
q27_1mea	Lobbying is positive because it provides the information needed (0 = disagree, 1 = agree).
q27_2mea	Lobbying is negative because the information is biased (0 = disagree, 1 = agree).
q27_3mea	Lobbying is positive because you get support from the concerned groupings (0 = disagree, 1 = agree).
q28mean	Are decisions improved when concerned interests are incorporated in policy formulation? (ranges from 1 = no, worse, to 4 = yes, mostly).
q41mean	Is it better that concerned interests participate in implementation? (ranges from 1 = strongly disagree to 5 = strongly agree).
q45mean	Participatory view of democracy: percentage expressing "The public should become actively engaged in parties, associations, local government, and so forth, to gain greater influence on politics."
q4amean	Extent to which external advisers are used in policy-making process (ranges from 1 = rarely to 4 = always).

Sources: World Income Inequality database (http://www.wider.unu.edu/wiid/wiid.htm); World Bank 2004.

Notes

1. One caveat should be mentioned: the Demstar survey was designed to address the issue of state transformation and administrative capacity. Thus, it touched on only some of the aspects of the responsive state. The issues at hand have made it necessary to aggregate the variables to the country level. For more information and for the questions themselves, see the annex.
2. It is reasonable to assume that the values of participatory democracy and inclusion in policy implementation go hand in hand. However, our data show that the two values are not correlated. We believe this lack of correlation arises because the policy makers and administrators in our sample, given the background of systemic communism, perceive democracy as only decision

making and accordingly have difficulty conceiving of a role for civil society organizations in implementation. Implementation is regarded as a mere technical-cum-administrative process.

3. Pearson correlation = 0.543; significant at the 0.05 level.
4. The question of corruption and its commonality, causes, and consequences in the surveyed countries is dealt with elsewhere (Pedersen and Johannsen 2006).
5. Pearson correlation = 0.691; significant at the 0.01 level.
6. Pearson correlation = 0.792; significant at the 0.001 level.
7. We are acutely aware that the implicit weights may need a full test because what we examine seems somewhat subjective. However, given the limited number of cases, we have chosen initially to adhere to the original questionnaire coding.
8. Are decisions improved when concerned interests are incorporated in formulation? (Pearson correlation = 0.709; significant at 0.005); participatory view of democracy (Pearson correlation = 0.920; significant at 0.000).
9. Pearson correlation = 0.712; significant at 0.004.
10. Pearson correlation = 0.570; significant at 0.033.
11. Pearson correlation = 0.773; significant at 0.001.
12. Mean (EU member 2004) = 1.25; mean (non-EU member by 2004) = 0.55; mean difference significant at 0.000.
13. INE (1): factor of Gini + 2 USD; initial eigenvalue of 1.352; percentage of variance explained 67.6. INE (2): factor of Gini + national poverty; initial eigenvalue of 1.393; percentage of variance explained 69.7.

References

Ágh, A. 2001. "Understanding Politics in Hungary." Demstar Research Report 2, Department of Political Science, University of Aarhus, Aarhus, Denmark.

Bernhard, M. 1996. "Civil Society after the First Transition: Dilemmas of Post-Communist Democratization in Poland and Beyond." *Communist and Post-Communist Studies* 29 (3): 309–30.

Blyth, M. 2001. "The Transformation of the Swedish Model: Economic Ideas, Distributional Conflict, and Institutional Change." *World Politics* 54 (1): 1–26.

Dahl, R. A. 1967. *Pluralist Democracy in the United States: Conflict and Consent.* Chicago: Rand McNally.

Deal, C., and J. Doroshow. 2003. "Corporate Astroturf and Civil Justice." *Multinational Monitor* 24 (3): 17–22.

Dunleavy, P., and B. O'Leary. 1987. *Theories of the State: The Politics of Liberal Democracy.* London: Macmillan.

European Commission. 2004. *Enlargement of European Union: Guide on the Negotiations.* Brussels: European Commission. http://www.evropa.bg/en/ic /services/download-publications/enlargement-of-the-eu.html.

Evans, P. 1995. *Embedded Autonomy: States and Industrial Transformation.* Princeton, NJ: Princeton University Press.

Foley, M. W., and B. Edwards. 1996. "The Paradox of Civil Society." *Journal of Democracy* 7 (3): 38–52.

Grabbe, H. 2001. "How Does Europeanization Affect CEE Governance? Conditionality, Diffusion, and Diversity." *Journal of European Public Policy* 8 (6): 1013–31.

Hellman, J. S., G. Jones, D. Kaufmann, and M. Schankerman. 2000. "Measuring Governance, Corruption, and State Capture: How Firms and Bureaucrats Shape the Business Environment in Transition Economies." Policy Research Working Paper 2312, World Bank, Washington, DC.

Hix, S. 2005. *The Political System of the European Union.* New York: Palgrave.

Howard, M. M. 2000. "Free Not to Participate: The Weakness of Civil Society in Post-Communist Europe." Studies in Public Policy 325, Centre for the Study of Public Policy, University of Strathclyde, Glasgow.

Johannsen, L. 2002. "The Responsive State." *Baltic Defence Review* 2 (8): 9–20.

Johannsen, L., and O. Nørgaard. 2005. "Policy-Making in Central and Eastern Europe: A Cross-Sectional Sector Perspective." In *Institutional Requirements and the Problem Solving of the Public Administrations of the Enlarged European Union and Its Neighbours,* ed. J. György, A. Barabashev, and F. van den Berg, 27–48. Bratislava: NISPAcee.

Johannsen, L., and K. H. Pedersen. 2005. "The Cohesion of European Democracy: The Consolidation of Democracy in Central and Eastern Europe." Paper presented at the European Consortium for Policy Research Joint Session of Workshops, Grenada, Spain, April 14–19.

Leftwich, A. 1995. "Bringing Politics Back In: Towards a Model of the Developmental State." *Journal of Developmental Studies* 31 (3): 400–27.

Lijphart, A. 1999. *Patterns of Democracy: Government Forms and Performance in Thirty-Six Countries.* New Haven, CT: Yale University Press.

Lindblom, C. 1977. *Politics and Markets.* New York: Basic Books.

Linz, J. J., and A. Stepan. 1996. *Problems of Democratic Transition and Consolidation: Southern Europe, South America, and Post-Communist Europe.* Baltimore, MD: Johns Hopkins University Press.

Lyon, T. P., and J. W. Maxwell. 2004. "AstroTurf: Interest Group Lobbying and Corporate Strategy." *Journal of Economic and Management Strategy* 13 (4): 561–97.

Mansfeldová, Z., S. Nałęcz, E. Priller, and A. Zimmer. 2005. "Civil Society in Transition: Civic Engagement and Nonprofit Organizations in Central and Eastern Europe after 1989." In *Future of Civil Society: Making Central European Nonprofit Organizations Work,* ed. A. Zimmer and E. Priller, 99–119. Berlin: Leske+Budrich e-book.

Offe, C. 1981. "The Attribution of Public Status to Interest Groups: Observations on the West German Case." In *Organizing Interests in Western Europe: Pluralism, Corporatism, and the Transformation of Politics*, ed. S. Berger, 123–58. Cambridge, U.K.: Cambridge University Press.

Pedersen, K. H., and L. Johannsen. 2006. "Corruption: Commonality, Causes, and Consequences in Fifteen Post-communist Countries." In *Democratic Governance in Central and Eastern European Countries*, ed. A. Rosenbaum and J. Nemec, 311–36. Bratislava: NISPAcee.

Pedersen, K. H., and R. Zubek. 2005. "The State of the State in Poland." Demstar Research Report 17, Department of Political Science, University of Aarhus, Aarhus, Denmark.

Petracca, M. P., ed. 1994. *The Politics of Interests: Interest Groups Transformed.* Boulder, CO: Westview Press.

Pressman, J. L., and A. Wildavsky. 1973. *Implementation.* Berkeley: University of California Press.

Putnam, R. D., with R. Leonardi and R. Y. Nanetti. 1993. *Making Democracy Work: Civic Traditions in Modern Italy.* Princeton, NJ: Princeton University Press.

Rueschemeyer, D. 1998. "The Self-Organization of Society and Democratic Rule: Specifying the Relationship." In *Participation and Democracy East and West: Comparisons and Interpretations*, ed. D. Rueschemeyer, M. Rueschemeyer, and B. Wittrock, 9–25. Armonk, NY: M. E. Sharpe.

Schattschneider, E. 1960. *The Semi-sovereign People: A Realist's View of Democracy in America.* New York: Holt, Rinehart & Winston.

Szabó, M. 2005. "Civic Engagement in East-Central Europe." In *Future of Civil Society: Making Central European Nonprofit Organizations Work*, ed. A. Zimmer and E. Priller (eds.), 77–97. Berlin and Münster: Leske+Budrich e-book.

Weiss, L. 1998. *The Myth of the Powerless State: Governing the Economy in a Global Era.* Cambridge, U.K.: Polity Press.

World Bank. 1991. *Managing Development: The Governance Dimension.* Washington, DC: World Bank.

———. 2004. *World Development Indicators.* Washington, DC: World Bank.

Zimmer, A. 2005. "Civil Society Organization in Central and Eastern European Countries: Introduction and Terminology." In *Future of Civil Society: Making Central European Nonprofit Organizations Work*, ed. A. Zimmer and E. Priller, 11–27. Berlin and Münster: Leske+Budrich e-book.

CHAPTER 4

Integrating Macroeconomic Policies and Social Objectives: Choosing the Right Policy Mix for Poverty Reduction

Elliott Harris and Caroline Kende-Robb

To achieve equitable development and social justice for the poor, one must look beyond macroeconomics. Indeed, increased awareness of the need to scale up efforts to achieve the Millennium Development Goals (MDGs) has put the spotlight on the role of macroeconomic policy in achieving social as well as macroeconomic objectives. The macroeconomic policy stance espoused by international financial institutions, primarily the International Monetary Fund (IMF), is criticized as limiting legitimate efforts by developing countries to step up their poverty-reduction expenditures. This view is largely colored by the misconception that macroeconomic policy is driven only by considerations of macroeconomic stability. Preservation of macroeconomic stability is indeed a precondition for sustained economic growth, which is the single most important factor influencing poverty reduction. However, responsible and shared growth, embracing both social development and environmental sustainability, is needed to maintain the improvements in human welfare targeted by the MDGs (see IMF 2005 and World Bank; World Bank 2004b).

Moreover, only recently have poverty objectives been integrated explicitly into the design of macroeconomic frameworks alongside growth and

The authors acknowledge the helpful comments received from Sabine Beddies, Andy Norton, and Dan Owen (World Bank) and Peter Fallon, Paul Francis, Kirsty Mason, Mark Plant, and Anton op de Beke (International Monetary Fund), though we alone are responsible for any errors.

stability objectives—for example, in the IMF's policy advice and program support under the Poverty Reduction and Growth Facility (PRGF). Integrating social and poverty-reduction goals with macroeconomic goals is challenging because it is not simply about adding social policies to a pre-designed sound macroeconomic framework (see Elson and Cagatay 2000). Formulating integrated and sustainable macroeconomic and social policies requires an understanding of countries' diversity and social contexts, plus an interdisciplinary approach combining social, economic, environmental, and political analysis of the links between poverty, livelihoods, and macroeconomic policies.

The range of feasible macroeconomic options open to a country depends in part on the constraints imposed by its macroeconomic situation. However, even in the most constrained environment, there is usually scope for increasing the pro-poor bias of policy choices while respecting the imperatives of overall stability. This chapter explores the potential to formulate macroeconomic policies from a social perspective. It begins by setting out a conceptual framework for integrating macroeconomic policies and social objectives, based on a multidimensional analysis of the transmission mechanisms of macroeconomic policies and the assessment of their impact. It then discusses some of the choices and tradeoffs confronting the macroeconomic policy maker and the scope for positively affecting social outcomes even in constrained circumstances. After some examples of the tradeoffs implied by these different policy choices, it examines how the policy-making process can facilitate the integration of macroeconomic and social policies. Finally, it looks at some of the key challenges ahead in integrating macroeconomic and social policies.

Conceptual Issues

This chapter contends that macroeconomic and social policies must be integrated at the policy formulation stage. Macroeconomic policies and structural reforms can affect existing distributive relations and institutional structures and, as such, may affect social relations and poverty.[1] It is difficult to analyze the impact, in this respect, of the macroeconomic policy stance as a whole, but an assessment of the influence of individual policy changes is possible and should inform policy choice.[2] The design of policies should reflect the country's social objectives and the macroeconomic opportunities and constraints that affect the sustained implementation of those policies.

Moving toward an integrated formulation of macroeconomic and social policies raises several methodological challenges. The analytical underpinning is an interdisciplinary approach, which facilitates a more open, evidence-based policy-making process, in which the tradeoffs are explicitly discussed (Robb 2003).

The definition of poverty must reflect its multidimensional nature, and the impact of macroeconomic and social policies should be examined across this range of dimensions. Such an examination requires a broad range of analytical tools. A more refined, interdisciplinary analysis facilitates identification of the mechanisms through which policies affect different groups of people and allows a deeper understanding, before the policies are put into place, of their poverty and social impact. Even if the availability of data is a constraint, this analysis should provide the basis for an informed debate over policies and tradeoffs and should result in a more effective combination of policies.

In the past, poverty was measured using an income-based poverty line derived from traditional household surveys, and poverty analysis focused on classic statistical indicators of income, health, and education. However, this method failed to capture the many dimensions of poverty revealed by a multidisciplinary approach. Vulnerability, physical and social isolation, insecurity, lack of self-respect, lack of access to information, distrust of state institutions, and powerlessness can be factors as important to poor people as low incomes. Maximizing incomes may be less of a priority than increasing livelihood security and decreasing vulnerability (Chambers 1983). Consultations with the poor can also provide insights into the nature of coping strategies—particularly the role of local networks and social capital, as well as information on the effectiveness of public and private institutions.

The multidisciplinary analysis of the various dimensions of poverty illustrates that macroeconomic policies affect a wide range of socioeconomic groups in different ways. First, for example, some macroeconomic policies and reforms mean that women have to work longer and harder, often without remuneration.[3] These adverse effects may not be visible in economic statistics, but they are revealed in statistics on the health and nutritional standards of women and children (Elson and Cagatay 2000). Second, some reforms could intensify regional and ethnic tensions and conflicts if they deepen existing social, economic, and political inequalities or create new ones (Osaghae 1995, cited in Mohan and others 2000, provides an example from Nigeria).

Third, adjustment measures may affect specific groups disproportionately, depending on their livelihood strategies. For example, certain groups, such as artisan fishing communities and low-paid casual laborers who rely heavily on commercial transportation, may be particularly affected by petroleum price increases. Finally, such awareness helps in developing complementary or mitigating policies targeting specific vulnerable groups. Moreover, the poor are not a static or homogenous group: people fall in and out of poverty depending on their vulnerability. The impact of policies will thus change over time.

Weighing Macroeconomic Policy Choices

The extent to which a country's economic and social policy choices are constrained by economic factors depends in large part on the country's macroeconomic starting point. This starting point may influence resource availability and thus set the financial parameters for social policy interventions by the government.[4] The choice of policy instruments and the timing of any given macroeconomic adjustment or reform also depend on the country's ability to absorb the adverse impact of the macroeconomic imbalances that need to be addressed. Countries with a stable macroeconomic environment will be able to pursue social objectives far more aggressively. Countries still struggling to control key macroeconomic variables will have less choice over how much or how fast to adjust to macroeconomic imbalances or step up poverty reduction efforts (see table 4.1). Within the constraints of even the most difficult macroeconomic environment, however, countries can still make some choices. Moreover, some of the same considerations hold when the issue is stepping up the poverty-reduction effort. Furthermore, in different country contexts, the process of policy making can contribute toward social policy objectives. For example, in postconflict environments, an inclusive social policy-making process in itself can be stabilizing and regenerative. In other countries, a more open policy-making process can build voices and accountability across social groups to improve governance through more diverse and inclusive institutions.

A macroeconomic policy stance can be considered stable at different levels of key variables. For example, inflation could hold steady at 5 or 10 percent, and a fiscal deficit could be kept to 2 or 8 percent each year. What matters is whether the macroeconomic stance is sustainable over time, for which a longer-term perspective is necessary. Higher aid could

Table 4.1. Assessing the Scope for Macroeconomic Policy Choices: Country Typology

Type of country	Characteristics	Macroeconomic choices	Social policy choices
Postconflict and fragile states, such as Bosnia and Herzegovina, Sierra Leone, and Afghanistan	• Politically sensitive • Social stability objectives predominant • Weak or diminished institutional capacity • Limited technical capacity • Financial constraints	• Limited range of macroeconomic choices • Focus usually on the most fundamental macroeconomic objectives, such as reducing deficits and inflation to more manageable levels	• Donor assistance for relief and reconstruction, which may provide fiscal space • More justification and policy space for inclusive social policies • Flexibility in delivery mechanisms, which may provide opportunities to rebuild social institutions • Sensitivity to the country's social and political context necessary
Stabilizing states, such as Guinea and Bolivia	• Many macroeconomic constraints, such as high debt and deficits • Vulnerable to shocks	• Need to stabilize key macroeconomic variables • Mixture of instruments available but limited range of targets	• Ability to adjust more slowly and better protect social sector expenditures • Greater scope to increase reach of social policies. • Ability to adopt longer-term perspective, with a focus on social justice and change • Opportunities to build more responsive, inclusive, and accountable institutions to strengthen service delivery

(continued)

Table 4.1. Assessing the Scope for Macroeconomic Policy Choices: Country Typology (*continued*)

Type of country	Characteristics	Macroeconomic choices	Social policy choices
Mature stabilizing states, such as Vietnam, Bangladesh, and Tanzania	• Macroeconomic framework stable and under control • Still vulnerable to exogenous shocks • Access to significant external financing	• Wider choice of both instruments and targets • Scope to absorb higher inflation or larger deficits without endangering stability	• Challenge of managing the macroeconomic effects of scaling up aid • Opportunities to focus on those excluded from access to benefits of previous social policies and growth • Room to create stronger local governance
Emerging market states, such as Brazil, Turkey, and Sri Lanka	• More sophisticated macroeconomic policy formulation and effective institutions • Well-developed financial sectors • Access to international capital markets • Diversified structure of economic production, which reduces vulnerability to exogenous shocks	• Fewer constraints on policy or available instruments • Ability to mobilize both domestic and external resources • Different set of questions facing policy makers	• Ability to pursue more ambitious social policies • Often more difficult to access concessional external financing to scale up to meet the MDGs • Emphasis on more market-based social policies, with public resources targeted to ensure that the marginal are included • Room to create more diverse, participatory, inclusive institutions

Source: Authors.

finance an immediate increase in poverty-reducing spending, but policy makers must assess the ability to generate the domestic resources needed to sustain the scaled-up efforts after the increase in aid tapers off. They must also consider the implications of higher short-term spending on expenditure composition over time.

Moreover, within the range of sustainable outcomes, policy makers can choose between different levels and speeds of adjustment for certain key variables. For example, one level of the fiscal deficit might imply an increase in the level of public indebtedness from 30 to 35 percent of gross domestic product (GDP) over five years; another, slightly smaller deficit might limit the increase in indebtedness to 33 percent of GDP. The choice depends, in part, on other considerations, such as the use to which the extra public spending under the higher-deficit scenario is put. Similarly, the decision on how quickly to adjust to the level of the fiscal deficit considered sustainable over the long term might depend on how fast different categories of spending can be reduced, how much additional revenue can be mobilized, and what sources of additional financing are available, at what terms.

Instruments

In principle, a given degree of adjustment of a macroeconomic variable can usually be achieved in a variety of ways. For example, the fiscal deficit can be lowered by 1 percent of GDP by reducing expenditures or by raising revenues by that amount, or by some combination. However, the social consequences differ. Revenue increases may have direct and indirect distributional consequences, affecting different groups positively or negatively. Spending cuts may impair the government's ability to deliver some social services but may enhance the government's ability to sustain others. Which social expenditures are adjusted may have a differential impact on social outcomes. For example, the social impact of a reduction in current expenditures in primary education will be different from that of an equivalent cut in tertiary-level spending.

Timing

The pace of adjustment toward a given objective can be varied to manage the social impact. Adverse impacts of a rapid adjustment path can sometimes be alleviated by compensatory social safety net measures, but the ability to finance, formulate, effectively target, and sustain them is often limited in low-income countries (see Baden 1997; Subbarao and others 1997).

More gradual implementation of reforms may be necessary to allow the absorption of social costs or to give the economy the time to adjust to new opportunities. (Trade liberalization is a case in point.)

The decision to accept the consequences of a slower pace of adjustment may be justifiable from a short-term social perspective, but it should also take into account the cumulative adverse effects over time of partial adjustment or of no adjustment at all. For example, the government may prefer to keep the rate of inflation at a somewhat elevated level, but it should also take into account the likely resulting erosion of purchasing power of the poor.

Stability versus Growth

An appropriate macroeconomic policy stance is not the same as a rational and sustainable growth strategy, which would require the specification of sectoral policies in areas particularly important to the overall growth of the economy. It is difficult to use macroeconomic policy instruments to target growth in specific sectors without distorting resource allocation decisions or the proper functioning of markets, but they can be used to pursue growth more aggressively. In such cases, there must be due consideration of potential risks. For example, reducing interest rates to ease access to credit for private sector investment may spur growth, but if quality controls and prudential supervision are too lax, financial sector distress could result, thereby undermining long-term growth.

Pro-poor Growth

Finally, social and cultural factors can prevent the benefits of growth from being shared equitably. In turn, social inequities, such as gender inequality in education and access to assets, can keep growth below its long-term potential. Temporary social safety nets cannot resolve these problems. Thus, growth without policies that reduce inequality and improve the distribution of income and assets within a society (such as land tenure reform, pro-poor public expenditure, and measures to increase the poor's access to financial markets) will be only partially successful in reducing poverty.

Two factors that determine the impact of growth on poverty are its sectoral composition and its distributional patterns (Ames and others 2001). Growth generated through labor-intensive production in the sectors where the poor are concentrated (often the agricultural sector) is likely to have a faster and more durable impact on poverty. Macroeconomic policy makers need to be aware of how any given policy would affect these key sectors.

Growth can also be rendered more pro-poor indirectly, through public redistributive policies (predominantly, the tax system, public spending on goods and services or infrastructure, and public transfers and social safety net outlays).

Closer reflection is needed on the impact of distributional patterns on growth and poverty, and a better understanding is needed of how growth is affected by the extent of a country's social fragmentation, social exclusion, and democratization (see Ravallion 2002). Policy makers should consider explicitly the sources of sustainable growth and alternative policy options to achieve it, as well as the role of private sector investment in promoting pro-poor growth. Exogenous factors, such as climate variations, the HIV/AIDS pandemic, or the role of remittances, are also important. There is, moreover, a need for improved understanding of how fiscal and monetary policies can take into account the unpaid domestic economy that centers on welfare.

Examples of Macroeconomic and Structural Policy Choices

For governments to exploit what flexibility they have to enhance the sustainability of policy implementation requires awareness of how transmission mechanisms affect different groups.

Macroeconomic Policies and Poverty Goals

High and fluctuating inflation harms the poor more than the rich and can undermine economic performance.[5] However, tightening the stance of monetary policy to curb high inflation may have adverse short-term effects on real interest rates and, thus, on the real cost of borrowing, consuming, and producing. Moreover, targeting very low inflation could also harm the poor if the required adjustment restricts pro-poor spending and slows output growth.[6]

Policy makers also need to consider the different effects of anti-inflation policies across socioeconomic groups. For example, high interest rates diminish women's already scarce access to credit for production and household emergencies more than they do men's.[7] In terms of exchange rate policy, allowing an overvalued currency to depreciate can enhance export competitiveness and raise the local currency income of exporters, but it also raises the cost of imported inputs and consumables, hence eroding households' real purchasing power. Changes in exchange rates will thus have both income-raising and price-raising effects, giving rise to different net benefits or losses across socioeconomic groups. Key factors that determine the net effect are what the consumption basket is composed of and who purchases what within the household.[8] The social impact may also be indirect and vary across groups. For example, depreciation-induced increases in the costs of imported medicines may prompt poor people to use traditional local medicines or to go untreated. Attenuating measures may thus be necessary to protect some vulnerable groups, even though there is a net benefit for the society as a whole.[9]

Fiscal Policies and Poverty Goals

A sustained effort to reduce poverty cannot be funded by external resources alone. A substantial improvement in domestic revenue mobilization is needed in most developing countries, but progress is often slow. Moreover, tension could arise between the need to increase revenues and the social imperative of fashioning an equitable tax system. For example, greater reliance on the value added tax may generate additional resources with greater administrative ease, but it could have a regressive impact if applied to items consumed by the poor. The ability to make tax policies more pro-poor through the use of exemptions, zero ratings, or lower tax rates for the items used by the poor may also be constrained by the limited tax base and shortcomings in tax administration, as well as by the relatively large size of the informal sector (see box 4.1).

BOX 4.1

Ghana, 2005/06: Example of a Poverty-Focused Tax Policy

Ghana established a ring-fenced fund for using the budgetary revenue from fuel taxes to subsidize pro-poor expenditures. The social impact levy is publicized as an additional tax on fuel and is targeted at the elimination of school fees, expanded rural electrification, and expanded public transportation. The elimination of school fees has been widely acclaimed as a success (school attendance has risen as a result), and its transparency has prompted public complaints about (and sanctions for) head teachers who continue to impose fees. The cost of this program is £13 million, well below the level of money raised.

Source: Information provided by IMF staff.

Regarding public expenditure, the level and predictability of available resources, both domestic and external, determine a government's ability to fund and sustain social programs and pro-poor spending. However, the impact on poverty and social forces of a given level of spending depends on both its composition (the extent to which resources are allocated to pro-poor spending programs) and the efficiency of social service delivery mechanisms.[10] The quality and efficiency of government spending can be improved by concentrating on pro-poor budgets, flexible fiscal targets, strengthened public expenditure management systems, accountability, and a gender-equitable focus in public expenditure management and the budget process (see Norton and Elson 2002).

Deficit Financing

The size and financing of the fiscal deficit can also have direct and indirect social effects. Using domestic government debt instruments may affect interest rates and private sector access to credit less than recourse to bank financing. Sales of public assets can help finance a given year's deficit while avoiding direct monetary effects. However, interest liabilities will absorb an increasing share of available revenues as the debt stock grows, hence limiting the ability to fund future poverty-reducing and social expenditures. An evaluation of the social impact of how the government deficit is financed must thus include an assessment of the longer-term sustainability of the government debt and an analysis of the longer-term sustainability of fiscal programs.

Structural Policies and Poverty Goals

The overall impact of changes in macroeconomic policies depends, in part, on complementary structural reforms. However, these reforms often elicit far sharper criticism than pure macroeconomic policies, in part because their social impacts are often more readily observable. The choice of structural reforms and decisions on their timing and scope must thus take into account a range of different tradeoffs. Consider the following four potential reforms: privatization, trade liberalization, banking sector reforms, and petroleum price changes.

First, privatization (see box 4.2) can improve welfare by raising the efficiency and effectiveness of the delivery of key social services and utilities, such as water and electricity, and by reducing the drain of public enterprises on government budgets. However, privatization can also lead to job losses and retrenchment, and it can replace a state monopoly with

BOX 4.2

Cameroon, 2001: Example of a Poverty-Focused Privatization Operation

Cameroon's privatization program in the water and electricity sectors aimed to increase production, enhance efficiency, and expand the scope of basic services vital to the poor. Efforts were made to limit labor shedding by the national electricity company, SONEL (Société Nationale d'Electricité), and to negotiate compensation packages. In addition, the privatization of the agribusiness sector was expected to be instrumental in enhancing the participation of the private sector in the management and production of agricultural products.

Source: Robb 2003.

a poorly regulated private one that does not address legitimate social concerns such as the needs of poor and remote populations. Market-based utility rates can improve service provision, but they may also exclude the poor, directly affecting their health and welfare. The issue, therefore, is to ensure that privatization generates the expected fiscal savings and efficiency gains without undermining the delivery of services to the poor.

Second, while, overall, trade liberalization can generate growth and reduce poverty, transitional costs, in many cases, heavily affect the poor. They do so through price transmission (depending on whether the poor are net consumers or producers), enterprise profits (and so employment and wages), and taxes and spending (changes in the government's fiscal position) (see McCulloch, Winters, and Cirera 2001). Too rapid liberalization could also increase poverty and inequality, particularly when poor countries have been opening up their markets more quickly than rich countries (Oxfam 2002). Changing incentive structures may encourage farmers to switch to the production of a single cash crop, thereby heightening their vulnerability to crop disease, climatic variations, and declining world market prices and possibly threatening household and national food security. Such considerations argue in favor of a more managed process, with full liberalization delayed while social safety nets are put in place (see Kanbur 2001) or necessary changes in production structures are under way. Complementary policies, such as improved extension services, transportation, and access to water could also be considered. Analyzing the possible effects before implementation can help determine the need for slower implementation of reforms or for such complementary policies.

Third, banking sector reforms in low-income countries (restructuring bank balance sheets to reduce the burden of nonperforming loans, eliminating unproductive directed lending by state-owned banks, and reinforcing prudential regulation and banking supervision) can enhance efficiency and promote confidence and could increase the amount of credit available to the private sector. However, such reforms may also lead to reduced provision of banking services to rural areas and to the poor or to more stringent collateral and guarantee requirements that effectively exclude small businesses and private individuals from access to bank credit. The damage could be offset by complementary measures to improve access to credit by the poor, such as strengthening the supervision of microfinance institutions to facilitate a closer interface between these institutions and the formal banking sector.

Finally, reducing government subsidies on petroleum product prices is a frequently recommended expenditure reduction measure, particularly in times of rising international oil prices. Taxes on petroleum products are also usually an important and secure source of revenue. However, rising prices can affect the poor disproportionately, both through their fuel consumption[11] and through higher input and transportation costs. The impact on the poor could be mitigated to some extent by differential taxation of petroleum products used by poor and nonpoor groups or by provision of cross-subsidies to the former (box 4.3).

BOX 4.3

Ghana, 2002: Country Comparison of Poverty-Focused Policy Responses—Petroleum Prices

When petroleum product prices in Ghana were increased in 2001 to reflect the rise in import costs and new taxes, the impact on the poor was mitigated through cross-product price subsidization and staggered implementation of the taxes. Recognizing that kerosene consumption is heavily concentrated in the lower income brackets, the government tapered the increases implemented in February 2001 by product: gasoline prices were increased by 61 percent to help contain the increase in kerosene price to 45 percent. The reintroduction of the ad valorem and specific petroleum taxes was staggered to August and October, respectively, to take advantage of a fall in world oil prices, which allowed the taxes to be implemented without further increases in retail prices. The new petroleum price adjustment formula will preserve the cross-subsidization of kerosene prices.

Source: Robb 2003.

The Policy-Making Process

Opening up the public dialogue on macroeconomic and social policies between diverse stakeholder groups can deepen the understanding between these groups and help build consensus on the common priorities of social policy, as well as on the constraints on government intervention, financial or otherwise. Participation by civic groups and the poor in monitoring and evaluating policies promotes transparency and accountability and enhances people's awareness of their rights, and, in the long run, it may encourage them to demand better governance. Equally important is an open, ideally ongoing, dialogue among those responsible for formulating and implementing social and macroeconomic policies.

Policy-Making Context

Many factors affect policy makers' decisions to create, sustain, alter, or reverse policies. Rules, legislation, traditions, networks, ethnic alliances, patronage, political allegiances, donor influence, technical advice, and bureaucratic structures all interact to form a complex and fluctuating policy-making environment. Policy making is a negotiation between groups of unequal power, access to information, and influence. The poorest people are often marginalized, excluded from the process, or even disenfranchised, and they usually have the least influence on it. Appreciating this fact can lead to a better understanding of how such policy choices are made and of how different groups are affected by them.

Many complexities arise in the policy-making process. First, political structures can determine the extent of participation around policy choices and the policy options that are to be discussed in the public domain. Second, successful reform requires country ownership and social consensus. These elements are difficult to achieve when stakeholders have varying interests and when certain groups have easier access to relevant information and to decision makers. However, broader public participation in the formulation of policies can facilitate the process. It is important to clarify the roles and responsibilities of the various groups involved and to understand the institutional setting for both the policy dialogue and the accountability of the various actors.

One important issue is the role of external development partners in the domestic policy dialogue—particularly in the essentially political choice of policies. In aid-dependent countries, the importance of donor funding for social policy outlays and the associated conditions can skew the balance between a government's internal accountability to citizens and the country's external accountability to financiers. Maintaining the appropriate balance of accountabilities requires strong government leadership and donor willingness to accept it.

Including the Poor in the Policy-Making Process

There are three main reasons to include the poor in the policy dialogue.[12] The first is improved diagnosis of problems and better design and implementation of appropriate solutions, based on analysis by the poor themselves of their situation and priorities. Such analysis can differ fundamentally from what is assumed by policy makers. The second is a broader constituency for reform, underpinned by deeper understanding and ownership of policy choices. The third is empowerment of poor communities, which then cease to be merely the passive recipients of (sometimes misguided) state benevolence and donor assistance.

Consultations with communities have shown that the poor have a far greater capacity to appraise, analyze, plan, and act than many development experts have previously acknowledged. Consequently, over the past 10 years, the World Bank, in partnership with governments, civil society organizations, academic institutions and donors, has developed tools to enable policy makers to consult directly with poor people and to ensure that their views are reflected in a national public dialogue of potential policy reforms. This approach enables a better understanding by policy makers and stakeholders of the synergies among macroeconomic goals, growth, and poverty reduction objectives.[13]

Linking Macroeconomic and Social Policies through the Budget Process

Macroeconomic policies influence the amount of resources and thus, indirectly, the range of feasible instruments available for attaining social objectives.[14] These objectives and priorities must be translated into annual budget allocations for effective implementation and must be reflected in medium-term expenditure frameworks, which should frame the annual budgets. To encourage a public debate, policy makers could present various aggregate spending scenarios to reveal tradeoffs between different macroeconomic, fiscal, and social policy options. With this information, elected assemblies (national and local) and domestic interest groups could scrutinize plans and budgets and bargain over the allocation of resources with a clear understanding of the tradeoffs involved. Such debate would give citizens an understanding of what they should expect and demand and a firm basis for insisting on greater accountability of government.

However, many formal accountability mechanisms, such as elections, legislative oversight, and financial reporting mechanisms, have limitations.[15] Over the past few years, an approach called *social accountability* has been applied in many countries to complement and enhance conventional internal mechanisms of accountability. Social accountability highlights the broad range of action and mechanisms, beyond the formal institutions, that citizens can use to hold the state accountable. Examples are influencing and improving the public expenditure management process by demystifying and disseminating budget information, increasing people's awareness of their entitlement to services and information, and analyzing the implications of budgetary allocations for disadvantaged groups. Such actions promote the demand side of governance and can help to increase citizens' voices in public policy and budget processes.

Challenges Looking Forward

This chapter highlights some of the challenges of better integrating macroeconomic and social policies. Macroeconomic and financial policies and programming need to be formulated with an understanding of the institutional and social contexts as well as the economic situation. Moreover, the analysis and understanding of these links must be deepened, both globally and in the specific country context. There are several ways to move this agenda forward. Two of these are touched on here.

Opening Up the Policy Dialogue

A discussion of alternative macroeconomic policy options, in terms of both their impact on key macroeconomic variables and their consistency with social objectives, would highlight the implicit tradeoffs and facilitate the choice of policy mix. Similarly, a debate on social policy priorities that also examines resource availability and issues of medium- to long-term sustainability would highlight the macroeconomic implications of social policy choice. Such outcomes suggest the need for a regular exchange between the decision makers responsible for macroeconomic and social policies, using the results of multidisciplinary analysis to inform their choices.

In reality, the policy-making process is not purely technical: it often involves balancing the broader goal of equity with the welfare and interests of the various groups that can affect the reform process, which is often constrained by sociopolitical dynamics. Hence, it is necessary to understand the rules and incentives (expressed both as price-based incentives and in terms of less predictable organizational cultures and social norms) governing the formulation and implementation of policy reform. Such an understanding can help to define more clearly the respective roles of the various actors in the policy-making process.

Since the introduction of the poverty-reduction strategy approach, many governments have attempted to open up a policy dialogue around alternative policy options for promoting growth and reducing poverty among those concerned with formulating and implementing policy. These individuals include representatives of the key ministries and agencies responsible for macroeconomic and social policies, as well as representatives of the relevant stakeholder groups, including the poor. Better information sharing and capacity building and an improved institutional setting are all necessary. Each group's views on policy priorities, core benefits, costs, and tradeoffs of policy options should be discussed openly against the backdrop of the financing constraints, and those views should inform and influence the positions of other groups. This process cannot be linear but must go through several iterations. Ideally, the institutional framework for consultation should provide for regular interaction between the groups as part of the overall poverty reduction strategy process and the integration of macroeconomic and social policies.

However, despite the increasing openness in discussing poverty reduction objectives and policies and notwithstanding the greater flexibility in the design of macroeconomic frameworks, the institutional framework for such discussions is often inadequate. The necessary information may not be available to stakeholders in an accessible form, and potential participants may lack the technical or institutional capacity to evaluate macroeconomic tradeoffs and formulate feasible alternative policy options. Moreover, domestic policies are increasingly linked to global developments, and decisions may need to be made promptly, often without adequate time for wide-ranging public consultations. Also, some macroeconomic policy decisions (such as exchange rate or interest rate changes) need to be handled with sensitivity because public disclosure could induce preemptive behavior. Nonetheless, even where there is relatively little public debate around macroeconomic policies and decisions, the impact on poverty of macroeconomic policies and their consistency with social objectives must be explicitly considered, and the policies must be adjusted or supplemented with alternative options as necessary.

Analyzing Impact of Policies

Understanding the impact of macroeconomic and structural policies on poor people is complicated and multidimensional, and relationships are often difficult to establish in definitive terms. With existing methods and data, it is possible for policy makers to make explicit their underlying assumptions and to use country knowledge, including the results of Poverty and Society Impact Analysis (PSIA), in formulating policies (see Coudouel, Dani, and Paternostro 2006; Robb 2003; World Bank 2003; World Bank and DFID 2007).

PSIA is the analysis of the positive and negative distributional and poverty impact of policy change on the well-being of different groups in society, with a focus on the poor and vulnerable (World Bank 2003: 2). Most importantly, it can help ensure that discussions of policy choices are based on sound and widely accepted evidence, thereby minimizing the effect of ideology or interest-group politics. The debate around PSIA can also encourage the government and its external partners, including international financial institutions such as the IMF and the World Bank, to better explain the poverty impact and tradeoffs of their policy advice. PSIA should not be seen as an externally driven, one-off exercise, but as an integral part of the policy-making process, in which, ideally, civil society groups should be partners. It can be undertaken in advance to make assumptions more explicit upfront, it can be used during implementation to monitor whether public choices are having the expected effect, and it can assess afterward whether public actions were successful and encourage the use of this information in future policy design.

The challenge for PSIA is to integrate and analyze existing data, such as household surveys, participatory poverty assessments (PPAs), end-user surveys, administrative data, national statistics, and censuses.[16] Lack of data has sometimes been used as a reason for not linking poverty outcomes to policy decisions. However, in most countries, there is an untapped wealth of information, knowledge, and data. Even in countries with limited data, it is possible to assess at least some of the potential poverty effects and therefore contribute to a more informed debate.

In most noncrisis situations, there is time for the World Bank and other donors to help governments analyze policy tradeoffs and reform options as part of a country's poverty reduction strategy. The macroeconomic policy discussions between governments and the IMF could then draw on this analysis. However, there is still an analysis gap: many countries and donors lack capacity and experience to conduct a comprehensive PSIA of policies and reforms. Moreover, many donors still focus on assessing the impact of projects, as opposed to policies. Improved donor coordination is required, as are clearer lines of agreed institutional responsibility for the analytical work needed to inform policy choices.

Social science data are always partial—an imperfect reflection of a more complex reality. As a result, it is important to be realistic and selective and to let key questions drive the choice of methods and tools, not vice versa (see Woolcock 2001). In the past, poverty analysis was dominated by quantitative data derived from nationally representative household surveys. More recently, qualitative methods (such as participatory research, including PPAs) have contributed to a more multidimensional assessment of the nonincome or hidden aspects of poverty. These methods have improved the understanding of the noneconomic processes by which people fall into and get out of poverty and that mediate group and individual control over resources, and they have improved the identification of the priorities of the poor.[17] Best practice is to combine data from different sources for policy analysis, as in Mongolia (Dulamdary and others 2001), Uganda (Government of Uganda 1999), and Vietnam (Turk 2001).

It is important to extend the focus beyond economic concerns to explicit consideration of social, political, and institutional concerns (Cernea 1985, 1996).[18] Institutional analysis acknowledges that the formal or informal rules of the game governing group behavior and interaction in political, economic, and social spheres can mediate or distort—sometimes fundamentally—the expected outcomes of policy reform. Political analysis of the structure of power relations recognizes that the entrenched political interests of different stakeholder groups affect many aspects of policy debate and decision making, as well as the distributional impacts of economic reform. Social analysis looks at the social relationships that govern interaction at different organizational levels, including within households, communities, and social groups (World Bank and DFID 2007).

Conclusions

The objectives of this chapter are threefold. First, it stresses that macroeconomic and social policies need to be fully integrated at the conceptual stage, in full awareness of the tradeoffs and the impacts of macroeconomic policies on social forces and vice versa. Second, it demonstrates that this awareness requires a full understanding of the transmission mechanisms of policies and the different impact that given policies can have on different socioeconomic groups. Such an understanding can only be achieved through a multidisciplinary analysis that takes into account the economic, social, institutional, and political context. Third, it illustrates that it is possible to improve the pro-poor bias of macroeconomic policy even in the most constrained macroeconomic environments, through the choice of policy instruments, timing, compensating measures, or policy redesign.

This agenda now needs to be taken forward by focusing analytical efforts on previously neglected areas in an effort to better understand both the short- and long-term effects of policies. More coordinated and timely analysis can help governments, international financial institutions, and other development partners collaborate more effectively to design sound macroeconomic frameworks that serve the ultimate objective of equitable development and social justice for the poor.

Notes

1. *Macroeconomic policies* are generally understood as consisting of the primarily fiscal, monetary, and exchange rate policies that have a direct or indirect impact on key economic variables, such as the inflation rate, the exchange rate, the external current account balance or fiscal deficit, or the level of international reserves. These policies are usually formulated to affect the economy as a whole, but they often have different effects on different groups. *Structural policies* include policies aimed at improving the efficiency of resource allocation, strengthening economic incentives, removing impediments to the smooth functioning of markets and to private sector development, and expanding the overall productive capacity of the economy. They usually have a longer time horizon than macroeconomic policies, but the latter often require complementary structural reforms to generate their full impact.
2. For example, one would have difficulty assessing the effect of the present structure of taxation on poverty or on the welfare of a particular group, but one could make such an assessment for a planned change in that tax structure.
3. In most African countries, for example, women are the agricultural producers; providers of care to children, the elderly, and the sick; domestic workers; preparers of food; managers of the household budget; and community managers (Moser 1993). Most of this work is outside the formal labor market and is based mainly in subsistence production, informal employment, domestic or reproductive work, and voluntary or community work (Blackden and Bhanu 1999).

4. The macroeconomic situation can have a direct impact on domestic resource mobilization: a stable environment with strong prospects for growth is more likely to generate a sustained stream of government revenue that can be used for social policy than one characterized by uncertainty and disruptions. Macroeconomic stability also contributes to donor decisions to provide external aid, particularly in the form of general budget support.

5. Cashin and others (2001) present a useful overview of the research on macroeconomic policies and poverty reduction. Also see Killick (1999) and Stewart (1995).

6. In general, the IMF's PRGF-supported programs emphasize the protection of pro-poor spending in situations where public expenditures have to be reduced to help monetary policy contain inflation.

7. In some countries, women workers may be more likely to fall victim to unemployment because they predominate in the small and medium-sized enterprises, which are hardest hit by high interest rates and overall economic slowdowns. They are often laid off before men in both public and private downsizing.

8. For example, a currency depreciation may make export crops, usually under the control of men, more profitable, but it could also raise the costs of transportation, fertilizers, and other imported inputs in the food crop sector, where women are more often active, and lead to higher food prices, again affecting women, who are responsible for feeding the family within the household. The depreciation may thus not benefit the household as a whole, because income may not be pooled.

9. These measures may include temporary and well-targeted subsidies of key staples, more gradual pass-through of the exchange rate–related increase in the prices of key commodities or consumer goods through adjustment of the tax component of the domestic price, or a differentiated wage policy in the formal sector.

10. The *World Development Report 2004* (World Bank 2004a) identifies four main reasons government spending may not have the intended social outcomes: (a) governments may be spending on the wrong goods or the wrong people, (b) the money may fail to reach the front-line service provider, (c) the incentives to provide the services are often very weak, and (d) households may not take advantage of the provided services for social or economic reasons.

11. Moreover, when prices of petroleum products used as fuel by the poor rise, the rural poor, in particular, often resort to using wood or charcoal as a substitute, with negative long-term effects on the environment.

12. Participatory poverty assessments are a tried and tested tool for including the poor in the analysis of poverty.

13. Direct consultations with poor communities through participatory poverty assessments can reveal the many dimensions of poverty. Vulnerability results

when poor people are forced into low-paid, insecure, and often dangerous occupations, as well as when people are isolated and socially excluded, as with single pensioners in Armenia. Gender affects the perception of poverty. Women typically define their poverty differently than men. Crime and violence, including child prostitution (Zambia), drugs (Jamaica), and domestic violence (Mexico), can also affect poverty. Participatory poverty assessments in Ghana and South Africa point to the effect of seasonality on food security, access to water, and health. Finally, powerlessness can also affect the perception of poverty: lack of influence on government policies (The Gambia); distrust of state institutions, especially the police and the judiciary (Uganda); and lack of information on entitlements, rights, and the activities of local government (Vietnam).

14. The reflections should not be limited to the short-term availability of resources. The predictability and volume of resource availability over longer times will determine, in part, the extent to which traditional, entitlement-based instruments of social policy (such as pension schemes, medical and unemployment insurance, and consumer subsidies) can be introduced and sustained.

15. Moreover, some national assemblies may not be prepared to surrender their prerogatives in the budgetary process to a more open process involving other stakeholder groups.

16. PSIA can use tools and techniques from a wide range of social sciences, including social and environmental tools (for example, PPAs, social impact analysis, village-based studies, gender analysis, social capital assessment); economic tools (for example, benefit incidence analysis, poverty mapping, public expenditure tracking); partial equilibrium tools (multimarket models); and general equilibrium tools (such as the computable general equilibrium model and social accounting matrix).

17. Booth and others (1998) make a connection between contextual methods (for example, qualitative analysis) that aim to capture social phenomena within their social, cultural, economic, and political context and noncontextual methods (for example, household surveys) that are designed to collect information independent of the specific context.

18. The World Bank and the U.K. Department for International Development (DFID) propose an analytical framework that identifies six major trans-mission channels (employment, prices, access, assets, transfers, and taxes), as well as authority structures, decision-making processes, and power relations, that can affect and are themselves affected by policy reforms (see World Bank and DFID 2007: 10–13). See also Moser (1996) for a groundbreaking study on the impacts of adjustment policies and economic crises (for example, high inflation rates and changes in prices, wages, public spending, and the labor market) in four urban communities, complementing rich qualitative community-level data with panel quantitative surveys.

References

Ames, B., W. Brown, S. Devarajan, and A. Izquierdo. 2001. "Macroeconomic Policy and Poverty Reduction." Washington, DC: International Monetary Fund and World Bank.

Baden, S. 1997. "Economic Reform and Poverty: A Gender Analysis Report." Prepared for the Gender Equality Unit, Swedish International Development Cooperation Agency, Stockholm.

Blackden, M., and C. Bhanu. 1999. "Gender, Growth and Poverty Reduction." Technical Paper 429, World Bank, Washington, DC.

Booth, D., J. Holland, J. Hentschel, P. Lanjouw, and A. Herbert. 1998. "Participation and Combined Methods in African Poverty Assessment: Renewing the Agenda." Social Development Division, U.K. Department for International Development, London.

Cashin, P., P. Mauro, C. Pattillo, and R. Sahay. 2001. "Macroeconomic Policies and Poverty Reduction: Stylized Facts and Overview of Research." IMF Working Paper 01/135, International Monetary Fund, Washington, DC.

Cernea, M., 1985. *Putting People First: Sociological Variables in Rural Development*. London: Oxford University Press.

———. 1996. "Social Organization and Development Anthropology." Environmentally Sustainable Development Studies and Monographs 6, World Bank, Washington, DC.

Chambers, R. 1983. *Putting the Last First*. London: Longman.

Coudouel, A., A. Dani, and S. Paternostro. 2006. *Poverty and Social Impact Analysis of Reforms: Lessons and Examples from Implementation*. Washington, DC: World Bank.

Dulamdary, E., M. Shah, and R. Mearns, with B. Enkhbat and L. Ganzaya. 2001. "Mongolia: Participatory Living Standards Assessment." Report prepared for donors consultative group meeting by the National Statistics Office of Mongolia and World Bank, Paris, May 15–16.

Elson, D., and N. Cagatay. 2000. "The Social Content of Macroeconomic Policies." *World Development* 28 (7): 1347–64.

Government of Uganda. 1999. *Poverty Status Report*. Kampala: Planning and Economic Development.

IMF and World Bank. 2005. *Global Monitoring Report 2005: Millennium Development Goals—From Consensus to Momentum*. Washington, DC: World Bank.

Kanbur, R. 2001. "Growth and Trade: The Last Redoubt?" Cornell University, Ithaca, NY. http://www.arts.cornell.edu/poverty/kanbur/EasterlyWBReview.pdf.

Killick, T. 1999. "Making Adjustment Work for the Poor." ODI Poverty Briefing 5, Overseas Development Institute, London.

McCulloch, N., A. Winters, and X. Cirera. 2001. *Trade Liberalization and Poverty: A Handbook*. London: Centre for Economic Policy Research.

Mohan, G., E. Brown, B. Milward, and A. Zack-Williams. 2000. *Structural Adjustment: Theory, Practice, and Impacts*. London: Routledge.

Moser, C. 1993. *Gender Planning and Development: Theory Practice and Training*. London: Routledge.

———. 1996. "Confronting Crisis: A Comparative Study of Household Responses to Poverty and Vulnerability in Four Poor Urban Communities." Environmentally Sustainable Development Series and Monographs 8, World Bank, Washington, DC.

Norton, A., and D. Elson. 2002. *What's Behind the Budget? Politics, Rights, and Accountability in the Budget Process*. Oxford, U.K.: ODI Publications.

Osaghae, E. E. 1995. "Structural Adjustment and Ethnicity." Research Report 98. Nordiska Afrikainstitutet, Uppsala, Sweden.

Oxfam. 2002. *Rigged Rules and Double Standards: Trade, Globalization, and the Fight against Poverty*. Oxford, U.K.: Oxfam International.

Ravallion, M. 2002. "Looking beyond Averages: A Research Program on Poverty and Inequality." Development Economics Research Group, World Bank, Washington, DC.

Robb, C. 2003. "Poverty and Social Impact Analysis—Linking Macroeconomic Policies to Poverty Outcomes: Summary of Early Experiences." IMF Working Paper 03/43, International Monetary Fund, Washington, DC.

Stewart, F. 1995. *Adjustment and Poverty: Options and Choices*. London: Routledge.

Subbarao, K., K. Ezemerari, J. Braithwaite, C. Graham, and A. Thompson. 1997. *Safety Net Programs and Poverty Reduction: Lessons from Cross-Country Experience*. Washington, DC: World Bank.

Turk, C. 2001. "Linking Participatory Poverty Assessments to Policy and Policy Making: Experience from Vietnam." Policy Research Working Paper 2526, World Bank, Washington, DC.

Woolcock, M. 2001. "Social Assessment and Program Evaluation with Limited Formal Data: Thinking Quantitatively, Acting Qualitatively." Social Development Briefing Note 68, World Bank, Washington, DC.

World Bank. 2003. *A User's Guide to Poverty and Social Impact Analysis*. Washington, DC: World Bank. http://go.worldbank.org/IR9SLBWTQ0.

———. 2004a. *World Development Report 2004: Making Services Work for the Poor*. Washington, DC: World Bank.

———. 2004b. *Responsible Growth for the New Millennium: Integrating Society Ecology and the Economy*. Washington, DC: World Bank.

World Bank and DFID (U.K. Department for International Development). 2007. *Tools for Institutional, Social, and Political Analysis (TIPS): A Sourcebook for PSIA*. Washington, DC: World Bank.

PART II

STRUCTURAL INEQUALITIES AND
POLICY EXPERIENCE

Addressing Exclusion: Social Policy Perspectives from Latin America and the Caribbean

Mayra Buvinić and Jacqueline Mazza

Social policy can neither be formulated nor advanced when entire groups of the population are excluded from mainstream society, a situation that is endemic in Latin America and the Caribbean. Exclusion has multiple historic, cultural, social, and economic roots, and it results in the denial of basic citizen rights to individuals on the basis of gender, ethnicity, race, or other distinguishing group features.

In recent years, governments in Latin America and the Caribbean have addressed exclusion with a growing array of public policy initiatives. This chapter reviews the experience with these policies and highlights good practices and unresolved challenges. It draws especially on the rich Latin American and Caribbean experience with women's inclusion and group interventions at three levels:

- Constitutional frameworks and national policies that provide the basic structure for inclusive societies
- Institutional arrangements for promoting and enforcing laws and policies
- Proactive programs that seek to counter specific forms of exclusion.

The Nature of Exclusion in Latin America and the Caribbean

What Is Social Exclusion?

Social exclusion can be understood as "the inability of an individual to participate in the basic political, economic, and social functioning of the society in which she lives" (Tsakloglou and Papadopoulos 2001). More concisely, it is "the denial of equal access to opportunities imposed by certain groups of society upon others" (Behrman, Gaviria, and Székely 2003). The first definition highlights the range of behaviors affected by exclusion, showing its multidimensionality. The second points to its two most distinguishing features: it affects culturally defined groups, and it is embedded in social interactions.

Social exclusion occurs if group membership has a sizable impact on an individual's access to opportunities and if social interactions between groups occur in a power-subordinate relationship. The group feature provides a case for reconsidering the focus on individual poverty and inequality that is so prevalent in the development agenda and focusing instead on the neglected dimension of group or "horizontal" inequalities, which reduce individual welfare over and above individual inequality (Stewart 2001).

Social exclusion is more closely related to the concept of relative poverty than of absolute poverty. It is, therefore, inextricably linked with inequality. It refers not only to the distribution of income and assets (as poverty analysis does) but also to social deprivation and lack of voice and power in society. In Latin America and the Caribbean, this lack of voice and power is perhaps best reflected in the low representation of excluded groups in political decision making. For instance, in Brazil, Afro-descendants make up 45 percent of the population but only 4.5 percent of Congress (Buvinić and Roza 2004).

The relational feature of exclusion highlights the importance of social and cultural assets, rather than just economic ones, in the analysis of poverty. It also underscores the active and deliberate nature of exclusion (Sen 2000). Exclusion is imposed in an arbitrary fashion: people are excluded not because of what they do, but because of who they are, beyond individual agency or responsibility.

It is generally agreed that social exclusion has both spatial and intergenerational dimensions. Residential segregation in Bolivian cities, for example, shows the spatial segregation of exclusion: indigenous people in segregated indigenous neighborhoods fare worse (in terms of income) than those in mixed neighborhoods (Gray-Molina, Pérez de Rada, and Sojo 2003). This spatial segregation element suggests the advantages of decentralization schemes and policies that use territorial targeting. The intergenerational dimension of exclusion locks people into poverty conditions over generations. In Latin America and the Caribbean, this disadvantage is perhaps most visibly reflected in the consistently lower educational attainments of indigenous children.

Common Features of Excluded Populations

Social exclusion is carved in the history of Latin America and the Caribbean. It is a product of colonial exploitation of native resources and people, including the African slave trade and forced labor of indigenous peoples. It is also the product of decades, if not centuries, of persistent inequality. In terms of income, countries in the region are among the most inequitable in the world. In the late 1990s, the wealthiest 20 percent of the population received 60 percent of the income, whereas the poorest 20 percent received only about 3 percent (Bouillon, Buvinić, and Jarque 2004).

Colonialism and slavery, combined with inequality and demographic and authoritarian legacies, have resulted in the exclusion of sizable numbers of people from mainstream society in most countries of the region. Precise numbers are difficult to come by, but approximately 40 percent of the region's population is of African descent, 10 percent is indigenous, another 10 percent has disabilities, and the number of intraregional migrants has grown considerably (Buvinić 2004). In many countries in the region, the excluded are the majority, not the minority, of the population.

Populations with a history of exclusion have different origins, social identities, and agendas, and the source of their exclusion is unique. However, they also share common features and mechanisms of exclusion. These common features include suffering from invisibility in national life, poverty, stigma and discrimination, and the cumulative and intergenerational transmission of exclusion.

Invisibility. First, and perhaps most characteristically, socially excluded groups are invisible in official statistics (censuses and government surveys). Latin America and the Caribbean countries know more about the diversity of industrial production than about the diversity of their people. The numerical invisibility of socially excluded groups reflects and reinforces their exclusion. Less than a third of countries in the region have official statistics on Afro-descendants, for example, even though they constitute approximately 30 percent of the region's population (between 80 million and 150 million people). Countries often collect some information on indigenous peoples, but it tends to be insufficient and unreliable.

In recent years, Mexico and Paraguay have instituted special censuses to provide more comprehensive information on the characteristics and needs of indigenous peoples. Only Brazil, Chile, and Nicaragua have begun systematically to collect information on people with disabilities, who are estimated to constitute between 5 percent and 15 percent of the region's population. Information is especially lacking on the conditions of women among the poor: their access to assets and their participation in informal labor and product markets.

Poverty. Combining poverty with disadvantage, excluded groups are overrepresented among the poor. In Bolivia, Guatemala, and Peru, ethnic groups constitute 60 percent of those who live below the poverty line (IDB 2003; Patrinos 2000). Afro-descendant populations in Brazil (*pretos* and *pardos*) have significantly lower human development (measured by the human development index) than their non-African counterparts (Pantano and Deutsch 2001). Women in excluded populations have lower earnings and well-being than all other groups.

The poverty of socially excluded groups is permanent rather than transitory. Moreover, unless it is purposefully addressed with a range of social investments, it persists over generations, locking individuals into poverty. For example, in Guatemala, in 1998, 58-year-old nonindigenous women had completed nearly two years more schooling than had indigenous women of the same age. For 23-year-old Guatemalan women, the difference was even greater, at two and one-half years (Duryea and Pagés 2001).

Stigma and discrimination. The poverty and deprivation resulting from social exclusion often produce stigma and discrimination. Power differences lie at the core of stigma, because groups with little power cannot stigmatize others (Link and Phelan 2002). Stigma dramatically influences the distribution of life chances. It can be a self-fulfilling prophecy and lead to self-exclusion. It can produce direct discrimination. There is growing research evidence on the stigma associated with living with HIV/AIDS (Aggleton, Parker, and Maluwa 2004; WHO 2002).

Discrimination, often a consequence of stigma, is another characteristic shared by excluded groups. Discrimination can result from societal imposition or from "self-discrimination," when the legacy of past discrimination discourages individuals from seeking certain jobs, walking into health clinics, or demanding their rights. In Latin America and the Caribbean, there is substantial evidence that wage discrimination in the labor market affects women, indigenous people, and Afro-descendants (Arias, Yamada, and Tejerina 2002; Patrinos 2000). This discrimination persists when education and experience are controlled for.

In addition to wage discrimination, resulting in pay differentials for the same job, members of excluded groups are less likely to obtain jobs in sectors with better pay, as processes of occupational segregation segment the labor market (Deutsch and others 2004). Torero and colleagues (2004) analyze earnings differentials in urban Peru, using a 1 to 10 scale of racial intensity. They find evidence of occupational segregation and wage discrimination. Predominantly white individuals have better jobs (in the service sector) and earn higher wages than predominantly indigenous individuals.

Cumulative disadvantages. Finally, socially excluded populations suffer cumulative disadvantages: a person experiences an even greater disadvantage if he or she exhibits two or more of the features that lead to group exclusion. In Honduras, the Garifunas, an Afro-descendant and indigenous population, have one of the highest rates of HIV/AIDS in the region. The stigma associated with HIV/AIDS builds on and reinforces gender prejudices. So women tend to be blamed more than men for having HIV/AIDS, and they suffer more stigma than their male counterparts (UNAIDS 2002).

The situation of the average woman in Latin America has improved markedly in recent decades. However, disaggregated data show that black, indigenous, and other women in socially excluded groups have been left behind, with many suffering compound discrimination. They are excluded from jobs for women because of their race, and they are excluded from jobs for men because they are women (Crenshaw 2000). In Brazil, in the late 1990s, white men had the highest labor market earnings, while black women had the lowest. White women did better than black men, but only because they had significantly more education. When schooling levels were equal, white women did worse than black men. This finding suggests that the intergenerational transmission of low educational attainments severely constrains opportunities for Afro-descendants, but if educational attainments were equal, gender would trump race in restricting labor market opportunities (Mezzera 2006).

Promoting Inclusion

Social inclusion, much like gender equality, affects how societies function as a whole. It needs to be integrated into a range of policies, as well as in day-to-day services and cultural practices. Most traditional social and economic policies, such as those for health and education, can draw on a defined toolbox of policy instruments, practices, and programs. There is no such readily defined toolbox or single responsible institution for inclusion. Indeed, the embedded nature of exclusion calls not for simple refinements to existing policies but for a deeper rethinking of how development operates at three basic levels: legal and national frameworks, institutional arrangements, and specific programs and policies.

Legal Frameworks and National Policies

The group aspect of discrimination resulting from social exclusion calls for a rights framework based on collective rather than individual rights. In contrast to an individualized view of nondiscrimination and equality, collective rights call for policies that actively seek to redress the subordination of the displaced group. In this context, affirmative policies and positive discrimination become fair instruments (rather than unjust or discriminatory to those who do not receive benefits from these policies) to combat the structural inequality that affects excluded groups (Saba 2004).

The principal instruments for enshrining these collective rights are international and national laws, with international laws providing the "macro" or universal framework. At least 29 international conventions and declarations relate to discrimination, most of them ratified by most Latin American and Caribbean countries. They include United Nations (UN) conventions on basic universal human rights and the rights of excluded groups, such as women, children, and racial or ethnic minorities, as well as International Labour Organization conventions on the rights of workers, declarations on race and racial prejudices, and others. These conventions, once ratified, take precedence over national law. (Unlike conventions, declarations do not require ratification.)

Vehicles to protect and enforce these rights include the periodic progress reports that governments are required to submit to regional agencies (for example, the Inter-American Commission on Human Rights and the Inter-American Court of Human Rights), as well as international meetings (for example, the UN Women's Conference and the UN Conference on Racism).

In response to the recent history of repressive regimes in Latin America and the Caribbean, the inter-American human rights system of the Organization of American States has largely devoted its resources to countering the violation of basic civil and political rights through imprisonment, torture, and murder. The protection of social rights has taken second place in the work of the Inter-American Commission on Human Rights and the Inter-American Court of Human Rights (Rossi 2003). This situation is changing, and the commission has heard the first cases of discrimination against women, but there is still a long way to go before the system as a whole protects social- and group-based rights. The commission hears individual petitions, but countries are still sometimes reticent to recognize the precise obligations that they have assumed in terms of social rights.

However, the heart of constitutional and legal protection for inclusion lies at the national level. Over the past decade and a half, a number of countries in Latin America have adopted constitutional frameworks that recognize excluded groups as distinct groups in the sovereign nation, acknowledging and sanctioning ethnic and cultural diversity. This trend marks a significant step toward social inclusion. An example is the 1991 constitution of Colombia, which defines Colombia as a multicultural nation. Other countries have enacted national laws against discrimination based on race (Brazil and Ecuador), ethnicity (Peru), or gender (Chile). Of course, implementation is the key to ensuring that rights on paper become inclusion in practice. Mexico, which approved a comprehensive antidiscrimination law covering groups excluded by reasons of gender, ethnicity, disability, sexual preference, and religious preference, along with an antidiscrimination commission, could serve as a model for comprehensive country legislation in the region (CONAPRED 2004; IAD 2004).

Many of these national antidiscrimination laws are difficult to implement because they do not mandate the allocation of adequate public budgets for enactment. Fiscally strapped governments in the region have been reluctant to back legislation with financial resources, thereby substantially reducing the effect that such legislation can have and failing to send the important symbolic message that the state does not tolerate exclusion.

Constitutional and legal protections work with key national policies to set the framework from which policies and programs can address specific causes of exclusion. Two central, national-level functions of a government committed to promoting inclusion (functions that are, therefore, foremost in the advocacy agendas of most civil society organizations) are (a) counting excluded groups in national statistics and (b) enacting land and property rights protections as part of a national framework of citizen rights. Counting excluded populations in censuses and surveys provides the government with basic information for allocating resources, designing policies and programs, and enforcing the law. Many governments in the region have begun to include questions about excluded groups in their statistical systems. Counting the excluded also involves ensuring the birth and adult registration of all citizens; without identity documents, excluded groups are routinely denied access to a host of rights and services, including basic education and health (IDB 2006).

Access to productive assets (land and capital) helps to counter the structural poverty of excluded groups, which stems in particular from unequal access to income-generating assets. A new generation of land titling and land reform programs in the region benefits women, indigenous peoples, and Afro-descendants and recognizes collective and community land ownership. For instance, in contrast to the gender-blind land reform programs of the 1960s and 1970s, land titling programs in the 1990s increased individual women's ownership of land significantly. The percentage of women registered as landowners rose from 20 percent to close to 40 percent (Deere and León de Leal 2001). Only through national legislation can the land and property rights of excluded populations receive systematic, transparent, and uniform protection.

Institutional Arrangements

Institutional arrangements provide the vehicle through which governments promote social inclusion, and these arrangements, in turn, are supported by the participation of civil society organizations.

Government mechanisms. Governments have different institutional options when it comes to promoting the inclusion of excluded groups and enforcing the law. One is to use the existing government capacity, without any extra resources. A second option is to devote additional resources to help mainstream the promotion and enforcement functions in existing government agencies. This option may entail the addition of staff members or staff functions in these agencies but not the creation of a new office. The third, more common option is to create an agency, office, or council exclusively devoted to some or all these tasks. Countries that have sizable indigenous populations, such as Bolivia, Ecuador, and Mexico, have agencies to protect the rights of indigenous peoples. Recently, Brazil created the Secretaria Especial de Políticas de Promoçao da Igualdade Racial (Ministry for the Promotion of Racial Equality, or SEPPIR) and Mexico established the Consejo Nacional para Prevenir la Discriminación (National Council to Prevent Discrimination, or CONAPRED).

The region (indeed the world) has more than two decades of experience, with government ministries ("national machineries") that were established to promote women's inclusion and empowerment. In the region, 18 countries have such offices, and in eight countries, the offices have ministerial ranking (those in Brazil, Chile, Costa Rica, Guatemala, Honduras, Panama, Paraguay, and Peru). Most have been established through legislation or an executive or ministerial decree. In addition, 16 countries have set up parliamentary commissions devoted to women's issues, and 5 (Argentina, Bolivia, Colombia, Nicaragua, and Peru) have a women's ombudsman or a staff in the ombudsman's office in charge of gender issues (Buvinić and Roza 2004).

Much of the writing on the performance of these national machineries draws attention to their continuing marginality or fragility, in terms of budgets, institutional capacity, and government influence (INSTRAW 2005; UNDAW 2004). However, the gender inclusion record in the region is quite impressive, very probably at least partly thanks to the actions of these offices. The record includes significant advances, which are reflected in the ratification by all countries of the Convention on the Elimination of All Forms of Discrimination against Women and the regional adoption of the Belém do Pará convention to combat violence against women. In addition, many countries have enacted national legislation on equality of opportunity and on violence against women, have mainstreamed gender issues and accountability in public expenditures, and have implemented affirmative action programs (ECLAC 2004; IDB 1998). In the view of the Economic Commission for Latin America and the Caribbean, "the mainstreaming strategy is bearing fruit" (ECLAC 2004: 77).

Two elements seem to be central to the effective functioning of these women's offices: the highest level of support or patronage from the executive branch of government (which translates into budget support) and strong alliance with women's organizations in civil society. A third, rarely mentioned factor is the rapid "modernization" of Latin American and Caribbean societies, with the shedding of traditional perceptions or attitudes about the place of women.

A Gallup poll of voters in major cities in 2000, sponsored by the Inter-American Development Bank (IDB), picked up these changing mores, showing the positive attitudes of younger, more educated generations of voters toward women in political office (Buvinić and Roza 2004). These modern attitudes were ratified in Chile's 2005 presidential election, when a woman was elected president on her own merits. A favorable political environment appears to have been a further supporting factor. A majority of the women's offices in Latin America and the Caribbean were established as a consequence of the return to democracy in the region in the early 1990s; in general, these offices have performed better as part of a larger transformative government, which broke with the status quo and increased democratic processes (Grown, Rao Gupta, and Kes 2004). Thus, in addition to government support and strong ties to nonstate actors, both political and cultural openings may help explain the successes of these national machineries devoted to gender equality.

Promotion and enforcement are two main functions of agencies with social inclusion mandates. They can be housed in the same or different agencies. Mainstreaming the concerns of the excluded group in government ministries is a principal vehicle for promotion. It is a good response to the inherent institutional fragility and lack of resources of these agencies (which represent one or more excluded groups that have little voice in mainstream society). Mainstreaming should increase the positive effects of government interventions and prevent "legacy" or unintended negative impacts of interventions on the excluded groups. In theory, over time, effective mainstreaming should obviate the need for a separate agency or function for promotion. However, the experience of government women's organizations suggests that mainstreaming is a long-term proposition and that technical soundness, instrumental rationales, and financial incentives all help advance the process. This experience has also revealed that successful mainstreaming does not eliminate the ongoing need for these agencies and their promotion and vigilance functions.

It goes without saying that government agencies' function of enforcing rights needs to be permanent, because the potential for rights infringement always exists. The unanswered question is whether it makes more sense to have an umbrella agency, such as CONAPRED in Mexico, to promote and oversee the rights of all excluded groups or separate agencies for different excluded groups, as in most countries. The idea of an umbrella agency has the appeal of potentially increasing the efficiency and effectiveness of the government function, especially because of its larger support base, its greater convening power, and the potential synergies from sharing best practices in inclusion across different groups. A potential downside is the loss of uniqueness and group identity.

Civil society organizations. Advocacy agencies in civil society, including nongovernmental organizations (NGOs) and grassroots organizations, support government institutions. They are central to the promotion, vigilance, and enforcement of group-based social rights. They help sustain the interest of the government and society in general in the social inclusion of disadvantaged groups, and they provide a safe and nurturing environment in which members of excluded groups can thrive. Effective action is usually the result of powerful alliances between such groups and their government counterparts.

In Latin America and the Caribbean, the advancement of women's rights largely resulted from coordinated advocacy by women's organizations in the 1980s and 1990s. Powerful indigenous organizations have lobbied effectively for indigenous rights, especially in Andean countries. More recently, organizations promoting the rights of Afro-descendants, persons with HIV/AIDS, and those with disabilities are influencing public policy and public institutions. These organizations have drawn strength from the region's return to democracy; in turn, they nurture the democratic process. In Honduras the collaboration of Afro-descendant and indigenous organizations, bolstered and embodied by the Garifuna peoples, who belong to both, has strengthened national civil efforts to combat discrimination.

Proactive Programs and Policies

In addition to the national legal framework and appropriate institutional arrangements, specific public policies and programs are needed to ensure that excluded groups have access to opportunities and services to overcome exclusion. Multiple interventions are key; policy in a single sector is not enough, because exclusion results from the cumulative dynamics of multiple denied opportunities. The cumulative nature of exclusion means that one missed entry point—say, poor maternal health or early school leaving—can combine with other missed entry points (or discrimination) to contribute to the persistence or reassertion of exclusion.

From a social policy standpoint, then, it is important to consider a series of key policy entry points over the life of individuals (Marshall and Calderón 2006). Doing so adds a layer of complexity to social policies. Evidence from Latin America and the Caribbean indicates that national governments that have political momentum behind social inclusion can bundle interventions across a wide spectrum of policies. Brazil, Colombia, Honduras, and Mexico offer important examples.

The chapter looks at three key sets of social policies—affirmative action, education, and labor markets and employment—in order to demonstrate the interrelated nature of pro-inclusion policies and the importance of not focusing exclusively on a single policy instrument. Education, in particular, has received attention as a focal point for inclusion in the region. Labor markets have seen less attention, but seeking gains in labor income and productivity is critical to unlocking a range of other types of exclusion, such as spatial exclusion, access to land or credit, and access to basic social protections.

Affirmative action. Discussion of public policies to promote social inclusion can too easily become mired in a debate over affirmative action. Affirmative action policies—understood as proactive policies intended to overcome past subordination and redress societal inequalities, whether based on race, gender, or other sources—are fundamental tools in the inclusion policy toolbox. They must, however, operate within a larger set of national policies and programs.

Although experience in the region remains limited, affirmative action–style policies can be found in many sectors (Buvinić 2004). For example, in Chile, people with disabilities are given 10 extra points when applying for public subsidies or housing programs; Brazil maintains quotas for entry into university for black and indigenous persons; and at least 11 countries in the region guarantee political representation in the form of apportioned seats in the national legislature on the basis of gender, race, or ethnicity (depending on the country). A compendium compiled by Afroamerica XXI (2005) of affirmative action and legal tools relevant for Afro-descendants in Latin America lists such tools in 10 countries. The most common instruments, where instruments exist, are quotas for political representation (principally gender-based quotas) or education. There are no specific affirmative action tools in the region related to private sector employment or to corporate or land ownership.

However, affirmative action is not the principal or only tool of inclusion policy, and even when enacted, it often needs to be supplemented by other interventions. Htun (2004), for instance, concludes that gender quotas in the region can promote representative parity, but only if attention is paid to the development of enforcement mechanisms, to interaction with election rules, and to the specifics of the quota laws. The same can be said of educational quotas. They go nowhere unless the quality of primary and secondary schooling is also improved, and minority students are given support in preparing for university entrance and affording school financially. Attention to enforcement is crucial in making affirmative action truly effective. In an extensive review of U.S. affirmative action policy, Bergman (1996) finds that the policy's limited effect on the labor market can be explained largely through inadequate enforcement by U.S. agencies.

Affirmative action policies can also play a larger societal role by bringing issues of discrimination and identity to the forefront. An admissions director at a Brazilian state university explains:

> "The biggest advantage of this quota system is that it has broken this myth of a nonracial society. Brazilians have by and large always believed there are no white Brazilians or black Brazilians. But the debate over quotas has forced everyone to confront the fact that racism, discrimination, and social exclusion are alive and well here" (Jeter 2003: A01).

Rethinking education. Excluded populations, by virtue of their poverty and more limited access to financial capital, seek inclusion largely through improved education and employment. Although the bulk of European inclusion policy rests on intervening in the labor market, Ocampo (2004) argues that exclusion begins earlier in Latin America, through lack of access to quality education and low rates of school completion. Education is a well-known tool for breaking intergenerational disadvantage. Inclusive education, however, differs from the education currently provided in much of the region (Verdisco, Calderón, and Marshall 2004). It includes broad-based incorporation of racial, ethnic, and excluded groups in primary, secondary, and tertiary education, without major inequities in participation, especially at the tertiary level; minimal variations in school quality; targeted learning interventions to diminish educational performance differences across ethnic, racial, gender (cross-cutting), and other lines associated with exclusion; and a high degree of physical access to schools, to ease access for socially excluded populations.

A basic starting point for inclusive education is officially registering children for school. In many Latin American and Caribbean countries, school registration depends on formal birth certificates or proof of parental citizenship or birth, both of which are often unattainable or nonexistent for rural, excluded populations. Not only does registration affect school attendance, but, as already discussed, it also affects voting, land ownership, and a host of other entry points for overcoming exclusion.

Experiences in the region to date have covered a range of different aspects of inclusive education. Interesting efforts include the following:

- Providing bilingual education (in Bolivia, Ecuador, and Honduras).
- Expanding physical access and introducing innovative pedagogy to include people with disabilities in regular classrooms (Mexico's 2002 "inclusion in higher education" program).

- Adapting curricula to stress multiculturalism and the contributions of Afro-descendants and indigenous cultures (Colombia's Ministry of Education chair on Afro-Colombian studies).
- Offering educational subsidies, scholarships, and admission quotas to students from excluded groups (the reserved places in Brazil's state university for *pardos* and *pretos*).
- Linking education and school attendance with programs to eradicate the worst forms of child labor (in the Dominican Republic, where indigenous, migrant, and Afro-descendent children are disproportionately represented among child laborers).

The low educational attainment of most excluded groups in the region (women are the exception) underscores the importance of schooling in inclusion initiatives. These initiatives need not only to embrace, but also to go beyond education objectives. In many Latin American and Caribbean countries, women have greater educational attainment than men, but these gains have not translated into the labor market (Marshall and Calderón 2006). Education is not the silver bullet for eroding social exclusion, especially when that exclusion is associated with gender, ethnicity, and race. It needs to be paired with labor market and other interventions to enhance assets and opportunities.

Inclusive labor markets and employment. Labor market exclusion involves a range of attributes: the inability to generate a livable family income, the devaluation of or lack of recognition for one's daily work, discrimination, and a lack of basic legal protections on the job. Although many factors interact in creating social exclusion, labor market exclusion prompts a chain of social and economic effects that deepen and solidify exclusion more broadly. These effects include physical segregation in marginal neighborhoods, social stigma associated with poor-quality jobs, unsafe working conditions, and early school leaving, which has a lifelong impact.

Across the region, what is striking is the lack of significant labor market gains by women, despite their average high educational level, because of persistent exclusion from key occupations, formal sector employment, and better and higher-quality jobs. Occupational segregation (the clustering of women in lower-paying fields such as teaching, domestic service, and office work) is pervasive and shows no signs of abating, despite other advances. Deutsch and others (2004) find that occupational segregation by gender did not decrease in the Latin American countries studied during an eight-year period (1989–97), despite important economic shifts in occupational structure and macroeconomic circumstances. This finding suggests that culture and tradition are as important as economic factors in determining the over- or underrepresentation of women—especially those who are less educated—in the occupational structure.

The rapidly growing informal sector, where one in two workers in the region now works, presents a crisis of low-quality employment for excluded populations. More than half of female workers in the region are informally employed, with particularly high informality rates among indigenous women. Women's average earnings in informal employment are lower than in formal sector work, and female informal workers lack maternity employment protection and other benefits available to women working in the formal sector (Barrientos 2004).

Often, labor market policies and programs in the region have not been designed, analyzed, or evaluated in terms of promoting greater inclusion. Targeting in labor market programs, if it is undertaken at all, has typically been based on income (programs for the poor); gender (smaller, specialized interventions); or, more commonly, self-targeting for the poor (job training or placement services with eligibility criteria that fit mainly the poor or offer wage levels so low as to appeal only to the very poor). Exceptions are larger training programs for disadvantaged youth, women, and people with disabilities. Examples of IDB-financed projects include a Mexico labor market loan that funds training for people with disabilities in firms; technical training for disadvantaged youth and women (for example, in Argentina, Chile, Panama, and Peru); and technical assistance to Argentina, Chile, and Uruguay to help expand the labor force participation of the blind. Labor market policies and programs in the region can be strengthened to support greater social inclusion in a number of key ways. These pro-inclusion efforts can draw on lessons from the labor market program experience in the region and elsewhere, in the following respects:

- *By improving labor market data and analysis on excluded populations.* Household and labor market surveys, as well as data collection on program beneficiaries, are important statistical inputs to an understanding of how labor market exclusion works in any national context and how labor markets affect different groups. Generally, only gender data on program beneficiaries have been collected, so very little is known about the differential effects of programs on excluded groups.
- *By using traineeships for improved labor market insertion.* One of the important lessons to emerge from a series of youth and women's training initiatives in the region (for example, in Argentina, Chile, Mexico, Peru,

Panama, and the República Bolivariana de Venezuela) is that combining classroom training with traineeships within firms results in improved labor market placement. For disadvantaged youth, job skills are less of a barrier to an entry-level position than the lack of a social network and work record. Evaluations of the Argentina Joven project indicated an increase in both job placement and income for disadvantaged youth over a control group that did not participate in the program.

- *By improving antidiscrimination laws and labor protections.* Many countries in the region have broad civil protections against discrimination on the books, as well as more specific legislation related to the labor market, but implementation and enforcement are very limited. Three key problems, common to the region, are lack of government enforcement, lack of a civil legal tradition defending individuals, and large informal sectors outside the protection of labor codes. National antidiscrimination policies in the region need to be strengthened through more vigorous attention to enforcement, citizen education, legal services for the poor, and extension of antidiscrimination protection to all, regardless of employment status.

- *By reforming labor intermediation systems to link workers to jobs and training.* These systems are a relatively neglected tool for advancing the labor market performance of excluded populations. Labor intermediation activities serve both workers and employers by promoting a more efficient match of worker to job. Recent reforms in both the Organisation for Economic Co-operation and Development (OECD) and in Latin American countries are prompting new models of intermediation services, which expand the range and type of services and involve private and nonprofit providers more directly.[1] Labor intermediation services can adapt universal services to the needs of excluded populations or provide specialized assistance to render the service more accessible to excluded groups.

- *By improving school-to-work transition and skill deficits.* The labor market cannot help excluded populations leapfrog the severe disadvantage they face when they enter the labor market with fewer years of education and lower-quality schooling. This initial disadvantage accumulates in the labor market, as workers with low skills receive little investment in skill development on the job and are rarely able to return to education later. Reform of training institutions to ensure greater linking to private sector employment and greater emphasis on low-income workers, plus school-to-work transition programs targeted at excluded populations, are needed to make Latin American labor markets more inclusive.

- *By expanding employment opportunities through business ownership.* Minority-owned businesses tend to hire a greater proportion of minority employees and may be a more effective way of reducing employment disparities between different racial and ethnic populations. The most fundamental step in advancing such employment growth is the development of specific efforts to foster and support minority business ownership and expansion. In the United States, affirmative action attention is moving from government procurement preferences for minority-owned businesses toward promotion of greater supplier diversity. This approach is pursued both to open up new markets to minority-owned firms and to improve the market access of many companies to minority customers (Boston 2006).

Conclusion

Traditional approaches to social policy often fail to take account of the complex processes of exclusion, which deny groups access to the very services and opportunities promoted by social policy. Social inclusion cannot be advanced, however, by focusing the inclusion lens on only one type of social policy or on state and nonstate actors separately. Lessons from Latin America and the Caribbean have made it clear that multiple sources of inclusion need to be addressed through constitutional and legal frameworks and national policies, institutional arrangements, and specific policies and programs. Although such a three-level framework may appear complex at first, in practice it is precisely these diverse types of intervention that result from political processes that promote inclusion. The key for policy makers is to set the priorities within such a framework for a specific national context.

Experience with legal frameworks and national legislation indicates that legislating on group social rights sets the basic conditions for inclusive societies, but that such legislation needs to be complemented by effective enforcement and regulation, as well as legal training. Key national policies include strengthening the collection of statistics on the excluded and increasing their access to productive assets.

Mainstreaming the concerns of excluded groups in agencies or ministries appears to have worked in the case of gender exclusion, but it requires the presence of a government agency or function devoted to coordination and vigilance. The success of such an agency depends on strong support from the executive branch, close alliance with nonstate actors, and both political and cultural openings.

In the past, education has been touted as the basic building block toward social inclusion, but it is no silver bullet. The record from Latin America and the Caribbean shows that, even when broader educational coverage and attainment is achieved, exclusion can be reasserted in the labor market where excluded groups suffer from centuries-long discrimination and earn fewer returns for the same human capital assets. Complementary interventions are required, especially to improve the long-term performance in the labor market of excluded groups and to sustain their livelihoods.

Promoting inclusion through affirmative action and labor market and education policies and programs requires rethinking and recasting current policies, drawing on many of the initiatives mentioned here. It requires strengthening the role of NGOs as representatives of the excluded. Public officials in the region are beginning to understand that inclusion, even in education and labor markets, can be promoted only through interrelated initiatives in the social, economic, legal, and cultural spheres. It is the sustained combination of policy and program interventions, operating on the different levels described in this chapter, that offers a means to propel social policy more purposefully toward social inclusion.

Note

1. See Mazza (2003) for a more thorough discussion of the international models for labor intermediation services.

References

Afroamerica XXI. 2005. *Compendio Normativo de Acciones Afirmativas a Favor de las Comunidades Afrolatinoamericanas.* Washington, DC: Afroamerica XXI.

Aggleton, P., R. Parker, and M. Maluwa. 2004. "Stigma, Discrimination, and HIV/AIDS in Latin America." In *Social Inclusion and Economic Development in Latin America*, ed. M. Buvinić and J. Mazza, with R. Deutsch, 287–306. Washington, DC: Inter-American Development Bank.

Arias, O., G. Yamada, and L. Tejerina. 2002. "Education, Family Background, and Racial Earnings Inequality in Brazil." Working Paper, Poverty and Inequality Unit, Sustainable Development Department, Inter-American Development Bank, Washington, DC.

Barrientos, A. 2004. "Women, Informal Employment, and Social Protection in Latin America." In *Women at Work: Challenges for Latin America*, ed. C. Piras, 255–92. Washington, DC: Inter-American Development Bank.

Behrman, J. R., A. Gaviria, and M. Székely. 2003. "Social Exclusion in Latin America: Perception, Reality, and Implications." In *Who's In and Who's Out: Social Exclusion in Latin America*, ed. J. R. Behrman, A. Gaviria, and M. Székely, 1–24. Washington, DC: Inter-American Development Bank.

Bergman, B. 1996. *In Defense of Affirmative Action*. New York: Basic Books.

Boston, T. D. 2006. "Does Supplier and Employment Diversity Help Disadvantaged Businesses: A Review of Good Practices in the USA that Could Be Useful for Latin America." In *Advancing Equity in Latin America: Policy into Practice*, ed. C. Nelson and S. Richards-Kennedy, 109–16. Washington, DC: Inter-American Development Bank.

Bouillon, C., M. Buvinić, and C. Jarque. 2004. *Building Social Cohesion in Latin America and the Caribbean*. Washington, DC: Inter-American Development Bank.

Buvinić, M. 2004. "Introduction: Social Inclusion in Latin America." In *Social Inclusion and Economic Development in Latin America*, ed. M. Buvinić and J. Mazza with R. Deutsch, 3–32. Washington, DC: Inter-American Development Bank.

Buvinić, M., and V. Roza. 2004. "Women, Politics, and Democratic Prospects in Latin America." Technical Papers Series, Sustainable Development Department, Inter-American Development Bank, Washington, DC.

CONAPRED (Consejo Nacional para Prevenir la Discriminación). 2004. "Ley para Eliminar la Discriminación." In *Comisión Ciudadana de Estudios contra la Discriminación*. Mexico City: CONAPRED. http://www.conapred.org.mx/index.php.

Crenshaw, K. 2000. "The Intersectionality of Race and Gender Discrimination." Background paper presented at Expert Group Meeting on Gender and Race Discrimination, Zagreb, Croatia, November 21–24.

Deere, C. D., and M. León de Leal. 2001. *Empowering Women: Land and Property Rights in Latin America*. Pittsburgh, PA: University of Pittsburgh Press.

Deutsch, R., A. Morrison, C. Piras, and H. Ñopo. 2004. "Working within Confines: Occupational Segregation by Gender in Costa Rica, Ecuador, and Uruguay." In *Women at Work: Challenges for Latin America*, ed. C. Piras, 187–226. Washington, DC: Inter-American Development Bank.

Duryea, S., and C. Pagés. 2001. "Human Capital Policies: What They Can and Cannot Do for Productivity and Poverty Reduction in Latin America." In

American Foreign Economic Relations: Policy Dilemmas and Opportunities. Miami, FL: North-South Press.

ECLAC (United Nations Economic Commission for Latin America and the Caribbean). 2004. "Roads towards Gender Equity in Latin America and the Caribbean." Report of the 9th Regional Conference on Women, Mexico City, June.

Gray-Molina, G., E. Pérez de Rada, and C. Sojo. 2003. "Residential Segregation in Bolivian Cities." In *Who's In and Who's Out: Social Exclusion in Latin America*, ed. J. R. Behrman, A. Gaviria, and M. Székely, 25–43. Washington, DC: Inter-American Development Bank.

Grown, C., G. Rao Gupta, and A. Kes. 2004. *Taking Action: Achieving Gender Equality and Empowering Women.* London: Task Force on Education and Gender Equality, United Nations Millennium Project, United Nations Development Programme.

Htun, M. 2004. "Lessons from Gender Quotas." In *Social Inclusion and Economic Development in Latin America*, ed. M. Buvinić and J. Mazza, with R. Deutsch, 335–48. Washington, DC: Inter-American Development Bank.

IAD (Inter-American Dialogue). 2004. Race Report: Constitutional Provisions and Legal Actions Related to Discrimination and Afro-Descendant Populations in Latin America. Washington, DC: IAD.

IDB (Inter-American Development Bank). 1998. "Institucionalidad para Mujer y Género en América Latina y el Caribe." Regional Study, Women in Development Unit, Sustainable Development Department, IDB, Washington, DC.

———. 2003. "Strategy Document on Poverty Reduction and Promotion of Social Equity." Poverty and Inequality Unit, Sustainable Development Department, IDB, Washington, DC.

———. 2006. *Building Opportunity for the Majority.* Washington, DC: IDB.

INSTRAW (United Nations International Research and Training Institute for the Advancement of Women). 2005. "Institutional Mechanisms for the Advancement of Women: New Challenges." INSTRAW Progress Report, INSTRAW, Santo Domingo. http://www.un-instraw.org/en/images/stories/Beijing/institutionalmechanisms.pdf.

Jeter, J. 2003. "Affirmative Action Debate Forces Brazil to Take Look in the Mirror." *Washington Post*, June 15, A01.

Link, B. G., and J. C. Phelan. 2002. "On Stigma and Its Public Health Implications." Paper presented at the conference on Stigma and Global Health: Developing a Research Agenda, Bethesda, MD, September 5–7.

Marshall, J. H., and V. Calderón. 2006. "Social Exclusion in Education in Latin America and the Caribbean." Technical Papers Series, Sustainable Development Department, Inter-American Development Bank, Washington, DC.

Mazza, J. 2003. "Labour Intermediation Services: Lessons for Latin American and Caribbean Countries from International Experience." *CEPAL Review* 80 (August): 165–83.

Mezzera, J. 2006. "Gênero, Raça, Emprego e Rendas." International Labour Office, Brasília, Brazil.

Ocampo, J. A. 2004. "Economic Development and Social Inclusion." In *Social Inclusion and Economic Development in Latin America*, ed. M. Buvinić and J. Mazza, with R. Deutsch, 33–40. Washington, DC: Inter-American Development Bank.

Pantano, J., and R. Deutsch. 2001. "Índices de Desarrollo Humano Desagregados por Etnicidad." Methodological Note, Sustainable Development Department, Social Development Division, Inter-American Development Bank, Washington, DC.

Patrinos, H. A. 2000. "The Costs of Discrimination in Latin America." Working Paper, Human Capital Development and Operations Policy, World Bank, Washington, DC.

Rossi, J. 2003. "Mecanismos Internacionales de Protección de los Derechos Económicos, Sociales y Culturales." In *Derechos Sociales: Instrucciones de Uso*, ed. V. Abramovich, M. J. Anon, and C. Courtis, 355–68. Mexico City: Doctrina Jurídica Contemporánea.

Saba, R. 2004. "(Des) Igualdad Estructural." In *Visiones de una Constitución*, ed. J. A. Amaya, 479–514. Buenos Aires: Universidad de Ciencias Empresariales y Sociales.

Sen, A. 2000. "Social Exclusion: Concept, Application, and Scrutiny." Social Development Paper 1, Asian Development Bank, Manila.

Stewart, F. 2001. "Horizontal Inequalities: A Neglected Dimension of Development." Paper presented at the Annual Development Lecture, United Nations University World Institute for Development Economics Research, Helsinki, May 25–26.

Torero, M., J. Saavedra, H. Ñopo, and J. Escobal. 2004. "An Invisible Wall? The Economics of Social Exclusion in Peru." In *Social Inclusion and Economic Development in Latin America*, ed. M. Buvinić and J. Mazza, with R. Deutsch, 221–45. Washington, DC: Inter-American Development Bank.

Tsakloglou, P., and F. Papadopoulos. 2001. "Identifying Population Groups at High Risk of Social Exclusion: Evidence from the ECHP." Discussion Paper 392, Institute for the Study of Labor, Bonn, Germany.

UNAIDS (Joint United Nations Programme on HIV/AIDS). 2002. "HIV and AIDS Related Discrimination, Stigmatization, and Denial." UNAIDS, Geneva.

UNDAW (United Nations Division for the Advancement of Women). 2004. "The Role of National Mechanisms in Promoting Gender Equality and the Empowerment of Women." Report of the Expert Group Meeting, Rome, November 29–December 2.

Verdisco, A., V. Calderón, and J. H. Marshall. 2004. "Social Exclusion in Education in Latin America and the Caribbean." Inter-American Development Bank, Washington, DC.

WHO (World Health Organization). 2002. "Fighting HIV-Related Intolerance: Exposing the Links between Racism, Stigma, and Discrimination." WHO and Joint United Nations Programme on HIV/AIDS, Geneva.

CHAPTER 6

Recognition and Distribution: Equity and Justice Policies for Disadvantaged Groups in Latin America

Martín Hopenhayn

How can an increasingly global society be reconciled with communities defined by identity and territory? This question, which is fast gaining significant momentum, puts the issue of identity and culture in the eye of the hurricane. There is, after all, a tension between global rationality, on the one hand, and belonging to a space with its particular ethnic-ethic codes (Touraine 1997), on the other. In this context of globalization, cultural identities and factors come into conflict (Castells 1999), and ascribed categories, such as gender and ethnicity, gain recognition as main components of everyday experience. (Garretón 2000). Consequently, a full-fledged debate is taking place today on the capacity to incorporate increasing social and cultural pluralism into the definition of citizenship (Kymlicka and Norman 1997).

In this context, the demands of groups defined by identity, culture, or ascription are acquiring unprecedented influence in national and international politics. Ethnicity, gender, territory, and generation, as grouping criteria, pose increasing challenges in the political justice and social justice spheres. In this sense, "social exclusion cannot be perceived solely as a synonym for marginality and lack of material goods, but as a dynamic complexity that alludes to the material, but also to a community's sense of belonging, the enjoyment of economic growth benefits and access to symbolic and material goods, as well as the respect for diversity (and integration in diversity)" (Bello 2004: 73).

Cultural, territorial, and ascription factors become relevant to active citizenship, understood in a republican sense as the practice and demand for participation and belonging. Therefore, the greater the presence in the political sphere, mass communication, and the collective imagination, the greater the advances in civil, political, social, economic, and cultural rights will be. Political citizenship and social well-being are two complementary aspects, as are the assertion of difference and the promotion of equality. If, on the one hand, poverty and exclusion are enhanced by these ascribed characteristics, on the other, citizens are increasingly aware of their right to diversity and identity. Furthermore, there is an asymmetry between those who make themselves heard because they are in a position of greater political power and collective negotiation, thus attaining the tutelage and protection of their rights, and those who, being less powerful and influential, are not able to exercise these same rights. Therefore, an order based on social rights should strive to counterbalance power and influence relations among different social groups, so as to avoid the vicious circle in which the most excluded, socially and culturally, are politically the weakest.

The following pages will address the challenges that identity- or ascription-defined groups pose to public policy in Latin America, a context characterized by acute inequalities in access to social well-being and justice. Given the scenario of identity demands in the political context of Latin American countries, the main challenge lies in combining recognition policies in the political, cultural, and juridical areas with distribution policies in the areas of social policy and access to productive assets. The idea is to bring about a gradual shift from the vicious circles that mutually degrade recognition and resource distribution, to virtuous circles of greater political recognition and benefit from redistribution policies.

Cultural Denial and Social Exclusion

Structural Inequality

This section begins by highlighting the link between inequality and cultural and ascriptive conditions. Indigenous peoples, those of African descent, women, and other groups defined by culture or ascription have been the most deprived in terms of social citizenship and public voice. Race, ethnicity, territory, and age confer sociocultural specificity on the demands for social citizenship by the groups that claim it. Thus, inequality goes hand in hand with difference.

When it comes to understanding the cultural variables involved in social inclusion and exclusion, nothing could speak more eloquently than the case of ethnic minorities, where discrimination is based on race and ethnicity. It is the case that most clearly portrays the problems with reference to citizenship's cultural dimension in Latin America. It touches on power distribution and productive resources, as well as on social protection and social promotion networks. On the one hand, ethnic minorities have invariably been an extreme incarnation of the link between cultural denial and social exclusion. Indicators concerning indigenous peoples also provide a barometer of the inequality affecting other groups that are discriminated against or excluded, such as those of African descent, women, youth, or migrants.[1] On the other hand, as we shall see, ethnic minorities pose the most critical juridical and political issues in terms of cultural demands, as they question the very rationality of social distribution, the individual basis of law, and the sovereignty of the nation-state.

Sociocultural Discrimination and Exclusion

Examining slavery and the colonial domination of Afro-descendant and indigenous groups helps us understand contemporary economic, political, and social exclusion processes. In Latin America and the Caribbean, historic denial of the other's culture and identity has been perpetuated in various ways in the exclusion patterns characterizing the dynamics of modernization (Calderón, Hopenhayn, and Ottone 1996). The denial of the other because of race and ethnicity laid a cultural foundation over which exclusionary, undemocratic policies were constructed. Latin American and Caribbean countries have sustained spurious forms of modernization with full, partial, and negated citizens.

This cultural denial is carried over from the racial other to women, peasants, and migrants. Even today, indigenous peoples and Afro-descendants are the poorest in the region, exhibiting the worst socioeconomic indicators, scarce cultural recognition, and lack of access to decision-making spheres. Most studies show that indigenous peoples in Latin America live in conditions of extreme poverty (Psacharopoulos and Patrinos 1994; Hall and Patrinos 2005; Hopenhayn and Bello 2000).

In Latin America, the indigenous population represents between 8 percent and 10 percent of the region's total population, while Afro-descendants account for approximately 30 percent. The poverty of indigenous peoples is primarily attributed to the liberal reforms of the 19th century, which aimed to introduce the notion of the private property of land (Plant 1998).

Predominant factors behind the poverty of these groups include a progressive loss of land, the breakup of community economies, reduced access to education and health services, and labor insertion structure and dynamics. Indigenous peoples and Afro-descendant populations get lower wages for jobs comparable to those done by the rest of the population and are more likely to work in the economy's informal sector without social protection or unionization.

As a consequence, there is a much greater incidence of poverty's ethnic and racial minorities than in the rest of the population. As figure 6.1 shows, the difference ranges from 1.6 times higher (Colombia) to 7.9 times higher (Paraguay). (This range excludes Costa Rica and Haiti, where the ethnic condition does not seem to imply any difference in the levels of indigence.) Other characteristic features of these groups that add to their members chances of being under the poverty line are the larger size of their households (although these percentages are lower for Afro-descendants) and, in most countries, the fact that they often live in rural areas.

Figure 6.1. Latin America and the Caribbean: Incidence of Extreme Poverty in Indigenous and Afro-Descendant Individuals as a Multiple of the Incidence in the Rest of the Population

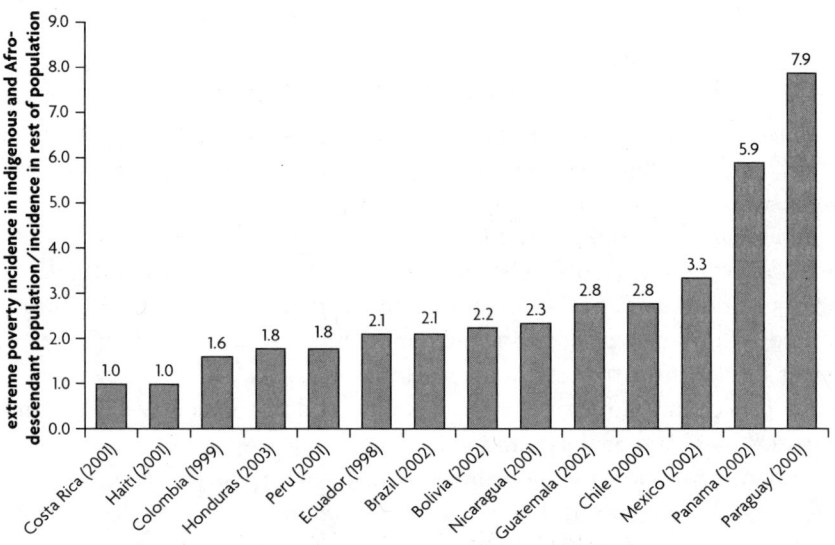

Source: United Nations Economic Commission for Latin America and the Caribbean, based on special tabulations of household surveys in the respective countries.
Note: The extreme poverty measure is US$1 per day.

Employment

Employment quality and salary gaps can also contribute significantly to these inequalities. For example, in Brazil, the percentage of Afro-descendant workers in precarious employment was much higher than that of white workers for every year from 1992 to 2001 and for both sexes and all age groups. For Afro-descendants between the ages of 16 and 24, the figure was always more than 70 percent, going up to 76 percent for Afro-descendant women (Borges Martins 2004).[2] In Bolivia, indigenous workers account for 67 percent of precarious jobs and 28 percent of semi-skilled jobs. Only 4 percent of indigenous workers are employed in jobs that require greater skills (Valenzuela 2004).

Education

Lack of access to education is another factor behind the inequality and exclusion affecting indigenous peoples and ethnic and national minorities. Although the threshold of educational achievement has risen in indigenous and nonindigenous populations, the gap between those two groups persists in most countries (see figure 6.2). In particular, more nonindigenous individuals complete the different school levels, and there is also a wide educational gap between urban and rural locations.

In Brazil, Afro-descendants and mestizos face the greatest difficulties in access to and progress and permanence in the educational system. They also tend to attend poorer quality schools, resulting in greater failing rates and inferior learning compared with those of whites. In the early 1990s, only 1.8 percent of the adult black population had completed the 15 years of minimum schooling that correspond to a university diploma in the Brazilian system. For whites, the figure was 8.2 percent. Despite the progress made, by 2001 the percentage had barely increased, reaching only 2.5 percent, compared with 10.2 percent of the white population (Borges Martins 2004).

Indigenous populations tend to present higher illiteracy rates than do nonindigenous groups, with particularities according to specific ethnic groups, age, and sex. Furthermore, indigenous literacy has increased at a lower rate in rural than in urban areas. In Brazil, in the early 1990s, illiteracy rates for the black population were more than double those of the white population, reaching three times the whites' illiteracy rates for the younger age bracket (15–24 years) (Borges Martins 2004). In Guatemala, despite a gradual increase in school attendance, illiteracy has been declining at a rate of less than 1 percent a year since 1989. In 2002, 64.5 percent

Figure 6.2. Latin America: 15- to 19-Year-Olds Who Have Not Completed Primary Education, by Ethnic or Racial Group, 2002

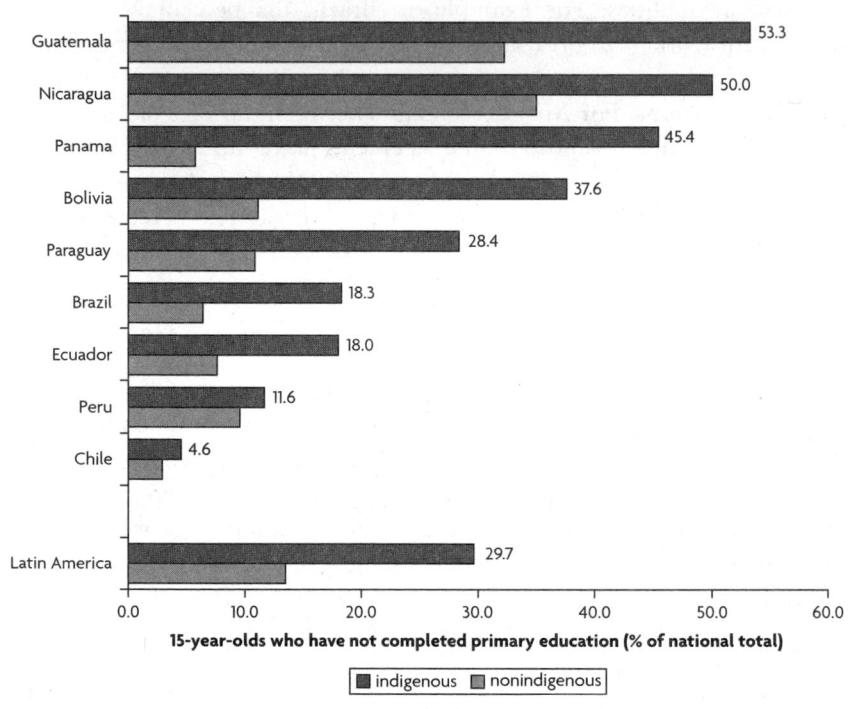

15-year-olds who have not completed primary education (% of national total)

indigenous   nonindigenous

Source: UNESCO 2004.
Notes: The bars for Latin America show the simple average for countries.

of indigenous men were literate, but in women the rate was still only 36.8 percent, and it was even lower for rural indigenous women: 31.1 percent (Adams 2005).

Health

When it comes to health, indigenous people remain worse off than the population in general, in terms of greater nutritional vulnerability, lower life expectation, and greater child mortality. Indigenous households, particularly in rural areas, face high illness risks attributable to precarious living conditions and the limited availability of health care services, water, and basic sanitation. In 2000, life expectancy at birth in Brazil was equivalent to that in Mexico or Hungary (71 years), but for blacks the figure was comparable to Guatemala or India (65.7 years)

(Borges Martins 2004). In Bolivia, 30 percent of the indigenous population does not have access to basic medication, while 41 percent of deliveries are not attended by specialized health care professionals. Instead, they are attended by "midwives," who are the best representatives of the traditional medical system.

Chronic malnutrition affects 50 percent of children under five years old in rural indigenous homes in Bolivia (Valenzuela 2004). In Guatemala, chronic malnutrition among indigenous individuals is at least three times that suffered by nonindigenous people. Between 1995 and 2002, the figure barely dropped, from 36.4 percent to 34.0 percent compared with 11.1 percent in nonindigenous communities (Adams 2005).

Gender Inequalities

Documentation of gender inequalities in Latin America is ample. These gender differences act invariably to the detriment of women and affect their access to the labor market, their working conditions, their vulnerability in their domestic situation, and their full exercise of citizenship and reproduction rights. A greater number of women than men live in impoverished homes in the region, especially in the actively employed age group, from 20 to 59. From a statistical perspective, because it measures household rather than individual income, the cutoff point used to determine who is poor and who is not reduces the visibility of a broad contingent of the female population. These women, even when they do not live in households regarded as poor, are poor and vulnerable to poverty on an individual basis, in terms of income distribution, roles, and risks among members of the household. This inequity arises because they have less access to economic resources and less economic autonomy. Figure 6.3 illustrates the distinction, when individuals rather than households are considered.

Combining gender and race variables, it is clear that indigenous and Afro-descendant women are situated in the lower social strata, with lower incomes and low investment returns in education. Although these inequalities also affect indigenous men, additional factors increase the vulnerability of indigenous women. These factors include difficulties with reproduction control, child and maternal mortality rates, disadvantages with regard to medical and nursing care, and environmental degradation.

A lower proportion of indigenous women use birth control, the use of modern methods being more frequent among nonindigenous populations, even in rural areas, than in indigenous populations. For example,

Figure 6.3. Sex Distribution by Quintiles for Urban Areas: Simple Average for Latin American and Caribbean Countries

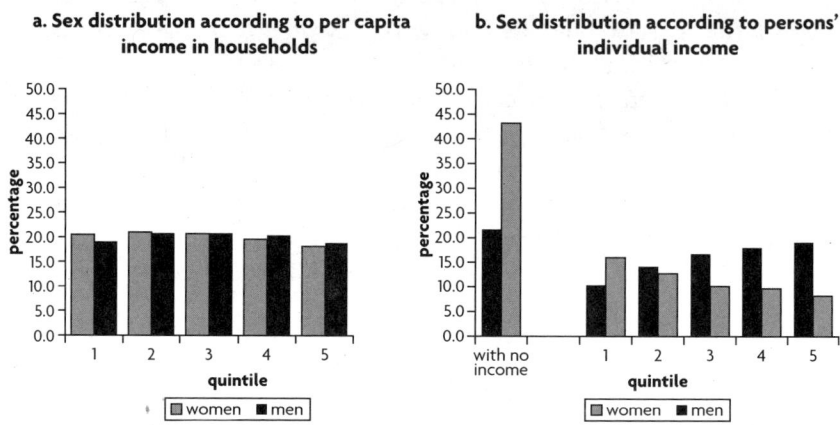

a. Sex distribution according to per capita income in households

b. Sex distribution according to persons' individual income

Source: United Nations Economic Commission for Latin America and the Caribbean, Women and Development Unit, based on special tabulations of household surveys in 15 Latin America and Caribbean countries.
Note: Data are for people 15 years of age and older.

in Guatemala, in 1987, only 5.5 percent of indigenous women used birth control methods, although 43 percent had heard of them. In 2002, the number of indigenous women who used birth control increased to 23.8 percent, of which 16.6 percent used modern methods. Among non-indigenous populations, the use of contraceptive methods increased from 34 percent in 1987 to 52.8 percent in 2002. Of these, 43.2 percent used modern methods (Adams 2005). In Bolivia, the total fertility rate for indigenous populations (per 1,000 live births) fell from 6.8 in 1987 to 6.1 live births per woman in 2002, while in nonindigenous populations it declined from 5.0 to 3.7 percent over the same period.

Access to pre- and postnatal care has had an enormous influence on child mortality rates in indigenous groups. Although rates are still high in these groups, they have dropped across the region. In Bolivia, mortality rates for children under 1 year old continue to be the highest in South America (64 per 1,000 live births), while the mortality rate for children age 5 and under is 83 per 1,000 live births (Valenzuela 2004). In Guatemala, in 2000, this rate was 49 per 1,000 for indigenous populations and 40 for nonindigenous ones. Mortality in children age 5 and under showed a parallel reduction, even though the figure for indigenous populations was 69 per 1,000, still higher than that of nonindigenous groups (52 per 1,000) (Adams 2005).

Core issues, such as birth control and child mortality, are beginning to arouse interest among indigenous women. One reason for indigenous women's incapacity to resort to birth control methods is lack of access to relevant information, often because of inhibitory factors such as mono-lingualism and illiteracy. Illiteracy is not a minor issue, and it has various nuances. No other group displays the educational gender gap, to the detriment of women, as clearly as the indigenous one. However, contravening it requires reverting prejudice or biases in the culture of many of those indigenous peoples. Thus, the cultural mediation of social citizenship operates in a problematic and contradictory way.

Location

The incidence of poverty and extreme poverty, as well as the lag in health and education, is much more pronounced in rural than in urban areas. In Latin America, by 2005, indigent groups[3] accounted for 33.5 percent of the rural population, compared with 11.9 percent in urban areas (see figure 6.4). However, mainly because of the region's growing urbanization, there have been more indigents in urban than in rural areas since 2002. According to 2005 estimates, 48 million out of a total of 89 million people in extreme poverty in Latin America live in urban areas.

Young People

Although their poverty rates do not exceed the population's average rates, young people deserve attention, because they face greater social integration difficulties. Although they have more years of formal schooling, their unemployment rates are two to three times that of former generations. In other words, they have become integrated into the accredited processes of acquiring knowledge and human capital formation but face obstacles in entering the spaces in which this human capital can be exercised—that is, the world of labor.

In 1990, only 25.8 percent of people age 20 to 24 in Latin America had completed secondary education; in 2002, this figure was 34.8 percent. However, at the start of the decade, average adult unemployment in the region amounted to 6.7 percent, rising to 15.7 percent for young people (UNECLAC and OIJ 2004). Moreover, the number of formal years of schooling required to obtain jobs with good prospects of future social mobility have soared. For example, in 2002, on average across the region, the percentage of those age 15 to 29 with 10 to 12 years of schooling (which far exceeds the Latin American average) working in low-productivity jobs was 38.1 percent for men and 45.6 percent for women (UNECLAC and

Figure 6.4. Latin America and the Caribbean: Evolution of Indigence by Geographic Area 1990–2005

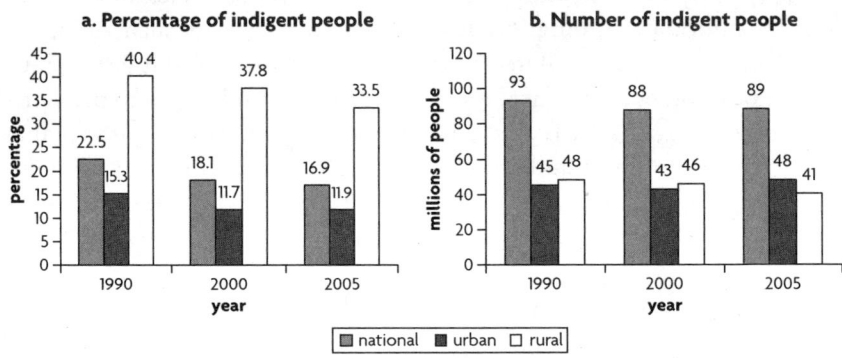

Source: United Nations Economic Commission for Latin America and the Caribbean, based on household surveys of the respective countries.
Note: Data are based on 19 countries in the region. The 2005 figures correspond to a projection.

OIJ 2004). With higher education, yet enduring higher unemployment or lower-quality employment, young people must surely live through this paradox with a sense of injustice, insofar as the educational process itself has conveyed the idea that greater achievements translate into better-options for future employment.

Underlying these forms of inequality is an accumulation of systemic disadvantages and discrimination embodied in everyday practices. It is important to look at the progress of most of the countries in the region in the past decade with regard to ethnicity, gender, and youth. Advances have been made in terms of political institutions, legislation and justice, and social policies, which take into account ascriptive variables, creating a positive influence on groups facing vulnerabilities or disadvantages. However, the step from de jure to de facto is not evident. Social and power gaps that condemn these groups to greater poverty and exclusion or that impose greater social integration barriers on them than on other groups in society are strongly upheld.

Ascriptive and Cultural Factors: Between Social Rights and Proactive Multiculturalism

The presence of social rights in political agendas, both domestic and international, is becoming stronger and challenges the capacity and will of states regarding the distribution of assets throughout society and its different socioeconomic groups. Together with such social rights and demands, indigenous people in different countries have been raising their voices to claim collective cultural rights. Such claims refer to the recognition of the other's own ways of giving sense, order, and content to personal and community life.

Cultural Citizenship and Recognition of the Other

The lack of social citizenship in Latin America is linked to the lack of cultural recognition. The indicators discussed previously speak for themselves. Moreover, the systems of resource and asset allocation instituted by the state are not governed by the rationale of collective aspirations, which carries more meaning for some of the groups defined by culture, ethnicity, or race.

From the perspective of indigenous peoples, a core concern is juridical regulations, because the rights accredited by the state are based on juridical individualism rather than collective rights. This distinction leads to a growing problem in societies that is becoming increasingly complex in cultural terms: a specific group's own sense of collective belonging (the most paradigmatic case is that of ethnic minorities who are self-defined as peoples) may not correspond to the assumed "universal" reference point of belonging to a nation. Thus, for example, the right to political organization and participation, in a framework of identity recognition and respect, can be as important for certain groups as other social rights, such as access to a decent job or to quality education.

The human rights doctrine and the democratic-liberal principles that assert the universality of rights and equality of all people under the law therefore encounter difficulties in capturing the situation. Indigenous peoples, for example, are proposing nonuniversal third-generation rights of a collective nature (rights of the people and not of persons), contradicting the individual-liberal nature of universally recognized rights. Furthermore, the struggle against inequalities based on ascriptive categories demands institutionalized positive discrimination to benefit disfavored groups.

The idea is that citizen equality should be complemented by mechanisms to correct origin-based inequalities (that is, unequal conditions stemming from accumulated and sustained prior discrimination) if it is to have a real, rather than merely formal, effect on the political and social citizenship of discriminated groups. The combination would allow women, ethnic groups, and other minority groups that are excluded or discriminated against to exert their different status without perpetuating their history of being unequal.

Toward a Proactive Multiculturalism

The growing visibility and strength of social demands—which are no longer age-old calls for access to employment or social protection but now center on identity or the more symbolic dimensions of distribution—pose challenges for the state in responding to the cultural particularities of social citizenship. The growing differentiation of group of individuals, according to changes in society that lead to a more diversified occupational structure and a wider scope of styles and ways of media communication, and the greater prominence of the so-called identity issue, implies that citizens are increasingly addressing the matters of assertion of difference, recognition policies, and promotion of cultural, gender, generation, and territorial diversity.

Ethnic minority, gender, youth, and migrant groups demand to be recognized in their singularity and in terms of their specific rights or the specific implementation of universal rights. Affirmative action and positive discrimination, compensation for historic damage, right to self-government, and differentiated policies in education are some examples. Citizenship is being rethought, not in terms of equality, but in terms of differences—or, rather, in terms of equal and different individuals.

Within this framework, proactive multiculturalism is a political force capable of moving forward in the direction of greater equality of opportunities, as well as a larger space for the assertion of differences. Proactive multiculturalism needs to reconcile nondiscrimination in the cultural field with social distribution to address inequalities. The challenge lies in ensuring compatibility between people's self-determination with the differentiation of culture and values, the participation and public voice of cultural and gender actors in public deliberation, and economic and social policies to implement second-generation rights, reducing the gap in terms of income, assets, ascription, human security, and access to knowledge.

Social Citizenship: A Recognition Issue with Redistribution Implications

In the recognition–redistribution dialectic, data collection and dissemination constitute an increasingly relevant issue. Census data on indigenous, Afro-descendant, and migrant populations must be updated and household surveys implemented to collect information on their socioeconomic conditions and perception of discrimination. These data must, in turn, enable the creation of indicators that will permit states, nongovernmental organizations, and different political interest groups to propose policies conforming to the situation of groups that perceive themselves as socially and culturally discriminated against.

An initial problem lies in the categories being used. For census purposes, when it comes to indigenous and Afro-descendant populations, there is no consensus regarding the use of a self-ascription criterion or preestablished definitions (table 6.1). For example, some censuses define ethnic belonging solely on the basis of spoken language, even though it is clear that age-old cultural submission or acculturation makes ethnic minorities reluctant to use or acknowledge the use of indigenous language.

As regards gender, recall that figure 6.3 reveals a difference in terms of regressive income distribution for women when household income is broken down into individual incomes within the household. This type of analysis is an infrequent exercise, although it is decisive in detecting income-related sex inequalities. With regard to young people, there is a marked lack of surveys in Latin America to inform society on the specific problems that they undergo.[4]

This information gathering has an undeniable political component: for the affected parties, it means disclosing their situation and constitutes a form of recognition in relation to others. Furthermore, without reliable data, periodic indicators, and measurements, it is impossible to make political decisions about how to tackle discrimination and target resources to groups that endure multiple exclusions based on ascriptive factors. Therefore, in terms of information, recognition and redistribution are two

Table 6.1. Census Criteria to Identify Indigenous Populations in Latin America and the Caribbean

Self-identification	Belonging	Use of indigenous language	Self-identification and language
Brazil, 2000	Chile, 2002	Mexico, 2000	Belize, 2000
Panama, 2000			Argentina, 2001 (at home)
Costa Rica, 2001			Bolivia, 2001
Honduras, 2001			Ecuador, 2001
Jamaica, 2001			Guatemala, 2002
R.B. de Venezuela, 2001			Paraguay, 2002

Source: United Nations Economic Commission for Latin America and the Caribbean Population Division.

sides of the same coin: in an information society in which social policy increasingly needs a social cartography, becoming statistically visible is part of the process of constructing social citizenship.[5]

Redistribution Fields with Sociocultural Implications

Several areas, in which access to assets and resources by different social groups requires state redistribution policies, have cultural implications. Education, health, labor, territory, the environment, and justice will be discussed here.

Multiculturalism in Education

Given the virtuous circles between higher education, socio-occupational mobility, and better income, education is regarded as the primary mechanism to reduce future inequalities and overcome intergenerational poverty reproduction. Allowing access to quality education and promoting educational achievement and effective learning provides greater opportunities for better living standards, greater labor options, and greater effective freedom to undertake life projects. In this sense, education is not just a social and cultural right; it is also an asset that promotes the realization of other rights. By the same token, an education gap perpetuates the income gap in terms of a decent job, access to well-being, and participation in the public sphere.

The educational models implemented up to now have resulted in two forms of discrimination. In the sphere of achievements and progress, indigenous peoples and Afro-descendants are clearly disadvantaged. One of the historic functions of education has been the promotion of cultural homogeneity among the population according to the widely prevalent model of the nation-state, which until recently conceived cultural unification as integral to territorial sovereignty.

Today, governments are aware that access to quality education with a multicultural emphasis is one of the key levers to promote social citizenship in indigenous and Afro-descendant populations, as well as among women. The promotion of bilingualism and literacy are core tools in creating a greater prospect of equality. The implementation of linguistic policies that enable training of indigenous groups without requiring them to relinquish their ethnic identity, language, and culture is a first step in overcoming the old education models. New approaches—interculturality, multiculturalism, bilingualism, and respect for cultural diversity—are increasingly being implemented in countries including Bolivia, Guatemala, Mexico, Paraguay, and Peru.

Bicultural–multicultural education aims to convey respect for cultural differences within a society and in the world in general (García Castaño, Pulido Moyano, and Montes del Castillo 1998). Also, importantly, school texts and syllabi that eradicate prejudice and stereotypes about black people, as well as incorporate elements that value indigenous and Afro-descendant cultures, are needed. The idea is to open a space for cultural pluralism and tolerance that respects and preserves existing cultures and rejects cultural assimilation processes.

In Chile, the Intercultural Bilingual Education Program[6] does more than contemplate the implementation of an intercultural bilingual educational system. It also finances 24,000 indigenous scholarships for students who have good academic performance and are living in poor socioeconomic conditions; implements programs for curricular innovation, teacher training, and preparation of teaching material for intercultural bilingual education in primary schools; and improves the infrastructure of schools with a high concentration of indigenous students. In addition, the Digital Literacy Program for Indigenous Communities,[7] part of the Inter-American Development Bank–financed Origins Program, seeks to train members of indigenous communities in Chile in computer technology. Part of this project contemplates the incorporation of the Infomóvil, a mobile computer room offering computer education classes. The idea is to provide indigenous peoples with home-delivered digital training.

In Bolivia, Law 1565, enacted as part of the Educational Reform of 1994, has had important implications for bilingual education. This law guarantees bilingual education to all Bolivian citizens. This initiative originated in a pilot experience carried out in 1990. In Peru, the National Directorate for Intercultural Bilingual Education was created to guarantee the organization and administration of intercultural bilingual education at all levels and modalities in the country. On the basis of this initiative, the Ministry of Education and Microsoft Peru have implemented a new software in Quechua, the Language Interface Pack Kit. This kit will be available to more than 3 million Quechua speakers.

School education also needs to grow closer to youth culture, especially since the latter is much closer to the audiovisual industry than to school programs. The huge gap between youth culture and school routines reinforces, instead of processing, conflicts between youth and the main socialization institutions accredited by society. Finally, in the case of women, it is necessary to complement the equality in achievement shown by women in Latin America with school socialization patterns that foster greater gender equality in values and everyday practices within schools. Schools should open a space for cultural pluralism and tolerance that will encourage respect and help preserve existing cultures and eliminate forms of discrimination and devaluation of groups defined by culture or ascription.

An educational model with a multicultural emphasis must create new teaching contents, values, and practices. The core elements in this are respect for ethnic and cultural diversity, civic education based on a full and extensive citizenship, curricular relevance in relation to the diverse social and cultural realities of the children who attend school, and encouragement of communication practices based on respect for others, gender equality, and mutual understanding.

Adaptation of Health Services to Sociocultural Realities

Improving health care coverage involves several challenges. First, health care must have a good outreach in rural areas to provide for indigenous populations who are scattered to benefit from health care services and prevention strategies. Second, health care protocols must be adapted to help overcome linguistic and cultural barriers between the indigenous population and health care professionals. Third, efforts must validate and incorporate traditional health systems, building bridges between official medicine and the traditional medicine that patients are acquainted with.

As the Pan American Health Organization (PAHO) notes, respect for cultural diversity and real knowledge about the needs of the various communities are the pillars of achieving health equity among indigenous peoples.[8] Indigenous peoples face a complex reality when it comes to health. In the first place, the indigenous population is quite scattered, located in rural, marginal urban, or border areas, rendering access quite difficult. Second, the great majority of health care professionals are not prepared to deal with the cultural diversity of indigenous peoples. Third, indigenous communities present health problems far beyond the national average.[9] As a way of addressing these difficulties, PAHO proposes a five-point approach:

1. A holistic approach to health
2. The indigenous peoples' right to self-determination
3. The indigenous peoples' right to systematic participation

4. The respect for and revitalization of indigenous cultures

5. Reciprocity in relationships.

Progress in this direction has been mixed. As far back as 1978, the World Health Organization asked national governments to study and progressively implement traditional medicine to complement official medicine. The countries that have made the best advances in this area are Mexico, Cuba, and Guatemala (Hauser and others 1997).

It is necessary to acknowledge and promote traditional medicines and pharmacopoeia, accepting the use of alternative medicines known for their effectiveness. Traditional medicines not only benefit health, but also facilitate the reintegration of communities into their own culture. States must safeguard, through specific policies and legislation, the promotion and protection of the natural pharmacopoeia heritage held by the communities. Such policies are necessary to promote environmental sustainability and biodiversity, to preserve ancestral wisdom and knowledge in health care, and to respect the intellectual property rights of indigenous groups.[10]

Women, especially rural and indigenous women, must be assured of their reproductive rights. Information, culture, and access factors account for the lags in this area. It is necessary not only to extend information coverage but also to ensure that it is internalized by those to whom it is targeted and to eradicate the sexist prejudices that cause women to feel inhibited about making effective use of modern birth control methods.

Young people have a very low probability of becoming seriously ill or dying from endogenous causes. Currently, the mortality rate of Latin American young people age 15 to 24, calculated as 134 per 100,000, is just over half that for the group age 25 to 44. However, there is a juvenile morbidity-mortality profile resulting from factors such as the higher prevalence of accidents, physical assaults, sexually transmitted diseases, and unwanted and premature births. Out of every 100 young men dying in Latin America, 77 die as a result of external causes (accidents, homicides, and suicides). For young women, the figure is 38 out of 100 (UNECLAC and OIJ 2004). Very healthy inside and very exposed on the outside, young people do not find the answer to their specific risk profile in health services or in preventive health care. Their health-risk problems are linked to socially negative stigmas that cause them to be less than welcomed by the health system. Often, the vague boundary between what may be considered either a health issue or a behavior issue, or between illness and social disgrace, situates young people too far away from the appropriate services to look after their health emergencies.

The case of adolescent pregnancy is a dramatic one, particularly when one takes into account that, despite the sharp fall in the region's average fertility, adolescent fertility remains high and has even increased in some countries. Unwanted pregnancies in young women lead to stigmatization and school desertion, as well as to extremely precarious economic and family trajectories throughout their lives. To compound the problem, adolescent fertility occurs much more frequently among women with lower educational levels, which reinforces the dialectic of exclusion. Therefore, it is essential that health policies take a two-sided approach. On the one hand, they need to accept and acknowledge the problems involved in this situation, providing the necessary support to break the link between adolescent pregnancy and school desertion. On the other, it is important to provide clear and exhaustive information in schools on pregnancy prevention, stressing the responsibility of men in this matter.

Extension of Work Opportunities and Social Protection

In the employment arena, women, youth, indigenous people, migrants, and Afro-descendants face a clearly disadvantageous position (and frequently, discrimination). States need to enforce laws on nondiscrimination, check that equal tasks receive equal remuneration, and ensure that everybody obtains the social security rights and benefits to which they are entitled, as well as health benefits and compensation for work-related accidents or illness. To promote greater equality in access to work and in working conditions, policy makers will need to, wherever possible, consider affirmative action measures or positive discrimination.[11]

Historically, integrated social sectors (which work as the axis of integration and exercise of rights) incorporated various social protection mechanisms against the risks that jeopardize work, such as disease, old age, lack of knowledge, and unemployment. Employment laws have focused on men, because men were traditionally and culturally designated as providers. The focus has tended to be on men who hold a formal, dependent, and wage-earning job, preferably organized under a union. This 20th-century social citizenship, which functioned on the basis of formal and unionized work, therefore left two groups without the possibility of effectively exercising their rights: women[12] and an abundant contingent of nonorganized, informal workers. Currently, the rural population, indigenous peoples, Afro-descendants, young people, migrants, and women are much more likely to be in informal, temporary, unprotected, and nonunionized jobs.

The region needs to reformulate its approach to security and protection. The concept of security, within this framework, encompasses new spheres and social categories, including age and ascriptive categories such as gender and ethnic minority status. Transformations in the working world exacerbate precariousness in groups that have invariably been discriminated against in the workplace, while changes in the family structure and in the age pyramid reformulate the relation between active and passive populations, providers, and dependents. As economic volatility and external shocks increase the population's vulnerability, social protection is increasingly inadequate. Labor and social protection policies must aim to provide greater coverage to historically excluded groups.

Territory, Autonomy, and Justice: An Emblematic Case

In the indigenous discourse, land and territory are deeply linked to historical destiny. It is an unalienable relation, because culture and language disappear with the disappearance of indigenous groups' land, as well as their vast knowledge about its resources (Bello 2004). Territorial and autonomy rights create an emblematic link between social citizenship and culture. Two reasons account for this link. First, the ownership of land and territories demanded by indigenous peoples is based on common or unwritten law and on the claim against usurpation. These ownership claims are fresh in the historical memory of these peoples but are not recorded in the land registers currently in force, which rule the modern nation-state. Second, for indigenous peoples, ownership of land and territories represents more than a residential and productive asset: it is a key factor that confirms their identity and the continuity of their mores, and it is their collective belonging referent. Their stake on the land is not only a matter of quality of life, but also a matter of identity.[13]

Traditionally, many indigenous peoples have owned their land collectively or with complex systems for allocating responsibility, using many possible combinations of ownership. Given this identity feature, public policy should promote titles based on shared usage and mores, such as the provisions established by communities in Mexico for the purpose of protecting communal territories. Jurisdictional mechanisms (territorial courts) should also be created to help prevent more subtle forms of discrimination related to indigenous territorial issues.

Land ownership of indigenous peoples is a key factor in the cultural dimension of social citizenship. It questions the liberal system of rights by claiming common-law rights (by customary use and not by law) that are collective but not universal (instead of individual rights with a universal scope) and that are based on self-regulation. At the same time, the claim of indigenous peoples on the land is often indivisible from the demand for self-determination and autonomy, because it comes from groups that define themselves as peoples and that attribute to themselves their own systems of deliberation, legislation, and justice anchored in territorial definitions. In the face of this demand for autonomy, the state is wary of the eventual creation of subnational states in detriment of that sovereignty that is the essence of the nation-state.

With the causal link between territory ownership and an administrative and judicial system set forth by indigenous peoples, the modern construction of citizenship is being questioned. Social citizenship and political citizenship cannot be embedded in the liberal model of rights or in the model of the welfare state but must be embedded in individual and collective rights, where demandability and justice is taken off the hands of the state (Bello 2004).

Conciliation is, therefore, not easy. Some countries have made progress by way of an autonomy that will not conflict with the general body of rules of the nation state (that is to say, not just any judicial system or self-government system). On the other hand, International Labour Organization (ILO) Convention 169, subscribed to by some governments in the region and resisted by others, advocates the establishment of measures and action programs enabling indigenous peoples to administrate and manage their own territories and natural resources. There also are some Afro-descendant populations who are redefining their exclusion in terms of culture and advocating similar forms of self-determination.

None of the special legislations in Latin American countries grant indigenous authorities full autonomy in matters of administration and justice, as the argument as long as it does not violate the Constitution or human rights international treaties turns out to be the minimum common denominator for granting any autonomy. The model adopted by the more progressive states in this matter is that of neocommunitarian liberalism, proposed by Kymlicka (1996), according to which external protection is a must when there are internal common-law rules that violate individuals' fundamental human rights. The argument has considerable weight from the perspective of universal human rights ethics: a state cannot allow a self-regulated community, by virtue of its common-law rights, to consider as normal in its daily life that which, at the constitutional level of that state, has been established as a crime or a violation of the law.

A classic dilemma usually set forth in this respect is that of women's right to equality, which is not always supported by self-regulated communities on the basis of use and custom. Indeed, in some communities, physical punishment of women may even be sanctioned. In many indigenous regions in Latin America, custom systematically denies women the right to own land or assets.

Regulatory and judicial systems based on custom may be incompatible with universally recognized economic, social, and civil rights. Thus, some of the common or unwritten laws have also been considered to be archaic and rigid, too localized and complex, making more generalized reform initiatives difficult to implement. They may even not be legitimate at a local level (for example, initiatives imbued by colonial legislation), and they may have derived from abusive chieftainships (*cacicazgos*) or clientelistic mechanisms that use local chiefs to maintain control. Therefore, though custom may be recognized, it must not become an obstacle for other fundamental human rights to come fully into force.

The most important issue is to build a consensus in terms of procedural ethics, beyond the realm of cultural differences, that will ensure that differences and resolutions are effectively respected and complied with, whether they may have been negotiated or adjudicated. The values and beliefs in conflict are immeasurable, but they are not untranslatable. It is in this translation of rights that the effort to improve justice for indigenous peoples must be focused, especially in territorial terms.

Environment and Cultural Heritage

Indiscriminate felling of native forests, oil extraction, and construction of dams and reservoirs have devastating consequences for indigenous groups and their surroundings. Hence, the demand for territorial rights has become the most visible aspect of the indigenous crisis at an international level. The effort has been assisted by the concern of international and multilateral organizations, such as the Organization of American States, the World Bank, and the Inter-American Development Bank, as well as by a set of instruments that could make operational the demands of indigenous peoples. These instruments include ILO Convention 169 and Agenda 21 of the Earth Summit.

In South America as a whole, much progress has been made toward recognition of indigenous peoples' ancestral rights in terms of territory, environment, possession, administration, and use of resources. In countries such as Bolivia and Brazil, this recognition has been incorporated into the constitutions of the respective countries. In ratifying ILO Convention 169, they have appropriated a corresponding set of rules and regulations. This set of distinctly expressed rules and regulations captures, in its scope and meaning, the current need to recognize territorial rights and the autonomy of indigenous peoples to use their territories at will.

However, to date many of these declarations are more de jure than de facto, without having had any real effect on indigenous peoples. Indigenous people continue to endure the degradation of their habitat, as a result both of land overuse caused by the scarcity of land and of large development projects. A basic measure to open political negotiation spaces for indigenous peoples regarding these problems is their constitutional recognition in the positive law of modern states.

With this in mind, the management of natural resources and the preservation of biodiversity of indigenous lands are also central issues. Increasing demand for new agricultural land; patenting of phyto-pharmaceuticals by transnational consortia; mining, aquifer, and oil concessions; and excessive lumbering—all threaten the survival of indigenous peoples. According to the framework laid out in Agenda 21 of the Earth Summit, the states must establish regulatory frameworks as well as participation processes to work with communities in the implementation of joint action and management plans for their land, natural resources, and biodiversity preservation.

It is necessary to establish precisely delimited regulatory frameworks for informed participation by indigenous communities in projects that affect them directly. Currently, there are several specific actions, including demarcation of indigenous territories; restitution; protection; sustainable management of natural resources (such as forests, water, and phytopharmaceuticals); land extensions; and territorial management through indigenous development areas, which are taking place in Chile, Colombia, Ecuador, Guatemala, Guyana, and Mexico.

On the other hand, given that rural and peasant women in general—and indigenous women in particular—are highly skilled in the use of certain natural resources, certain processes of degradation and contamination of the natural environment are likely to have a special impact on them. They experience the loss of resources required for their subsistence and subsequent displacement to other geographic areas in conditions of poverty and precariousness (Bello 1998). These women's knowledge, derived from their specialization, is essential to preserve biodiversity. By the same token, their role in the sustainable management of natural resources is a central factor in ending the vicious circle of poverty in the rural sector.

Therefore, it is important to incorporate gender concerns and perspectives in all policies and programs intended to favor sustainable development in indigenous territories. This effort implies a heightened awareness of gender on the part of the institutions concerned and the implementation of redistributive policies to channel resources to women in order for them to undertake greater responsibilities in projects and programs. The idea is to assimilate the knowledge and traditional practices of rural women into the sustainable use of resources when environmental management programs are developed. It is also essential to achieve the active participation of women in decision-making processes related to the environment, at all levels—as administrators, project makers, planners, executors, and evaluators of environment-related projects (Bello and Rangel 2000).

De Jure and de Facto: The Emblematic Case of Indigenous Peoples

The main juridical problem in sanctioning any kind of discrimination, whether because of ethnicity, migrant status, or gender, and in promoting greater space for the assertion of difference and social inclusion of these ascriptive groups is that of the demandability of rights.

This area is where the gap between rule and reality becomes, for ethnic minorities, particularly dramatic. De jure, indigenous peoples constitute a relatively privileged minority from a legal perspective. Probably, there is no other vulnerable population whose rights have been recognized with such scope and understanding, and the same reflected in the plethora of constitutional rules and special public policies benefiting the indigenous peoples in Latin America. De facto, however, indigenous populations are the most unprotected, mainly because they do not have access to the institutional means to pursue the enforcement of the rules.

This situation calls for more than simply the implementation of mechanisms aimed at mediation or finding alternative solutions to conflicts. There must also be a strengthening of the adjudication means in civil matters affecting indigenous and Afro-descendant populations (Nader 2002), so they get easier and faster access to judicial mechanisms and, by association, the fulfillment of their fundamental rights.

The main problems related to territorial justice concern the chronic deferments they experience in access to and attainment of title deeds for land, water, and every other resource found in the subsoil and soil. Daes (1999) describes the most common territorial problems as lack of recognition by states of the rights of indigenous peoples over lands and territories, lack of demarcation, failure to apply recognition and protection laws, problems associated with claims for devolution, expropriations, forced displacements and relocations, and lack of integral protection of environmental and territorial resources.

One of the feasible reforms of the judicial system, similar to those being implemented in penal reform matters or the creation of family courts in Chile, involves the creation of territorial courts to coordinate the handling of environmental queries and conflicts, demands from indigenous peoples, and problems associated with access to and distribution of resources or with tangible or intangible cultural heritage. Such courts would considerably reduce the interstitial spaces for discrimination and racism, which generally take place in the semidarkness of various public offices. Another access mechanism for which there is a precedent is the specialized advocates (for children, as is the case in Bolivia, or for indigenous peoples, as in Guatemala).

Judicial reforms are necessary to facilitate the demandability of rights, so that all sanctions and benefits contained in the law are complied with. At present, there are obstacles in the form of costs and intermediation that hamper this demandability. Many Latin American countries do not allow self-representation, which effectively restricts the poorest sectors' access to justice. Legal assistance would increase access to justice, as would also the existence of mediation community centers, justice of the peace offices, or mobile courts. The mobile courts introduced in remote areas of Brazil in 1999 have been replicated in Chile and Mexico. In Guatemala, 24 mediation centers have been created using mediators who are fluent in Spanish and Mayan. The social movements themselves provide whatever is required so that people may claim their rights in a formal situation.

Although indigenous peoples' advocate organizations in Guatemala report to the public defenders office, their particular composition and their access to indigenous-language-speaking attorneys grant them a special sensitivity regarding the rights of indigenous peoples. They also perform their work under the explicit mandate of ILO Convention 169, creating jurisprudence that may serve as a precedent in future. The indigenous advocate project includes many facets, such as promoting the use of the language, assessments, and work of experts, as well as acting as a multiplier of rights through various workshops, radio programs, and roundtables.

Another notable aspect of indigenous advocate organizations is their involvement in training activities. On the basis of research carried out on the application of indigenous peoples' law and constitutional law, paradigmatic cases have been constructed that are used to sensitize the operators. Also, in collaboration with the Supreme Court of Justice and the Judicial Studies School, training workshops have been carried out both for judicial officials and for indigenous leaders and authorities. Undoubtedly, indigenous advocacy is an institution to be recommended when the time comes to coordinate both justice systems while respecting indigenous law. At the same time, indigenous advocacy favors the use of the language and takes part of the conflict away from the judicial system, which, in turn, helps to clear the justice administration system.

In Chile, the new Code of Criminal Procedure introduces a new persona—the translator—for cases in which the accused cannot express themselves clearly in Spanish. The new code also considers that, in cases involving members of the same ethnicity, custom may have the validity of law, acting as a mitigating circumstance in penal matters. With this in mind, experts prepare anthropological reports for the judge's deliberation at the time of pronouncing judgment.[14] Furthermore, the government has incorporated alternative methods of solving conflicts into the justice system. This approach allows for mechanisms such as mediation, arbitrage, conciliation, and negotiation, which facilitate processing group demands that previously had various access barriers, ranging from language to territorial marginality.

These examples, while encouraging, are limited in scope and coverage. Enabling more inclusive judicial reforms remains a challenge across much of Latin America.

Policy Implications

This chapter illustrates the challenges of multiculturalism and social diversity in societies where particular groups are systematically disadvantaged. It documents the inequality effects of ascriptive, territorial, and other social characteristics that stem from the structural and institutional constraints that prevent members of those social groups from benefiting equally from economic and social opportunities. The chapter argues that, in part, this inequality arises from a built-in bias within laws, regulations, and public institutions that privilege individual over collective rights, the formal sector over informal workers, and cultural homogeneity over multiculturalism. The chapter argues for a more holistic approach to social citizenship, beginning with recognition of identity and the right to diversity in how people organize themselves, identify themselves, and choose to exercise their rights.

The policy implications for Latin American countries are not dissimilar to those for many other developing countries that are multicultural. However, given the high levels of inequality associated with ascriptive categories, the two main messages are provisions in the policy and institutional framework for proactive multiculturalism and adaptation of entitlements to local cultures and institutions, as well as gender differences. For countries where such differences are stark, structural inequality will probably need to include measures of affirmative action. In others, ensuring cultural sensitivity in public institutions might significantly improve access to public goods and services.

Notes

1. In much the same way as it has become commonplace to say that indigenous women in Latin America suffer a triple discrimination—for being women, poor, and indigenous—it can also be stated that the case of indigenous and Afro-descendant populations embodies an accumulation of discriminations characterizing the situation of a number of excluded and discriminated groups.
2. The differences observed in average remuneration originate in the job market and are prompted by occupational segmentation and an important element regarding salary discrimination based on race. In Brazil, between 1992 and 2001, the salaries of black workers were 51 percent below of those of white workers. Disaggregating data by sex, black men's wages never reached even one-half of white men's wages, and although the gap is slightly less in women, the average remuneration for black women was never more than 53 percent of white women's remuneration. For both sexes and for every year during the 1992 to 2001 period, remunerations for the black population amounted to 60 percent to 80 percent of the income of whites with the same educational level (Borges Martins 2004).
3. The term *indigent* refers to households in extreme poverty whose earnings are insufficient to pay for the basic nutritional goods that underpin the poverty line in that country.
4. Up to 2003, only Chile, Colombia, and Mexico had undertaken youth surveys with the coverage required to be considered in the preparation of public youth policies.

5. Likewise, the United Nations has proposed a racial equality index, which, like the human development index, would provide visibility and comparability for national situations with regard to social citizenship lags for ethnicity- and race-defined minorities.

6. More information about this program is available online at http://www. risalc.org.

7. More information about the Digital Literacy Program for Indigenous Communities is available online at http://www.origenes.cl/diarionota77.htm.

8. More information about the initiatives of PAHO is available online at http:// www.paho.org/spanish/ad/ths/os/Indig-home.htm.

9. An example is infant mortality. In Mexico, indigenous children present an infant mortality rate of 59 per 1,000 live births, which is twice the national infant mortality rate. In Honduras, the maternal mortality rate at the national level amounts to 147 per 100,000 live births; however, in regional departments where the indigenous population prevails (Colón, Copán, Intibucá, Lempira, and La Paz), it fluctuates between 190 and 255 per 100,000 live births. Likewise, in Guatemala, chronic malnutrition reaches 67.8 percent among indigenous peoples and 36.7 percent among those who are nonindigenous. In the United States, the indigenous population tends to present higher rates with respect to alcoholism, obesity, and diabetes. See http://www.paho.org/spanish/ ad/ths/os/Indig-home.htm for more information.

10. There are many ongoing research projects in the Amazon rainforest studying traditional medical practices and the use of pharmaceuticals to verify their validity in the Western world. But the idea is not to just legitimize and disseminate this heritage of knowledge. It is also essential to ensure that its intellectual property rights remain where it belongs: with the ethnic groups and in the areas where it has been developed for centuries. At present, conflicts over the patents for this knowledge are also a central political conflict in which the citizenship rights of original peoples is at stake.

11. International Labour Organization Convention 169 states, "Governments must adopt, within the framework of their national legislation and in cooperation with the peoples concerned, special measures to guarantee workers belonging to those peoples an effective protection in matters of contracting/hiring and employment conditions, insofar as they are not effectively safeguarded by legislation applicable to workers in general" (part III, "Contracting and Employment Conditions," article 20, no. 1).

12. Even if, well into the 20th century, women were still left out of the protection systems associated with work, their own demands and struggles resulted in them being recognized as workers, with their own specific features (pre- and postnatal maternity leave and leave for children's illnesses are among the most significant successes achieved). However, they encountered severe limitations with respect to social security coverage in periods of unemployment, their

integration into labor training, matters related to child care and supervision, and their participation in the social insurance system.

13. The same occurs with the quilombo "remanescents" in Brazil, who demand their right to the land, as well as with Afro-descendants who have been displaced by violent conflicts in Colombia.

14. Anthropological expert work and cultural mitigating factors are not problem-free. An action that is considered to be a felony from the perspective of universal law (for example, wife battering) may be remitted or attenuated during judgment if it is proven that the felony is not so from the perspective of an ethnic group's common law.

References

Adams, R. 2005. *Etnicidad e igualdad en Guatemala*. Social Policies Series 107. Santiago: United Nations Economic Commission for Latin America and the Caribbean and German Agency for Technical Cooperation.

Bello, Á. 1998. "Mujeres rurales, indígenas y medio ambiente: acuerdo y políticas." In *Cartilla N°5*, publication of the Centro de Estudios para el Desarrollo de la Mujer, CEDEM, Santiago, Chile.

———. 2004. *Etnicidad y ciudadanía en América Latina: La acción colectiva de los pueblos indígenas*. Santiago: United Nations Economic Commission for Latin America.

Bello, Á., and M. Rangel. 2000. "Etnicidad, 'raza' y equidad en América Latina y el Caribe." Santiago: United Nations Economic Commission for Latin America the Caribbean.

Borges Martins, R. 2004. *Desigualdades raciales y políticas de la inclusión racial, resumen de la experiencia brasilera reciente*. Social Policies Series 82. Santiago: United Nations Economic Commission for Latin America the Caribbean.

Calderón, F., M. Hopenhayn, and E. Ottone. 1996. *Esa esquiva modernidad: Desarrollo, ciudadanía y cultura en América Latina y el Caribe*. Caracas: United Nations Educational, Scientific, and Cultural Organization and New Society.

Castells, M. 1999. *La era de la información: Economía, sociedad y cultural*. 2nd ed. Madrid: Alianza Editorial.

Daes, E. I. 1999. "Indigenous People and Their Relationship to Land." Working Paper E/CN/Sub.2/1999/18, United Nations, Geneva.

García Castaño, F. J., R. Pulido Moyano, and A. Montes del Castillo. 1998. "La educación multicultural y el concepto de cultura." *Revista de Educación Bilingüe Intercultural* 13, Organization of Ibero-American States for Education, Science, and Culture. http://www.oei.org.co/oeivirt/rie13a09.htm.

Garretón, M. A. 2000. *La sociedad en que vivi(re)mos: Introducción sociológica al cambio de siglo*. Santiago: LOM Ediciones.

Hall, G., and H. A. Patrinos. 2005. *Indigenous People, Poverty, and Human Development in Latin America: 1994–2004.* Washington, DC: World Bank.

Hauser, R. M., X. Montecinos, and M. Quintanilla. 1997. "METSAL (Por una interculturalidad en salud)." Cuadernos de la Academia 6, Department of Research and Applied Social Studies, Universidad Academia de Humanismo Cristiano, Santiago.

Hopenhayn, M., and A. Bello. 2000. *Discriminación étnico-racial y xenofobia en América Latina y el Caribe.* Social Policies Series 47, Santiago: United Nations Economic Commission for Latin America the Caribbean.

Kymlicka, W. 1996. *Ciudadanía multicultural: Una teoría liberal de los derechos de las minorías.* Barcelona, Spain: Paidos.

Kymlicka, W., and W. Norman. 1997. "El retorno del ciudadano: Una revisión de la producción reciente en teoría de la ciudadanía." *Revista Agora* 7 (Winter): 5–43.

Nader, L. 2002. *The Life of the Law: Anthropological Projects.* Berkeley: University of California Press.

Plant, R. 1998. "Issues in Indigenous Poverty and Development." Inter-American Development Bank, Washington, DC. http://idbdocs.iadb.org/wsdocs/getdocument.aspx?docnum=363750.

Psacharopoulos, G., and H. A. Patrinos. 1994. *Indigenous People and Poverty in Latin America: An Empirical Analysis.* Washington, DC: World Bank.

Touraine, A. 1997. *Pourrons-nous vivre ensemble? Égaux et différents.* Paris: Fayard.

UNECLAC (United Nations Economic Commission for Latin America and the Caribbean) and OIJ (Organización Iberoamericana de Juventud). 2004. *La juventud en Iberoamerica, tendencias y urgencias.* Santiago: ECLAC and OIJ.

UNESCO (United Nations Educational, Scientific, and Cultural Organization). 2004. *Universal Conclusion of Primary Education in Latin America: Are We Really So Near the Goal?* Santiago: UNESCO Regional Education Office for Latin America and the Caribbean.

Valenzuela, R. 2004. *Inequidad, ciudadanía y pueblos indígenas en Bolivia.* Social Policies Series 83, United Nations Economic Commission for Latin America and the Caribbean, Santiago.

CHAPTER 7

Local Participatory Democracy in Latin America: Lessons from Mexico and Colombia

David Recondo

In Latin America, the concept of "participatory democracy," or rather "citizen participation," first appeared in the second half of the 1980s, at a time when initial steps toward decentralization were being taken. This held true in particular for Brazil and Colombia, but also for Bolivia and Ecuador. In other countries, such as the Central American nations and Mexico, decentralization occurred during the same period, but references to participatory democracy were less explicit. Yet even in the latter cases, decentralization was always presented as a vehicle for greater democratization. Narrowing the gap between citizens and political decisions was considered a guarantee of both democracy and administrative efficiency. The reasoning behind the decentralization measures was that if citizens were to be involved in decisions concerning the allocation of public funds, these allocations—because they would correspond more closely to the beneficiaries' needs—would appear more legitimate and would thus be more efficacious.

This chapter will first provide an insight into the decentralizing, participatory wave. It will then explore the effects these measures have had on the indigenous regions of Mexico and Colombia. The reason for choosing this particular context for analysis is that, in these areas, such decision-making processes existed well before the participatory policies were introduced in the 1980s. In these cases, the state sought to include traditional practices in the modern framework of a decentralized handling of public affairs. Yet, inevitably, the process ran into obstacles: terminology gave rise to contradictory interpretations and procedural misunderstandings. Those contradictions and misunderstandings mark the limits of government policies designed to promote citizen participation; at the same time, they account for the innovative situations created when such policies are grafted onto local procedures.

The State and the Promotion of Citizen Participation: Efficiency versus Legitimacy

In Mexico, decentralization first became a subject of political debate in the 1970s, but it was not until the early 1980s that the first reforms were implemented. President Miguel de la Madrid (1982–88) made decentralization his primary objective by pushing for amendment of article 115[1] of the federal constitution and taking steps to decentralize the health and education sectors. However, those measures were largely symbolic because they were not accompanied by an increase in funds allocated to the federated states and the municipalities. It was only from 1989 onward that the federal government undertook a genuine decentralization of its budget. The National Solidarity Program (Programa Nacional de Solidaridad, or PRONASOL)[2] of President Carlos Salinas de Gortari (1988–94) and the Nuevo Federalismo (New Federalism),[3] launched by President Ernesto Zedillo Ponce de Léon (1994–2000), involved a redistribution of federal government funds, of which an ever-increasing proportion was administered directly by the municipalities.

In Colombia, President Belisario Betancur (1982–86) instigated the first decentralizing reform. In 1986, the Colombian legislative assembly passed Law 11, which provided for the election of mayors (*alcaldes*) by direct suffrage and extended the powers of the municipalities.[4] The law also established a number of procedures based on participation.[5] However, it was in 1991, when a new constitution was enacted, that the participatory aspect of reform was given primary importance. Article 1 of the constitution declares, "Colombia is a constitutional social state organized in the form of a unitary republic, decentralized, ... democratic, participatory, and pluralistic." The municipalities were granted new powers authorizing them to fix their own administrative rules, raise taxes, and control the handling of funds transferred by the central government. With regard to the native communities, Law 60 of 1993 reestablished the *resguardo*[6] as a separate "territorial entity," to be administered by the "traditional" authorities in *cabildos indígenas* (indigenous municipal councils). The law also provided for the transfer of special funds—through the municipalities or the departments in which the *resguardos* were located—that were to be allocated according to decisions by the members of the *cabildos*, in consultation with the inhabitants of each of the territories concerned.

The evolution was much the same in the two countries, even if the conditions and historical context differed considerably. In Mexico, decentralization was the equivalent of municipalization, even though the federated states also benefited from substantial transfers of powers and financial resources (particularly for social policies, education, and health). In Colombia (at least in regions inhabited by the indigenous population), the *resguardos* (those newly created and those already officially recognized by the state) were, along with the municipalities, the primary beneficiaries of decentralization with regard to administrative autonomy. In both cases, local management of the funds transferred by the central government was subject to direct decision-making participation by the inhabitants of the community in question. The institutional context that the law stipulated for this process was the *cabildo abierto*[7] in Colombia and the *consejo de desarrollo social municipal* (council for municipal social development) in Mexico. Apart from the difference in title, the principles on which these new institutions were based and the ways in which they functioned were similar. The local authorities were called on to organize meetings with all the citizens of their district, including delegates of local organizations (associative, cooperative, and so forth) and representatives of private companies, government departments, or public agencies directly concerned with the funds being transferred. In most cases, the meetings were held annually. Later the chapter will explore how the institutions functioned in greater detail. What is of interest at this juncture is the similitude of the timing of participatory decentralization in the two countries and the institutional structures adopted.

The similarities were obviously no coincidence. Parallel evolutions taking place in neighboring countries indicate that the movement was widespread and based on common factors. Without going as far as establishing a hierarchy or a relation of cause and effect, one can recognize two essential ingredients in this process. First, in Mexico, as in Colombia, the decline in state tax revenues brought about by changes in the global economy (in particular, the fall in oil prices in the early 1980s) paralyzed the patronage system that, thanks to the permeability of the dominant political parties, had ensured a form of social mobility and thus the legitimacy of the regime. In the two countries, patronage (a system of asymmetric exchange of favors within a pyramidal structure) was the principal motor of integration and political stability. It is this relationship that explains how the Partido Revolucionario Institucional (Institutional Revolutionary Party, or PRI) managed to extend its hegemony over a period of more than 70 years. The lavish oil revenues and agrarian reform (or rather, the promise of agrarian reform) enabled the postrevolutionary regime to maintain vast networks of loyal supporters over the years. Similarly, in Colombia, even if the regional oligarchies had traditionally been stronger than their Mexican counterparts, the bipartisan system of the National Front,[8] established in 1958, retained its ascendancy by building on a hierarchical network of patronage that linked the local bosses and the leaders of the two parties through myriad intermediaries at all levels of the political and administrative structures.

The change in global economic conditions and the excessive debt burdens of both countries combined to cut off the funding for the patronage network, causing it to crumble into a multitude of micronetworks that were barely interconnected. The restructuring measures advocated by the international financial agencies only accentuated this tendency, because to profit from new credits, governments had to implement austerity budgets and privatize a number of public or semipublic enterprises that hitherto had served as sources of patronage funding. Politics continued to operate on a patronage model, but one that was dismantled and increasingly incapable of guaranteeing the stability of a hierarchical system that was falling apart.

A second factor explains the recourse to decentralization and procedures that provided for nonpartisan citizen participation: namely, the extensive changes that had affected the two societies. In Mexico, from the 1930s to the 1950s, the state pushed through a developmental program that, in a few decades, transformed a society consisting mainly of peasants into an industrialized, urbanized nation. A sizable working class emerged, closely controlled by the PRI. Middle-class city dwellers, the primary beneficiaries of the regime, grew in geometric proportions throughout the 1950s and 1960s. The policies favoring the indigenous population, established in the 1940s, contributed to the formation of a new cultivated indigenous elite in search of qualified jobs and political representation. This diversification of Mexican society resulted in the emergence of new social agents that stood outside the corporatist channels of the national populist regime. Confronted by an increasingly closed political system, these protagonists became spokespersons for social reforms and identity claims similar to those of social movements in northern societies. The demand for democratization was often tinged with a certain simplistic ideology by those who claimed to be Marxist but made a point of indicating their rejection of armed combat. In addition, movements within the Catholic Church close to the post–Vatican II option in favor of the poor also thought highly of community organization. They actively supported such organizations in the form of grassroots religious communities and looked with favor on the indigenous communities, which they found to embody the spirit of early Christian communities. In a convergence of crosscurrents, these approaches to politics coincided in the 1980s with the arrival of neoliberal ideas, imported by the new technocratic elite trained in the United States. Such approaches were taken up by a political class eager to compensate for the erosion of patronage contacts and to find substitutes for the centralized corporatism that it no longer had the means to finance.

In Colombia, the situation was quite different. The state had never embodied a national-populist project and, therefore, had never served as the primary motor of economic development and (trans)formation of society. The liberal and conservative party networks of allegiance predated the development of the central government, unlike in Mexico, where the state was behind the creation of the PRI. In addition, the disintegration of the patronage system was, to a greater degree, due to the paralysis of a bipartisan system that was no longer capable of representing a society in the throes of profound change. Another factor should be cited: the increasing strength of irregular armed forces (guerrillas and paramilitary militia) and their control of whole regions of the nation, as well as the exponential increase, from the 1980s onward, of drug trafficking (the two phenomena being closely linked). The war economy and drugs provided alternative financial resources for patronage networks; the state and the political parties were reduced to competing on an equal footing with others for control of the territory and the monopoly of legitimate violence.

In both cases, the result was similar: a widespread conviction that alternative forms of territorial administration and political participation had to be found. Once again, in the two countries, protagonists whose motives were in no way similar appeared to converge, as if by design, on the same strategic objective: to create procedures and forums for collective debate. For some, these innovations would be the means to circumvent a swollen and corrupt government; for others, they would provide political institutions with renewed legitimacy. For the state itself, the quest for greater efficiency in the management of public funds (the quest to do better with less) corresponded with the aim of winning back a certain measure of legitimacy that the worn-out recipes of patronage were no longer capable of providing. From the viewpoint of the peripheral civilian agents (regional social movements, indigenous organizations, nongovernmental organizations), the ideal of local democracy, freed from the meddling of a patronage system deemed both unproductive and restrictive, suited their aim of finding better ways to handle the allocation of public funds, however sharply those funds might be reduced.

Finally, the decision by international financial sponsors to upgrade the level of credits and development aid helped turn the ideal of participatory democracy into a standard model and spread it throughout Latin America, in conjunction with the decentralizing reforms and new antipoverty programs being initiated. However, the influence of international organizations (such as the World Bank, the International Monetary Fund, the Inter-American Development Bank, and the United Nations Development Programme) and of multilateral organizations (the European Union and the Organization of American States) must not be overestimated. Although multilateral organizations played a crucial role in the spread of new standards of good governance—the fact that foreign aid was granted only if certain management techniques were adopted provided an aura of legitimacy—it would be a mistake to assume that the participatory norms and practices were dreamed up from nowhere by institutional experts and approved by government elites anxious to find favor with their generous benefactors.

The modes and techniques of governance were developed through a dialectical process that drew on diverse social and ideological currents (in this case, the grassroots ideology of popular movements of the 1970s and 1980s, the Christian and indigenous neocommunitarian movements, the neoliberal conception of a modest, decentralized state, and so on). These currents converged during a period of economic penury, a fact that rendered them all the more pertinent in that they promised both material and symbolic benefits. The international agency experts (some of whom had taken part in the antiestablishment movements of the preceding decade) brought with them ideas influenced by their experiences in the field. Their recommendations concerning the advantages (both political and financial) of direct citizen involvement in the administration of the decentralized public budgets were favorably received by top-ranking international civil servants. The approach also confirmed their own conclusions concerning the paralyzing nature of bloated state governments and the built-in corruption of state administrators and regional political leaders. From that point on, the actions undertaken by the international organizations had a snowball effect; decentralization and participation became the twin watchwords, extending to regions that had never known such procedures. When the United Nations pointed to the participatory budgeting process of Porto Alegre as a best practice, prompting its adoption by several cities in Latin America and elsewhere,[9] the effects of such feedback between local societies and international bodies became more apparent.

Vicissitudes of Participatory Decentralization in Indigenous Regions

A comparison between two regions heavily populated by indigenous communities (the state of Oaxaca[10] in Mexico and the Cauca department[11] in Colombia) illustrates the ambiguous results of decentralized participatory policies. In each case, the government transferred a portion of the national budget to the municipal authorities (traditional or not). The local authorities, in consultation with the inhabitants of the communities concerned, would determine the distribution of these funds. In both countries, these provisions were phrased in terms that vaunted the merits of a diversity of ethnocultural forms of expression, including a diversity of deliberative practices. In other words, the decisions concerning public spending would be made in accordance with traditional customs (the *usos y costumbres*). The rules governing transfers amounted to full-fledged acceptance of the diversity of participatory procedures. However, the terms in which acceptance was phrased considerably limited the leeway accorded the local authorities and local population. Nonetheless, the transfers did produce a new dynamic that reinvented community participatory traditions.

The Recognition of Traditional Local Institutions

In the Program for National Development, 1995–2000, Mexican President Ernesto Zedillo introduced the New Federalism as "the form of political organization best suited to reinforce democracy, reaffirm national unity, and promote a more balanced and just society" (Secretaría de Hacienda y Crédito Público 1995: 59). Included in the plan was a revamping of functions, responsibilities, and budgetary resources in favor of the federated states and the municipalities. Both the federated states and the municipalities were to benefit from greater prerogatives in fiscal matters; in particular, the administrative powers of the municipalities were reinforced. The federal congress passed a decree in August 1997 that made New Federalism the official government program. Unlike the PRONASOL, which embodied a form of decentralization that benefited civil society, New Federalism emphasized the redistribution of responsibilities and resources among the three levels of government. The reform that had been carried out in education and health care was extended to include other areas of public policy: social development, agriculture and rural planning, ecology and the management of natural resources, communications and transportation, tourism, energy, and agrarian reform. The program also provided for a complete overhaul of the fiscal system, ensuring an improved distribution of the federal budget and increased opportunities for the states and municipalities to raise their own tax receipts.

The *municipio* deserves particular attention. An increasing number of antipoverty programs were directly assigned to the municipalities through the Fondo de Desarrollo Social Municipal (Fund for Municipal Social Development, or FDSM). The FDSM took over the core programs that had been included in the Fondos Municipales de Desarrollo (Funds for Municipal Solidarity, or FMSs), which were created in 1989. These programs were designed to finance urban and rural infrastructure projects that opened up roads, built schools, installed systems for drinking water or irrigation, and so forth. The mode of operation was relatively simple: in each municipality, the authorities were required to set up a *consejo de desarrollo social municipal* (council for municipal social development, or CDSM),[12] which included representatives of the *agencias municipales*[13] along with representatives of local grassroots organizations, when appropriate. The mayor presided over the CDSM, which was responsible for consulting the inhabitants of the municipality about which public works were to be given priority. Projects were chosen from a "menu" similar to the one established for the FMSs. The menu included a fairly complete list of basic infrastructure equipment that could be financed with FDSM aid. The requirement that the inhabitants of each locality participate in the elaboration of the municipal development plan was thus clearly stated, but no explanation was furnished on the exact role this participation was to play in the decision-making process. Was it to be simply a question of asking the inhabitants for their opinion, with the municipal authorities (and particularly the mayor) keeping the real decision-making power? Or was it to be a genuine consultation, with the local authorities obliged to adhere to the assembly's recommendations? The question remained open. The result was the adoption of a wide range of procedures, with the collective deliberations accorded differing degrees of importance in the final decision.

In fact, in the indigenous regions of Oaxaca, the CDSM and the collective planning of public works were merely superimposed on the traditional procedures of community assemblies. In other words, the CDSM amounted to another name tag that, in the first instance, did not result in creating a new method but described what the authorities and the community were in the habit of doing. This traditional process of consultation was an inheritance of the colonial period, but one that had undergone profound transformations over the centuries. Contrary to what Indianist rhetoric and a certain school of *engagés* anthropologists would have us believe, the traditional forms of deliberation were, from the very beginning, hybrid in nature: the consensus method (*el acuerdo*) derived from the talk sessions of African society was often combined with the principle of majority rule determined by individual voting. The endless discussions among elders, during which everyone spoke simultaneously with the oldest and most respected member, produced a synthesis to which all the assembly members could agree. This tradition gradually gave way to a more systematic method of deliberation, whereby a number of spokespersons or opinion leaders presented their proposals in turn. The proposals were then submitted for general debate until one of them was adopted by majority vote, but not necessarily unanimously. The balance between the consensus principle and the majority vote principle could vary from one assembly to the next, depending on the issue that was to be decided, but unanimity was always an important community ideal. Thus, with regard to questions crucial for the survival of the community, such as mapping the land and determining its use, the authorities and the most prestigious leaders of the community were always called on to seek the solution that would, to the greatest degree possible, take into account every person's opinion. However, votes were always taken in the course of debate, even if they were simply a way of ratifying agreements that had already won majority approval. The vote itself could take various forms (raising hands, marking ticks on a blackboard, or using ballots), but it was almost always public (Recondo 2007b).

Procedures used in assembly decisions have a history that is rarely retraced by ethnologists eager to interpret them as vestiges of a pre-Columbian past. However, it is possible to trace how procedures developed and the uses to which they were put. Consultation as a decision-making method—one limited to the elders or those having occupied posts of responsibility (either religious or civil)—dates from the introduction of the *repúblicas de indios*[14] and the *cabildos*, corporate bodies that were supposed to represent the indigenous population and liaise with the colonial authorities from the

15th century onward. For nearly a century, the *cabildos'* duties were monopolized by a noble caste, descendants of former *caciques* or Indian chiefs. Gradually, the category of those who exercised these responsibilities was opened to all adult males of the community, commensurate with their contribution to the financing of Catholic rites. The hierarchical relations underwent change, and the assemblies soon began to function as forums for collective decision that were not limited to the authorities. In fact, the assemblies were no longer chosen by the elders but elected by all the adult members of the community. Before decentralization, the majority of public works in most indigenous municipalities were carried out by villagers in the form of community service. Widespread poverty contributed to the institutionalization of the community assemblies (open to all) as decision-making bodies, to the detriment of the *cabildo* or the council of elders. From the authorities' point of view, a decision applied only if the majority of the people were prepared to contribute to its implementation; the participation of community members was thus a way of guaranteeing that they would take part in implementing the measures adopted.

Deliberative procedures observed today in the indigenous communities of Oaxaca also bear the traces of the modifications introduced in 1930 by schoolteachers and the civil servants involved in agrarian reform. The formation of a quorum, the preparation of an agenda, the election of moderators and assessors at the start of each assembly, and the taking of minutes were procedures borrowed directly from the postrevolutionary agrarian assemblies set up to manage the *ejidos*, or community lands. They were also similar to the procedures governing the assemblies organized by the teacher's union. The ear-splitting cacophony described by the anthropologists gave way to mutual exchanges of opinions, closely controlled by rules of procedure destined to reassure the state representatives of the legality of the decisions made.

Thus, participatory decentralization was grafted onto these deliberative traditions, which were already the result of fusions. The CDSM is the equivalent of a *cabildo* sitting in full session. It convokes the community assembly at the start of each year to inform members of the amount of the annual budget. In certain municipalities, the authorities present their proposals, which are then voted on by the assembly; in other municipalities, the members themselves suggest the projects to be undertaken. In all cases, the projects are prioritized. The decisions are made by a vote, in which all the members participate, except the authorities who preside over the meeting. The minutes of the assembly are then annexed to the description of the projects selected and sent to the central administration for approval.

In Colombia, the process was similar. Decentralization took place in two stages. The procedures established by the 1986 reform (in particular, the local action juntas) were similar to the Mexican procedures, the only difference being an increased emphasis on consultation and supervision, rather than actual decision making. Nevertheless, a reform of this nature, as in Mexico, provided the opportunity to introduce (if the local authorities agreed) procedures for concerted programming of public funds. The process was a delicate one, depending mainly on the willingness of the mayors, who could ultimately ignore the recommendations of the juntas. Nonetheless, it represented a significant change, given that the Colombian government had always exercised highly centralized control. It was not until the new constitution came into effect in 1991 that participatory decentralization became one of the primary elements (at least in symbolic terms) of the country's political system. As mentioned earlier, the Colombian political system was known from then on as a participatory democracy. In this regard, it was the first Latin American country (before even Bolivia and the República Bolivariana de Venezuela) in which citizen participation, other than voting, was the established norm for government procedures on a nationwide level. The methods of democratic participation were stipulated in article 103 of the constitution: "elections, plebiscites, referendums, consultation of the people, open municipal councils, legislative initiative, and repeal of mandates" (Government of Colombia 1998: 51). At the local level, the open municipal council (*cabildo abierto*) served as the framework for citizens to share in the decisions made by the authorities. This disposition went well beyond the former juntas because, from this point on, public expenditures could not be programmed without the local population's agreement. On the face of it, the Colombian reform would appear to carry the process further than the reform in Mexico. Citizen participation in decisions was no longer simply an option, with the municipal authorities, promoted to the rank of the Mexican CDSMs, free to uphold or to ignore the recommendations formulated by the inhabitants summoned to the annual meeting. It would seem then that the standards set by the framers of Colombia's 1991 constitution went well beyond what had previously existed, whereas in Mexico (at least in the case of the indigenous municipalities) the recourse to village assemblies (analogous to *cabildos abiertos* in Colombia) was common practice even before decentralization was inaugurated.

The novelty of the Colombian participatory process was heightened by another key innovation: the creation and official recognition of *resguardos*, an institution of colonial origin akin to the Mexican *repúblicas de indios*. The traditional *cabildos* were granted a legal status that they did not possess before 1991. Statute 60, adopted in 1963, provided provisional guidelines for the functioning of these "indigenous territorial entities" and, in particular, for the management of the public funds that were transferred to them. A regional planning law (Ley de ordenamiento territorial) was supposed to be adopted at the same time, but in 2007, it still had not been passed. The current regulations have nonetheless made it possible for the *cabildos* to manage, through the municipalities or the departmental governments, the funds, over which they have sole control and which they can allocate as they please, in the areas specified by the law. As in Mexico, a menu of acceptable projects is drawn up, but the traditional authorities, within these fairly flexible limits and in consultation with the citizens of the *resguardo*, are free to elaborate their own spending programs. Unlike the Mexican case, however, it is explicitly stated that "citizen participation" must be implemented in accordance with the traditions of each *resguardo*—which means that no standard set of procedures has to be respected. In a strictly formal sense, the indigenous authorities are not required to go through the motions of setting up a CDSM, as is the case in Mexico. They only have to transmit their projects to the central administration of the municipality, without specifying the manner in which they have been decided.

In fact, in Cauca, traditional procedures are similar to those of the indigenous *municipios* of Oaxaca. These communities have long been familiar with assembly procedures; the most varied questions, touching on matters of general interest, are systematically submitted for discussion. The assemblies are broader based than the *cabildos*, which remain select, collegial groups. All eligible adults (including women in most cases) participate. It is these assemblies that decide the projects or public works to finance on the budget allocated to the *resguardo*. The methods of deliberating resemble those used in the Oaxaca communities; they are derived from the same hybrid origins, fashioned over time by successive borrowings and reformulations. Decisions are ratified by a roll call vote after lengthy discussions during which conflicting opinions—sometimes radically opposed—are presented in turn. Even if a consensus is the ideal, majority rule is sufficiently anchored in custom so that, in most cases, the vote determines which proposal will be selected, rather serving as an indication of unanimous agreement.[15]

Supervised Participation

Yet in Mexico and Colombia, participatory decentralization suffers from the same shortcomings: not only is there little leeway in choosing how funds are spent, but the higher-level administrative authorities (the state governors in Mexico; the mayors and departmental governors in Colombia) supervise the local authorities (the indigenous *municipios* and the *resguardos*). These two factors considerably limit the control that the assemblies exercise over the decisions to be made.

Even if, in Colombia, the list of areas in which the funds can be spent is more inclusive, the due dates for payments to be respected, and the accounting rules laid down by the central administration, create a situation similar to that in Mexico.[16] Because spending is on an annual basis, communities and community leaders tend to select construction projects that can be completed in less than a year since, unlike longer-term projects in, for example, education or agriculture, the results are easier to quantify. They also choose short-term, hard-built projects because local authorities generally have mandates that are brief (annual or triannual), and therefore there is no municipal administration capable of following up on long-term planning.

The case of Colombia is exceptional: the *resguardo* authorities cannot directly manage the budget that has been transferred. It is the mayor of the municipality in which the *resguardo* is situated (or, if the *resguardo* overlaps two departments, the governor of one of the departments) who is entitled to receive and administer the funds. The funds are undoubtedly placed in a separate account and reserved exclusively for each *resguardo*, but the *resguardo* officials cannot dispose of them without the authorization of the mayor or the governor in question. Once the *resguardo* assembly has established its spending program, the mayor must approve it. In principle, the mayor is supposed to verify only that the planned expenditures fall within the areas specified by law and to ensure that the money has been spent as planned. But *resguardo* officials often complain of the pressure exercised by mayors regarding the choice of projects or, in classic patronage style, the demands they make for political or material favors in return. For more than 10 years, community spokespersons have been asking that the *cabildos* and the *resguardos* be placed on the same footing as municipalities and be authorized to handle their budget in a totally independent manner.

In addition to the supervision by higher authorities, a second factor has acted to "parasitize" participatory procedures. Widespread patronage, in both Mexico and Colombia, still plays the determining role in political relations, despite the profound changes that the governments and the regimes of the two countries have undergone. Even if the majority of patronage networks have disbanded, patronage has not necessarily disappeared; on the contrary, it has intensified as the "bosses" acquire more autonomy and as resources diminish. The participatory provisions were often presented as a way to promote the development of a form of citizenship free from the shackles of patronage. It was thought that the deliberative assemblies would provide the solution, because they would bring together autonomous individuals (or at least individuals bound only by horizontal solidarity) who would convince their fellow citizens—or be convinced by them—on the basis of reasoned argument. However, this ideal, akin to Habermas's model of society, is far from the realities of the community in which the inequalities of social status and the relations of dependence combine to maintain a dense, fluid network of patronage ties. The forums for participation—in this case the assemblies—are not immune to the unequal balance of power and influence. In fact, the combination of decentralization policies and the bonus accorded to participatory methods of decision making has contributed to further multiply micronetworks of patronage that have found fertile breeding grounds in the relative autonomy of the *municipios* (in Mexico) and the *resguardos* (in Colombia).

New Forums for Deliberation

The joint policies of decentralization and promotion of citizen participation have had positive as well as negative effects on local deliberative procedures. The veneer of a new terminology, when applied to traditional procedures, has also contributed to the emergence of a new dynamic of participation and new areas for its implementation.

First, in certain cases, the allocation of financial resources, together with the regulations governing the participatory process, has breathed new life into participation by transforming the assembly from a gathering reserved for a limited number (elders, municipal officials, males, inhabitants of the central administrative district of the municipality, and so forth) into one that includes a sizable number of people who, until then, had been excluded from the decision-making process. It is true, for instance, of the Sierra Norte municipalities in Oaxaca or the Pacific coast municipalities. Until 1990, assemblies in those two regions were controlled by the municipal authorities, together with a few of the more affluent families with better political connections. The caciques or local "bosses" were commonplace, even if they had less power than their predecessors did between 1930 and 1970, when the institutionalization of the postrevolutionary regime was in full swing. In addition, the only assemblies that included a majority of citizens were those for designating the municipal authorities—once a year (Sierra Norte) or once every three years (Pacific coast). Even in the case of these assemblies, the level of attendance was often low. Most of the time, the assembly served only to ratify decisions that the community leaders and authorities had already made. It was not a genuine forum in which decisions were reached through deliberation. Whole sectors of the community were excluded from the assemblies: women, inhabitants of outlying districts, religious dissidents, and nonnatives. The citizens who had the right to speak and vote were therefore relatively few and did not represent the inhabitants of the municipality as a whole.

The rehabilitation, in 1995, of traditional methods of designating the municipal officials, followed by the participatory municipalization of that part of the federal budget earmarked for the development of basic infrastructures and antipoverty programs, contributed to revitalize the procedures of the community assemblies. The change did not always come about peacefully. On the contrary, in most, cases the marginalized elements of society mobilized to demand the right to examine the way in which the municipal budget was being distributed. The inhabitants of the outlying districts were the most vehement in this regard. For example, in Santiago Ixtayutla in the Pacific region, where the assembly was limited to about 12 inhabitants of the central district with close ties to the merchant families, the inhabitants of the outlying districts (who until then had been penalized by an arbitrary, unfair allocation of public resources) organized a vigorous protest movement in 1998 and 1999 that brought about a radical change in the assembly's prerogatives and mode of functioning.

This example is interesting because the struggle for participation in political decisions did not result in the rejection of local traditions but rather a reinvention of those traditions. The "candidates" for inclusion in decision making contrived new procedures for participation in the name of traditions that they accused their adversaries (the caciques) of having betrayed. Some authors have spoken of "the paradoxical invention of modernity" (Bayart 1996: 48) when describing the ways in which social, cultural, or political innovations have often been accompanied by invoking or "recycling" certain values and forms of behavior anchored in the past, although the past referred to might well have been "reconstructed or simply invented" (Bayart 1996: 48). This observation particularly holds true for Europe from the end of the 18th century onward. The development of the modern state and colonial expansion went hand in hand with "a process of ritualization and formalization" of "fragments of a more or less fantasized past" in both the mother country and the colonies (Bayart 1996: 49). The same holds true for contemporary Mexico. The insistence on identity recognition—and particularly the call for the defense of tradition—contributed to redefine the public arena and transform the political system.

Santiago Ixtayutla[17] is a particularly interesting example. Protesting against the municipal authorities' strict control over decision making, more than 2,000 inhabitants of the central administrative district and the outlying communities demanded that the elections be annulled and an assembly including "all the citizens of the *municipio*" be held.[18] The novel feature of this movement is that the protesters accused the outgoing mayor and his allies (both local and regional) of having violated community law in naming his successor.[19] It was rumored that the mayor (who had been designated, according to tradition, by the elders) had been assassinated—by bewitchment. In making their claims, the protesters were reaffirming that, before the caciques had changed the rules, elections were held in the following way: the elders named the municipal authorities, taking into account the careers of those who had already exercised community responsibilities. The choice was then submitted to a village assembly, whose role was to ratify the decisions already made by the elders, rather than to elect other candidates. Nothing had changed so far. The Ixtayutla procedures resembled those of most of the traditional rural and Indian *municipios*, in which the officials were designated by a relatively small group of elders and central district inhabitants. The protesters seemed to be siding with their adversaries when they declared that "traditionally the Ixtayutla communities do not take part in the election of authorities." "True," admitted one of their spokesmen, "but that's the way it was before the caciques broke community law." Since then, he continued, the caciques had corrupted the elders by offering them money or other material benefits to influence their decisions. To put an end to this corrupt tradition, the protesters proposed that the elections of municipal authorities be determined by an assembly that included all the communities of the *municipio* and that the elders "serve once again as counselors to the authorities."[20] What transpired was a perfect example of "the invention of a tradition" (Hobsbawm and Ranger 1993). The protesters claimed to be the defenders of a tradition that the caciques had violated, while inventing another tradition that had little basis in custom. The general community assembly is seen as a genuine forum for deliberation and election, and the elders are merely counselors and not the ones who decide. In other words, recourse to a form of legitimacy based on tradition provided a way to promote far more active and open citizen participation—including that of women—in the election of local authorities (Recondo 2007a: 156–79).

Whereas, in this case, the conflict was limited to the designation of municipal officials, it nonetheless formed part of a more general dynamic that has redefined the methods of community decision making. The protest movements have gone beyond election issues to embrace the whole conception of the purpose and functioning of deliberative procedures. In all such cases, decentralization, coupled with government recognition of traditional forms of participation, has contributed to foster this reinterpretation of political mores so as to make them more participatory.

Similar developments took place in the Cauca region of Colombia. The transfer of funds directly to the *resguardos* resulted in considerable restructuring within the communities. Although the situation varied greatly from one *resguardo* to the next, forums for deliberation took on renewed importance. From that time forward, investing in the deliberative process was worth the time and trouble, because it was a matter of selecting which projects and districts would benefit from the transferred funds. Simultaneously, the influx of public money fostered more competition for election to posts in the *cabildos* or in the associations that grouped together several *cabildos* and that were created to share the resources allocated by the central government. The very idea of what constituted power and how it was to be exercised was transformed by these developments. The posts carried with them not only symbolic rewards (prestige) but also material rewards: the indigenous authorities of the *resguardos* were in a position to derive personal profit from transactions (bribes, overbilling in allocating building contracts, and so forth) with the complicity of the regional authorities (the mayor or department governor) who were in charge of administering the funds. These types of arrangements became commonplace once the new administrative procedures were established.

However, the influx of money also stimulated the formation of organizations above the community level. In an area lying north of Popayán, in Cauca, the indigenous authorities created an association of *cabildos* (the *asociación de cabildos del norte del Cauca*), which included officials of several municipalities (Toribío, Jambaló, and Santander de Quilichao) and several *resguardos* of the region. Transmunicipal coordination enabled the association members to swing the balance of power with the department governor in their favor. In addition, the legal status of the association was such that it could negotiate supplementary budget transfers from the central administration, as well as from international organizations, such as the Inter-American Development Bank or the United Nations Development Programme. In this Cauca department, the indigenous authorities constructed what amounted to a participatory pyramid with three levels: *cabildos*, district councils, and regional councils. Every two years, the *cabildos* of each region of Cauca designate the delegates who will sit on the district council; the district council, in turn, chooses the delegates who are to become members of the Cauca Regional Indigenous Council. This system, established in 1990, now functions smoothly. It facilitates the coordination of projects and public policies that concern the totality of the indigenous districts, making the most of the funds that are transferred without the constraints that the narrowly focused policies of the *resguardos* imposed. At the same time, negotiations are conducted at every level of the pyramid, because the members of the district councils meet in assembly every year and a regional congress is held every four years. The regional council provides a fitting occasion for the indigenous authorities to draw up a four-year development plan.

Conclusion and Policy Recommendation

The comparison between the ways in which participatory decentralization has been implemented in the indigenous regions of southern Mexico and the ways in which it has been implemented in southwestern Colombia provides a striking example of the ambiguities inherent in the dissemination of political norms today. At first glance, the same hierarchical relations (between the central government and the local governments, but also between the local governments and civil society) and the same provisions for participatory planning of public expenditures appear to have been imposed on very different existing political procedures. With similar conditions set for the distribution of development funds, one could conclude that the result would conform to a single model with identical decision-making procedures, which were technical and managerial in nature rather than political. Yet a closer analysis reveals the complex ways in which the new procedures for participation in decision making have been appropriated and developed on the basis of traditional models that are themselves in constant mutation. The development and implementation of participatory procedures then appear as a complex set of interactions between protagonists (on the local, state, and international levels) and the wide range of political practices they bring to bear. Finally, none of the actors and the practices involved emerges unaffected by the hybridization of participatory cultures that these complex transactions produce.

The comparison also provides a second lesson. Paradoxically, it is in Colombia, where the official pronouncements concerning participatory democracy are the most eloquent and frequent, that local decision making is more closely supervised by the higher levels of government. In Mexico, where the purely administrative aspects of decentralization have taken precedence over the participatory element, the municipalities have been able to breathe new life into their deliberating procedures, while maintaining a conventional façade for the benefit of outside observers.

What lessons can be drawn from this comparative analysis? Beyond procedural and mere institutional design, some practical observations arise:

1. Development agencies should not think in relation to "best practice." Participative decentralization is certainly a necessary means to promote social development, but no standard model will likely be suitable to all regional and local contexts worldwide. Therefore, any development strategy should acknowledge local and specific conceptions and practices of governance and should avoid exporting a standard model elsewhere as a turnkey solution. Only a bottom-up process of participatory decision making is likely to create the basis for a more even and sustainable development. Ready-made devices, imported and imposed by central governments onto local constituencies, cannot lead to any virtuous change.

2. The bottom-up focus of development strategies should not neglect the importance of the state and the need for a legitimate central government that is capable of steering the overall process of territorial development. Decentralization paradigms should not be conceived as a means to bypass the state, but rather to consolidate it. In Latin America, like in most countries of Sub-Saharan Africa, decentralization has had the negative effect of further undermining already feeble states. The overall concept of "stateness" should therefore be considered more thoroughly.

3. Any development promotion strategy should overtly consider power and politics. Decentralization and participation are not just about reducing bureaucracy and making it more efficient. Above all, they are a matter of power sharing and should be considered as such. The participation paradigm must therefore be linked to an institutional design that guarantees transparency and accountability in public management, so as to prevent the exacerbation of patronage and corruption.

4. Any sustainable development requires a constant and lengthy process of external assistance. The latter should be conceived as a real (not just

rhetorical) accompaniment to the strategies set up by the local actors to promote development. International, multilateral, and bilateral assistance have often been applied on a short-term basis. Long-term aid, equivalent to at least a generation, is essential to enable the socialization—and therefore overall acceptance—of new "traditions."

Notes

1. Article 115 of the Mexican federal constitution determines the organization and attributions of the *municipios* (municipalities). See Instituto Federal Electoral (2000: 103–10).
2. The PRONASOL, an antipoverty program established in 1988 by Carlos Salinas de Gortari, was intended primarily for the construction of basic infrastructures in the underdeveloped regions (urban or rural) that were most in need.
3. New Federalism was a national program of decentralization and social policy. Contrary to the PRONASOL, which advocated, above all, a form of decentralization that would benefit civil society, the New Federalism program emphasized the reallocation of responsibilities and resources among the three levels of the federation (the central government, the federated states, and the *municipios*). The reforms in education and health care were expanded to cover other public programs: social development, agriculture and rural development, ecology and the management of natural resources, communications and transportation, tourism, energy, and agrarian reform. In addition, the program provided for in-depth reform of the fiscal system to ensure a better distribution of the federal budget and grant the states and municipalities the means to raise tax revenues of their own.
4. Law 11 was enforced following the municipal elections of 1988. Until then, the mayors had been named by the state governors. Until 1991, state governors were named by the president of the republic.
5. The law created *juntas de acción local* (local action juntas, or JALs) in the recently created inframunicipal subdivisions called *comunas* (in the urban municipalities) or *corregimientos* (in the rural municipalities). JALs consist of seven members, who are elected by universal suffrage. Among other duties, JAL members are expected to propose projects for inclusion in the municipal planning and to supervise the functioning of public services. The law also included provisions for "consultation of the people" and "municipal referendums."
6. The term *resguardo* refers to a colonial institution that set aside parcels of land consisting of several hectares; previously, these areas were mostly inhabited by Indians, who enjoyed a certain degree of government autonomy, as well as collective control over land use. One or more *resguardos* can be included within one municipality or can straddle two municipalities or even two departments.

The number of *resguardos* has constantly risen since they were first written into the constitution. The most recent statistics available list 638 *resguardos* covering nearly 300,000 square kilometers, close to one-fourth of the nation's territory (1,141,748 square kilometers).

7. Literally, "open municipal council," *cabildo abierto* refers to municipal council meetings that are open to all inhabitants of the municipality in question.

8. The liberal party and the conservative party took turns occupying the presidency and shared the administrative posts between them.

9. Porto Alegre's participatory budget was considered by the United Nations as one of the 40 most commendable urban innovations in the world and was singled out by the Habitat II Conference in Istanbul in 1996. This conference included the adoption of participatory budgets as one of its recommendations.

10. Oaxaca is one of the 32 federated states of Mexico; it is situated in southern Mexico, bordering the state of Chiapas. It has a population of 3.5 million, of which roughly 50 percent (1.2 million) are Indian (INEGI 2000).

11. Cauca is one of Colombia's 33 departments; it is situated southwest of Bogotá and has a population of 1.3 million, of which 15 percent (190,069) are Indian (DNP 2001).

12. *Consejo de desarrollo social municipal.*

13. The Mexican municipalities are subdivided into administrative districts called *agencias municipales* or *agencias de policía*, depending on the number of inhabitants. In the rural municipalities, they are most often villages that are independent of the central municipal district. The village inhabitants meet in assembly to choose their authorities, as is the custom in the central administrative districts. Neither the mayor nor the council members of the central district have any say in the village elections.

14. The *repúblicas de indios*, or Indian republics, are a sort of substitute for the *municipios* in regions where the Indian population is in the majority.

15. Definitions of citizenship vary from one community to the next. As a general rule, a person is a citizen (which entails both the right and the obligation to attend community assembly meetings) if he is the head of a household (adult or not) having fulfilled the collective community requirements (community work, dues, and so forth). The participation of women varies greatly. In certain municipalities, they have been citizens since 1930 or 1940; elsewhere, it is only recently that they have acquired the right to deliberate and vote in the village assemblies. Today, in Oaxaca, women are active citizens in 70 percent of the traditional *municipios*. See Velásquez Cepeda (2000).

16. The funds transferred to the *resguardos* are invested in everything from education to land acquisition, including the financing of basic infrastructure, improvements to living conditions, culture, justice, or institutional development. See the official site of the Departamento Nacional de Planeación (National Planification Department), http://www.dnp.gov.co/, under the heading "Desarrollo territorial".

17. This municipality is nestled in the mountains close to the Pacific coast.
18. See the January 16, 1999, edition of *Noticias* (a regional daily newspaper).
19. See the January 18, 1999, edition of *Cantera* (a regional daily newspaper).
20. See the January 18, 1999, edition of *Cantera* (a regional daily newspaper).

References

Bayart, J. F. 1996. *L'illusion identitaire*. Paris: Fayard.

DNP (Departamento Nacional de Planeación). 2001. *Población y área indígena por departamento*. Bogotá: DNP.

Government of Colombia. 1998. *Constitución Política de Colombia*. Bogotá: 3R Editores.

Hobsbawm, E., and T. Ranger. 1993. *The Invention of Tradition*. New York: Cambridge University Press.

INEGI (Instituto Nacional de Estadística Geografía e Informática). 2000. *XII Censo general de población y vivienda*. Mexico City: INEGI.

Instituto Federal Electoral. 2000. *Constitución Política de los Estados Unidos Mexicanos*. Mexico City: Instituto Federal Electoral.

Recondo, D. 2007a. "From Acclamation to Secret Ballot: The Hybridisation of Voting Procedures in Mexican-Indian Communities." In *Cultures of Voting: The Hidden History of the Secret Ballot*, ed. R. Bertrand, J.-L. Briquet, and P. Pels, 156–79. London: CERI-Hurst.

———. 2007b. *La política del gatopardo: Multiculturalismo y democracia en Oaxaca*. Mexico City: Ediciones de la Casa Chata (CEMCA-CIESAS).

Secretaría de Hacienda y Crédito Público. 1995. "Plan nacional de desarrollo 1995–2000." Secretaría de Hacienda y Crédito Público, Mexico City.

Velásquez Cepeda, M.-C. 2000. *El nombramiento: Las elecciones por usos y costumbres en Oaxaca*. Oaxaca, Mexico: Instituto Estatal Electoral.

Policy Reform and Culture Change: Contesting Gender, Caste, and Ethnic Exclusion in Nepal

Lynn Bennett

What actors *believe* may be just as important as what they *want*.
—John L. Campbell (2004: 90)

This chapter examines an ongoing collaborative effort by the World Bank and the U.K. Department of International Development (DFID). The objective of this collaboration has been to influence public policy in Nepal toward greater gender, caste, and ethnic inclusion and to support the government of Nepal in the messier, longer-term process of implementing these policies and trying to make them a reality on the ground. Those who have worked on social policy in South Asia know that the formal laws and policies are often equitable and even progressive, reflecting increasingly shared global norms of social justice. Yet the mechanisms and incentive regimes through which these laws and policies are supposed to change the behavior of the dominant groups and increase access to opportunity for the subordinate groups are rarely given the necessary attention. Nor is there sufficient focus on understanding the configuration of ideas and interests that drives the current inequitable structure of power and opportunity or on supporting the emergence of alternative ideas and new alignments of interests.

As a result, the oft-cited "implementation gap" yawns between what is on the books and what happens on the ground. Because the nuts and bolts of implementation and accountability for results have not been spelled out, old ideas and interests fill the gap with business as usual. This chapter examines the interests and the ideas that have supported centuries of

197

gender, caste, and ethnic discrimination in Nepal and the ways in which these interests and ideas have been changing over the six decades since the fall of the autocratic Rana regime in 1951. Because the author's background is in anthropology rather than economics or political science and because the realm of ideas and meaning systems and their influence on policy outcomes has generally been given less attention, less stress will be laid on the interests of various Nepali actors (what they want) than on their ideas (what they believe) and how these ideas are changing.

The Nepal Gender and Social Exclusion Assessment and the DFID Social Inclusion Action Program

The first phase of the World Bank–DFID collaboration, which began in 2002, has just been completed (box 8.1). It focused on producing the Nepal Gender and Social Exclusion Assessment (GSEA). DFID met part of the costs for a World Bank lead anthropologist to collaborate with the National Planning Commission (NPC) on framing the issue and forming the assessment team. DFID, the World Bank, and the Danish government supported a series of studies, including primary research,[1] by a team of primarily Nepali researchers, many of them from excluded groups. As the results of these studies emerged, they were submitted for discussion and review by stakeholders from each of the excluded groups and policy makers at different levels, in a series of more than a dozen workshops.

BOX 8.1

Ingredients for Influencing through the Policy Research Process

1. *Choosing the team.* Though it is good to bring in international perspectives on some issues, it is even more important to engage local researchers for most of the work and to go beyond the "usual suspects"—that is, those who generally consult for the World Bank and other international donors. The GSEA used some scholars who are well known in development circles in Nepal but also drew on academics, activists, journalists, and writers—people who did not always produce a standard product but had independent ideas, deep commitment to the issue, and credibility with a broad range of citizens. The GSEA also ensured that the team was diverse in terms of caste,

(continued)

BOX 8.1

Ingredients for Influencing through the Policy Research Process (*continued*)

gender, and ethnicity. Thus, an excellent editorial team was necessary to pull the diverse contributions and the different styles together into a single report.

2. *Creating the DFID–World Bank partnership.* The collaboration between DFID and the World Bank brought together the comparative advantages of each agency and underlined the seriousness with which each views the issue of social exclusion.

3. *Taking time and paying attention to the process, with continuous stakeholder consultation, debate, and dissemination.* Twelve consultation workshops were held during the process. Different stakeholder groups and team members gave many informal presentations on the inclusion framework.

4. *Developing data stories.* Narratives are important, but they are much more powerful when backed by numbers. National datasets were reanalyzed by caste, gender, and ethnicity, and additional primary research was carried out to generate some of these data stories.

5. *Creating logical and more manageable classifications of caste and ethnic groupings.* The 103 social groups included in the last census were reorganized into seven major groups. The "other" category, which had accounted for 20 percent of the population (and nearly all of the most vulnerable ethnic groups with fewer than 10,000 members), was reduced to only 1 percent. This grouping has been adopted by the Central Bureau of Statistics.

6. *Working on multiple levels, from the national and sector policy levels to the nitty-gritty of implementation.* A key is for team members to be able to contribute to all aspects of the country program from the perspective of inclusion. Social inclusion became a key pillar of both the DFID Country Assistance Programme and the World Bank Country Assistance Strategy. The messages of the GSEA were reinforced in the Poverty Reduction Support Credit's concern with affirmative action in the civil service and in the health and primary education sectorwide approaches, where indicators of inclusive access have become key to the release of tranches.

7. *Internal outcome monitoring.* Based on the GSEA conceptual framework, DFID has developed and implemented a system of livelihoods and social inclusion monitoring for all its programs. All DFID-supported programs now report on what they are doing to (a) increase assets and services for the excluded, (b) increase the voice and influence of the excluded, and (c) change the rules of the game in terms of policies and implementation mechanisms that create a more level playing field for women, Dalits, Janajatis, and Madhesis.

The GSEA report[2] examines gender, caste, and ethnicity as three interlocking factors that influence individual and group access to assets, capabilities, and voice based on socially defined identity. After presenting the historical and sociocultural background (including the caste system), the report examines the links between poverty (economic, human development, and political) and social exclusion. It draws first on national data (reanalyzed by caste, ethnicity, and gender) and then presents the results of primary research that measures empowerment and social inclusion and is based on a survey carried out in 60 villages. This research clearly documents the persistence of caste, ethnic, and gender hierarchies and the link with poverty in rural Nepal. The GSEA then examines how state and civil society institutions have responded to social exclusion and to political and social changes in contemporary Nepal. Separate chapters are devoted to examining exclusion in the law and in the education and health sectors. Two approaches to more inclusive governance are also examined: one from the bottom up (local self-help and user groups and federations of these groups) and one from the top down (affirmative action). Finally, strategies and actions are identified to promote progress toward a more inclusive and equitable society.

The analytical framework of the GSEA sees pro-poor social change as a result of action from below to empower the poor and socially excluded, as well as action from individuals within the power structure to bring greater equity and inclusion to the institutions that determine access to assets, opportunity, and voice for different social groups. It highlights three domains of change through which donors can support governments and civil society actors in bringing about greater inclusion:

- Improving access to assets and services for the poor and excluded
- Increasing voice and influence of the poor and excluded
- Supporting changes in the rules of the game, which have always favored the elite.

The second phase of the DFID–World Bank collaboration is the three-year Social Inclusion Action Program. Conceived as a means of following up on the recommendations to government and civil society in the GSEA and deepening the focus on inclusion in DFID's other programs, this program is being reformulated to make it more responsive to the recent political changes in Nepal—and to take advantage of the increased interest in "inclusive democracy" after the people's power movement in April 2006 forced the king to hand power back to Parliament and opened the way for peace talks with the Maoist insurgents.

Looking at the Process

This chapter does not deal extensively with the findings of the GSEA, although some of the most important data stories documenting the link between social exclusion and different dimensions of poverty have been summarized in boxes 8.2 and 8.3, and a few key policy recommendations are also discussed in the final section. Rather, the idea is to shed light on the process of social policy change by tracing the emergence of new ideas and institutional forms that have entered the national discourse since Nepal opened up to outside influences after the fall of the Rana regime. At the time of writing, the rebel Maoists have been brought into an interim government in preparation for elections to a Constituent Assembly that will formulate a new state structure and lead to the election of a new government.

Nepal stands at the confluence of three worldviews or systems of meaning: one based on mutually reinforcing caste, feudal, and patriarchal hierarchies; another based on Marxist and Maoist ideology; and a third mélange of postenlightenment ideas about democracy, the rule of law, competition, accountability, civil liberties, and human rights. The outcome is unpredictable. These different and often mutually incompatible ideas are circulating in the minds of diverse Nepali citizens with diverse interests, levels of education and exposure, and power bases. As the peace process unfolds, Nepal will forge from this fluid mix of ideas and actors a new social contract between the state and its citizens. This contract will not be a path-dependent replication of Nepal's past, but neither will it be a radical break. It will not be entirely homegrown, nor will it be taken lock, stock, and barrel from outside. Rather, it will be something uniquely Nepali that has been negotiated, contextualized, and creatively reinvented from these ingredients.

What lies ahead for Nepal can be viewed as policy reform at the most fundamental level. Many dimensions of the social contract need to be worked out, but the focus here is on the social policies Nepal will need to establish to overcome the persistent legacy of interconnected caste, ethnic, and gender-based exclusions. Although *policy reform* sounds technocratic, almost any policy reform that takes hold is part of the deeper and more mysterious process of cultural and institutional change. The

BOX 8.2

Caste and Ethnic Dimensions of Poverty in Nepal

Poverty headcount dropped 11 points between 1996 and 2004—from 42 percent to 31 percent. Moreover, poverty has dropped across regions, quintiles, rural and urban populations, and caste and ethnic groups. However, as the accompanying figure shows, there are major differences by caste and ethnic groups.

Poverty Headcounts by Caste and Ethnicity in Nepal, 1995–96 and 2003–04

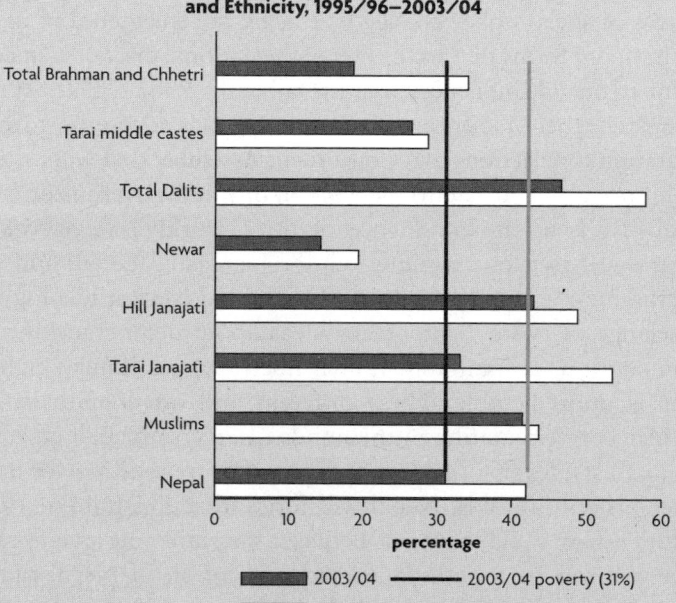

Trends in the Incidence of Poverty by Caste and Ethnicity, 1995/96–2003/04

Source: Based on data from the National Living Standards Survey II, 2003/04, Gajurel.

The result is a caste penalty: per capita household consumption in Brahman and Chhetri households is 42 percent higher than in Dalit households. Is this just because of differences in background variables such as location (urban or rural and the region), education, occupation, dependency ratio, landholdings, and remittance income? Not entirely. Even controlling for all these factors, per capita income is still 15 percent lower in Dalit households than in Brahman and Chhetri households. This "caste penalty" translates to Rs 4,853 less per person per year. Muslim and Janajati households face similar penalties of 13 percent and 14 percent, respectively.

Source: World Bank and DFID 2006: 21.

BOX 8.3

Political Poverty: Participation in Governance

Efforts to increase women's participation in elected government after 1990 have largely failed. Women have never gained more than 6 percent of the seats in the lower house. Even in the upper house, where members are appointed, their proportion has mostly hovered at 5 percent. They make up only 7.1 percent of the Communist (Unified Marxist-Leninist) Central Committee membership and 9.6 percent and 7.3 percent, respectively, of the central committees of the Nepali Congress and rightist Rastriya Prajatantra Party. At the level of local government, the law mandates that one of the five ward committee members and 20 percent of the municipality members be women, but in the more pow-erful village development committees and district committees and councils, women's representation falls to between 3 percent and 7 percent. Women make up roughly 8 per-cent of the civil service and less than 1 percent of the officers at and above first-class level. Their representation in the executive and judiciary branches is even lower.

During the Panchayat period and the first 10 years of multiparty democracy, Brahmans and Chhetris were able to maintain a presence in the legislature of about 60 percent (see the accompanying figure), and Newars maintained a presence of just under 10 percent. Janajati and Madhesi presence is limited and does not match their proportions in the population. Dalits, however, are almost entirely absent from Parliament and have had only one representative during the multiparty period. Given the dominance of the Brah-man and Chhetri group in the legislature, it is not surprising that men from that group have continued to dominate cabinet appointments. Their domination has also increased in civil service—from 70 percent to 90 percent between 1985 and 2002.

Ethnic, Caste, and Gender Representation in the Nepali Parliament, 1959–99

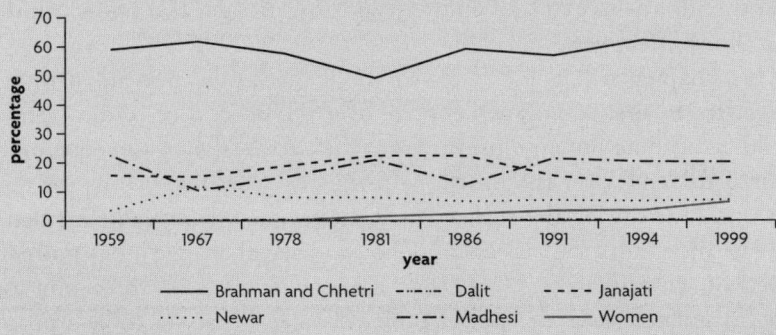

Source: Lawoti 2002.

(continued)

BOX 8.3

Political Poverty: Participation in Governance (*continued*)

Applicants to civil service positions are also overwhelmingly (83 percent) Brahman and Chhetri. Candidates from this group are more than twice as likely to be chosen as Newars, nearly three times more likely than Janajatis, and more than four times more likely than Dalits. The pattern extends to the judiciary; the Brahman and Chhetri and the Newar groups hold virtually all positions.

Source: World Bank and DFID 2006: 31–32.

shape that such reforms take is invariably influenced by local contexts and by the creative agency of individuals and groups, be they blockers or champions of the reform in question. Therefore, the outcomes of policy reforms are often far less predictable than development practitioners like to admit. It is increasingly clear that successful policy reform, be it economic, sectoral, political, or social, must address not only the formal rules and procedures that are written down and enforced by law, but also the thicket of informal behaviors and deep-seated norms, values, and networks of political alliances and obligations that stand between the formal policy statement and its actual implementation. In short, successful policy change is social change.

Once the nontechnical political and cultural dimensions of policy change are recognized, several extremely difficult questions follow. Can cultural change be induced consciously? Should DFID, the World Bank, and other donors try to contribute to cultural change? If so, how can they do so most effectively?

This chapter will come back to these questions, but an instinctive answer to the first is no. Such control over the process of cultural change would be nothing but an illusion. From the perspective of someone on the ground in Nepal over the past four turbulent years (as well as for more than a decade during the earlier Panchyat regime when the king ruled as absolute monarch), the process of policy and social change looks more like a kind of self-organizing chaos than a linear progression through a logically formulated series of "public policy choices." It seems to be a process through which many individual change entrepreneurs and stakeholder groups come to realize that the current institutional configuration is no longer tenable and needs to be changed. This realization can come about as a result of increasingly apparent internal contradictions, the emergence of violent conflict, or external economic, political, or ideological shocks—or some combination of these, as has happened in Nepal. In a process that Campbell (2004) calls "bricolage," these change entrepreneurs draw on the existing stock of institutional logics or "rules of the game," either locally available or sometimes brought in from elsewhere. They put these pieces together in a new way to create and negotiate new rules of the game that better suit their interests and values. The process of negotiation involves not only being able to make an effective case for change on the cognitive and normative level to the general public but also understanding the prevailing configuration of power—that is, whose interests will be threatened by the change and whose might possibly be served by it. A critical aspect of the policy reform and social change process is being able to forge pragmatic alliances by linking the new institutional logic with the interests of those who are in a position to implement it.

Looking at Institutions

Institutions are critical to equity and prosperity because they establish the distributional rules of the game: they structure access to the assets, capabilities, and opportunities that allow people to meet their needs, manage risks, and make progress toward achieving their aspirations. This chapter follows North's definition of institutions as the "formal rules of the game in a society, or the humanly devised constraints that shape human interaction" (North 1990: 45). However, the focus here is on the dimensions of meaning and value and the power differentials that are embodied and perpetuated by institutions. Thus, the game metaphor is extended to address such questions as these: Why do people play this game? What is the prize for winning? Who sets the rules, and who is the referee?

As with North's (1990) concept (which includes codes of conduct, norms of behavior, and conventions, the concept of institution used here overlaps to a significant degree with at least certain concepts of culture. The practical notion of culture presented by Rao and Walton (2004) is useful in understanding culture in relation to development. These authors view culture as fundamentally "about relationality—about the dynamics of relationships between individuals within groups, between groups, and between ideas and perspectives" (Rao and Walton 2004: 4). They also understand culture as continually contested and subject to change: Culture "is not a set of primordial phenomena permanently embedded within national or religious groups, but rather a set of contested attributes, constantly in flux, both shaping and being shaped by social and economic aspects of human interaction" (Rao and Walton 2004: 4).

In most of the world today (and certainly in Nepal), we encounter inequitable institutions. The distributional rules of the game vary for diverse individuals and groups on the basis of their social identity. This observation may sound discouraging, but our knowledge of the reciprocal relationship between people and their institutions gives us hope. People are born at a certain time and place into the complex web of institutions that not only largely determine their initial asset endowments but also shape their thinking and behavior—even how they think of themselves and the kind of future they are able to imagine for themselves and their children. Yet these same institutions have themselves been created by people and are continually contested by other people. The fluidity of the situation is what saves the process of institutional change from total path dependency and opens the way for human agency and the possibility of transformational change.

Many of these overlapping institutions reinforce each other, sometimes in negative ways. However, institutions can also compete with each other for legitimacy and power, thus opening up space for structural change. Individuals and groups that are disadvantaged in some way by the prevailing distributional rules under one institutional setup continually use these competing institutions to negotiate ways to meet their own needs and aspirations. Because they are socially constructed, institutions are dynamic. Hence, inequitable distributional rules established by one or even a set of interlocking institutions can be negotiated and changed.

During the Shah-Rana era (1768–1951), Nepal had no alternative institutions or ideologies backed by any economic and political power equivalent to the feudal regime. Especially during the rule of the Rana oligarchy (1846–1951), the Nepali caste system and the patriarchal gender system of the dominant group were reinforced by the state. It was an era of consolidation of power and entrenchment of social inequity, as can occur when competing worldviews lack sufficient political and economic power to challenge the dominant view.

Both formal and informal institutions shape the opportunity structure within which individuals and groups must act. Formal institutions have written rules encoded in law and so are ultimately backed by the power of the state. Thus Nepal's laws governing marriage, citizenship, and inheritance; the policies that structure the public education or health systems; the court system; and the regulations that shape the national and local systems of elected government are all formal institutions. The informal institutions include behaviors, values, and norms that are deeply embedded in Nepal's particular social and historical context. They include much of what are often referred to as the "sociocultural context." The caste system is one of these informal institutions, although, as noted previously, until 1963 it was also a formal system backed by the law of the land (see figure 8.1). Other informal systems operating in Nepal include the various gender systems of different social groups and the hangover of feudal patronage networks and expectations that still influence the way more formal government organizations and institutions work.

One of the most ingrained of the informal rules of the game, identified in table 8.1, is the *binti* system. *Binti* means a request or favor asked of a powerful person by someone lower in the hierarchy. The cognitive logic behind this system is that if you are obedient and loyal to those above you (your parents, your husband, your landlord, a government official,

Figure 8.1. Caste and Ethnic Dimensions of Poverty: The Caste Hierarchy in Nepal under the 1854 Muliki Ain

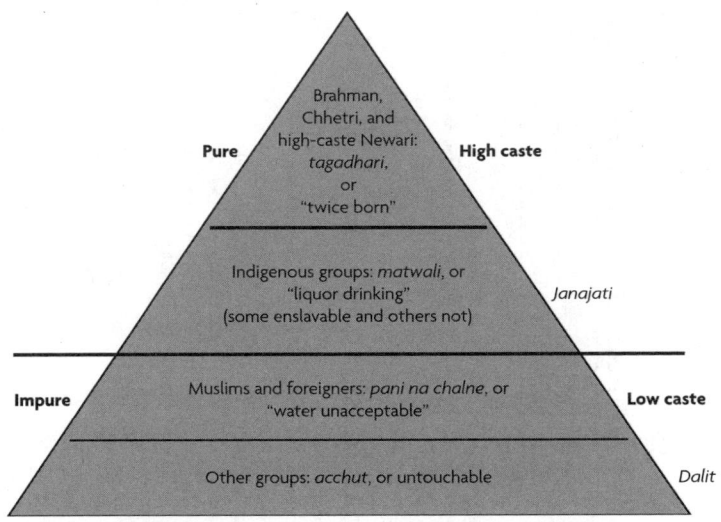

Source: World Bank and DFID 2006: 6.

Table 8.1. Transformation of Cognitive Logic and Values and Shifts in Formal Institutions and Political Power

Power configuration	Formal rules of the game	Informal rules of the game	
	Legal and policy regime	Cognitive logic	Norms and values
Feudal-religious configuration: The Shah-Rana regime (1768–1951) is a feudal, land-based economic and political system backed by a normative system of Hindu patriarchal and caste hierarchy. Little space exists for competition of institutions.	The *Mulki Ain*, or Country Code, formulated in 1854, unifies the Nepali nation by using the Hindu caste system as an organizing principle. Legalized inequality is established on the basis of gender, caste, and ethnicity. Diverse indigenous ethnic groups are incorporated into the caste hierarchy in the middle rungs.	• If an individual is obedient and loyal to those above him or her (parents, husband, landlord, king, gods), they will take care of the individual, but fair treatment cannot be expected. • People and gods are organized in a hierarchy based on their relative ritual purity. • Purity creates power by disciplining and controlling desires and needs of the body (for example, sex and eating). The stricter the behavior, the purer and more powerful the person or group becomes. • The king (*sarkar*) is the state (*sarkar*). • The individual is a subject to the state. • The individual can do little in his or her lifetime to improve circumstances, which are determined by *karma*, or actions in past lives. Obedience to *dharma*, or the precepts of religion, in this life will lead to a better rebirth in the next.	• Personal ritual purity pleases the gods and is a legitimate basis for higher social and political status. • Those lower in the hierarchy should respect and obey those above them. • Those in higher positions have a duty to look after those in lower positions. • Women should be modest (show *laaj*, or shame) about their bodies and sexuality. • Janajatis should accept their status below the "twice-born" Hindus. • Low castes should be obedient, make sure they avoid polluting those above them, and stick to their caste-specific occupation. • At the same time, philosophically, all humans are recognized as part of the Supreme Being, or *Atma*, and caste, gender, and other distinctions are recognized as illusion.

Competition between democratic and feudal institutions (1951–2006)	• The 1953 and 1990 constitutions speak of caste, gender, ethnic, and religious equality, but contradictions remain. The 1990 constitution also transforms the king into a constitutional monarch, but the king still controls the army, and ambiguities allow resumption of absolute rule. • The state is described as a Hindu kingdom. • Nepal opens up to diplomatic and foreign aid missions and from the 1960s on becomes more and more heavily aid dependent. Over time, a group of foreign-educated "technocrats" in the government begins to coalesce around an economic reform agenda and to wish to see government rather than donors setting the development agenda.	• Old cognitive logic continues to dominate behavior of most Nepalis in state as well as societal relations. • The belief that individual lives are determined by karma is challenged by hope for improvement in this life based on individual effort and public policies and programs. • The idea of merit rather than just loyalty becomes source of pride to at least some civil servants. • More young people are educated and exposed to other modes of behavior: in social service clubs like the Rotary Club and Jaycees; through newspapers, television, and the Internet; through merit-based opportunities for education abroad under the Colombo Plan and Fulbright; and through Peace Corps and other young volunteers, development workers, and tourists. • Maoists radically reject old feudal, patriarchal, and caste-based social, economic, and political relationships and ways of doing business. • Mainstream parties and civil service resist entrance of women, Janajatis, Dalits, and Madhesis—and many NGO workers continue to practice the old behavior by favoring seniority, members of their own caste, and family members despite democratic rhetoric.	• Tacit beliefs and values of dominant Hindu worldview remain strong in most areas. • Among the middle class, emphasis on ritual aspects of the Hindu belief declines, but hierarchic power relations and interpersonal behavior remain strong in many areas. • Ideas about democracy and equal citizen's rights are taking hold. • In gender relations, especially in urban areas and through women's self-help groups in rural areas, change is evident. • The Hindu hierarchy is challenged by the Maoist ideology of radical equality and economic redistribution. • The government is expected to provide civil liberties, follow democratic norms, and be accountable to the electorate. • Discourse on human rights is widely understood and accepted. • Little emphasis is placed on the individual and group obligations that need to accompany rights. • A tendency exists to turn the party or the state into the all-powerful benefactor or patron.

Source: Author's representation.

the king, or the gods), those above you will take care of you. They may not treat you with respect and their favor is uncertain and must be constantly cultivated, but you will be in safe "in the shade of a great tree," to paraphrase a Nepali saying.

For Nepalis, *binti* and many of the institutions, values, and norms in the two right-hand columns of table 8.1 are simply accepted as the natural way of doing things. Changes in these ways of thinking, behaviors, and values generally lag the more rapid shifts in the configuration of power and even in the formal legal and institutional regimes, often by decades and in some cases even by centuries. Most contemporary polities reveal a volatile "soup" of different cognitive logics and different ideas of what is right and how people should behave toward each other. Some individuals and groups will remain attached to older worldviews, perhaps out of self-interest or simply because of lack of exposure. Other groups will seize certain aspects of new ideas—often those that favor their own interests—but ignore others that entail new obligations. The process of negotiating change will span generations, even when there is a broadly accepted social contract.

Central to the GSEA analysis is the idea that individuals and groups are defined—and define themselves—in terms of the multiple layers of institutions that surround them. Exclusion and disempowerment take place at various levels. One level is the psychological: within the mind of the individual, where negative or positive definitions of identity are internalized. To a large extent, the rules, norms, beliefs, and behaviors laid down by institutions define who the individual is, how that individual is valued by society, and what that individual can or cannot do. In Nepal, because these institutions have been defined primarily by the dominant male high-caste group, they can be very disempowering for a woman, a Dalit, or a member of a linguistic or religious minority.

Critical sites of empowerment and social inclusion may vary for different categories of marginalized people (figure 8.2). For example, for women, the home is a key site where norms, beliefs, and behaviors have to be changed to enable them to exercise their agency. Community norms and formal national laws must also be changed, but change in the domestic site is fundamental. For Dalits, the local community is where caste-based discrimination is likely to be most strongly enforced and harshly experienced. However, Dalit women, subordinated in both the gender and the caste domains, encounter discrimination in the home as well as in the community and the state.

Figure 8.2. Sites of Empowerment and Inclusion

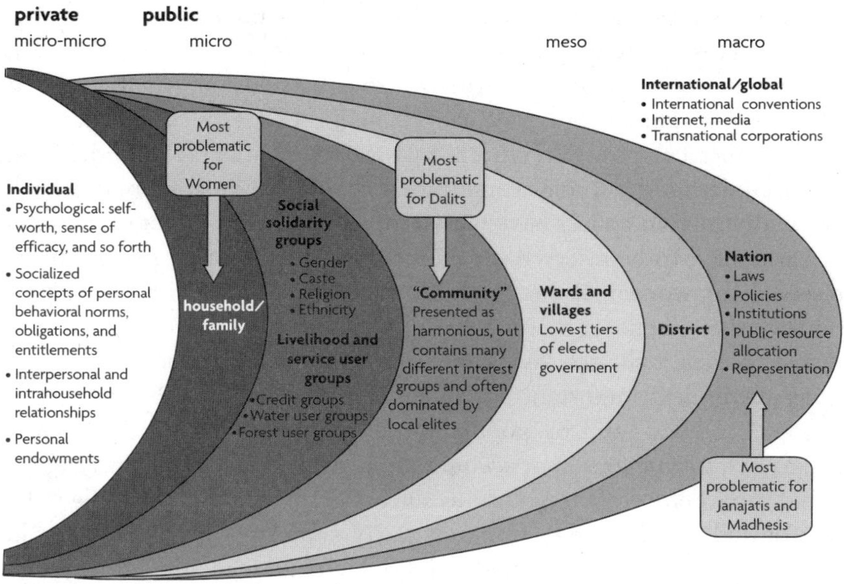

private   public
micro-micro   micro   meso   macro

International/global
• International conventions
• Internet, media
• Transnational corporations

Most problematic for Women

Most problematic for Dalits

Individual
• Psychological: self-worth, sense of efficacy, and so forth
• Socialized concepts of personal behavioral norms, obligations, and entitlements
• Interpersonal and intrahousehold relationships
• Personal endowments

household/family

Social solidarity groups
• Gender
• Caste
• Religion
• Ethnicity

Livelihood and service user groups
• Credit groups
• Water user groups
• Forest user groups

"Community"
Presented as harmonious, but contains many different interest groups and often dominated by local elites

Wards and villages
Lowest tiers of elected government

District

Nation
• Laws
• Policies
• Institutions
• Public resource allocation
• Representation

Most problematic for Janajatis and Madhesis

Source: World Bank and DFID 2006: 13.

The Historical and Political Context of Social Exclusion in Nepal

Nepal, a fledgling democracy and one of the poorest countries in the world, has for the past 10 years been engulfed by a Maoist insurgency in which more than 13,000 people have died. In late 2005, Nepal was caught in a three-way struggle between the Maoists; the king, who had used the insurgency as a pretext for reinstating absolute monarchy; and the democratic political parties, whose corruption and failure to deliver improvements in the lives of most Nepalis during their 12 years in power had largely discredited them. Then, in November 2005, the six main parties began informal discussions with the Maoists about a possible alliance against the king. When, in April 2006, the new Seven Party Alliance called for a major rally in Kathmandu, the king, citing the danger of Maoist infiltration, declared a curfew to keep people off the streets. However, the world watched as people—many from outside Kathmandu and probably Maoist linked—ignored the curfew and poured onto the streets of the city in protest that lasted 19 days. Finally, after one partial attempt to placate the crowd failed, the king gave up power and called for the reinstatement of the dissolved Parliament. This was the *Jana Andolan II*, or the Second People's Democratic Movement (figure 8.3).

Politicians in the reinstated Parliament, belatedly grasping the deep resentment over the many forms of social exclusion, swiftly passed legislation responding to 4 of the 12 major GSEA recommendations. First, women can now pass citizenship onto their children. Second, Nepal has been declared a secular state (rather than a Hindu kingdom). Third, affirmative action polices have been adopted, with 33 percent of the seats in Parliament to be reserved for women and a total of 45 percent to be reserved for women, Dalits, Janajatis, and the people with disabilities. Finally, the practice of untouchability has been declared illegal and punishable (though such laws have been on the books since 1963).

However, it is important not to get carried away by the euphoria of "people's power" and by popular proclamations, many with no clear means of implementation or accountability spelled out. Nepal has experienced three democratic revolutions since 1951, when the Rana oligarchy was ousted by the Nepali Congress Party supported by India. The old Muliki Ain, or County Code, of 1854, which had made the caste system

Figure 8.3. Efforts to Build Democratic Institutions in Nepal: A Time Line

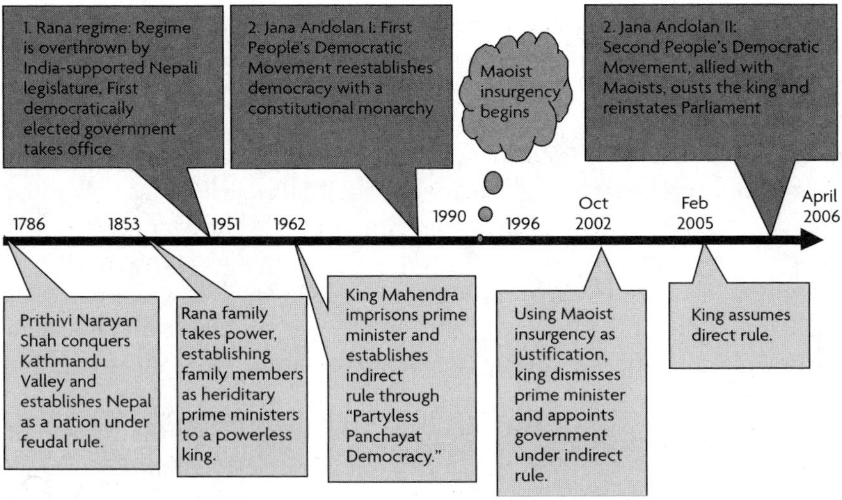

Source: Author's representation.

and gender subordination the law of the land, was abolished then. The new constitution and country code proclaimed all citizens equal regardless of their caste, tribe, or sex. Nevertheless, in 1962, the king imprisoned the prime minister and established direct rule though a system of "Party-less Panchayat Democracy." During the Panchayat regime (1962–90), the state attempted to build a modern and unified nation. Although directly ruled by the king, Nepalis were for the first time beginning to think of themselves as citizens rather than subjects. The rhetoric, if not the reality, of democracy was introduced. However, the diversity of languages, gender, kinship systems, and spiritual outlooks were framed as barriers to development, and efforts were made to merge them into a common, modern Nepali culture. Cultural unity was projected as essential to nation building and the maintenance of independence.

Unlike the old Rana regime, which had isolated itself from outside influences, the king believed that foreign aid was necessary to deliver on the promise of modernization and thereby maintain legitimacy for the monarchy. Hence, he could not keep Nepal isolated from the rest of the world. In the 1960s, development agencies from many countries established their offices in Nepal and began development projects in many sectors. Education levels increased and, for better or worse, new ideas and ways of doing business were brought in by these aid agencies and by increased media exposure and travel abroad for a slowly expanding middle class.

Scholarship programs such as the India-sponsored Colombo Plan and the American Fulbright Program awarded opportunities to study abroad, based on merit rather than caste status and family connections, to students who ordinarily would never have had such a chance. Some of these students came back with doctoral degrees and joined the civil service, forming a small core in government with both the professional training and the mindset to view their role from a technocratic rather than a feudal perspective. Young foreign volunteer workers (including those in the Peace Corps), along with workers from development agencies, spread out to the rural areas, bringing exotic new ideas and behaviors that affected the thinking of some rural government workers and many young students. In the urban areas, television came in, and even in the rural areas, radios became increasingly common, as did access to print media. Video parlors, even in remote district centers, also brought in new images and ideas from Hindi and English movies.

In the spring of 1990, when the people rose up in protest against the king's rule, multiparty democracy was reestablished through the first *Jana Andolan*. The new constitution established Nepal as a more inclusive state. It describes the country as "multiethnic, multilingual, and democratic," and states that all citizens are "equal irrespective of religion, race, gender, caste, tribe, or ideology." The statute also gave all communities the right to preserve and promote their languages, scripts, and cultures; to educate children in their mother tongues; and to practice their own religion. However, this constitution retained contradictions, in addition to its ambiguities on the status of the king and the control over the army. In particular, it explicitly protected what it called "traditional practices," which left room for the continuation of caste-based discrimination.

The 1990 constitution reaffirmed the principle of equality under the law and provided diverse groups space to express their opinions openly and to assert their identities and rights as citizens. Democratic Nepal allowed space for another major development: the growth of civil society organizations, especially those based on ethnic and caste identity. The post-1990 period also witnessed the dismantling of the old projection of a single Nepali culture based on that of upper-caste Parbatiyas.[3] Self-chosen terms such as *Adivasi Janajatis*, or "indigenous nationalities," emerged to displace those—such as *tribal* and *Matwali* (liquor drinker)—that had been used to describe indigenous ethnic groups. The previously *achut* (untouchable) or *sano jat* (small caste) groups at the bottom of the Hindu caste hierarchy took the name *Dalit* (oppressed, broken, or crushed) from the Dalit movement in India.

As shown in table 8.1, many hierarchical institutions, including powerful informal networks, behavioral norms, and expectations, remained unchanged. The unitary, centralized, and noninclusive state structure also remained largely unchallenged. Not surprisingly, much of the formal machinery of the state remained under the control of male Brahmans and Chhetris from the traditionally influential Parbatiya group and of the urban-based and generally well-educated Newars. A related reason for the failure of the democratic transition to be genuinely inclusive was that the political parties were unable or unwilling to represent and articulate the demands of less powerful Nepalis. Feudal, caste, and patriarchal hierarchies, including an emphasis on age-based seniority that prevented the emergence of new leadership, continued as the informal organizing principles of the parties' internal structures and their ways of operating. Those left at the margins were women, Dalits, and Janajatis, as well as other groups such as the Madhesi and the small Muslim population.

The inability of the polity to be inclusive led to the radicalization of the demands of those who felt neglected by the new political order. Although actually motivated by internal discontent after failing to win sufficient seats in Parliament in the second election, the Communist Party of Nepal (Maoist) sensed the growing discontent of ordinary people, especially the poor and excluded. After launching their People's War in February 1996, the Maoists were quick to capitalize on this discontent. They have accordingly provided important symbolic recognition to disaffected women, Dalits, and Janajatis and brought the demands of those groups into the public debate.

Social exclusion gained prominence in official public discourse in 2003, after inclusion was made one of four pillars of the Poverty Reduction Strategy Paper (PRSP), which is also Nepal's Tenth Plan. As a result, there is now greater understanding that social exclusion is a structural problem and that solving it requires the state to define and ensure citizenship rights to all rather than continuing to dispense inadequate and insecure welfare handouts in the old *binti* mode. What is not yet clear (and will be critical to the success of the "new Nepal") is whether, in return for these rights, Nepal's citizens can shift from a mindset of dependency and patronage to one of individual and collective responsibility as the price for their rights.

At present, the 1990 constitution has been abrogated by "people power"; an "interim constitution" is in place, but a new social compact between the state and its citizens has not yet been articulated. Hence, the desired outcomes listed below the question marks in the different columns in table 8.2 are far from certain. The balance between citizen's rights (to equal access to services, physical security, proportionate representation, and so on) and their responsibilities (in terms of paying taxes and obeying the law) has not been established. Without them a functioning democracy cannot survive, and there is danger that the logic of patronage could reemerge thinly disguised as the rule of the street but manipulated by competing interest groups—including, most notably, armed Maoists. Therefore, in addition to the fundamental shifts in the structure of governance and economic opportunity that will be negotiated in the coming months and years, attaining the inclusion goal of the PRSP and the *Jana Andolan II* requires changes in the cognitive logic as well as the underlying hierarchical norms.

Table 8.2. Uncertainty and Hopes for the Emergence of Democratic Institutions

	Formal rules of the game		Informal rules of the game	
	Power configuration	Legal and policy regime	Cognitive logic	Norms and values
	• "People's Power" (post–April 2006): An alliance between the Maoists and the six parties forces the king to return power to parliament as a first step toward an interim government with Maoist representation and the election of a constituent assembly to form a new constitution that will restructure the state and secure the peace. However, the army is still loyal to the king, the seven-party alliance has weak legitimacy, and the Maoists are now able to call on "the street" in power negotiations. **?**	• The reinstated parliament passes a number of populist pro-inclusion acts and proclamations, but inequities continue in practice (for example, no women are on the negotiation committee), and the details of implementation on affirmative action and other issues have not been worked out. • Once the constituent assembly has been elected, a new constitution will be drafted. **?**	• "People power" or "right makes might" is a common perception. • Patronage systems and old hierarchies continue to operate. **?**	**?** • Bedrock Hindu values continue to structure the worldview of most Nepalis, but with more and more emphasis on the egalitarian strands in the tradition and no formal involvement of the state, which is now secular. • Open debate takes place on the pros and cons of Marxist versus "liberal democratic" and other democratic systems and on the role of the state. • The principle of proportionate representation is interpreted and integrated into the structure of the state and the electoral system. • Human rights values are reflected in law and practice.
	• An interim government including the Maoists has been formed—although the Maoist's Young Communist League operates outside the law and stages frequent violent clashes against the government. **?**	• Special time-bound policies are established to level the playing field for historically excluded groups. • Systems of checks and balances are built into governance. • A robust system is established for monitoring inclusion outcomes. • Results-based budgeting is implemented. • Parties become more inclusive and transparent. • Power and funds for many government roles are delegated to the local government or recognized and accountable citizens' groups.	• Mix of new and old logic continues as in table 8.1. Ideally, more and more Nepali citizens are educated and able to observe and judge for themselves what kinds of institutions (or "contracts" between individuals, between social groups, and between the state and its citizens) actually deliver improved welfare for the majority, and they vote accordingly.	• A greater sense of mutual responsibility between citizens and the state is institutionalized, for example, through increased tax compliance. • Open competition takes place between individuals, firms, and ideas. • Corruption becomes unacceptable—enough to topple a government.
	• A constituent assembly is to be elected to draft new constitution.			

Source: Author.

Policy Influence, Culture Change and the Role of Donors

Tables 8.1 and 8.2 attempt to identify some of the internal and external ideas as well as the power configurations that are likely to influence the overall governance structure of Nepal and, specifically, the pace and success of the social inclusion process. Looking at this array, which captures only a small portion of the influences in play, one would find it heroic indeed to assert that any specific cultural change can be "induced," as one might induce a chemical reaction in a test tube or a supply response in a market. Perhaps great leaders like Gandhi or Mao have brought about rapid changes in the cognitive logic and values of multitudes of people, but even those changes are found on deeper examination to have been part of larger processes of historical change, with the actual changes on the ground that resulted from their leadership being perhaps less complete or unidirectional than their vision.

Ordinary individuals, like social development specialists in agencies such as the DFID and the World Bank, know that specific desired cultural changes cannot be induced by anyone and certainly not by outsiders. Too much human agency is involved in the creation of new meanings and cognitive logics and the shift of values that is at the core of culture change for this process to be controlled. Yet the presence, ideas, and, in particular, funding of outsiders is not neutral, either politically or culturally. Legitimately or not, they are players on the battlefield of ideas and contribute to cultural change even when espousing purely technocratic policy reforms.

The question is do development workers know what they are doing? What can they do to increase the chance that support to government or nongovernmental organizations (NGOs) has the intended consequences? What can they do to see that the formal economic and social policy changes being promoted are not dead in the water because they challenge informal networks and embedded cultural values and ways of thinking that operate below an outside agency's radar screen? In other words, how can development workers acknowledge the cultural dimension of policy change and factor that into country strategies to increase the chances of contributing to reducing poverty and social exclusion?

These questions have no general or universal answers. Local specifics in terms of history and culture are critical to the process. Even in Nepal, where there has been an attempt to take account of these specifics, question marks and hopes dominate the discussion (table 8.2) and no predictions can be made. However, the following observations, which are based on the Nepal GSEA experience, may be made as a rough travel guide.

Ever since Nepal embarked on the project of development six decades ago, a gap has persisted between (a) government policy pronouncements in support of equity and social justice and (b) action on the ground. Even during the multiparty rule of 1990 to 2002, the mechanisms of democratic accountability—including the link between voter and party politician—remained weak. This observation is confirmed in table 8.3, which compares the promises made to the Dalits in the Ninth Plan (1997–2002) with the actions that have ensued. Almost nothing has happened to change life for ordinary Dalit citizens.

The Tenth Plan and PRSP's commitment to social inclusion and good governance, plus the progress on a number of reform fronts over the past few years, has been extremely encouraging. However, the optimism generated by a visionary document and by the efforts of reform-minded leaders in certain parts of government must be tempered by the experience of how things often work in other parts of the system—especially the middle levels of the bureaucracy and district level and below. At those levels, the formal institutions and the progressive reform policies crafted by high-level and often reform-minded government officials interact with the old cognitive logic and the informal networks and values based on relations of kinship, party affiliation, business interests, caste, ethnicity, and gender. Very different rules of the game govern those relations, and their conflicting demands and value frameworks can lead to perverse and unintended results during the implementation process.

In the development community, this phenomenon—which neither donors nor government can ignore—is politely called the *implementation gap*. However, such language avoids any clear attribution of responsibility for the failure or any hint about the reasons behind it. A better term is *elite resistance*, which is similar, but more subtle than the more familiar term, *elite capture*.

When it comes to changing patterns of exclusion based on social identity, the influence of these informal institutions can be especially strong. As noted earlier, these institutions are actually systems of meaning and value through which individuals and groups define their very identity. Policy changes at this level are not technocratic; they challenge fundamental power relations and ways of interacting with others that follow from those relations. In terms of figure 8.2, they go to the innermost core of self-identity.

Table 8.3. Implementation Status of Major Policy Commitments for Dalits in the Ninth Plan

Policy commitments	Implementation status
Education	
Establish a higher education scholarship fund.	Fund is not established.
Allocate special seats for higher education in agriculture, forestry, engineering, and medicine.	Very limited seats (two per semester) in medicine were provided during the planning period, and no seats in other disciplines.
Appoint literacy mobilizers in all districts to reach Dalits and make compulsory primary education more effective.	Policy has not been implemented.
Appoint at least one teacher in each secondary school.	Policy has not been implemented.
Health	
Provide basic health service for Dalits by conducting mobile health clinics.	Policy has not been implemented.
Conduct special programs like population education, child health, and family planning directly targeting Dalits.	Policy has generally not been implemented.
Training and capability enhancement and others	
Modernize traditional Dalit occupations through training.	Policy has not been initiated (although an International Labour Organization project was carried out in several municipalities).
Provide special loans to trained Dalits to carry out their traditional businesses.	Policy has not been implemented.
Conduct special employment programs targeting Dalits and provide tax exemption to industries that employ a certain proportion of Dalits.	Policy has not been implemented.
Institutional arrangements	
Establish a strong and independent Dalit and Oppressed Community Council.	Council is not established yet. Instead, the National Dalit Commission, a body with limited autonomy, resources and power, was established through a cabinet decision at the end of the planning period, and after the term of the first commission, nearly a year passed before the appointment of a new commission.
Establish Dalit and oppressed committees in all 75 districts to make recommendations and give approval for Dalit-related programs of the village development committees within districts.	Committees have not been established yet.
Special provision	
Mandate expending a certain percentage of the funds provided by the government as a grant to district- and village-level local government bodies for the development of the Dalit community.	Generally the provision has not been implemented. The district- and village-level government bodies were under no obligation to submit or keep records of programs and budgets related to this provision, and the Local Development Ministry has no information on how much money was spent under this provision during the plan period.

Source: Bennett and others forthcoming: chapter 15.

Though it is more comfortable to think of the implementation gap as attributable to lack of government or NGO capacity—and therefore something that can be addressed through painless donor-funded training, study tours, and new computers—the major causes of poor implementation probably lie deeper. Those who have long benefited from the status quo are often reluctant to see the old system change. The impunity and ease with which so many of those in positions of authority can circumvent formal rules and policies suggest that powerful informal systems, behaviors, and norms are still very much at work in Nepal, and that groups whose objectives differ from those officially espoused by the state still find it easy to call on these systems.

Given this situation, what can donors do to address the informal systems that block pro-poor change? A few ideas are listed here.

Focus on the Mechanisms of Accountability

Many of the GSEA policy recommendations (World Bank and DFID 2006) have to do with closing the implementation gap. Most are focused on strengthening the mechanisms of political and administrative accountability. The most pressing need is for restoration of elected government at all levels—one would hope after thorough internal party reforms and reforms in the electoral system to improve representation and accountability to the electorate. Linked to this need is that for affirmative action in the civil service, which will increase the diversity of those who make the critical decisions about how policy is implemented. The final element is to continue the PRSP emphases on close monitoring of the link between expenditures and outcomes and on making sure that inclusion is a required outcome. This work is being done through the NPC's unrelenting focus on the Poverty Monitoring and Analysis System (PMAS) as a tool for results-based budgeting tied to the medium-term expenditure framework (MTEF). The PMAS can be strengthened by insisting that sectoral ministries also report progress disaggregated by caste, gender, and ethnicity and by using a range of social accountability tools to increase civic involvement and instill greater transparency in the allocation and use of public resources at the local level. Such mechanisms have the added advantage of offering a check to the threat of local elites capturing the lower tiers of elected government.

Although this discussion emphasizes the incompleteness of the transition to accountable, democratic institutions, it should be noted that, by and large, civil liberties have been protected in Nepal since 1990. Even during the period of the king's direct rule—and despite efforts to control the press through legislation and withholding of government advertising—a vibrant press continued to report what was seen and to editorialize openly against the regime. For more than a decade, there has been freedom of association, allowing, for example, the flourishing of civil society groups focused on ethnic, caste, and gender inequities. The discourse on inequality, human rights, and governance has become much more sophisticated. The expectations of instant utopia that followed the coming of democracy in 1990 have been tempered by greater realism, at least in some quarters, about what the state can and cannot do and by better understanding of the hard economic constraints Nepal faces—despite what has often seemed to the public like a limitless supply of donor funding.

Some important foundations of democratic governance have been laid in the past 14 years. The major strength of the Tenth Plan and PRSP is that the plan seeks to build on these foundations. One is the MTEF, which ties the entire PRSP exercise to the discipline of a rolling three-year budget and annual budgeting exercises. Together with the emphasis on developing a strong poverty monitoring and analysis system, this effort will allow government to move to results-based budgeting. Although the modalities have not all been worked out, the monitoring system provides for the collection and analysis of data by caste, ethnicity, and gender specifically to track performance on the PRSP's inclusion pillar.

Combined with freedom of the press and freedom of association, these emerging systems for allocating, managing, and tracking public funds can also be the critical foundations of accountability and good governance. Tools like the MTEF may seem rather technocratic and uninspiring. Citizens' report cards and social audits may sound like the latest civil society fad. Supporting such approaches, however, is part of what donors can do to close the implementation gap.

Recognize and Support Elite Reformers in Government

Donors can also realize that, just as all NGOs are not necessarily motivated by genuinely egalitarian visions of society or committed to transparency and accountability in their own operations, so government also contains individuals with different motivations and mindsets. Even though, as with most of civil society, government servants are mostly men from the privileged groups, it is important not to assume that they are all prisoners of the old cognitive logic and therefore part of the problem. In Nepal, an important group of government workers see themselves as technocrats and have, over the past five or six years, led a number of reforms that have at least begun to dismantle some of the old networks of favoritism and crony capitalism holding back Nepal's economy. Despite layers of inertia and open resistance, this group has pushed through banking reform, educational reform, and support for new mechanisms that channel substantial funds directly to community groups.

Those Nepali citizens, in government and in civil society, who are pushing for reforms in support of social inclusion have already begun the process of redefining themselves in terms that emphasize the egalitarian elements in their own tradition[4] and blending these elements with increasingly shared global democratic norms. However, other Nepalis from the dominant group have not yet engaged in the difficult process of examining, critiquing, and reformulating their inherited traditions in a more contemporary egalitarian frame. Many in government—and indeed in civil society—either do not understand their own ingrained habits of thought or, with varying degrees of self-awareness, are simply resistant to the loss of privilege and to the deep-seated changes in their own self-definition that would be required in order to realize the goal of social inclusion.

For these reasons, state-sponsored reforms, such as the proposed affirmative action policies that support the shift to a more inclusive society, must be cast in a long-term framework. Donors need to take the long view, resist donor fatigue, and convince their capital cities to stay the course and take a back seat as the process unfolds. This country-led process must draw in a broad spectrum of government and civil society groups to engage in a series of debates on why and how these far-reaching social changes should come about.

Recognize That Poverty Reduction Will Not Be Achieved without Culture Change

Donors who profess to support poverty reduction should not pretend that they are not in the business of sociocultural change. Sociocultural change is what development is, as surely as it is changes in the economy or changes in governance. Slicing a global poverty reduction and development project into economic, political, and sociocultural segments is a distortion of reality that will make donors less effective on the ground. They cannot be content with policy changes and sectorwide programs that ignore the informal rules of the game. The work must involve not only supporting change in the formal rules but also engaging with the cognitive logics and the deep-seated values and norms that guide the way people practice these rules. Donors must be in a position to support those who are leading change in that dimension as well.

Notes

1. The primary research on measuring empowerment and social exclusion was supported by the government of Norway through the Trust Fund for Environmentally and Socially Sustainable Development Poverty Window and by the governments of Norway and the Netherlands through the Trust Fund for Gender Mainstreaming at the World Bank.
2. The 700-page draft report has been widely available since June 2005 and will be published shortly (Bennett and others forthcoming). In May 2006, the summary report, *Unequal Citizens: Gender, Caste, and Ethnic Exclusion in Nepal*, was published (World Bank and DFID 2006).
3. *Parbatiya*, which means hill dweller, is the name used to described the Hindus who migrated into the Nepal middle hills over many centuries and finally, in 1768 under the command of Prithivi Naryan Shah, conquered the Kathmandu valley and established rule over the diverse Mongoloid ethnic groups that had inhabited the middle hill and mountain regions of the territory that became Nepal. In contrast to the Parbatiya are the *Madhesi*, or plains dwellers, who live in the Tarai region bordering India and share many cultural and linguistic characteristics Indians from across the border.
4. Because Hindu culture and religion are so closely linked with patriarchal ideology, patrilineal land inheritance, and the concepts of ritual purity and pollution embodied in both the caste system and in gender relations, the predominant Hindu view of the world is a very hierarchical one. However, a more intimate knowledge of Hindu traditions reveals the presence of strong opposing egalitarian values and many rituals and social movements that recognize these values and contest the ontological validity of both caste and gender hierarchies. See Bennett (1982) and Parish (1997).

References

Bennett, L. 1982. *Dangerous Wives and Sacred Sisters: The Social and Symbolic Roles of High Caste Hindu Women in Nepal*. Columbia University Press: New York.

Bennett, L., P. Onta, S. Tamang, M. Thapa, and others. Forthcoming. *Unequal Citizens: Gender, Caste, and Ethnic Exclusion in Nepal*. Kathmandu: Himal Books.

Campbell, J. L. 2004. *Institutional Change and Globalization*. Princeton: Princeton University Press.

Lawoti, M. 2002. "Exclusionary Democratization: Multicultural Society and Political Institutions in Nepal." Doctoral thesis. Graduate School of Public and International Affairs, University of Pittsburgh, Pittsburgh, PA.

North, D. C. 1990. *Institutions, Institutional Change, and Economic Performance*. Cambridge, U.K.: Cambridge University Press.

Parish, S. 1997. *Hierarchy and Its Discontents: Culture and the Politics of Consciousness in Caste Society.* Delhi: Oxford University Press.

Rao, V., and M. Walton. 2004. "Introduction: Culture and Public Action." In *Culture and Public Action: A Cross-Disciplinary Dialogue on Development Policy*, ed. V. Rao and M. Walton, 3–36. Stanford, CA: Stanford University Press.

World Bank and DFID (U.K. Department for International Development). 2006. *Unequal Citizens: Gender, Caste, and Ethnic Exclusion in Nepal—Summary Report.* World Bank and DFID, Kathmandu.

CHAPTER 9

Citizens, Identity, and Public Policy: Affirmative Action in India

Arjan de Haan

The aim of this chapter is to develop a framework for assessing whether public policy institutions are inclusive, whether they promote inclusive practices and attitudes, and how donors can promote institutional change. In many contexts, deep-rooted differences and inequalities continue to pervade what are, on paper, progressive public policy practices. Yet donors have paid little attention to how public policy institutions omit and influence broader societal patterns of exclusion and inclusion. Drawing on the author's experience working for the U.K. Department for International Development (DFID), the chapter looks primarily at India—particularly Orissa—where social differentiation has been reinforced by policy and political practices in several ways:

- Through categories and classifications used
- Through official inaction or delays
- Through the attitudes of officials
- Through modes of representation, including through civil society organizations.

The chapter focuses on policies for affirmative action. Although not a major part of the international development debate, affirmative action is important (a) because of the role it has played in the processes of nation building and construction of citizenship and (b) because affirmative action policies are usually key to advocacy efforts by marginalized groups. Moreover, by examining perhaps not very widespread but nonetheless illustrative practices that focus on inclusion, the chapter may help build a framework for understanding the ways that other public institutions function—including outside the social hard sectors.

The chapter begins by placing the key themes of the discussion within current international development debates. It focuses in particular on social development and policy, poverty analysis, and rights-based approaches. It then examines processes of nation building in the South and the ways in which notions of justice and citizenship have been incorporated, with particular reference to India. This discussion is followed by a brief analysis of affirmative action, which arose out of strong urges to enhance justice for marginalized groups, met with considerable success, and provided the basis for new forms of political contestation, thereby reinforcing processes of identity formation. It discusses the discrepancy between official policy statements and practices and attitudes in implementation, including how progressive policy frameworks may not be enough, how they need to be accompanied by changes in perceptions and attitudes, and how they thus require a renegotiation of the social contract. Finally, while acknowledging that the role of international agencies is limited, the chapter considers the risks that donor support may reinforce exclusionary practices.

International Development Debates

Social development advice and analysis in the international development debate has remained captured in a project approach. The reasons are manifold:

- Marginalization of social development in macrolevel policy dialogue and public expenditure management (a problem that is partly addressed within Poverty Reduction Strategy Paper approaches)
- Continued strong focus on safeguard questions
- Residual approaches to safety nets and poverty analysis
- Relative lack of engagement of the social development studies literature with questions of policy.[1]

Few, if any, studies have looked at the ways "street-level bureaucrats" (Lipsky 1980) interact with citizens and representative (and not-so-representative) organizations or at the policy makers' perceptions and motivations. Often, we know too little about the institutions responsible for making the policies and programs that directly impinge on the well-being of poor (and nonpoor) people—even though, according to Nick

Stern (2002), these institutions are key to the post–Washington consensus. Attempts to support the capacities of such institutions are limited, and approaches to social funds, particularly with donors' spending pressure, have tended to neglect the strengthening of mainstream social policy institutions.

How poverty analysis has evolved is relevant for the way policy and institutions are understood in the development debate. With the critique of structural adjustment, efforts to measure poverty have been intensified, and the understanding of poverty has moved beyond the money-metric to include aspects of human development, vulnerability, and subjective or participatory definitions of poverty. The *World Development Report 2006* (World Bank 2005) stresses that equity is relevant not only in the sphere of outcomes or opportunities, but also in institutions and processes, for example, in the area of justice systems. This chapter underlines the importance of institutions in maintaining poverty and disparities, while concurring with Eyben (2005), that we need to move beyond a "categorical" understanding of inequality that focuses on measurable differences or disparity between categories of individuals as measured by an observer, and incorporate a "relational" perspective of society that focuses on people's experiences of inequalities and on the power relations at work in society.

A rights language has entered the development debate (including in the *World Development Report 2006*), but definitions and usages of the terms have varied considerably (Nyamu-Musembi and Cornwall 2004; Piron with O'Neil 2005). Research from a human rights perspective often finds it difficult to use a paradigm that is different from a more traditional poverty paradigm (see, for example, Bandyopadhyay and Mukherjee 2004). Although policy documents on rights-based approaches exist in the DFID, frameworks on rights have found little acceptance across the organization, neither in the toolkit of economists nor among governance advisers or public sector specialists. Where it is used, the rights language tends to be normative, often disconnected from an understanding of policy processes—and particularly the politics of policy making.

In the context of a discussion on rights, the absence (by and large) of debates on race within international development studies is relevant.[2] Sarah White (2002) has challenged the color-blind stance of development, stressing that development may be regarded as a process of racial formation, and that social categories are actively constituted through development intervention.[3] This challenge does not appear to have been taken up in international development approaches, despite the outcome of the World Conference Against Racism, held in Durban, South Africa. Initiatives under the "diversity" banner have been restricted to development agencies themselves and are largely separated from programming. As a result, essential elements of policy processes have remained marginal to international development approaches.

Can a social policy framework help highlight a policy angle? Development studies literature is divided over the usefulness of such a framework. For example, research from the Institute of Development Studies in Sussex, United Kingdom, almost entirely rejects a social policy notion. It proposes that a livelihoods framework would be more suitable, because it would reflect the diverse conditions and comparative unimportance of state provisions for well-being in the South (Devereux and Cook 2000). Research at Bath University in the United Kingdom (the work of Ian Gough in particular—see chapter 2) has engaged more intensively with the social policy language, but this research, too, is ambivalent about the usefulness of such language—in part because of critique by Southern partners in the research program (Gough and Wood with others 2004). In contrast, the United Nations Research Institute for Development highlights the importance of social policy, especially for late industrializers in the process of nation building, and the ways in which economic and social policies interact; however, it is very critical of the role of international agencies (Kwon 2005; Mkandawire 2004).

Despite these and other criticisms, a social policy notion can be useful to strengthen our understanding of how mainstream policy is developed and implemented at a macrolevel, and how state institutions interact with communities and civil society. A social policy agenda as envisaged here is not about bringing social issues into the debate, which has received sufficient attention. Rather, it is a way to help move social development forward and elevate social issues to the level of macroeconomic and public expenditure technical work and policy advice—although ensuring those issues remain outside the sphere of conditionality—and move them out of the replere of residual safety-net approaches.

For this purpose, and building on work by Aina (1999) and recent discussions within the African Union (2006), *social policy* here is defined as an integrated set of deliberate public policy instruments and related institutions. For social development analysis, this definition implies strengthening understanding of how policy is developed and implemented.[4] Such a social policy framework implies an understanding of the political forces and coalitions that shape policy formulation and implementation. These politics are path dependent, and policy making often moves in parameters of national histories and cultures of policy making, illustrated, for example, in preferences for targeting or universalism. Perceptions of justice and inequality are part of such political histories, as discussions on lagging regions in Ghana and Nigeria demonstrate. Moreover, addressing disparities and other aspects of social policy is at the core of nation-building agendas. This goal is illustrated in the political history of affirmative action in India, in Malaysia after ethnic riots, and in South Africa's rainbow nation.

Within such a broad social policy framework, this chapter focuses specifically on inclusive institutions: to what extent public and social policy institutions are inclusive; how they define citizens; and what role, if any, the international community can play to enhance inclusion in the way these partner institutions operate. Institutions are defined to include both formal and informal rules and practices. These questions are explored with reference to the discrepancy within the Indian policy framework, where the Indian constitution has been progressive in eliminating discrimination, but the forms of social differentiation it purported to address have by no means disappeared. The key concern here is to highlight elements in the functioning of public policy institutions that actively, if unintentionally, reinforce disparities.

Nation Building and Citizenship: Affirmative Action in India

Social policy is embedded in processes of state formation and nation building, which set the parameters within which we understand the inclusiveness of institutions. As posited by Mamdani (1996, 2001, 2005), processes of nation building are relatively new, and social contracts, therefore, are relatively unstable.[5] They inevitably involve decisions about inclusion or exclusion of groups. Such processes have historical origins and are path dependent. Hutu-Tutsi differences in Rwanda were actively created under colonial rule, following the colonial ruler's urge to identify an intermediate group for indirect rule, thereby overcoming practical problems in separating the two identities to create mutually exclusive categories. Whereas in Rwanda these differences were reinforced to extremes, in Tanzania social integration and nation building were key to the experience in the first decades after independence (Wangwe 2005).

In many countries, affirmative action has been a central, albeit understudied, part of nation building, together with integration of ethnic diversity, rebalancing of the economic power of majorities, and integration of minorities. Ghanaian and Nigerian states' institutions, fiscal instruments, and civil service appointments are examples of the strong emphasis toward inclusion, even though lack of accountability and patronage politics have probably limited positive benefits from these policies.[6] Whereas East Asian states—and particularly their inclusive social policies— have focused mainly on nation building, in Malaysia affirmative action was a crucial element in reconfiguring the country's nation-state. After severe ethnic riots in 1969, affirmative action primarily focused on restoring the imbalance of economic power between the ethnic Malays and the Chinese and Indian settlers, with a clear productivist orientation through the New Economic Policy (Yusof 2006).

India's diversity was a main consideration for postcolonial state formation, and affirmative action or "reservation" became a central part of nation building as a result of political compromise operating in the newly forming nation. Reservation entailed a form of political representation that resulted from the compromise between Mahatma Gandhi and Bhimrao Ramji Ambedkar—who became responsible for drafting the relevant sections of the constitution—and, compared with the option of separate electorates, was interpreted by many Dalit activists as a defeat.[7] Later, policies of reservation became integral to the extension of democracy (Alam 1999) and in the rise of caste politics that have given much more agency to deprived groups (castes much more than Adivasi or religious groups).

The government of India's approach to historically marginalized groups draws on provisions made in the Indian constitution, which contains explicit obligations for protecting and promoting their social, economic, political, and cultural rights: "The State shall promote with special care the educational and economic interests of the weaker sections of the people and, in particular, of the Scheduled Castes and the Scheduled Tribes, and shall protect them from social injustice and all forms of exploitation" (Directive Principle of State Policy, article 46). The constitution officially abolished untouchability and any disability arising out of its enforcement. It mandates positive discrimination in government services, and state-run and sponsored educational institutions and legislative bodies. Amendments to the constitution promoted representation of scheduled caste men and women in local governance structures. Affirmative action thus encapsulates contradictions, particularly opposing principles of liberal and egalitarian justice. Although the constitution is explicitly secular (avoiding reference to religious symbols and emphasizing equality of all citizens), it requires state agencies to recognize castes and tribes through the provisions for advancement of scheduled castes (SCs) and scheduled tribes (STs), which are based on group taxonomies rather than, for example, forms of individual means testing or universalism. (These provisions were later extended to other backward castes, or OBCs.)

Policies for marginalized groups exist in three areas: human rights protection, economic empowerment and poverty alleviation, and affirmative action. First, legal safeguards against discrimination include enactment of the Ant-untouchability Act of 1955 (renamed Protection of Civil Rights Act in 1979), under which practices of untouchability and discrimination in public places and services became a legal offense. The Scheduled Caste/Tribe Prevention of Atrocities Act of 1989 provides legal protection against violence and atrocities by high castes. These policy measures are monitored though annual reports, which consistently show high levels of violence directed against protected groups.

The second policy area focuses on economic empowerment of deprived groups, through education and antipoverty programs. States make special provision for the advancement of deprived groups through reserved seats for SC and ST students, financial schemes, scholarships, special hostels, concessions in fees, grants for books, remedial coaching, and so forth. Nodal departments implement income-generating programs under the rubric of poverty reduction, and apex financial organizations develop entrepreneurial skills and provide credits for deprived groups. The Special Component Plan (SCP), an umbrella program intended to tailor public schemes to different needs,[8] provides financial allocation equivalent to the percentage of deprived groups in the population from the general sectors in state and central plans.

The third and most controversial area is reservation policy, which operates in government services; admission into public educational institutions; and seats in central, state, and local legislatures and bodies. Over time, the scope of reservations has expanded to include government housing and spaces for commercial activities. Some services are excluded from reservation—chiefly the judiciary and defense. Special provisions to enhance the SCs' and STs' capabilities to compete for government jobs accompany the reservation, including relaxation of minimum age and suitability standards, relaxation in fees, provisions for preexamination training, separate interviews, and inclusion of experts from SC and ST backgrounds in selection committees. The constitution provides for reservation of seats for SCs and

STs in central and state legislatures, and local bodies at district, *taluk,* and village levels. Reservation is proportional to population shares, and statutory provisions to enhance political participation (for example, smaller election deposits) complement the constitutional provision. Unlike reservation in government service, a time limit for political reservation exists, which is extended every 10 years.

Affirmative action is confined to government and government-aided sectors of services and educational institutions. Private enterprises and educational institutions have been excluded from the purview of the policy. Since coming to power in 2004, the coalition government has initiated a debate on reservation in the public sector. Activists' concerns over the decline in employment in public services since the 1990s under economic policies of liberalization have partly informed that debate. Because opinions on the desirability of such an extension are predictably diverse, the government has emphasized a process of consultation before proceeding with legislation.

Successive Five-Year Plans indicate gradual public policy changes.[9] Initially, the focus was on enforcement of legislation to prevent atrocities and on targeted and additive programs to the general development schemes—under an assumption that overall development programs would be tailored to specific needs at field level. Nevertheless, the Fifth Plan concluded that development expenditure was insufficiently focused, and the SCP was introduced as a means of allocating funds from the general budget. During the 1990s, when a rights and empowerment discourse found currency, the plan committed itself to a three-pronged strategy of social empowerment, economic empowerment, and social justice. Finally, analysis for the most recent Five-Year Plan highlighted how processes of forced integration into mainstream society for backward and isolated Adivasis have been central to problems of exclusion.

A number of official bodies monitor these programs (Thorat 2005). At the central level, the Ministry of Social Justice and Empowerment for Scheduled Castes, Other Backward Castes, and Minorities is responsible for addressing and monitoring programs—with corresponding departments at state level. In the 1990s, national commissions were set up to facilitate SCs, STs, OBCs, minorities, and *safai karamcharis* (scavengers) in claiming their rights. Monitoring tends to have a strong quantitative focus (for example, numbers of students from deprived groups) and is input oriented, paying little attention to, for example, changes in attitudes. Policy changes, as highlighted in plan documents, have not been accompanied by radical changes in monitoring frameworks. Compared with the rich body of literature in the United States or the United Kingdom, or to the extensive Indian debates on poverty trends, remarkably little academic or independent analysis exists regarding the effect of reservation policies.

National data indicate that disparities between social groups continue to exist. Despite the existence of extensive policy frameworks, significant gaps in poverty rates, in particular, continue to prevail. Statistical analysis has shown continued "discrimination," in the sense that differences in poverty rates cannot be explained by differences in recorded indicators of capabilities (de Haan and Dubey 2003). Although social differentiation has indeed changed remarkably—albeit with enormous variation across India—significant disparities remain.

Popular debates have stressed the negative impacts of affirmative action—in terms of decline in efficiency and "creamy layer" of the few who have benefited from reservation—but much evidence exists regarding positive benefits. Weisskopf's (2004) comparison of affirmative action in the United Kingdom and India, for example, highlights the positive effects relating to access to and performance in education (see also Deshpande 2004; Galanter 1984). Microlevel evidence also shows the enormous effect that access to education and jobs has on the status and confidence of individual members of deprived groups and how these individuals help other family members raise their socioeconomic status.

Although policies have affected (albeit unintentionally) the formation or reaffirmation of group identities and radically changed the country's politics, their effect on informal rules and practices is less clear. These issues are explored next.

Identities Reaffirmed

Independence brought optimism about the potential for economic and social progress, including, in India, the expectation that caste would soon disappear. Caste was seen as a barrier to progress and as incompatible with democracy, but there was optimism that the system would soon dissolve—although the existence of caste and the desirability of affirmative action were heavily debated. According to H. V. Kamath, member of the constituent assembly:

> before 10 years ... there will be no socially and educationally backward classes left, but that all the classes will come up to a decent, normal human level, and also that we shall do away with this *stigma* of any caste being Scheduled. This was the creation of the British regime.... (Shah 2001: 3)

One of the most remarkable developments counter to such expectations half a century ago, however, has been the reaffirmation of social identities, particularly caste and tribe. In this context, it is important to underline that social identities are not given and unchanging. Although it is commonly stated (Deshpande 2004) that the caste system is thousands of years old, a historical perspective (Bayly 1999) reveals constantly evolving categories, changing substantially under subsequent phases of state formation (including during the 1990s and the rise of *Hindutva*). What constitutes caste, *jati*, and tribe has been the subject of widespread scholarly, activist, and political debate, and who belongs to target groups for government programs is thus less clear than often assumed.

The postcolonial government used the 1931 Census to decide who would be included in the schedules. For SCs, this decision focused on backward communities in terms of untouchability and "polluting" status, combined with economic, educational, and local political criteria; for STs, key indicators referred to spatial and cultural isolation, combined with socioeconomic deprivation. Currently, the national commissions for SC and ST are responsible for considering castes for inclusion in or exclusion from the schedule, which then requires ratification in Parliament. Group classifications have gone through various stages of reformulation, scheduling, and descheduling; they have been widely debated, with the process becoming politically sensitive, particularly with the introduction of the OBC category.

The ways in which policies for social justice have been implemented have led to a reaffirmation of identities. SC and ST categories and targets have become part of the official vocabulary, including of civil society organizations, and of course reservation, including in senior positions. Specific policies have contributed to the articulation of groups as caste, to struggles of inclusion in schedules, and, in some cases, to complicated processes of claims for and subdivision by groups to be included in or excluded from lists and reservations (Assadi and Rajendran 2000; Balagopal 2000).

Also, "caste politics," or the "democratic incarnation of caste" (Shah 2002: 28), has followed the official approach to social groups, in turn reinforcing it. On the rise since the 1970s, caste politics have usually been associated with the decline of power of the Congress Party and represent a new phase in contestation of Indian citizenship and justice (often vulgar vote-bank politics). The attempt by Vishwanath Pratap Singh's government in 1990 to implement the Mandal Commission report, extending the reservations to OBCs, added a much stronger and controversial dimension to the role of caste in politics. Quotas at the *panchayat* level of the electoral system, introduced through the 73rd constitutional amendment, have had enormous effects.

These processes have given much more voice to the previously deprived groups, making the democratic process a messy one, but also leading to a stronger articulation and reaffirmation of identities, particularly of castes, including higher castes (Alam 1999). Reaffirmation of caste identities highlights what may be a major dilemma in instruments of social policy and in terms of modes of national integration. The point is not that the way the policies have evolved in India has made the process messy or that the complexities make the process unworkable (given administrative capacity, this does not appear to be the case). The key point is that, whereas the policies were set up to reduce the importance of the disparities, they appear to have strengthened the awareness of differences and strengthened these differences as social identities. Hence, an assessment of the inclusive character of institutions needs to take account of the dynamic contexts in which they operate. The effect of formal policies is determined as much by the contexts in which they operate as by their publicly stated intentions.

Social Policy, Attitudes, and Norms

The reversal of the use of categories and their adoption by discriminated groups is not unique: most racial categories in the West have undergone similar processes. A question that follows directly, however, is have these reversals brought about changes in attitudes among dominant or majority groups? This question has been central to much of the thinking on diversity within the United Kingdom, for example. Although reliable analysis of such changes within India is not available, the conclusion by Xaxa (2003: 45) with regard to tribal groups is relevant:

> The constitution of course promises to integrate and provide them space for participation and share in state institutions. However, the state administrative machinery is manned mainly by personnel from the dominant communities, is indifferent, discriminatory, and even hostile to the entry of the tribal people in these modern institutions. They are not only kept excluded but also discriminated through various kinds of administrative recruitment procedures and practices.

The discrepancy between official policy and practices is highlighted in the language and terms used in the private sphere. The language of caste, or *jati*, is commonly used, most notably in marriage advertisements, where "caste no bar" is the exception rather than the rule (the constitution abolished untouchability but not caste). Similarly, the language of tribe continues to be used widely, including by nongovernmental organizations (NGOs) and human rights advocates reporting, for example, "tribals shot by police." Although not all usage is derogatory, it does homogenize. In official parlance, SC and ST are usually clubbed together, even though the nature of deprivation and policy effects differ (Xaxa 2001). ST and Adivasi categories neglect the enormous heterogeneity of hundreds of groups across India, varying from majority groups in the northeast to very small communities in often environmentally marginal areas.[10]

The use of this language in itself is not wrong or inequitable (the quote about "tribals," of course, highlights a concern about human rights violations), but there appears to be little reflection on the usage of terms, and, overall, the language illustrates the exertion of power. Thus, a significant difference exists between the political correctness that prevails in Europe and North America (reflecting at least a conscious public policy effort to address discriminatory behavior, although this effort by no means guarantees abolishing racism) and that in India, where the continuous and largely unreflective use of categories and terms accentuates differences and power.

Many social science studies and journalistic reports have documented the continued existence of discriminatory practices and attitudes. Large regional variations exist, and individual stories show slow and often intangible, yet important, symbolic changes, including those brought about by reservation policies. Studies on administrative practices appear to be lacking, while regular official monitoring reports and reviews exist but have a strong focus on inputs. Statutory bodies are thought to be fairly ineffectual, partly because functionaries are often political appointees. In any case, few would dispute Thorat's (2002) conclusion, which discusses data at the all-India level and studies in Andhra Pradesh, Karnataka, Gujarat, and Orissa, that traditional caste norms still govern social behavior by high castes.

Two decades ago, Galanter (1984: 550) concluded:

> [Al]though preferential treatment has kept the beneficiary groups and their problems visible to the educated public, it has not stimulated widespread concern to provide for their inclusion apart from what is mandated by government policy.... This policy has encouraged a tendency to absolve others of any responsibility for their betterment on the ground that it is a responsibility of the government.[11]

Thorat (2002), too, although a fervent supporter of affirmative action, notes that legal measures by beneficiary groups do little to change embedded inequalities. Moreover, in terms of targeted actions, Galanter (1984) and many others stress that when compensatory discrimination produce a self-sustaining dynamic of inclusion, there are fewer counterdynamics related to resentment, manipulation, and low self-esteem.

Four questions thus arise when assessing affirmative action, and they have wider relevance in the assessment of inclusive institutions:

• First, are the policies enough to change attitudes, in this case deep-rooted discrimination (an issue discussed in the next section with reference to Orissa)?
• Second, do the policies become goals in themselves rather than instruments for empowerment?
• Third, with regard to choices between developmental and preferential affirmative action, does the negative impact of targeted measures in terms of stigma outweigh the positive benefits of inclusion within programs?
• Finally, because group-based policies can lead "citizens [to] embrace group-based identity and consciousness" (Loury 1999), has that effect been considered?

The political context and how these questions as political contestation have arisen out of particular histories should be assessed.

Public Policy Responses to Disparities: Orissa Focus

Orissa is not only one of India's poorest states, but it is also marked by large differences between regions, highlighted by perennial reports on starvation deaths. Regional disparities overlap significantly with differences between social groups, particularly through the concentration of Adivasis in noncoastal Orissa. Comparison of public policy responses across Indian states is critical to understanding those disparities (de Haan 2008).

As elsewhere in India, a broad set of policy instruments exists for rural development and the alleviation of poverty, but institutions appear to work less in areas where they are most needed. Uptake of central funding is often less in India's poorest states because of a lack of matching funds, limited administrative capacity, and lack of political commitment. A poor state such as Orissa usually does badly in terms of use of funds— an issue often publicized in the press but without notable effect. It also has large numbers of unfilled vacancies in the poorest areas. Moreover, little evidence and knowledge exist about the performance of such programs, which arguably can be attributed to a lack of accountability or sustained advocacy.

The special development program for Orissa's southwestern region illustrates many of the problems with policy implementation. For decades, the region received a great deal of political interest, resulting in an area-specific program started in the late 1980s, multisectoral and long term, with substantial central funding. Existing reviews reveal numerous implementation problems: it adds to the complexity of mushroomed programs with overlapping objectives that overstretch the bureaucracy, and spending has been slow, leading to redesign. Even in 2003 (IAMR 2003), the program headquarters was understaffed and use of funds was in the range of 75 to 80 percent, varying across sectors.

Orissa's disparities have historical and deep institutional roots. It is generally regarded as a quiet and law-abiding state, not marked by the messy processes of Bihar and Uttar Pradesh, for example, and not suffering from casteism. Chief ministers are not generally associated with corruption and maladministration, as in other poor states. Arguably, however, this lack of conflict and corruption is the result of unchallenged social structures that are extremely discriminatory against social groups—perhaps particularly tribals—and the absence of political or advocacy structures representative of their interests. Orissa's political and administrative elites have a remarkably small social base (high-caste Brahman-Karan, coastal-based) and are unchallenged, partly because Orissa is a young state with ongoing patterns of internal colonization (Mohanty 1989/90).

Targeted policies are likely to be ineffectual against such deep-rooted constraints and do not normally feature highly on policy and reform agendas. Historically, forest policies have prioritized state revenue generation, and recent progressive reforms have been unable to break through vested interests. Land policies have undergone dramatic transformation on paper, but they lacked the teeth to provide secure access for poor people. Development-induced displacement, with a very patchy record of resettlement and rehabilitation, has undermined the livelihoods of many. Decentralization to *panchayat* levels is less developed than in most Indian states, and districts are largely ineffective as units of planning.

Public policies continue to exclude in a number of ways. State politicians have shown remarkable indifference to some of the worst excesses of poverty in the state. The relative inaction of politicians to reports about starvation deaths during 2001 and 2002 was striking compared with, for example, actions by Bihar's chief minister. Responses to these crises focused mainly on long discussions about whether deaths occurred as a result of starvation or otherwise (eating of mango kernels) and on relief efforts, thereby continuously ignoring the structural nature of deprivation. Moreover, the crises did not lead to a call for a fundamental inquiry into existing and well-funded programs.

Orissa politics is centralized, and the state leadership reflects little representation or articulation of the interests of deprived groups. Elected representatives from deprived groups in Orissa have done little to change the dominant elite nature of politics, bringing into question the influence of affirmative action (political reservation) in this particular context. Although the "creamy layer" created by affirmative action is not necessarily a negative outcome, whether the form of political representation has been in the broader interests of the poorest remains questionable in Orissa's case. The predominant nature of civil society organizations in Orissa (partly because of its commercialization after the 1999 supercyclone) and the way government officials relate to them underline the lack of representation within the state.

Categories used in the government development and poverty-alleviation programs highlight Orissa's poverty profile, but they do so in a way that arguably contributes to marginalization within the policy debate. It is generally accepted that tribal areas are poor, often in a way that assumes that Adivasis are poor because they are tribal. Styles of governance, particularly in tribal areas, remain a reflection of the pattern of internal colonization. Rew (2003) highlights that the government at the turn of the century was an adversary, insensitive to local context, and a solid and person-like entity. Stereotypes surrounding tribal populations still prevail. Senior officials do little to hide discriminatory attitudes toward subaltern groups, including people who obtained senior positions (probably) through reservation.

Thus, progressive policies are no guarantee that institutions function inclusively, and, in the case of Orissa, the tangible effect of constitutional provisions addressing injustices against marginalized groups is small. Beyond that, however, progressive instruments can become tools for further or continued disempowerment. Apart from frequently blaming tribal people for eating mango kernels, debates on starvation deaths—while functioning in relief mode (with colonial public policy origins) and locking advocacy efforts into claims for distribution of food—have continued to deny the structural nature of deprivation (and reinforce the categories of difference used). The ways in which policies toward the poorest areas have been formulated and implemented have continued to reinforce political disparities between the coastal-based elite and inland tribal populations. These inequalities pervade all institutions as well as economic and political relations. Demands on public policy institutions to promote inclusion are thus of a tall order.

International Agencies

International agencies have essentially failed to address questions of social differences and discrimination (Bennett 2005; Brown and Stewart 2006). Questions about power relations or problematic categories are usually not addressed, and some of their practices may actively reinforce social differences.

Much of the policy dialogue has been marked by silence. Affirmative action has generally stayed outside the radar of donors; welfare ministries have not received much attention either. Budget support discussions, a fairly new instrument within India, do little in terms of interrogating sector-level policy instruments—despite the potential importance of the cross-cutting Central Component Plan. In Orissa's case, the lack of organized voice among deprived groups (and adverse government–civil society relations) has led to a near absence of dialogue between civil society and donors.

Furthermore, many of the mainstream social development instruments do not build in a critical assessment of effects on social differentiation. An example is the role of safeguards relating to involuntary displacement of indigenous people, which, of course, has made lending more sensitive to effects on marginalized groups. However, in the author's experience of appraising multidonor support to primary education in India, the application of safeguard requirements can contribute to an objectification of marginalized groups and, in fact, limit discussions on inclusion.[12]

Another example is budget analysis and participation in budgeting—areas that have developed rapidly in the past 10 years and that are often supported by international organizations such as the United Nations Development Fund for Women, the International Development Research Centre, and DFID. In India, examples of both gender and tribal budgeting exist (Utkal University 2003). Although gender falls outside the social differentiation discussed in this chapter, highlighting that most of the analysis has focused on allocations and shortfalls in actual expenditure for women in state and central budgets is important. A few organizations have focused on tribal budgets; in the case of Gujarat, for example, injustices in financial allocations to tribal areas have been emphasized.[13] These advocacy efforts critically assess governments' commitments, including differences between stated objectives and implementation, but do not question the categories used or the potential effects of their use.

Other parts of donor-supported programs strongly emphasize targeting socioethnic and socioeconomic groups. Discussions on the pro-poorness of electricity provision focused on numbers and proportions of SC and ST users. Similarly, targeted livelihood projects, such as watershed development, include social category indicators of landownership and water access. Targeting predominates in primary education programs. Building on NGO-led experiences such as Lok Jumbish, which successfully reached remote tribal groups in Rajasthan, the centrally sponsored primary education program (Sarva Shiksha Abhiyan) was designed to universalize primary education. This focuses on bringing primary education to the last remaining deciles of the population, often implying Adivasi communities (an aspect reinforced by donors' poverty focus). Clear output targets are set, and elaborate delivery and monitoring mechanisms ensure strong control over the delivery of services. Local participation is critical to the programs. It is an essential element for delivery, particularly in remote areas, and a way of adapting the program to local needs, for example, with respect to translations into local languages.[14]

Targeted programs have had considerable success in India, partly because existing administrative systems allow for effective management. Moreover, they play a central role within the context of inclusive policies. In the case of primary education, a targeted approach to remote rural communities may well be the only or best way to deliver the constitutional commitments to education, at least as a temporary strategy. Designed with strong progressive advocacy and providing, in principle, space for diversity, the primary education program has enormous emancipatory potential and forms an indispensable condition for broader empowerment.

At the same time, the question remains whether the instruments risk reinforcing the stigma and discrimination of targeted groups. At least the donor debate has a strong focus on quantitative outputs, with less attention to quality and, in particular, content of education and attitudes of teachers, which have been key elements of strategies to address discrimination and stereotypes elsewhere.

Conclusion

Three key lessons emerge from the discussion of the specific form of affirmative action that exists in India and the use of caste and tribal categories in public policies. First, constitutional commitments and expectations of progressive leaders to abolish social differentiation and stigma differ markedly from the continued use of terminology and practices showing that caste has been transformed but certainly not disappeared and that tribe has remained a largely unquestioned category. Second, affirmative policies by themselves have not been sufficient to change attitudes toward deprived groups, as highlighted in public language, as well as in behavior and attitudes of officials. Tribe and caste in India, far from being traditional, have evolved through the operation of nationally specific politics and policies, including practices of targeting, unintentionally contributing to re-creation and reinforcement of separate and separating identities. Third, in conditions where severe social inequalities permeate institutions, reducing feedback and accountability, such policies are less likely to be effective, and the adoption of categories designed to achieve justice may, in fact, contribute to reinforcing inequalities by objectifying groups and the way in which elected representatives are integrated into the political system.

Nevertheless, such targeted and affirmative actions are not undesirable—far from it. They exist as important instruments for advocacy, and targeted policies within an inclusive system play important roles. The question is how the use of such categories can become emancipatory, and under what conditions identities can come to signify differences rather than inequalities. This question implies significant changes are needed, both within the public institutions and in the relationship between the state and its citizens. These processes of change may be messy (as in Bihar's social churning over the past decades) and may stretch the current boundaries of the state's influence in social and private spheres.

What role donors play requires further investigation. Nevertheless, they already play an important role—particularly when the poverty focus reinforces targeted approaches based on, or involving, social categories. In general, donors need a better understanding of the social and political dynamics in which their support is embedded, and particularly of the inequalities within public institutions that potentially reinforce social disparities.

Notes

This chapter was written while the author was on special leave from DFID and a visiting fellow at Guelph University, Canada. Ideas expressed in the chapter do not necessarily reflect DFID policy.

1. These arguments are further developed in *Reclaiming Social Policy* (de Haan 2007b).

2. The fact that international rights approaches have remained within a civil liberties paradigm, as opposed to what may be called egalitarian human rights, may have reinforced this absence.

3. Recent work by Eyben and Moncrieffe (2005), building on Wood (1985) and other researchers, emphasizes the power of labeling in development practice (Eyben and Moncrieffe 2005; Moncrieffe and Eyben 2007). Some of the analysis here draws on the author's contribution to Moncrieffe and Eyben (2007), titled "Labelling Works: The Language and Politics of Caste and Tribe in India" (de Haan 2007a).

4. The author's experience at DFID has highlighted an urgent need for greater understanding of macrolevel institutions responsible for the delivery of policy, including public finance processes, or, for example, the complexities of Indian central and state responsibilities for social policies, including allocations for targeted groups or regions.

5. The following discussion draws heavily on Mamdani (1996, 2001, 2005) and emphasizes colonialism's legacy of bifurcated power, which mediated racial domination through tribally organized local authorities, reproducing racial identity in citizens and ethnic identity in subjects.

6. See Bangura (2005), Ibrahim (2006), and Mukherjee and Adamolekun (2005) for Nigeria; Ghana does not have such explicit forms of affirmative action, but its regional policies reflect the need to include different ethnic groups within macrolevel institutions (Shepherd and others 2004).

7. Minority leaders have to rely on support from the general population and hence are still subject to pressure from powerful (higher-caste) leaders. During the 1950s, affirmative policies were widely contested. Ram Manohar Lohia favored addressing discrimination but thought the policy of uplift of deprived groups was capable of yielding poison, because more influential groups may monopolize benefits and protect their position and because elections might become acrimonious (Shah 2002).

8. Evidence points to poor performance of funds, including nonuse of monies, fund diversion, and difficulties in monitoring because resources are spread across ministries. In states with high percentages of deprived groups, incentives for diversion of funds may be larger.

9. Shalini Bahuguna highlighted these changes in the DFID (2002).

10. Gender analysis of tribes has also tended to homogenize the category and has neglected the fundamental changes imposed on these groups and implications on gender relations (Xaxa 2004).

11. Galanter (1984: xviii) describes India's compensatory discrimination policy from the viewpoint of the courts, stating that courts "act as a balance wheel channeling the compensatory policies and accommodating them to other commitments; but it is the political process that shapes the larger contours of these policies and gives them their motive force. Official doctrine—judicial pronouncement or administrative regulation—proved an insufficient guide to the shape of the policies in action and the result they produced."

12. For example, in the case of multidonor support to India's primary education program, Sarva Shiksha Abhiyan, the secretary opposed and deemed unnecessary the safeguard requirement to produce a tribal plan because the focus of the entire program was on deprived populations, including tribal groups. Focus on the safeguard requirement, in fact, limited in-depth engagement with the program—further research would be required to show whether this experience was exceptional.

13. See http://www.disha-india.org/.

14. This approach has gained much support for the national program from the international community, including Nordic donors for the NGO initiatives in Rajasthan, the World Bank, the European Union, and DFID. The program is described on the government of India Web site, http://ssa.nic.in.

References

African Union. 2006. "Meeting Social Development Challenges: Social Policy Framework in Africa." African Union, Addis Ababa.

Aina, T. A. 1999. "West and Central Africa: Social Policy for Reconstruction and Development." In *Transnational Social Policies: The New Challenges of Globalization*, ed. D. Morales-Gómez, 69–87. London: Earthscan.

Alam, J. 1999. "What Is Happening Inside Indian Democracy?" *Economic and Political Weekly* 34 (37): 2649–56.

Assadi, M., and S. Rajendran. 2000. "Karnataka: Changing Shape of Caste Conflict." *Economic and Political Weekly* 35 (19): 1610–11.

Balagopal, K. 2000. "A Tangled Web: Subdivision of SC Reservation in AP." *Economic and Political Weekly* 35 (13): 1075–81.

Bandyopadhyay, R., and A. N. Mukherjee. 2004. "Impact Assessment of Poverty Alleviation Programmes from Human Rights Perspective: A Case Study of Bolangir District, Orissa, India." Paper presented at the Second International Law Conference, Indian Society of International Law, New Delhi, November 14–17.

Bangura, Y. 2005. "Ethnicity, Inequality, and the Public Sector: A Comparative Study." United Nations Research Institute for Social Development, Geneva. http://unpan1.un.org/intradoc/groups/public/documents/UNTC/UNPAN018646.pdf.

Bayly, S. 1999. *Caste, Society, and Politics in India from the Eighteenth Century to the Modern Age.* Cambridge, U.K.: Cambridge University Press.

Bennett, L. 2005. "Gender, Caste, and Ethnic Exclusion in Nepal: Following the Policy Process from Analysis to Action." Paper presented at the Conference New Frontiers of Social Policy: Development in a Globalizing World, Arusha, Tanzania, December 12–15. http://siteresources.worldbank.org/INTRANET-SOCIALDEVELOPMENT/Resources/Bennett.rev.pdf.

Brown, G., and F. Stewart. 2006. "The Implications of Horizontal Inequality for Aid." Paper presented at the United Nations University–World Institute for Development Economics Research Conference on Aid: Principles, Policies, and Performance, Helsinki, June 16–17.

de Haan, A. 2007a. "Labelling Works: The Language and Politics of Caste and Tribe in India." In *The Power of Labelling: How People Are Categorized and Why It Matters*, ed. J. Moncrieffe and R. Eyben, 143–59. London: Earthscan.

———. 2007b. *Reclaiming Social Policy: Globalization, Social Exclusion, and New Poverty Reduction Strategies.* Basingstoke, U.K.: Palgrave Macmillan.

———. 2008. "Disparities within India's Poorest Region: Why Do the Same Institutions Work Differently in Different Places." In *Institutional Pathways to Equity: Addressing Inequality Paths*, ed. A. Bebbington, A. Dani, A. de Haan, and M. Walton, 103–6. Washington, DC: World Bank.

de Haan, A., and A. Dubey. 2003. "Extreme Deprivation in Remote Areas in India: Social Exclusion as Explanatory Concept." Paper presented at the Chronic Poverty and Development Policy Conference, University of Manchester, Manchester, U.K., April 7–9.

Deshpande, A. 2004. "Affirmative Action in India and the United States." Background paper for *World Development Report 2006: Equity and Development.* Washington, DC: World Bank. http://siteresources.worldbank.org/INTRANET-SOCIALDEVELOPMENT/Resources/Affirmative_Action_India_Ashwini.pdf.

Devereux, S., and S. Cook. 2000. "Does Social Policy Meet Social Needs." *IDS Bulletin* 31 (4): 63–73.

DFID (U.K. Department for Information Development). 2002. "Caste in South Asia: Social and Economic Exclusion." Briefing for the secretary of state, DFID India, New Delhi.

Eyben, R. 2005. "World Development Report 2006: Equity and Development—Response." Institute of Development Studies, Sussex, U.K.

Eyben, R., and J. Moncrieffe. 2005. "The Power of Labelling in Development Practice." Policy Briefing 28, Institute of Development Studies, Sussex, U.K.

Galanter, M. 1984. *Competing Equalities: Law and the Backward Classes in India.* Berkeley: University of California Press.

Gough, I., and G. Wood, with A. Barrientos, P. Bevan, P. Davis, and G. Room. 2004. *Insecurity and Welfare Regimes in Asia, Africa, and Latin America: Social Policy in Developmental Contexts*. Cambridge, U.K.: Cambridge University Press.

IAMR (Institute of Applied Manpower Research). 2003. "Evaluation Study of RLTAP in the KBK Region in Orissa." Study sponsored by the Planning Commission, Delhi.

Ibrahim, J. 2006. "Affirmative Action: Nigeria." Policy Brief 15, Inter-regional Inequality Facility, Overseas Development Institute, London. http://www.odi .org.uk/inter-regional_inequality/papers/Policy%20Brief%2015%20-%20Ni geria.pdf.

Kwon, Huck-Ju, ed. 2005. *Transforming the Developmental Welfare State in East Asia*. London: Palgrave Macmillan.

Lipsky, M. 1980. *Street-Level Bureaucracy: Dilemmas of the Individual in Public Services*. New York: Russell Sage Foundation.

Loury, G. C. 1999. "Social Exclusion and Ethnic Groups: The Challenge to Economics." Paper presented at the Annual World Bank Conference on Development Economics, Washington, DC, April 28–30.

Mamdani, M. 1996. *Citizen and Subject: Contemporary Africa and the Legacy of Late Colonialism*. Princeton, NJ: Princeton University Press.

———. 2001. *When Victims Become Killers: Colonialism, Nativism, and the Genocide in Rwanda*. Princeton, NJ: Princeton University Press.

———. 2005. "Political Identity, Citizenship and Ethnicity in Post-colonial Africa." Keynote address, World Bank conference on New Frontiers of Social Policy: Development in a Globalizing World, Arusha, Tanzania, December 12–15. http://siteresources.worldbank.org/INTRANETSOCIALDEVELOPMENT /Resources/revisedMamdani.pdf.

Mkandawire, T., ed. 2004. *Social Policy in a Development Context*. London: Palgrave Macmillan.

Mohanty, M. 1989/90. "Class, Caste, and Dominance in a Backward State: Orissa." In *Dominance and State Power in Modern India: Decline of a Social Order*, vol. 2, ed. F. Frankel and M. S. A. Rao, 321–67. Delhi: Oxford University Press.

Moncrieffe, J., and R. Eyben, eds. 2007. *The Power of Labelling: How People Are Categorized and Why It Matters*. London: Earthscan.

Mukherjee, R., and L. Adamolekun. 2005. "Implementing Affirmative Action in Public Service: Comparative Administrative Practice." World Bank, Washington, DC.

Nyamu-Musembi, C., and A. Cornwall. 2004. "What Is the Rights-Based Approach All About? Perspectives from International Development Agencies." IDS Working Paper 234, Institute of Development Studies, Sussex, U.K.

Piron, L.-H., with T. O'Neil. 2005. *Integrating Human Rights into Development: A Synthesis of Donor Approaches and Perspective*. London: Overseas Development Institute. http://www.odi.org.uk/rights/publications.html.

Rew, A. 2003. "Why Has It Ended Up Here? Development (and Other) Messages and Social Connectivity in Northern Orissa." *Journal of International Development* 15 (7): 925–38.

Shah, G., ed. 2001. *Dalit Identity and Politics*. New Delhi: Sage.

———. 2002. "Caste, Hindutva, and Hideousness." *Economic and Political Weekly* 37 (15): 1391–93.

Shepherd, A., and E. Gyimah-Boadi, with S. Gariba, S. Plagerson, and A. Wahab Musa. 2004. "Bridging the North-South Divide in Ghana." Background paper for *World Development Report 2006: Equity and Development*. Washington, DC: World Bank. http://siteresources.worldbank.org/INTRANETSOCIAL DEVELOPMENT/Resources/North_South_Divide_Ghana_Shepard_et_al.pdf.

Stern, N. 2002. "Dynamic Development: Innovation and Inclusion." Presented at the Munich Lectures in Economics, Center for Economic Studies, Ludwig Maximilian University, Munich, November 19.

Thorat, S. K. 2002. "Oppression and Denial: Dalit Discrimination in the 1990s." *Economic and Political Weekly* 37 (6): 572–78.

———. 2005. "Affirmative Action Policy in India: Dimensions, Progress, and Issues." Paper presented at a workshop at the United Nations Economic Commission for Africa, Addis Ababa, July 2–11.

Utkal University, School of Women Studies. 2003. *Proceedings of International Workshop on Gender Budget Initiatives in Orissa*. Shovan, Bhubaneswar: Utkal University.

Wangwe, S. 2005. "Culture, Identity, and Social Integration: The Tanzania Experience in Social Integration." Paper presented at World Bank conference on New Frontiers of Social Policy: Development in a Globalizing World, Arusha, Tanzania, December 12–15. http://www.worldbank.org/socialpolicy.

Weisskopf, T. E. 2004. Affirmative Action in the United States and India: A Comparative Perspective. London: Routledge.

White, S. 2002. "Thinking Race, Thinking Development." *Third World Quarterly* 23 (3): 407–19.

Wood, G. 1985. "The Politics of Development Policy Labelling." *Development and Change* 16 (3): 347–73.

World Bank. 2005. *World Development Report 2006: Equity and Development*. Washington, DC: World Bank.

Xaxa, V. 2001. "Protective Discrimination: Why Scheduled Tribes Lag Behind Scheduled Castes." *Economic and Political Weekly* 36 (29): 2765–72.

———. 2003. "Adivasis in India." Paper prepared for the U.K. Department for International Development, New Delhi.

———. 2004. "Women and Gender in the Study of Tribes in India." *Indian Journal of Gender Studies* 11 (3): 345–67.

Yusof, Z. A. 2006. "Affirmative Action: Malaysia." Policy Brief 13, Inter-regional Inequality Facility, Overseas Development Institute, London. http://www.odi .org.uk/inter-regional_inequality.

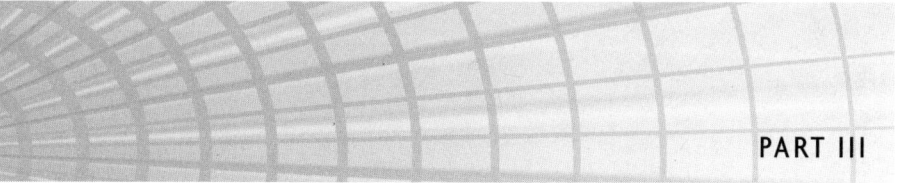

PART III

INCLUSIVE INSTITUTIONS

CHAPTER 10

Taking Culture into Account in the Delivery of Health and Education Services

Alexandre Marc

This chapter examines how cultural diversity and identity affect public service in the delivery of basic services—in particular in health and education—and how local governments can respond to this challenge. Over the past 20 years, recognition has grown of the importance of cultural and ethnic diversity in the design and implementation of development programs. The increasing cultural diversity[1] of societies throughout the world and the key role culture plays in identity formation present a major challenge for national and local governments, as well as providers of public services, in designing policies and ensuring social cohesion and integration.[2] Many basic services are delivered at community level.

This chapter focuses on education and health and uses the findings to draw more general conclusions about the challenge of taking into account cultural diversity in the delivery of services at the local level. This challenge should be seen in the framework of the broader issue of citizenship and citizens' rights in today's world. In the past, nation building has run counter to recognizing cultural diversity in a large number of countries. Today, with the advancement of globalization, nation-states are being challenged to adopt a more diverse view of citizenship that would recognize cultural differences among citizens. The debate around the mastering of the official language as a requirement for citizenship is only one example of this broader discussion.

Nurturing Cultural Diversity: A Priority for Policy Makers

Governments have been increasingly under pressure from citizens and international and grassroots organizations to design policies and programs in support of cultural diversity. This opening up to multicultural policies has been particularly significant at the local level in the provision of basic services.

This chapter explores culture as a framework that influences values and societal norms with the understanding that cultures are evolving, flexible, and variable. Cultures constantly adapt, sometimes faster and sometimes slower. "Hybridization" phenomena are also taking place, whereby cultures adopt aspects of other cultures and individuals belonging to one culture assimilate some trait of another culture (Douglas 2004).

The increased awareness of cultural and ethnic diversity is due to two parallel phenomena. First, migration—both international and national—creates many mixed communities with people of different origins and cultures living collectively under the same local administration. In addition, the ties that migrants maintain today with their countries and communities of origin are much stronger than in the past, mainly because of the rapid expansion and accessibility of various means of communication. Second, today, throughout the world, ethnocultural minorities are demanding greater recognition and accommodation of their cultural practices and identities. In the past decade, international agencies—in particular the United Nations (UN) and the Council of Europe—have moved actively to recognize cultural diversity, rights of minorities, and cultural rights.

The increased demand for recognition of cultural diversity in public policies has given birth to the concept of multicultural citizenship. It is the approach advocated in the United Nations Development Programme (UNDP) *Human Development Report 2004* on cultural liberty (UNDP 2004). Today, some policy makers and academics clearly see the need to supplement traditional human rights with minority and cultural rights to avoid conflicts and support social cohesion and integration. The new multiculturalist model is viewed as different from the three classical models for creating cohesive nations: communitarian, assimilationist, and integrationist.

The theory of multicultural citizenship has influenced multicultural policies. In his book *Multicultural Citizenship*, Will Kymlicka (1995: 6) writes, "I believe it is legitimate, and indeed unavoidable, to supplement traditional human rights with minority rights. A comprehensive theory of justice in a multicultural state will include both universal rights, assigned to individuals regardless of group membership, and certain group-differentiated rights or 'special status' for minority cultures." Multicultural citizenship preserves a central core of common human rights valid to all citizens but complements these rights with specific rights for minority groups; these rights will allow minorities to exercise their universal rights because they will be less discriminated against.

Acknowledging cultural differences is essential for the following reasons:

- Cultural minorities are often among the poorest groups, and to improve their well-being, it is important to recognize their cultural specificity and avoid cultural discrimination.
- Many studies have shown that culture positively influences collective and individual agency. As a result, culture should be taken into account in the design of policies.
- Understanding and promoting some of the cultural attributes of groups can reduce conflicts.

Nevertheless, risks can be associated with considering local culture in programs and policies. The main risk is of reducing the autonomy and liberty of choice of some subgroups in a given society, such as women, youth, or lower castes. It can also keep unfair and ineffective institutions alive, as well as isolate communities from the majority culture.

Little has been written about service delivery and cultural diversity at a local level. This gap seems to be an important omission in the design of social policy. The following sections look at the specific cases of education and health care.

Education

Education is probably the most culturally embedded service provided to the population. Only very recently has education been seen as an institution primarily concerned with preparing children for integration into the labor market. Public education was initially set up to teach certain conceptions of the world that were supposed to influence human values and behaviors. Education was, in most cases, in the hands of religious authorities. When public education became a mass phenomenon in the 19th century, its main objective was the creation of a national identity through the establishment of common values for all citizens and support of the nation-state. At the same time, it was supposed to provide the skills necessary to feed the industrial revolution. Today, school remains the place where children's social identity is shaped. It is much more than a preparation to confront the labor market; it is where future citizens are formed. Therefore, claims for recognizing cultural diversity are, not surprisingly, strongest in the field of education.

Multicultural Education

Multicultural education is a broad term that includes the following components:

- Education in languages other than the majority language
- Changes to curricula to reflect the history and culture of minority groups
- Support to students from minorities when under particular pressure caused by their cultural specificities
- Changes to pedagogical methods to take into account cultural differences.

In multicultural education, the main challenges are (a) to create structures that support the development of one's group identity while fostering common ground between groups that are part of the broader society and (b) to ensure efficiency so that education also provides skills useful in the labor market. The various concepts supporting multicultural education are well presented by James A. Banks (2001).

During the past decade, multicultural education has progressed rapidly throughout the world, with notable progress in Latin America and Eastern Europe. In Sub-Saharan Africa, however, where the majority of children have a mother tongue other than the official language, multicultural education is still limited.

The nature and source of the demand for multicultural education are important to understand. Multicultural education usually has a strong ideological appeal, and elites often call for it for political reasons. This factor should not be viewed negatively, because elites have always been at the forefront of social changes. However, such reforms need to be understood and accepted by the intended beneficiaries at local level. Kogila A. Moodley (2001), who wrote on multicultural education in Canada, believes that multicultural education can be important but that it often overlooks the prime goals of "equality of opportunity" and "equality of condition." She argues that multicultural education need not challenge the hegemony education and emphasizes that "competence," not culture, is the main concern of parents in minority groups. They often prefer a curriculum of basic skills and success in subjects needed to survive in the nation rather than condescending, diluted versions of their culture, taught secondhand by an "inauthentic group member." She supports multicultural education but advises care in the way it is implemented.

Teaching in the Mother Tongue

Discussing education is difficult without examining a country's language policies and the way nation building and citizenship are conceived in the countries concerned. Language is probably the most important vehicle of a culture. As Will Kymlicka and François Grin (2003: 11) write:

> So when a language group fights to preserve its language, it is never just preserving a tool for communication: it is also preserving certain political claims, autonomous institutions, cultural products and practices, and national identities. Conversely, of course, when the state attempts to impose a dominant language on minorities, it is never just imposing a language: it is also imposing a set of political and cultural claims about the primacy of the state, the need for common rules and centralized institutions, the need to learn new history and literature, and the construction of new nation-state loyalties and identities. Language disputes are never just disputes over language.

In a democratic society, the need clearly exists to recognize that people have varying interests in relation to language; what is important is accommodating these interests. At the same time, having all members of a nation communicate easily with each other and putting the state in a position to interact with citizens in an effective manner are legitimate considerations.

Teaching in a culture's mother tongue has proved effective. Success is measured not only in terms of identity recognition but also in terms of cognitive development and ability to learn other subjects in the future. A World Bank study (Dutcher and Tucker 1977: 5) conducted in 1977 stated:

> The most important conclusion of the research and experiences reviewed in this paper is that, when learning is the goal, including that of learning a second language, the child's first language (that is, his or her mother tongue) should be used as the medium of instruction in the early years of schooling. The first language is essential for the initial teaching or reading and for comprehension of subject matter. It is the necessary foundation for the cognitive development upon which acquisition of the second language is based.

Another report from the United Nations Children's Fund (UNICEF) supports these findings in the context of poverty reduction. According to that study (Mehrotra 1998), in a situation where the parents are illiterate, if the medium of instruction in school is language that is not spoken at home, the problems of learning in an environment characterized by poverty are compounded, and the chances of dropout increase correspondingly. In this context, the experience of high achievers has been unequivocal. The mother tongue was used as the medium of instruction at the primary level in all cases. International research also suggests that bilingual education, particularly at the early childhood stage, supports cognitive development that helps learning in general—not only learning languages—at an older age.

Other evidence indicates that learning in a mother tongue increases interest in school participation and encourages school enrollment and attendance. The case of New Zealand illustrates this finding notably. The introduction of Māori immersion education (education in the Māori language) in 1982 was a success in many ways. Not only has the size of the sector grown so much that students in New Zealand can now attend Māori-language education from preschool through primary and secondary schools, but also it has created an incentive for other schools to start teaching Māori. Today, an estimated 80 percent of Māori children learn their mother tongue to varying degrees and in various forms in the primary and secondary levels of education (see chapter 11 by Ringold). No in-depth assessment has yet been made, but according to evaluations carried out in New Zealand, the extension of Māori-language teaching has had a strong effect on the ability of students to perform in class.

When researchers assess the effects of bilingual education, they also must consider children's interest in learning a second language. Interest depends on issues of identity and the perception of the relevance of the second language. If the second language is seen as the language of the invader, as was the case for Russian in the Baltic states under the Soviet Union, then not much energy is likely to go into learning the majority language, especially if someone can get by without mastering it. Lack of interest will also exist if the second language is not seen as bringing any solid prospects in terms of future livelihood. In Romania, the Hungarian minority community often sees its future as involving migration to Hungary or another European Union country, which are considered to offer better prospects than Romania. This perspective does not encourage families to invest in their children's education in Romanian.

Changes to the Curriculum

Learning in one's mother tongue and teaching local languages at school are only one aspect of multicultural education. Introducing an understanding of minority cultures in the curriculum is also central—not only in history, geography, and literature, but also in other specific areas, such as music, artistic expression, and local trades. Some argue that this cultural appreciation needs to go hand in hand with multilingual education. Learning about their own culture allows children to perceive the sense and meaning of learning a different language. Currently, a big debate is in progress about how the curriculum should be adapted to reflect the various cultures of a country, especially in cases with a history of conflict between the various cultures composing a nation. Many argue that having an additional curriculum on the culture of one group, in the form of separate books and classes, increases that group's sense of difference and alienation from the majority culture, which therefore undermines social cohesion. Having books that actually integrate the geography, history, and arts of various groups within the same nation is preferable.

Adaptation of the curriculum is also linked to a debate on pedagogical methods, with some specialists arguing that different cultures have different methods and abilities of learning (King and Schielmann 2004).

Cultural Differences in the Classroom

How should teaching be organized when different sociocultural groups are in the same community? Should minorities be taught in separate schools at primary level to facilitate the teaching of the specific culture of the subgroup and avoid in-class discrimination; should all students be in the same school, with some classes taught separately; or should all students learn the same things? The debate is raging among specialists in multicultural education. Hungary, the most advanced country in Eastern Europe for multicultural education, is supporting three types of schools:

- Schools where the teaching is entirely provided in the minority language
- Bilingual schools where both the national official language and the minority language are being taught
- Schools where the mother tongue is taught as a "foreign" language.

The Hungarian system of education is quite decentralized, and many schools have room for adapting the noncore curriculum. Because the development of multicultural education is still relatively new, assessing the merits of these different approaches is difficult at this stage.

In particular, the value of separate schools for minorities is the focus of much debate. In some countries, minorities attend separate schools from the majority population or are forced into special schools because they cannot perform well in majority schools, often because of language barriers. This is the case with the Roma population in Eastern and Central Europe. In many cases, these schools are actually schools for children with disabilities, therefore reinforcing the strong stereotype that Roma are intellectually inferior. By all standards, these are second-rate schools where the Roma students cannot learn properly. A number of indigenous populations in Australia, New Zealand, and Latin America were also placed in special schools. Because of the disastrous effects of these policies, the idea of special schools for minorities is today often viewed with skepticism. Some believe that these schools end up second rate because of a lack of financial means, their isolation from mainstream education, and the low quality of their teachers. In addition, when these schools target excluded minorities—such as the Roma, who live in urban ghettos—they can be vulnerable to violence and the influence of deviant behaviors.

Roma special schools, which are usually run by nongovernmental organizations (NGOs) but receive state support, are an interesting example. Some have been successful in attracting students to education who probably would have remained out of the school system without the opportunities opened up by these special schools.

Keeping children in the same school but with mediators, teaching assistants, and special classes on culturally sensitive subjects is often the preferred approach. It is seen as a way both to recognize that minority students face special problems of integration in the school and to ensure that the minority is not educated separately from the mainstream population. Finally, after-hours classes can be very helpful, where specific curricula related to the minority culture are taught and support is provided to allow the minority children to keep up in the standard class.

Cultural Diversity in Preschool

Multicultural issues are also critical in preschool. This stage is seen as vital for sociability and to prepare children for primary education. Preschool, if conceived as a transition period and not just a way to send children to school earlier, is important to create a peaceful and nonthreatening bridge between a minority culture and the mainstream culture. A program initiated by UNICEF with a local NGO in Albania, Kosovo, and Macedonia and boosted by funding from the World Bank, helped organize community centers for mothers and their children of preschool age. The beneficiaries are mostly Roma and Albanians living relatively isolated in their communities and often confined to their homes because of violence and blood feuds, especially in northern Albania. The program has been effective in getting mothers to accept the idea of schooling, as well as getting children to socialize with nonpeers in the security of their mother's presence.

Quality Education

In multicultural education, the main challenge is to ensure quality education for minority languages and other culture-related subjects. Problems maintaining quality education are usually linked to the following:

- Financial means to pay additional teachers and buy additional text-books
- Availability of teachers who have a solid understanding of the culture and are qualified to teach minorities
- Coordination between the central authority and local authority in implementation of new curriculum
- Outreach to parents and children of the majority population so that they understand the purpose of introducing new subjects to avoid backlash at the school level
- Establishment of a monitoring system that facilitates assessment of the effect of new curricula and allows for correction when mistakes are made.

The situation varies considerably according to each case. Very often, the more isolated and marginalized the community, the more difficult it will be to introduce new subjects to the curriculum. In the case of the Roma, for instance, work on standardizing the Romani language, which has many different dialects, is still needed. More Romani teachers need to be trained to convince families that the teaching is worthwhile and to explain to the majority population how they could benefit from having Romani children learn their own language and culture. As a follow-up to its national strategy to improve the Roma situation, formulated in 2001, the Romanian government adopted a set of programs focusing on these shortcomings

(Republic of Romania Government Decision 430/2001). It included the following:

- Affirmative action to support Roma entry to university
- Measures to increase the number of Roma-qualified teachers
- Outreach programs to stimulate interest in Romani studies
- Design of curricula, textbooks, and didactic materials for the study of Romani language and Roma history and traditions
- Recruitment of Roma school inspectors to monitor the quality of Romani education and assess the implementation of the program.

Some circumstances—for example, whether the minority is concentrated in certain areas or dispersed throughout a country—will affect both costs and quality. Countries usually require a minimum concentration of children to start bilingual education in a community. In Bulgaria, for instance, a minimum of 13 students is necessary for a teacher to be appointed for language classes. If a minority is well organized, with many NGOs and support from a neighboring nation, as with the Hungarians in Romania, then all of these obstacles become less serious. Experience shows that motivated NGOs can help in this area. The language immersion program of the Māori in New Zealand started with an NGO, which then spread its successful experience with the help of government funding.

Paradoxically, the groups that probably need multicultural education the most—groups that are marginal and poor with a high level of illiteracy—are also the ones for whom it is the most expensive and difficult to implement. Obviously, German, Hungarian, and to some extent Turkish minorities in Eastern and Central Europe are accessing bilingual education in most areas where they live. Maya, Quechua, Aymara, and Guarani in Latin America (Hall and Patrinos 2005), as well as Roma in Europe (Ringold, Orenstein, and Wilkens 2003), have more difficulty accessing bilingual education, which isolates them even more from opportunities to access education and services in general. Participation of parents is usually key to the success of multicultural education. Education does not end when children leave school; it continues at home, in large part through the interest and support of the parents. Ensuring quality education through parent monitoring is important. For this reason, mechanisms that allow parent participation, such as school boards, monitoring committees, and parent–teacher associations, are all central to quality education.

Participation is essential for multicultural education because persuading municipal governments and parents from the majority population that multicultural education can benefit the whole community is not usually easy. Beneficiaries might be dubious about the benefits of multicultural education and not see the practical benefits for their own children. Without important efforts to involve parents and without outreach to other stakeholders, multicultural education will fail.

Participation of other stakeholders in the development of multicultural education is also vital. Local governments and teachers can feel threatened by education reform, especially when it can change the power structure in a community. In Latin America, large teachers' unions have often opposed multicultural education; they see the recruitment of indigenous and local minority teachers as a threat to their existence and control. Having strong parent and community support for reforms usually helps counterbalance the power of conservative teachers' unions.

Health Care

Recent studies attribute part of the problems of poor health in indigenous populations and ethnic minorities to poor awareness by the medical establishment of cultural issues and the cultural environment in which illness and treatment are understood by the patient. According to researchers at the London School of Hygiene and Tropical Medicine, addressing the indigenous health crisis requires a more holistic vision of health research and interventions. Health services should be more integrated, with an indigenous outlook on health and well-being. These researchers also advocate continued research on the health of indigenous peoples, with a specific emphasis on including indigenous perspectives on health and incorporating their views into health policies (Stephens and others 2005).

Policies taking cultural diversity in health care into account have two main components: the first consists of measures to respect the cultural background of a patient; the second recognizes the value of the traditional curative practices of a population. These components can be combined, but usually the first component is the focus of health care programs designed to reach minority groups with strong cultural specificities. Again, as in the case of education, taking culture and cultural diversity into consideration in health care is consistent with the recent trend toward (a) preventive approaches over curative medicine and outreach and (b) general practices over hospital care.

Health and Culture

Recognizing that health and culture are interconnected—in other words, that the way people see their body and health is influenced by values and societal norms—is essential, not only for effective outreach and acceptance of medical care, but also to make prevention and cure more effective. Many surveys show that a lack of trust in the Western health care system is an important issue in the developing world, together with the high cost of treatment. Experience shows that action can be taken to help bridge this gap.

First, understanding the relationship between the body and the mind with regard to wellness and illness in a specific culture is essential when trying to improve prevention and access to health care, as well as effectiveness of treatments. Many cultures do not understand the separation of the body, the mind, and society as Western medicine does. Hiring health workers who originate from the culture concerned usually helps, but other public health specialists and personnel must make the effort to understand what cure and wellness mean in specific cultural contexts.

Second, language can be a barrier to health prevention and care. Health providers who speak the language of the minority group are essential, especially in areas where the knowledge of the national language is limited.

Third, respect for cultural specificities should be integrated into the public health system. Respect for cultural specificities means taking into account the way one's relationship with one's body is valued and considered in various cultures. Considering culture requires careful assessment of the gender dimension of health care. In some societies, for instance, it would not be socially acceptable for a woman to be examined by a male doctor and vice versa. Other barriers, such as being separated from the family, eating food that is prepared outside the family, and not being able to pray, can act as major deterrents in accessing health care. Some of these demands go against hygiene standards; therefore, some tradeoff usually needs to be made, but only after the psychological benefits of respecting one's culture have been taken into account. In any case, cultural specificity, even if negative, requires respect and consideration, if only to explain to the patient what might not be beneficial to his or her health.

Australia has made great efforts to introduce cultural awareness in the training of doctors and nurses working with the aboriginal population

(Beaton 1994). In 2001, the New Zealand Ministry of Health launched the Māori Health Strategy, He Korowai Oranga. One of the main innovations of the strategy is the introduction of Māori health providers. Workers are contracted to deliver services to the Māori population in the framework of Māori governance and management structure and in accordance with Māori values and culture (see chapter 11).

In Romania, the government has agreed to a number of measures to increase access to health care of Roma residents. These measures include activities that should facilitate the inclusion of Roma in health insurance participation and promotion of intercultural education among all categories of medical personnel. In an attempt to break down barriers between Roma communities and health providers, the government has adopted affirmative action measures and increased opportunities for Roma to become health care providers (for example, it has increased the number of Roma nurses, district nurses, doctors, and social workers through scholarships and training). Introducing Roma health mediators in Roma communities has been one of the most successful schemes. The scheme was initiated in 1997 by the NGO Roma Center for Social Intervention and Studies, and in 2001, the Romanian government officially adopted it. Health mediators work in Roma communities to help ease communication and understanding between Roma patients and the medical staff. They also keep Roma communities informed of their rights regarding access to health care. In 2005, health mediators were active in 150 communities and facilitated access to health care to 38,000 Roma (Andreescu 2005).

Traditional Medicine

Western medical institutions have only recently started to recognize the importance of traditional forms of medicines in large parts of the world. Some practices, such as acupuncture, use of medicinal plants, and manual therapies, are now widely acknowledged to be very effective in treating certain types of illnesses. The gap between traditional medicine and Western medicine is not as big as it seems, however. Some 25 percent of plants used in the manufacturing of modern drugs are used in traditional medicines and actually come from knowledge acquired from those medicines. Even some psychosymbolic curative systems, such as shamanism in Asia, traditional healers in Africa, and exorcism in Europe, can be effective in the treatment of psychological disorders. A recent report from the World Health Organization (WHO) points out that traditional healings are still a vital part of the healing strategies of indigenous communities. As such, they should either be recognized as a parallel system—equal but separate—as in India or be integrated into the medical education and practice of mainstream medicine, as in Bhutan, China, and Vietnam. Currently, most countries with indigenous populations outside of Asia do not have parallel or integrated health systems (Alderete 1999). Several studies have documented how combining traditional healing strategies with Western medicine practices has helped in the healing process of patients (Yoder 1982).

WHO (2002) adopted a traditional medicine strategy for 2002 to 2005. The strategy recognizes that traditional medicine is widely used and rapidly growing. The report estimates that in Africa 80 percent of the population uses traditional medicine and that in China it represents 40 percent of delivered health care. In Malaysia, an estimated US$500 million is spent annually on traditional health care, compared with about US$300 million on allopathic medicine. In Ghana, Mali, Nigeria, and Zambia, the first line of treatment for 60 percent of children with malaria is the use of herbal medicines at home (WHO 2002). The report cites two reasons for the strong popularity of traditional medicines: (a) it is accessible and affordable in comparison with Western medicine, and (b) it is embedded within wider belief systems.[3]

In Africa, the recognition of the importance of traditional medicines and traditional healers has also been linked to the emergency created by the AIDS epidemic. The very limited outreach of the Western medical system in rural areas of many developing countries and the lack of trust for cures—often seen as foreign to the local culture—are recognized as major issues in conducting effective outreach campaigns. Traditional healers are often seen as ideal promotional agents to encourage practices that could decrease the AIDS epidemic. This role, of course, requires strong collaboration between traditional healers and Western medicine practitioners, which is far from easy. In 2000, an African Regional Strategy on Traditional Medicine was adopted to respond to this challenge. Ministers of health confirmed the role that traditional medicine can play in health systems and services in terms of health promotion, diagnosis, treatment, and prevention of diseases.

The WHO strategy identifies four main challenges for states in their recognition of traditional medicines:

• The weakness of national policy and regulatory frameworks
• The lack of a good understanding of safety, efficacy, and quality issues

- Accessibility
- Support for a rational use of traditional medicine.

The strategy states that, today, only 25 of 191 members have developed policies on the use of traditional medicine.

In developing these policies, countries should also address intellectual property issues. U.S. and European pharmaceutical laboratories are actively involved in the study of traditional medicinal plants in Latin America and Asia, often in collaboration with national research institutions. Many collaborative agreements have been signed with governments for this type of research, but little attention has been given to the property rights of communities with knowledge of these plants.

Interest in medicinal plants is also a challenge for biodiversity conservation. Many of these plants are rare and are grown in very specific environments; overharvesting of this flora can quickly result in an extinction of plant varieties. For this reason, many research institutions are compiling detailed inventories of medicinal plants and creating informal policies of protection, as well as environmental safeguards.

Collaboration between Traditional and Western Medicine

Many issues surround the encouragement of collaboration between traditional and Western medicine, primarily different understandings of what the human being is. Traditional medicines usually favor holistic treatments, which are based on an understanding of the human being as strongly dependent on a symbolic and cultural environment.

> [Traditional medicine] therapies have developed rather differently [from allopathic medicine], having been very much influenced by the culture and historical conditions within which they first evolved. Their common basis is an holistic approach to life, equilibrium between the mind, the body and their environment, and an emphasis on health rather than on disease. Generally, the practitioner focuses on the overall condition of the individual patient, rather than on the particular ailment or diseases from which he or she is suffering (WHO 2002: 21).

The Western medical establishment is increasingly recognizing that the lack of a holistic approach is a shortcoming of allopathic therapies, but it still finds recognizing the true value of such approaches difficult and continues to exclude the holistic approach from most medical student curricula. More proof is probably needed of the value of traditional medicine.

The WHO strategy supports further research into traditional medicines through medical trials.[4]

Assessment of the legitimacy of traditional healers is also a major issue, especially in environments such as urban centers, where acculturation is strong. Traditional healers are usually known by the community and are under some sort of collective control. People know from whom these healers received their knowledge, how effective they have been in curing members of the community, and how legitimate they are according to local tradition and institutions. Today, many people are appointing themselves healers for economic or influential reasons, without any community control, particularly in urban centers where community control is often reduced and community checks and balances are eroded.

In the field of psychiatry, traditional medicine can be effective because of the highly symbolic and cultural context of some psychological illnesses. However, some approaches to healing, especially when witchcraft is involved, can be very negative for society, in particular those that ostracize individuals because they are named as culprits in the community. Again, these approaches tend to be much worse in environments where acculturation is stronger, such as large urban centers.

In many countries, the lack of communication between Western health care providers and traditional healers means that referral systems are weak. The ideal would be a greater coordination between both type of medicines, with some form of referral system and a better understanding and respect by medical practitioners of what traditional medicine can offer, and vice versa. For this outcome, much more research on medicinal plants and on other practices that accompany the prescription of plants by traditional healers is required.

Policy Implications

Policies and programs aimed at supporting cultural diversity have acquired a new visibility in the international arena over the past 15 years. Because impact analyses of programs and policies supporting cultural diversity are still scarce and because cultural diversity is a relatively new focus of attention for governments and international organizations, clear-cut policy recommendations are difficult to provide. How to nurture cultural diversity at local level while preserving cohesion, striving for equity, and avoiding conflicts is still open to debate. The nascent theory of multiculturalism tells us that the acknowledgment of cultural diversity itself will help achieve cohesion and equity and that its negation will do the reverse. Recognizing cultural diversity and fighting poverty are complementary activities. Because inequality is still strongly correlated with ethnic and cultural differences, reduction of world inequalities clearly requires recognition of cultural differences and the dynamics of interactions between different sociocultural groups within societies. Actions supporting cultural diversity also need to be integrated in overall social and economic policies to be effective. The answer is not to develop parallel policies but to mainstream the attention to cultural diversity within government policies and programs. Cultural diversity is handled best when integrated.

When one is designing policies and programs integrating practices issued from a specific culture in service delivery, a central preliminary step should be to assess how collective and individual aspirations are going to interconnect, what they will do for the power structure in the community, and—more broadly—what they will do to the functioning of existing institutions. Understanding how different systems expressing the cultural diversity of a society will work together is also important. Usually, they are not all based on the same set of values.

Policies for cultural diversity should not be imposed from the top; a bottom-up approach is needed. Cultural diversity cannot be driven only by elites. Policy makers and elites need to understand what the population—particularly the poor—feels and what policies supporting cultural diversity can do to improve the day-to-day situation of the people at the community level. Cultural diversity cannot be established through laws only; deep institutional changes are required as well. Recognizing a minority culture is a process that needs to be managed over time like any other institutional reform. Cultures adapt and change over time. Flexible policies are required so that corrections and improvements can be made along the way.

When a country decides to recognize different cultures and shape its services to meet aspirations for cultural diversity, it needs to understand the political motivations at play. The design of policies supporting cultural diversity can be politically motivated on premises that go against the interest of the minorities and cultural groups concerned. Cultural diversity is often the target of populist agendas, and, because it touches symbolic identities, it can create strong political divisions. These motivations should be clear, at least in the minds of the technicians designing policies.

Recognizing cultural diversity as multisectoral is essential. Supporting native languages does not make much sense if children never use this language outside narrow family circles. Recognizing customary law but not the language in which the law is expressed and applied is also not a wise strategy. Requesting health workers to speak a local language if it is not taught at school does not make sense.

These actions supporting cultural diversity at local level will always have very limited effect unless countries adopt a policy and legal framework that provides legitimacy for these actions and programs at the local level. Such a framework would prove the central government commitment while bringing together various sectoral policies.

When governments are establishing policies and programs supporting cultural diversity, participatory processes are critical, because all members of the communities concerned need to be part of the process to avoid exclusion. However, traditional forms of consultation can exclude some subgroups, so a full commitment should be given to include all stakeholders.

The design of programs and policies nurturing cultural diversity requires a careful balancing act between protecting individual human rights and recognizing cultural collective rights. Typically, every society will have fundamental individual rights that the society at large considers essential for all. Policy makers should agree that these fundamental rights cannot be challenged.

Another major issue is the cost of recognizing cultural diversity in service delivery, especially for poor countries. Costs are often not negligible, especially when the task requires training and capacity building; however, costs should be looked at together with benefits. Policies and programs dealing with cultural diversity usually require investment in the first years, but then they can be implemented over subsequent years with few additional costs to the normal sectoral budgets. Because of these start-up investments, donor support can play a big role.

Recognition of cultural identity and practices should not be seen as one-shot measures; it needs to be nurtured and adapted. Fresh objectives might emerge, and corrective measures will be needed. Whatever is done should be done with a long-term goal and with room for adjustment along the way.

Measurement and assessment of the effects of policies and programs supporting cultural diversity are still very limited. In the field of education, more analysis is available than in other sectors, but the focus is mainly on the effect of introducing local languages and teaching in the mother tongue.

Today, policies for the recognition of cultural diversity in the delivery of basic services to the population should be seen as part of the social response to globalization and as an effort to make globalization more equitable and human. In a growing number of countries, the recognition of such diversity is becoming one of the most important components of social inclusion policies.

Notes

1. The world's nearly 200 countries include some 5,000 ethnic groups. Two-thirds of countries have more than one ethnic or religious group making up at least 10 percent of the population (UNDP 2004).
2. The terms *social integration, social inclusion,* and *social cohesion* are used often in this chapter. These terms are not equivalent. *Social cohesion* refers to the way a group, a community, or a society reacts collectively to internal or external challenges. A cohesive society minimizes internal conflict, and its members collaborate effectively to resolve problems or face external threats. A cohesive society does not have to be culturally homogenous. The concept of *social integration* refers to the ability of individuals or groups to be part of a broader community or society economically, socially, and politically, and it assumes that members of the group or society share a number of common values and vision. *Social inclusion* refers also to the ability of individuals to be part of a broader group, but it gives less emphasis to the requirement of sharing common values and vision and focuses on the access to basic rights and basic functions.
3. On the fast development of traditional medicine in Africa, see in particular the very lively book by J. M. Gibbal (1984).
4. The WHO (2002: 23) strategy on traditional medicine points to a study undertaken by Peru's National Program for Complementary Medicine and the Pan American Health Organization (PAHO), which compared traditional medicine and allopathic medicine practices through the systematic follow-up of 339 patients for a year. Treatments of the following pathologies were analyzed: moderate osteoarthritis, back pain, anxiety-based neuroses, asthma, peptic acid disease, tension migraine headache, exogenous obesity, and peripheral facial analysis. The overall cost-effectiveness of the traditional medicine treatment was 53 to 63 percent higher than that of conventional treatments for selected pathologies.

References

Alderete, E. 1999. *The Health of Indigenous Peoples.* Geneva: World Health Organization.

Andreescu, V. 2005. "Cultural Diversity and Service Delivery." Case study for Romania. University of Louisville, Louisville, KY.

Banks, J. A. 2001. "Multicultural Education: Historical Development, Dimensions, and Practice." In *Handbook of Research on Multicultural Education*, eds. J. A. Banks and C. A. McGee Banks, 3–29. San Francisco: Jossey-Bass.

Beaton, N. 1994. "Aboriginal Health and a New Curriculum for Rural Doctors." *Medical Journal of Australia* 160 (4): 185–86.

Douglas, M. 2004. "Traditional Culture, Let's Hear No More about It." In *Culture and Public Action,* eds. M. Walton and R. Vijayendra, 85–109. Washington, DC: World Bank.

Dutcher, N., and G. K. Tucker. 1997. *The Use of First and Second Language in Education: A Review of Education Experience.* Washington, DC: World Bank.

Gibbal, J. M. 1984. *Guérisseurs et Magiciens du Sahel.* Paris: Métailié.

Hall, G., and H. A. Patrinos. 2005. *Indigenous Peoples, Poverty, and Human Development in Latin America: 1994–2004.* Washington, DC: World Bank.

King, L., and S. Schielmann. 2004. *The Challenge of Indigenous Education: Practice and Perspectives.* Paris: United Nations Educational, Scientific, and Cultural Organization.

Kymlicka, W. 1995. *Multicultural Citizenship.* Oxford, U.K.: Oxford University Press.

Kymlicka, W., and F. Grin. 2003. "Assessing the Politics of Diversity in Transition Countries." In *Nation-Building, Ethnicity, and Language Politics in Transition Countries*, European Centre for Minority Issues Series on Ethnopolitics and Minority Issues, vol. 2, eds. F. Daftary and F. Grin, 5–27. Budapest: Open Society Institute.

Mehrotra, S. 1998. "Education for All: Policy Lessons from High Achieving Countries." *International Review of Education* 44 (5–6): 461–84.

Moodley, K. A. 2001. "Multicultural Education in Canada: Historical Development and Current Status." In *Handbook of Research on Multicultural Education*, eds. J. A. Banks and C. A. McGee Banks, 801–20. San Francisco: Jossey-Bass.

Ringold, D., M. A. Orenstein, and E. Wilkens. 2003. *Roma in an Expanding Europe: Breaking the Poverty Cycle.* Washington, DC: World Bank.

Stephens, C., C. Nettleton, J. Porter, R. Willis, and S. Clark. 2005. "Indigenous People's Health—Why They Are behind Everyone, Everywhere?" *Lancet* 366 (9479): 10–13.

UNDP (United Nation Development Programme). 2004. *Human Development Report 2004: Cultural Liberty in Today's Diverse World.* New York: UNDP.

WHO (World Health Organization). 2002. *WHO Traditional Medicine Strategy, 2002–2005.* Geneva: WHO.

Yoder, P. S. 1982. "Biomedical and Ethnomedical Practice in Rural Zaire: Contrasts and Complements." *Social Science and Medicine* 16 (21): 1851–57.

CHAPTER 11

Accounting for Diversity: Policy Design and Māori Development in New Zealand

Dena Ringold

Māori are the indigenous people of New Zealand.[1] Theirs is a relatively small population (approximately 620,000) within a relatively small country. However, their contributions are substantial, both at home and internationally. Māori as a whole have made impressive gains and contributions across the economic, cultural, and social spectrum of New Zealand. More Māori participate at all levels of education than ever before. Māori unemployment is at a 20-year low, and Māori are working across the economy. There has been a cultural renaissance, and the use of the Māori language is on the rise.

However, not all Māori are benefiting from these upward trends. Some Māori remain unemployed or in low-level or unskilled jobs that are vulnerable to economic shocks. Māori are disproportionately represented among the poor, especially Māori children. As with indigenous peoples in other countries, there is a significant gap in life expectancy—in this case, eight to nine years—between Māori and non-Māori.

Recent Māori development approaches provide a valuable record of experience and innovation for New Zealand and other countries. The past 20 years have seen the emergence and growth of services developed, owned, and provided by Māori, as well as numerous initiatives to make mainstream programs more inclusive and responsive. This effort has

This chapter is based on work done by the author while an Ian Axford fellow in public policy, based at the Ministry of Māori Development in Wellington, New Zealand, February through July 2005.

271

included formulating policy strategies, building capacity within government departments for developing and delivering services, and diversifying service delivery considerably.

At the level of policy design and service delivery, New Zealand has sought to calibrate the extent to which policies should be universal, mainstreamed, and applicable to the entire society, as well as the extent to which they should be targeted to specific populations. These questions are directly relevant for other countries, developed and developing nations alike, that aim to improve the welfare of their own indigenous peoples, ethnic minorities, and vulnerable groups. Increasingly, the results suggest that both inclusive policies, reaching all New Zealanders, and policies recognizing the cultural distinctness and particular needs of Māori are necessary.

The State of Māori Development

Māori comprise a larger share of the total population than indigenous peoples in other countries (see table 11.1). According to Statistics New Zealand's 2004 estimates, 620,000 individuals identify themselves as Māori. That amounts to 15 percent of New Zealand's population of 4.1 million and is set to increase, with projections suggesting that Māori will make up 17 percent of the total population by 2021 (Statistics New Zealand 2005).

Growth is driven by higher-than-average fertility, intermarriage, and a younger age structure. Although Māori fertility has been declining and converging with non-Māori levels since the 1960s, it remains higher, at 2.7 births per woman compared with 1.9 births for non-Māori.

High rates of intermarriage underscore the increasingly diverse ethnic composition of the population. Nearly 25 percent of Māori children were born to non-Māori mothers in 2003, and 57 percent of Māori children have a parent who identifies with European ethnicity.[2] The Māori population is also significantly younger than the national average. In 2001, 25 percent of children in New Zealand were Māori. The median age of Māori is 22 compared with 37 for non-Māori (Statistics New Zealand 2005).

Economic Recovery and Māori

Recovery since New Zealand's recession of the early 1990s has made a difference to the living standards and welfare of all New Zealanders, including Māori. The recovery of the labor market since the economic

Table 11.1. Comparison of Indigenous Peoples, Selected Indicators, Latest Possible Year

	Māori (New Zealand)	Aboriginal and Torres Strait Islanders (Australia)	First nations peoples (Canada)	Native Americans and Alaskan natives (United States)[a]
Total population	620,000	458,500	1,319,890	4,400,000
Percentage of population	15	2.4	4.4	1.5
Life expectancy:				
Males (age)	69	59	69	67
Females (age)	73	65	77	68
Life expectancy gap[b]:				
Males (years)	9	18	7	7
Females (years)	8	17	5	12
Infant mortality (per 1,000 live births)	7	10	8	9
Employment rate (%)	59	42	43	53
Unemployment rate (%)	8	20	19	12

Sources: U.S. Centers for Disease Control and Prevention 2004, http://www.cdc.gov; Department of Labour 2005; Goldberg, Notson, and Nolan 2005; Health Canada 2005, http://www.hc-sc.gc.ca; Ministry of Health Nauenberg 2005; Statistics New Zealand 2005.
a. 2000 census data include those who reported more than one race.
b. Difference from nonindigenous population.

downturn of the early 1990s has been a key factor driving improved economic performance. Although New Zealand's unemployment rate was 11 percent in 1992, by mid-2005 it had reached 3.8 percent, the lowest rate in the Organisation for Economic Co-operation and Development (OECD).[3] Labor market expansion has been especially critical for Māori, who were most adversely affected by the economic reforms of the late 1980s and early 1990s. Māori unemployment peaked at 27 percent in March 1992, nearly 18 percentage points higher than non-Māori unemployment of 9.5 percent.

Māori employment levels have rebounded since the mid-1990s. Initially, Māori employment growth was driven by an increase in part-time employment. However, since December 2000, full-time employment growth has become the main source of employment. Employment rates of Māori women have outpaced those of Māori men over the past decade, at 4.6 percent and 2.8 percent annual growth, respectively. Rising employment has improved living standards. Average incomes of employed Māori increased 8 percent in real terms between 1997/98 and 2002/03, and 16 percent for all working-age Māori (Dixon and Maré 2004).

Diversity and Disparities

There is considerable diversity and heterogeneity within Māori society, which is organized tribally. Differences within the population emerge along various lines. Māori belong to *iwi* and *hapū* (tribes and subtribes) and to *whānau* (families),[4] each with its own distinctive history, traditions, and cultural attributes. In the 2001 census, some 75 percent of Māori identified themselves as affiliated with one or more of 106 *iwi*. Whereas some Māori identify strongly with their *iwi, hapū,* and *whānau*, others have less active connections.

Māori socioeconomic outcomes diverge depending on the type of ethnic identification. In the census and other datasets, Māori can be categorized as *sole Māori* (those who regard themselves as only Māori) or as *mixed Māori* (those who identify with more than one ethnic group). Analysis of the labor force survey found significant gaps in welfare between sole and mixed Māori. Mixed Māori were more likely to have labor market status similar to non-Māori, whereas sole Māori had lower employment chances (Chapple 1999).

Diversity is also geographic and regional. Māori living in rural areas lack the access to employment and education opportunities that are available to Māori living in cities (Maani 2002). Māori men and boys are increasingly falling behind in critical areas. Girls are more likely than boys to stay in school at age 16 and 17, and at the tertiary level nearly two-thirds of Māori students were women (64 percent) (Ministry of Education 2005b; 2005c). Māori men are also overrepresented among the prison population, 51 percent of which is estimated to be Māori. However, Māori women lag behind in other areas. Although the labor market status of Māori women has been improving, unemployment is slightly higher (3 percentage points), and their wages are below those of Māori men and non-Māori (Statistics New Zealand 2004; Te Puni Kōkiri 2005).

The past two decades have been a remarkable period of economic, social, and cultural transformation for Māori. Although the reforms and restructuring of the mid-1980s and early 1990s disproportionately affected Māori employment, economic recovery has brought unemployment down, and the share of low-income families with Māori adults has fallen. Participation in early childhood and tertiary education has escalated, and use of the Māori language and participation in cultural activities continue to increase. The period has also been characterized by increased economic and cultural diversification of Māori.

Policy Approaches to Māori Development

Recent approaches to Māori development provide a valuable record of experience and experimentation. Several key themes have characterized policy developments over the past two decades:

- A desire by Māori to take charge of their own development
- An ongoing interest in self-determination, autonomy, and involvement in the policies and programs that affect them
- A recognition that policy approaches need to consider the history, culture, and position of Māori as the indigenous people of New Zealand
- A need to tackle socioeconomic disparities between Māori and non-Māori.

The Treaty of Waitangi

The Treaty of Waitangi, signed in 1840 by Māori tribal (*iwi*) chiefs and representatives of the British Crown, sets a unique backdrop for policy in New Zealand. The Treaty paved the way for, and continues to shape, Māori participation in politics and public policy in New Zealand. Although debates about the actual meaning and intent of the Treaty continue to this day, it has provided an important framework for recognizing Māori as the indigenous people of New Zealand and has influenced relations between Māori and the Crown.[5] To a greater extent than indigenous and minority policy approaches in other countries, policies in New Zealand have taken into account the history and interests of Māori.

The principles of the Treaty of Waitangi have been incorporated into legislation as mechanisms for recognizing indigenous rights. The framework has also been influential in addressing the injustices of the colonial period. In 1975, the government established the Waitangi Tribunal to hear claims by Māori concerning breaches of the Treaty's principles. In 1985, the tribunal's jurisdiction was extended to cover claims from the Treaty's signing in 1840. The tribunal hears claims brought by Māori individuals and groups.[6] Settlements involve a formal apology by the Crown, as well as redress through recognition of the claimants' rights, financial settlement, return of assets, or all three.[7] The settlement process has had an important role in providing a forum for recognizing, airing, and acknowledging historical breaches of the Treaty.

Targeting and Tailoring

For policy discussions, it is useful to distinguish between targeting and tailoring of services. *Targeting* refers to the determination of eligibility for services and benefits, whereas *tailoring* refers to the design of services and benefits to respond to the needs of specific population groups. Tailoring can make policies and services more accessible, as well as more effective, for ethnic groups by involving them in delivery, increasing voice and empowerment, strengthening accountability, and incorporating culture— including language, values, and traditions.

Few policy targets in New Zealand are actually based on ethnicity to the extent that being Māori (or a member of another ethnic group) would affect an individual's eligibility to participate in the program or access the service. However, there has been a wealth of experience in tailoring services on the basis of ethnicity, particularly to Māori communities.

The distinction between services that are targeted through eligibility criteria and those that are tailored to consider the needs and preferences of beneficiaries is useful for considerations of policy design. Tailoring concerns the design and delivery of services. Tailored programs are generally self-targeted rather than exclusive. They are designed so that the intended beneficiaries are most likely to access the program or service. For example, Māori language education is not restricted to Māori, but Māori are most likely to participate. Similarly, services may be physically provided within Māori communities.

Services can be tailored in many ways: through the location of delivery (for example, within the community); the involvement of beneficiaries (for example, as service providers); and the content (for example, a school curriculum that incorporates local history and culture). Services in New Zealand have been tailored to ethnic groups—and to Māori in particular—through the devolution and decentralization of service delivery to communities, the participation of Māori in service delivery and governance, strengthened outreach and communication, and the incorporation of Māori culture into services.

In New Zealand, tailoring has included the emergence of separate, alternative Māori services, such as Māori immersion education and Māori health providers. There have also been concerted efforts to tailor mainstream services to Māori. In the context of service delivery, *mainstream* refers to services or systems that are intended for the population as a whole. Mainstream education involves public schools that are not specific to a population group, as with health or other social services.[8] Tailoring of mainstream services is important, because an estimated 80 to 90 percent of Māori receive health and education from mainstream services.

Because of the high diversification of services, there is no neat division of targeted, tailored, and mainstream policies. Targeted and tailored programs can be delivered within mainstream services—for example, through bilingual classrooms within mainstream schools or Māori health units in hospitals. An important distinction is between mainstream services (which may contain aspects of tailoring and targeting) and separate, or parallel, services (which exist alongside mainstream services). Tailoring has the potential to improve the quality of service delivery and outcomes through a number of channels, which are summarized in the following subsections.

Increasing efficiency and responsiveness. Many services in New Zealand have been devolved, or decentralized, to *iwi* providers, community groups, and other types of organizations. Devolution has the potential to improve the efficiency of services by making them more responsive and accessible to local needs and preferences. According to theory, local governments and organizations have more accurate information about the preferences of their constituents and can therefore better respond and tailor services to those needs and preferences. However, the efficiency argument for decentralization may be qualified by a loss of some economies of scale. Some localities may simply be too small to deliver services efficiently.

Decentralization may also undermine equality, as the provision of public services becomes more dependent on local resources, and there is a risk of increased regional inequality in the level and quality of services provided. Another potential pitfall is the risk that governance might substantially worsen because of capture by local elites or insufficient capacity for program management and service delivery.

Strengthening accountability. Devolution and increased participation of beneficiaries in governance and service provision also have the potential to strengthen accountability of services, and eventual outcomes. Public involvement can increase the demand for quality services and strengthen incentives for providers. In *World Development Report 2004: Making Services Work for Poor People*, the World Bank (2004) noted that accountability of services can be strengthened through greater responsiveness of politicians and policy makers, who, in turn, can influence the policies of service providers. There is also scope for strategies to strengthen the influence of citizens on service providers.

Facilitating empowerment. Improving outcomes depends on well-functioning institutions that respond to the needs of the population. Equally essential are mechanisms to ensure that all population groups can articulate their interests and participate in decision making. In *World Development Report 2000/2001: Attacking Poverty*, the World Bank (2000) identified empowerment as a central aspect of well-being, alongside opportunity and security. Strategies for tackling poverty and exclusion need to involve poor people in the decisions that affect them. Particular efforts are needed to reach out to groups that may be excluded for reasons of gender, ethnicity, or social status.

Strategies to promote empowerment include measures to make institutions more effective, as well as measures to enable participation and strengthen the ability of individuals and communities to engage with institutions. Building human and social capital is an important precondition. Education can increase the ability of the poor to articulate their interests and aspirations. Similarly, social networks and communities can increase opportunities for the poor to take charge of their own development.

Recognizing culture. Building cultural aspects, such as language and traditions, into policy and service design can function as a mechanism for the inclusion and empowerment of groups. Evidence is growing that programs and policies risk failure if they do not recognize the culture and perspectives of beneficiaries. In his book on culture and development, Amartya Sen discusses the channels through which culture influences development, including through the behavior and preferences of individuals and groups, which in turn affect economic success; through value formation; and through social and community interactions. He notes that culture can be an end in itself: "The freedom and opportunity for cultural activities are among the basic freedoms the enhancement of which can be seen to be constitutive of development" (Sen 2004: 39).

Culture can also affect the opportunities of different groups. The concept of *equality of agency* recognizes that different groups have different levels of influence attributable to the different social and cultural contexts in which they live. Groups can differ in their influence for reasons of history, discrimination, and gender. As a result, equality of access to social and cultural capital can be important, in addition to human and physical capital, for overcoming inequality and poverty. This concept implies a need for policies that consider group, as well as individual and agency, and for attention to different cultural perspectives (Rao and Walton 2004).

Tailoring Services to Māori

Services in New Zealand have been designed to be responsive to and effective for Māori in a number of ways:

- *Expanding Māori participation and ownership.* Growing Māori involvement in policy making and service delivery has been a major development of the past two decades. Māori are involved in governance and ownership of services as members of school boards and representatives on district health boards and primary care organizations. Māori own, manage, and deliver education, health, and social services and work as providers.
- *Devolving services.* Iwi, *hapū*, and urban Māori organizations have developed services and contract with various government departments.
- *Investing in Māori culture and values.* Aspects of Māori culture, values, and practice have been integrated into service delivery, both through separate Māori services and within mainstream services.
- *Strengthening outreach and communications.* Efforts have been made to improve the outreach of services and to tailor information to reach Māori communities by using language and culture in public information campaigns, embedding programs within local communities, and involving community members in delivery.
- *Increasing choice for all population groups.* An outcome of the diversification of service delivery approaches and providers has been increased choice. Along with the rest of the population, Māori have greater options to send their children to Māori schools and health providers.

The education and health sectors have supported alternative Māori providers owned and managed by Māori, Māori participation in governance, integration of culture into services, community involvement, and the development of the Māori workforce as education and health professionals.

Education

Māori students make up more than one-fifth of students in primary and secondary schools.[9] Raising Māori achievement in education has been a priority for policy makers, parents, and students alike. It has involved a combination of separate Māori medium programs, as well as concerted efforts to make mainstream education programs work for

Māori. Although New Zealand's education system performs well by international standards, the gap between high and low achievers is the widest in the OECD.

There have been significant efforts within the education sector to make schools more accessible and responsive to Māori. Māori medium education has allowed for the piloting of new approaches, some of which have been integrated into mainstream schools. This transfer of experience is critical, as between 80 and 96 percent of Māori students study in mainstream schools.[10]

The boundary between Māori medium and mainstream education is no longer clear cut. At the compulsory level, a growing number of mainstream schools have immersion and bilingual units. The Ministry of Education defines *Māori immersion education*, or *kaupapa matauranga Māori*, as education based on *matauranga* (traditional knowledge) and *tikanga Māori* (customs). It includes *kōhanga reo* (primary schools), *kura kaupapa Māori* (secondary schools), and bilingual immersion classes in mainstream schools (Ministry of Education 2005a).

Māori immersion education. Since the first *kōhanga reo* was set up in 1982, many Māori families have chosen to enroll their children in Māori language immersion schools (see box 11.1). The size of the Māori immersion education sector has grown, and it is now possible for students in New Zealand to participate in Māori-language education from preschool through secondary education. There are even some limited opportunities for study in the Māori language at the tertiary level.

Māori immersion education has multiple objectives. The *kōhanga reo* movement started with the goals of preserving the Māori language, teaching cultural traditions, transferring knowledge across generations, and providing education within a Māori cultural context. Māori schools and classes also aim to strengthen Māori ownership of education and respond to Māori interest in self-determination, or *tino rangatiratanga*, as embodied in the Treaty of Waitangi.

There are also important pedagogical rationales. International research suggests that, in certain contexts, bilingual education—particularly at the early childhood level—can improve children's language and cognitive development, as well as strengthen children's identity and self-confidence (Cooper and others 2004). Evidence from Latin America suggests that bilingual education for indigenous children can support school retention (Hall and Patrinos 2005).

BOX 11.1

Kōhanga Reo

The *kōhanga reo*, or "language nest" movement paved the way for Māori language education in New Zealand; it has been cited internationally for its contributions to language revitalization, early childhood education, and Māori development more broadly. The movement's example of a "by Māori, for Māori" service catalyzed Māori-led initiatives in other areas, including health and social services. In 1987, Koro Wetere, then minister for Māori affairs, stressed the importance of the movement for Māori development as a whole:

> The ultimate objective of Te Kōhanga Reo is nothing less than the rebirth of the Māori nation as an equal but separate element contributing to the common good of New Zealand society. (Ministry of Education 2005d.)

The first *kōhanga* was piloted outside Wellington in 1981. Although the primary objective was to support language retention by ensuring that children were immersed in the language from an early age, the approach was comprehensive, involving cultural, social, economic, and educational aspects and supporting the development and involvement of *whānau* through their involvement in the program. The program had an important effect on employment by creating opportunities, especially for Māori women, who were particularly disadvantaged in the labor market at the time. The approach also aimed to preserve and transfer Māori knowledge and culture across generations by having community elders teach children.

The design and philosophy of *kōhanga* are embedded in Māori culture and organization. Decision making and administration are modeled on *whānau* structures. Teachers (*kaiko*) are assisted by older women (*kuia*) and parents. The focus on parental involvement has brought many adult Māori back in contact with the language and with education. Many *kōhanga* were set up by *iwi* and *hapū* organizations at *marae* (community meeting space) and were linked with other activities involving the wider *whānau*.

The *kōhanga reo* movement spread rapidly. The government provided seed funding for five pilot centers. Within 12 months, 107 centers had been established with additional funding from the Department of Māori Affairs and the Māori Education Foundation. Seven years later, more than 600 *kōhanga* were in operation. In 2004, there were 513 *kōhanga reo* centers, enrolling 10,319 students. The numbers of *kōhanga* have declined because of consolidation of centers and because of the growth of other

(continued)

BOX 11.1

Kōhanga Reo (*continued*)

types of Māori early childhood programs. Each center is set up as an autonomous it is accountable to the Kōhanga Reo National Trust, which sets and manages policy for the organization.

The *kōhanga* movement has influenced mainstream education through its model of introducing language and culture into curriculum and pedagogy and through its strong emphasis on family and community. Aspects of the *kōhanga reo* curriculum have been adopted by other schools. Since its founding, *kōhanga reo* has inspired the establishment of other models of Māori-language preschools that are responsive to community needs. Many non-Māori have also sent their children to *kōhanga reo* and other Māori-language early childhood programs.

Sources: Ministry of Education, 2005d; Tangaere 1997; Tawhiwhirangi and others 1988.

In 2004, there were 513 *kōhanga reo* centers, enrolling more than 10,000 students, or 6 percent of children enrolled in early childhood education. Nearly one-third (30 percent) of Māori preschoolers were in *kōhanga reo* in 2004. Enrollments fell during the 1990s and early 2000s, but the majority of Māori children (80 percent in 2003) in early childhood education are in centers with some form of Māori medium education (Ministry of Social Development 2003).

The majority of children graduating from *kōhanga reo* continue their education in mainstream schools. However, there are a growing number of Māori schools and bilingual and immersion classes. Enrollments have fluctuated, along with enrollments in Māori medium education in early childhood, as age cohorts move through the school system. Four percent of Māori students were enrolled in *kura kaupapa Māori* schools in 2004 (5,976 students), and approximately 14 percent of Māori students were enrolled in some form of Māori medium education at the compulsory level.[11] Of these students, 43 percent were in schools or classes teaching in the Māori language 81 to 100 percent of the time, while the remainder were in classes using the Māori language more than 31 percent of the time.

A 2002 Education Review Office (ERO) summary of evaluations of 52 *kura kaupapa* found that some schools were highly effective at combining a focus on *kaupapa Māori*, effective teaching, governance, leadership, and *whānau* involvement. However, many schools still faced challenges in these areas. Most are relatively small, with an average of 84 students, compared with 267 students for all New Zealand schools. As a result, they faced issues common to other small schools, including isolation and limited capacity to leverage economies of scale. The reviews identified particular weaknesses in administration and governance; teaching practices, especially addressing individual learning needs; and staffing and personnel. Many of the schools lacked skilled and experienced staff members. Although *kura* are excluded from the requirement of employing only registered teachers, the demands on teachers in these schools can be greater than those on teachers in mainstream schools (ERO 2002).

Information on the socioeconomic backgrounds of students in immersion programs is limited. A 2004 study found that about 50 percent of participating children came from low-income households. Nearly one-fifth (19 percent) of students were in homes where neither parent was employed. Most of the parents who were employed were in professional jobs, a higher share than the total Māori population. The profile of families appeared to include a majority of lower-income families, as well as professional families on the upper tail of the income distribution (Cooper and others 2004).

Because of the newness of the sector, there is limited information and research on the futures of graduates of Māori immersion education compared with those of graduates from mainstream schools. There is evidence that a high share of 11th and 12th grade students in immersion schools achieved qualifications above the expected level (Ministry of Education 2005d). Such analysis is needed to determine whether these trends hold, controlling for factors such as the students' and parents' backgrounds. There is also a need to evaluate the further education and labor market outcomes of immersion and mainstream school graduates.

Education in mainstream schools. More than 80 percent of Māori students study in mainstream schools. In recent years, stakeholders at all levels, including the Ministry of Education, individual schools, *iwi*, and other partners, have put growing effort into raising the performance of Māori in schools. In its 2004 annual review, the ERO (2004) found that schools have been increasing their efforts to improve outcomes for Māori students over time.[12]

This has not always been the case. Focused initiatives to raise the performance of Māori in mainstream schools have accelerated in response to evidence that educational outcomes for Māori students were lagging. Māori achievement rates are, on average, lower than those of non-Māori children. Māori are also less likely to leave school with completed qualifications and are more likely to be stood down or suspended than their non-Māori peers (Ministry of Education 2005b, 2005d).[13] Research evidence identified the low expectations of teachers when it came to Māori achievement as one of the key factors contributing to poor performance of mainstream schools.

In its first review of Māori education in mainstream schools in 2001, the ERO found that only a minority of schools collected data to assess the achievement of Māori students or had established plans for making improvements. By 2004, most schools were collecting and analyzing achievement information of Māori and had some form of tailored initiatives focused on Māori students.

The ministry has supported a number of initiatives to improve outcomes for Māori within mainstream schools. These programs have focused on improving the quality of teaching through professional development. Strengthening community and family participation in schools has been another area of emphasis, through initiatives at the school level to involve parents, as well as growing Māori involvement in school governance and formal partnerships with *iwi* organizations.

The Māori immersion sector has influenced the way mainstream schools approach Māori education by demonstrating that bilingual education can be effective for Māori students and that Māori values and priorities can be incorporated into school management and teaching practices. However, persistent gaps in the educational achievements and attainments of Māori students point to the need for further efforts to reach Māori students and to ensure quality of education.

Achievement data showing a wider gap in results within the Māori student population than between Māori and non-Māori students underscore the increasingly diverse nature of the Māori student body. Ongoing attention is needed to make schools effective for high- and low-achieving students. Outcome evaluations of the educational and labor market status of Māori students, in both immersion and mainstream schools, are needed to understand what works and which quality improvements can be made.

Health Services

Significant and persistent gaps in Māori health status have intensified efforts to improve access and quality of health services for Māori. As with education, the health sector has been characterized by increasing choice and diversification in provider arrangements. A Māori health provider sector has emerged, and greater emphasis has been placed on improving Māori health outcomes within mainstream providers, particularly within primary care services, through tailored public health promotion activities, and through development of the Māori health workforce.

Māori health providers. Health services in New Zealand have been tailored to Māori through the growth of alternative Māori providers, as well as through efforts to improve health services for Māori within mainstream services. According to the 2005/06 application form for the Ministry of Health's Māori Provider Development Scheme, Māori health providers are "contracted to deliver health and disability services that target Māori clients or communities; are led by a Māori governance and management structure and express Māori kaupapa; and consider the wider issues of Māori development and how it might apply to their own organization."

Māori providers are variously arranged, set up by *iwi* and Māori organizations. There are currently around 250 providers, up from 20 in the mid-1990s. Māori health providers constitute a relatively small share of total health services. In 2004, an estimated 3 percent of the total health budget was spent on Māori health providers (Ministry of Health 2004).

Māori health providers aim to supply services appropriate and responsive to Māori health needs. Such services require a focus on Māori values and on the concepts of health and wellness within a *kaupapa Māori* (philosophy). Service delivery incorporates aspects of Māori customs, including use of the Māori language in consultation and for health promotion materials. Māori health providers tend to be smaller than other providers and have a strong community-based and not-for-profit philosophy.

Māori providers focus on primary services and public health promotion, as well as on mental health and disability. Providers vary notably in their size and in their services. Services include clinical services; community health programs; public health campaigns; vaccinations; disability support programs; mental health services, including residential care; community support; and Māori healing services. Māori health providers also offer services at multiple geographic sites and, in some cases, at mobile health units (Crengle 1999). Most are small in size and scope, but some have broader regional coverage. Geographically, they are concentrated on the North Island, where the majority of Māori live. Most patients of Māori providers are Māori, but non-Māori also access the services.

Māori providers appear to do well in reaching populations with poorer health status and high need. According to the National Primary Medical Care Survey, the majority of patients were from areas of high socioeconomic deprivation (Crampton and others 2004).[14] Crengle (1999) found that 77 percent of patients come from poorer areas, where nationally 56 percent of Māori live. Patients were also more likely to have a community services card, a means-tested card that is an indicator of low income. Māori providers charge lower copayments than other providers.

Because of their greater emphasis on holistic and *whānau*-based approaches, Māori providers are more likely to provide services that are multisectoral and go beyond basic health services, such as physiotherapy and social services. Māori health providers are more likely to involve community health workers and to provide complementary and alternative services (Crengle, Lay-Yee, and Davis 2004).

Mainstream services. Most Māori receive care through mainstream providers. The 2004 New Zealand Health Survey found that 14 percent of Māori had sought care from a Māori provider in the year preceding the survey. As a result, a major focus of the Māori Health Strategy has been on improving the effectiveness of mainstream services for Māori (Ministry of Health 2002). This effort encompasses a wide range of activities at all levels of the system, involving institutions such as primary care organizations, district health boards, Māori providers, *iwi* organizations, hospitals, and other health service organizations.

In particular, the Māori Health Strategy identifies the need for: close partnerships among district health boards, *iwi*, and Māori communities; effective working relationships with Māori providers; and improved collection of ethnicity data. Key areas of focus are (a) workforce development to increase the participation of Māori health professionals across the sector and (b) public health campaigns tailored to Māori communities.

As with education, Māori health services have become increasingly diversified over the past two decades. Although the size of the Māori health provider sector remains small, it has provided an opportunity for experimentation with different approaches to caring for Māori, as well as non-Māori. Further efforts are needed to evaluate results to determine lessons for Māori health providers and mainstream services more broadly.

Aspects of Māori health providers, including holistic, multisectoral approaches, community-based orientation, integration of Māori values and culture, and accessibility to low-income populations, have the potential to provide useful lessons for mainstream services. Tailored health promotion programs have also demonstrated that they can be more effective at reaching Māori.

Conclusions

The wide range of efforts to tailor services to Māori needs and preferences has been an important factor behind increased Māori access to and participation in education and health over the past two decades. *Tailoring* refers to how policies and services are designed to consider the needs and preferences of specific groups. Although there has been limited targeting of policies, whereby ethnicity restricts an individual's eligibility for participating in a program or receiving a benefit, there has been significant effort in New Zealand to tailor policies to Māori and to make them more accessible, effective, and responsive.

However, the distinction is no longer clear cut between targeted and tailored programs that are designed to consider the specific needs of Māori and mainstream approaches. Separate tailored services are available to non-Māori, as well as to Māori, while mainstream services incorporate aspects of tailoring, for example, by including Māori content and approaches in mainstream schools. Tailoring has included

- Increased Māori participation in delivery and governance
- Devolution of delivery to *iwi* and Māori organizations
- Incorporation of language and culture into policy design
- Strengthened outreach to Māori communities.

This valuable body of experience can be used in designing new policies for Māori in New Zealand, as well as indigenous peoples and ethnic minorities in other countries.

There have been some notable successes. Increased involvement of Māori in education (through school boards, community-based initiatives, and partnerships with *iwi* and Māori organizations) has motivated the demand for quality education among Māori and raised participation levels, particularly in early childhood and tertiary education. Māori leadership and ownership of schools, starting with *kōhanga reo,* can be a catalyst for parents' interest in lifelong learning. Greater Māori involvement in the health sector has also increased access and awareness of critical health risks.

Targeting and tailoring of services also present challenges, to be kept in mind especially in transferring the experience to other countries. First, tailoring entails costs. Poorer and developing countries will not have the resources to experiment with the wide range of service delivery models that currently exist in New Zealand. For example, the wide range of educational options incorporating various levels of Māori language usage is expensive and may not be feasible in many countries. Analysis of the costs and benefits of adopting targeted and tailored services would be essential in considering the tradeoffs.

Second, in addition to purely financial costs, political economy costs merit particular attention. In New Zealand, there has been ongoing public debate, most recently surfacing in the run-up to the 2005 elections, about the benefits of targeting and tailoring. Some have been concerned about the disproportionate attention being paid to Māori, despite the very small amount of resources that are devoted to these programs (Slack 2005). Addressing this concern calls for better information about the actual level of targeted spending and the rationale for targeting and tailoring.

Third, both tailoring and targeting are complicated by the wide diversity of the Māori population with regard to welfare and living conditions, culture, language, and preferences for services. Broadly targeting services to Māori may not be sufficient if there are specifically local concerns and needs. The approach of some *iwi* to developing their own educational programs reflects the need for tailoring at the local and community levels and for flexibility in service delivery approaches. These issues merit consideration in other countries.

Alternative Māori Services

Although alternative Māori services make up only a small share of the total sectors (for example, 80 to 90 percent of Māori participate in mainstream education and health services), their effect on policy design has been far reaching. They have given Māori opportunities to develop approaches based on their own priorities, culture, and traditions.

These approaches have provided examples for mainstream services to draw on in strengthening their consideration of diversity and improving effectiveness for Māori and other population groups. They highlighted shortcomings of mainstream services, demonstrated alternative approaches, and built awareness of the need to do things differently. Another important contribution of Māori services has been to build the capacity and capability of Māori organizations and service professionals.

It is important to recognize that these services still reach only a small number of Māori. They are also new, some still have limited capacity, and there has been little evaluation of their outcomes and effectiveness. In this context, there is a risk that alternative Māori services will be relied on too heavily to produce results for Māori. In other words, policy needs to continue to emphasize results for Māori within mainstream services.

Non-Māori Benefits

The diversification of service delivery has increased choice for the population as a whole. In education, the *kōhanga reo* movement opened the door for bilingual education, in which non-Māori also participate. In health, Māori health providers have led the way in community-based care and have been innovative in providing holistic care and integrating different types of services. Non-Māori have also benefited from the policy innovations developed within tailored Māori services. There is ongoing potential for lessons from these approaches to be scaled up into mainstream services.

Quality

Tailoring can improve access by making services more appropriate for Māori and expanding participation. It also has the potential to raise effectiveness and quality. There is growing recognition across sectors that the priority for policy makers, service providers, and Māori communities alike is shifting from access to quality. Access will remain a concern for some Māori—particularly those who are poor and excluded. However, the major concern is raising quality across services, which, in turn, can influence access by increasing demand. Improving quality requires greater focus on evaluation to shape policy.

Diversity and Equity

Internal diversity among Māori has implications for policy design. Involvement and participation of Māori in-service provision and governance can help ensure the consideration of different perspectives. Similarly, devolution to *iwi* and Māori organizations can help services become more responsive to local preferences and needs. However, increasing diversity can also make ensuring representative participation of Māori more complex. Having a single Māori member on a school or health board may not sufficiently reflect the range of different Māori views in a community or locality. Governance arrangements need to be effective to allow for sufficient consultation and integration of varying viewpoints.

Equity issues also require careful consideration in service delivery and policy design. Although an improved labor market and economic opportunities have increased Māori welfare, not all are benefiting. Some Māori are left behind and lack access to opportunities. Services need to be designed to ensure inclusivity. Similarly, while service delivery by *iwi* and Māori organizations has increased choice and opportunity for some Māori, these services are not evenly distributed, and not all are benefiting.

Capacity Building

In some respects, the number of institutions has grown faster than the number of people. Increased opportunities for Māori to participate on school boards, district health boards, and other entities have been important. However, the pool of Māori qualified for these positions has been small. Expectations that people would have the skills, background, and knowledge to play important roles have proved unrealistic (Durie 2005). Capacity building is essential for these governance and partnership arrangements to work and for increasing accountability and transparency.

Investment in Culture

Culture in itself can be an outcome for economic, as well as social reasons. In New Zealand, efforts to invest in and ensure the success of the Māori language and culture have an economic value, for example, through tourism, as well as the value Māori bring to New Zealand as the indigenous people. Culture can also be a means for improving other types of outcomes; for example, bilingual education can improve educational attainment and achievement. There is a rich body of experience in New Zealand for further research into the interactions between culture and development outcomes.

Political Economy Issues

As in other countries, issues of targeting and tailoring by ethnicity are politically sensitive in New Zealand. Even tailored policies, which are not exclusive to Māori or other ethnic groups, can be perceived to be based on ethnic preferences. The debate on race-based policies in 2004 was an issue in the lead-up to the 2005 election. These political debates have the potential to distract from policy discussions regarding what works in improving socioeconomic outcomes for Māori and all New Zealanders.

Better information about the actual level of targeted spending, eligibility criteria, and the rationale for targeting and tailoring could improve understanding across the population. There is also a need for greater appreciation of Māori success stories and an understanding of the particular issues of indigeneity and the role of the Treaty of Waitangi.

In sum, Māori development approaches provide a compelling record of experience and innovation for New Zealand and other countries with indigenous and ethnic minority populations. Among the most resonant themes are the desire of Māori to succeed on their own terms within an increasingly integrated and globalized world, the challenge of making policies inclusive, the importance of weaving diversity and culture into policy design, and the need to build on successes. Māori and non-Māori alike have much to gain from further study, analysis, and discussion of these experiences.

Notes

1. *Aotearoa* is the Māori name for the islands that make up New Zealand.
2. In the 2001 census, respondents had the option of identifying with multiple ethnic groups.
3. See the March 2005 quarterly data from the Household Labour Force Survey, quoted at http://www.stats.govt.nz/.
4. In New Zealand, *tribe* and *subtribe* are applied to what elsewhere in the literature are called *tribal lineages* and *sublineages*. The term *families* refers to extended families.
5. King (2003), Orange (1987), and http://www.treatyofwaitangi.govt.nz/ give a background of the Treaty.
6. See http://www.waitangi-tribunal.govt.nz/ for more on the work of the Waitangi Tribunal.
7. Details of the settlements are on the Web site of the Office of Treaty Settlements: http://www.ots.govt.nz.
8. For some, *mainstream* has negative connotations and is found to imply a value judgment that, for example, anything outside the mainstream is abnormal. No such judgment is implied in here.
9. *Primary school* refers to grades 1 to 8; *secondary school* refers to grades 9 to 15. This section focuses on preschool through secondary education.
10. The percentage depends on the level of education and definition of *Māori medium education*. In 2004, 4 percent of Māori students were studying in *kura kaupapa Māori* schools.
11. The majority are at the primary school level.
12. The ERO is a government agency responsible for reviewing and reporting regularly on the performance of New Zealand schools and early childhood centers.

13. A *stand-down* is the formal removal of a student from a school for a specified period. A *suspension* is the formal removal of a student from school until the board of trustees decides the outcome at a suspension meeting. Definitions can be found at the Ministry of Education glossary of educational terms (http://www.minedu.govt.nz).

14. The deprivation index (NZDep2001) is a small-area measure based on the 2001 census. *High deprivation* refers to the top two quintiles.

References

Chapple, S. 1999. "Explaining Patterns of Disparity between Māori and Non-Māori Employment Chances." In *Labour Market Bulletin 1999*, 70–100. Wellington: Department of Labour.

Cooper, G., V. Arago-Kemp, C. Wylie, and E. Hodgen. 2004. "Te Rerenga a Te Pirere: A Longitudinal Study of Kōhanga Reo and Kura Kaupapa Māori Students." New Zealand Council for Educational Research, Wellington.

Crampton, P., P. Davis, R. Lay-Yee, A. Raymont, C. Forrest, and B. Starfield. 2004. "Comparison of Private For-Profit with Private Community-Governed Not-for-Profit Primary Care Services in New Zealand." *Journal of Health Services Research and Policy* 9 (Suppl. 2): 17–22.

Crengle, S. 1999. "Māori Primary Care Services." Paper prepared for the National Health Committee, Wellington.

Crengle, S., R. Lay-Yee, and P. Davis. 2004. "Māori Providers: Primary Health Care Delivered by Doctors and Nurses." National Primary Medical Care Survey (NatMedCa): 2001/02 Report. Ministry of Health, Wellington.

Department of Labour. 2005. "Trends in Māori Labour Market Outcomes, 1986–2003." Fact sheet prepared for the Hui Taumata, Wellington.

Dixon, S., and D. Maré. 2004. "Understanding Changes in Māori Incomes and Income Inequality, 1997–2003." Motu Working Paper 04-12, Motu Economic and Public Policy Research, Wellington.

Durie, M. 2005. "Māori Development: Trends and Indicators." Presentation to the International Association for Official Statistics Satellite Meeting on Small and Indigenous Populations, Te Papa Tongarewa/Museum of New Zealand, Wellington, April 14–15.

ERO (Education Review Office). 2002. "The Performance of Kura Kaupapa Māori." ERO, Wellington.

———. 2004. "Māori Student Achievement in Mainstream Schools." ERO, Wellington.

Goldberg, H., S. Notson, and L. Nolan. 2005. "Measurement Issues Associated with the Health of the United States American Indian/Alaska Native Population." Paper presented at the International Association for Official Statistics satellite meeting on Measuring Small and Indigenous Populations, Wellington, April 14–15.

Hall, G., and H. A. Patrinos. 2005. *Indigenous Peoples, Poverty, and Human Development in Latin America: 1994–2004.* Washington, DC: World Bank.

King, M. 2003. *The Penguin History of New Zealand.* Auckland, New Zealand: Penguin.

Maani, S. 2002. "Education and Māori Relative Income Levels over Time: The Mediating Effect of Occupation, Industry, Hours of Work, and Locality." Working Paper 02/17, New Zealand Treasury, Wellington.

Ministry of Education. 2005a. "Educate: Ministry of Education Statement of Intent: 2005–2010." Ministry of Education, Wellington.

———. 2005b. "Māori in Early Childhood Education and Schools." Briefing note for the Hui Taumata 2005, Ministry of Education, Wellington.

———. 2005c. "Māori in Tertiary Education: A Picture of the Trends." Briefing note for the Hui Taumata 2005, Ministry of Education, Wellington.

———. 2005d. "Ngā Haeta Mātauranga: Annual Report on Māori Education 2004." Ministry of Education, Wellington.

Ministry of Health. 2002. "He Korowai Oranga: Māori Health Strategy." Ministry of Health, Wellington.

———. 2004. "An Indication of New Zealanders' Health 2004." Ministry of Health, Wellington.

Ministry of Social Development. 2003. "The Social Report 2004." Ministry of Social Development, Wellington.

Nauenberg. 2005. "Counting Australia's Indigenous Peoples." Paper presented at the International Association for Official Statistics satellite meeting on Measuring Small and Indigenous Populations, Wellington, April 14–15.

Orange, C. 1987. *The Treaty of Waitangi.* Wellington: Allen & Unwin New Zealand.

Rao, V., and M. Walton, eds. 2004. *Culture and Public Action.* Stanford, CA: Stanford University Press.

Sen, A. 2004. "How Does Culture Matter?" In *Culture and Public Action*, eds. V. Rao and M. Walton, 37–58. Stanford, CA: Stanford University Press.

Slack, D. 2005. *Bullshit, Backlash, and Bleeding Hearts: A Confused Person's Guide to the Great Race Row.* Auckland, New Zealand: Penguin.

Statistics New Zealand. 2004. "Labour Market Statistics." Statistics New Zealand, Wellington.

———. 2005. "Māori Population: Looking Out to 2021." Background paper prepared for *Hui Taumata 2005.* Wellington: Statistics New Zealand.

Tangaere, A. R. 1997. *Learning Māori Together: Kōhanga Reo and Home.* Wellington: New Zealand Council for Educational Research.

Tawhiwhirangi, I., R. Renwick, F. Sutton, and K. Irwin. 1988. *Government Review of Te Kōhanga Reo.* Wellington: Te Kōhanga Reo National Trust.

Te Puni Kōkiri. 2005. "Ngā Wāhine Māori i Te Rangai Mahi: Māori Women in the Workforce." Wellington: Te Puni Kōkiri.

World Bank. 2000. *World Development Report 2000/2001: Attacking Poverty.* Washington, DC: World Bank.

———. 2004. *World Development Report 2004: Making Services Work for Poor People.* Washington, DC: World Bank.

CHAPTER 12

Arenas of Child Support: Interfaces of Family, State, and Nongovernmental Organization Provisions of Social Security

Catrine Christiansen and Susan Reynolds Whyte

Over the past two decades, children have become a priority area in social policies and programs in Sub-Saharan Africa. This increasing attention reflects two significant issues. On the one hand, demography intersects with social problems. In most African countries, more than half the population is less than 18 years old, and substantial numbers are growing up in societies afflicted by extreme poverty, the HIV/AIDS epidemic, and armed conflicts. On the other hand, the Convention on the Rights of the Child (CRC) has, since its ratification in 1989, provided a framework for allocating international aid to strengthen local capacity, in public and private institutions, to address the needs of the younger generation of citizens. As well as adopting the CRC, many African governments have recently developed national policies on child security and taken action to enhance the institutional capacity to implement these policies at diverse administrative levels.

This chapter addresses current practices with regard to the provision of social security to children in conformity with the CRC, through government institutions and nongovernmental organizations (NGOs).[1]

This chapter is a revised version of a commissioned paper elaborated in collaboration with Bawa Yamba and presented at the World Bank conference New Frontiers of Social Policy: Development in a Globalizing World, Arusha, Tanzania, December 12–15, 2005.

It does so by examining the interaction of these practices with kinship networks and local patterns of child support in Uganda. In particular, it focuses on the inclusion and exclusion mechanisms that allow children to claim entitlements from family, government, or civil society organizations, concentrating on school-age children (ages 6–18).

The welfare of children and young people must be seen as a process of inclusion and exclusion shaped in two arenas: a family and personal network arena, where children find and give support for daily life and longer-term endeavors, and an arena made up of government and NGO policies and programs. The conflation of state and NGOs into one arena reflects the common situation of service provisioning in East Africa. A weak state apparatus has been reinforced by bilateral and multilateral donors and supplemented by NGOs in order to provide social welfare (Semboja and Therkildsen 1995).

In terms of the themes of this volume, children are citizens of both a nation-state and a domestic sphere. As citizens of Uganda, all children (defined by national policies as persons below the age of 18) have equal rights and obligations, whether boys or girls, urban or rural, from prosperous or poor families. The Ugandan government has signed all international conventions on child welfare and has implemented numerous policies and programs for both universal and more targeted welfare for children.[2] As individual citizens, they are entitled to social protection.[3] If, by analogy, one extended the concept of citizenship to the realm of family relations, it would make sense to speak of "domestic citizenship" (see Das and Addlakha 2001). One could recognize that children have rights and obligations by virtue of being part of a kinship network.

Values, resources, and expectations within the domestic arena are realized through relationships with kin, rather than by virtue of rights as an individual citizen of the state. Family support may have to be mobilized. It is based not on a legal convention, but on norms that can be disputed or may be difficult to follow for practical reasons.[4] Notably, kin-based support is, by its nature, targeted at particular children, whereas state provisions are universalizing in principle, in that they envision equality and equity for all (for example, health for all or education for all).

With social security cast in these terms, one can inquire about the interfaces between the two arenas and the relations between the two kinds of "citizenship." It is often those children who are least able to exercise their rights as state citizens whose entitlements within the domestic arena are weak. The constellation of kinship relations facilitates or impedes children in going to school, obtaining health care, and otherwise achieving social security. In other words, inclusion or exclusion in the domestic arena strongly influences inclusion in the state-NGO arena. This observation is recognized by policy makers who target programs toward vulnerable groups such as orphans or street children and who are very aware of segmentation and differentiation (Mkandawire 2006). The interaction between the two arenas may have further ramifications when universal or targeted policies and programs affect children's "citizenship" within the domestic arena. Although both arenas are analytically important, the emphasis here will be on families and local communities and the relevance of the state-NGO arena from their points of view.

This chapter draws on long-term ethnographic fieldwork, interviews with government and NGO staff at national and district levels, and reviews of published and unpublished literature. The authors' own ethnographic fieldwork has taken place in the eastern districts of Tororo and Busia. The data include household surveys in Tororo (1970, repeated in 1993 and 2002), surveys in 2003 and 2004 of 105 secondary school children regarding their social welfare networks, and a mapping of civil society projects[5] running in Busia district in 2004 (the majority focused on children and youth). The qualitative data consist of formal and informal interviews with families, children, and youth over several years, including, for instance, attitudes toward AIDS, stigmatization, and changing patterns of care for children who had lost one or both parents. Beyond the family sphere, Whyte (1997) has extensive data on the composite health care system, and Christiansen (forthcoming) has considerable data on religious organizations as vital, resourceful networks in the social fabric and in the local networks of social development.

The chapter begins with an introduction to the two arenas, focusing on the rationales and practices of child support. The next two sections discuss interfaces, using examples of targeted and universalistic provisioning of social security for children in Uganda (education for vulnerable children and the law against defilement, respectively). The criteria for social support established by various government policies and NGOs (for example, being an orphan) are compared with the needs for social support experienced by young people in particular kinship networks (for example, being a pregnant teenager). The final section will address children's double "citizenships" in a low-income country.

Policy Context of Child Welfare in Uganda

The upheavals besetting Uganda during the 1970s and the early 1980s led to a severe decline in the well-being of its people.[6] Basic human rights were violated, drastic reversals in socioeconomic achievements occurred, and the social development sector almost totally collapsed. Since the late 1980s, relative peace and stability have been restored in most of the country, and the past 15 years have seen considerable progress in terms of economic growth and development. Moreover, the HIV/AIDS infection rate has dropped from about 14 percent in 1995 to 7 percent in 2004. However, despite a national economic growth rate of 6.5 percent per year over the past 10 years, the quality of life for many—especially in rural areas—has not improved substantially. Available data indicate that many Ugandans are not accessing essential services, such as health care, education, water and sanitation, and information (Okuonzi 2004).

Unequal access to social services is a key concern of the social development sector, which deals with matters related to equality, inclusion, employment, adult literacy, vulnerability, and rights (Ministry of Gender, Labour, and Social Development 2003). From 2003 to 2008, the sector's focus is social protection as a contributor to social transformation. This focus encompasses initiatives that reduce economic and social vulnerability. Although social development is thought of as an overarching roof resting on several pillars, social protection is the application of these pillars to specific subgroups within the population: those who are considered poor, vulnerable, or marginalized. Children, in general, are an obvious group for social protection: 52 percent of the population is age 0 to 14 years (Uganda Bureau of Statistics 2001), but they make up 62 percent of the population living in absolute poverty (Ministry of Gender, Labour, and Social Development 2004a). In addition to economic poverty, many children face problems related to the HIV/AIDS epidemic and, particularly in northern Uganda, armed conflict. Thus, there is an immense need for social policies and interventions that contribute to favorable environments for children in general, as well as for children living in particularly difficult circumstances. Two examples are crucial in this context: the Universal Primary Education (UPE) program and the National Strategic Programme Plan of Interventions for Orphans and Other Vulnerable Children, 2006–2010 (NSPPI) (Ministry of Gender, Labour, and Social Development 2004a).[7]

The UPE policy was implemented in 1997 with the aim of eliminating user fees for primary education.[8] Initially, guidelines specified that each family could send four children to school without cost and that girls and children with disabilities should be given priority. However, such criteria proved difficult to enforce, and UPE came to mean free schooling for all. In other words, the government policy moved from being targeted to being universalistic. The program led to a dramatic increase in enrollment, from 49 percent in 1992 to 76 percent in 1997, across gender, economic, and geographic categories. For girls in particular, enrollment rates increased significantly, in some cases more than doubling, so that by 1999 the gender difference had virtually disappeared, with 74 percent of girls and 77 percent of boys attending primary school (Deininger 2003). UPE has also been successful in reducing bias based on wealth and urban or rural residence. However, the program still faces challenges in terms of reducing one of the highest student–teacher ratios in the world and the high rates of students who do not pass final primary level exams (Deininger 2003). Ensuring the long-term value of the advances made will also require increased attention to educational quality and measures to include the remaining 20 to 25 percent of children in primary schooling.

Within the NSPPI, access to primary education is identified as an essential component of social protection for vulnerable children, alongside health and psychosocial support. The program is to be implemented through local government institutions. However, these social sector institutions are severely underfunded (below 0.5 percent of district budgets and 1.0 to 2.0 percent of national budgets in 1999) and are inadequate to provide services related to children (Odongkara 1999). The situation is problematic because district social provisioning depends on resources from external donors such as the United Nations Children's Fund (UNICEF) and NGOs, yet local infrastructure is unable to coordinate resources from manifold organizations. This lack of coordination between the state and NGOs increases the risk of inefficiency and may, in some cases, undermine state activities (Mkandawire 2006).

According to the experiences of industrial countries, universal provisioning of social services is an important ingredient in the promotion of national cohesion, social cohesion, and equity (Mkandawire 2006; Townsend 2004). Among social policies, universal education is a key component. As the case of UPE in Uganda shows, the populace benefits across gender, wealth, and urban–rural lines. The first cohort of primary school pupils under the UPE program graduated in 2003, and the government is now determined to support postprimary education so that the gains of UPE can be sustained (Ministry of Finance, Planning, and Economic Development 2002).

Because the past decade has not yielded a substantial capacity building of the state sector in general and the social sector in particular, there is a risk that the multifaceted NSPPI will have only a limited effect in terms of enhancing opportunities for vulnerable children to access social services such as education. Although it is vital to target resources to the most vulnerable children, resources must also, in this context, be allocated to build the required institutional capacity to coordinate the provision at national and local levels (Kabeer and Cook 2000).

It may also be possible to target the poor through universal programs. According to a joint donor policy, provision of school meals is a key factor in facilitating girls (and presumably also boys) from the poorest households to attend primary school (UNICEF and UNAIDS 2004). Recognizing that many current UPE pupils would also benefit from food provision at school, UNICEF–Uganda and Save the Children Alliance are agitating strongly for the reintroduction of school meals as part of UPE. However, the public education sector does not have the necessary resources. In the experience of other poorer southern countries, universal programs of free school meals are likewise recognized as a social protection measure (Norton, Conway, and Foster 2002; Townsend 2004).

In sum, according to the government endorsement of international conventions and elaborated policies, children are, as citizens, entitled to benefit from social services. Against the background of a social sector that is still being built up, and given that the majority of children live in absolute poverty, universal programs that benefit children across gender, wealth, and urban–rural divisions may be the measures through which state institutions can provide for its young citizens. However, it is important to remember that a quarter of school-age children are still not in school. Moreover, when UPE, with its huge class sizes and poor quality of education, took effect, families who could afford to do so sent their children to private schools. Thus "domestic citizenship" affected the practice of state citizenship.

Family-Based Social Security Networks

The lives of Ugandan children unfold within a framework of kinship relations. It is through family that children are given a sense of identity and belonging. In the patrilineal societies of rural Uganda, children are members of their fathers' clans and are generally perceived as belonging to their paternal kinsfolk. It is important to note that kinship is gendered: boys and girls are ascribed different social positions, obligations, and entitlements within the family networks. Sons inherit land from their fathers, a practice that leads to the establishment of patrilocal enclaves, where children are brought up in proximity to their paternal kin. Boys learn that they will stay on that land and bring a wife to help cultivate it, while girls learn that they are supposed to join their husbands' homes when they marry (Meinert 2003). In most Ugandan societies, there is an expectation that bridewealth should be paid by the husband's family to that of the wife, as compensation to those to whom she belongs.

Although children belong to their father's kin, they are part of the wider family networks of both parents. The roles of the maternal kin have always been recognized as important in sharing the obligations of socializing the younger generation, but the recent increases in adult mortality, high rates of divorce, and children born outside wedlock have furthered the roles of maternal kin in providing care and access to resources (Christiansen 2005b; Whyte and Whyte 2004).[9]

In Eastern and Southern African contexts, childrearing has been conceptualized as a central dimension of extended family networks (for example, Kilbride and Kilbride 1990; Weisner 1995). This "shared social support" (Weisner 1995: 22) in childrearing means that children often live with relatives in another village or town for longer periods of time. A child of parents living in a rural area may live with relatives in town while attending a nearby school that offers a higher educational standard than the schools close to the rural home. Children—especially girls—may stay with busy and better-off relatives to help out with household chores (Meinert 2003). A woman may place a child with her own mother as a way of showing affection and to provide company and help with daily chores. However, in general, because of the patrilocal tradition in Uganda, children live near their father's parents; when children live with their mother's parents, it is because of special circumstances (Whyte and Whyte 2004).

Although fosterage (taken here as care by an adult other than a parent) is a well-established pattern in Uganda, it has become more widespread in recent years. In a rural village in eastern Uganda, a household survey conducted in 1970 and repeated in 1993 and in 2002 points to rising numbers and proportions of children in fosterage with relatives, primarily with their maternal grandparents (Whyte and Whyte 2004).

In the literature on fosterage in Africa, a distinction is often made between fosterage based on a voluntary agreement between the parents and the caretaker and fosterage reflecting a crisis situation, such as the death of the parents or their inability to care for the child (Goody 1982).[10] In the Ugandan context, however, the distinction between voluntary and crisis fosterage is not always clear, because the circumstances of the fosterage may change over time. Consider, for example, a mother who takes up work in a town where she cannot care for the child. She arranges to leave the child with her own mother. After some time, she dies in an accident or (the common cause) from AIDS. Although it is important to note that fosterage is a culturally valued practice, the increasing numbers and proportion of fostered children point toward general patterns of change. AIDS, unstable relations between parents, and poverty are considered to be the main factors leading to these changes (Christiansen 2005b; Hunter 1990; Whyte and Whyte 2004). In the districts of Arua, Soroti, and Lira in northern Uganda, the prolonged armed conflict and AIDS have led to a similar rise in fosterage with relatives (Ntozi and others 1999). In Uganda, 42 percent of children do not live with both their parents: about 17 percent live with only the mother, about 6 percent live with the father, and about 18 percent live with neither. Among the latter group, the parents are most often alive. Only 3 percent of such cases relate to the death of both parents (Uganda Bureau of Statistics 2001: 11). Such fosterage may indicate the inability of the parents to support their child.

When a mother or father becomes unable to provide for the children (for example, as a result of an accident, a disability, an illness, a death, or alcoholism), relatives help by taking children into their households or by contributing support in other ways, such as paying school fees, paying medical expenses, or providing necessities. People with more resources often support large numbers of needy children and poorer relatives. Such kin-based support and the common pattern of fostering, even when parents are alive, may explain why some children's lives do not change markedly when a parent dies. In northern Uganda, a large household survey found that 8 percent of children in Arua district were unaffected by the death of one or both parents, in terms of access to care and financial resources. These figures were as high as 11 percent in Lira district and 22 percent in Soroti district (Ntozi and others 1999). However, such statistics do also show that the majority (75 to 90 percent) of children experience negative changes in relation to the death of a parent. The failure of relatives to provide sufficient support is probably due more to poverty, in the sense of an inability to enter into the exchanges that define a social being, than to changes in sociocultural values.

Of 120 adolescents with diverse socioeconomic backgrounds who were enrolled in low-cost educational institutions in eastern Uganda by an NGO or a relative, most anticipated little or no support for their further education (Christiansen 2004). Many young people hoped for assistance from their own mothers (who were often peasants); others mentioned an older sibling, uncle, or aunt (usually in salaried employment). In group discussions and individual interviews, these adolescents expressed strong opinions about lack of unity and solidarity within kin-based networks, which they saw as intensified by high death rates and conflicts related to AIDS, such as property grabbing, accusations, and neglect. AIDS certainly exacerbates tensions within families; however, it is the prolonged wide-spread poverty and the disproportion between the few adults (who are expected to stretch their meager resources) and the many needy children that lead to a decline in interhousehold assistance between kin. This decline puts pressure on the single household to provide the everyday affectionate, socializing care (commonly ascribed to the role of the mother), as well as material resources (commonly ascribed to the role of the father). Thus, in practice, childrearing is becoming more a matter for the individual household, although the cultural ideal of shared responsibility persists (Christiansen 2005b). This increasing pressure for the individual house-hold to care for its members requires an understanding of intrahousehold dynamics and resource availability.

Household size and composition vary, but they often include, at least for a time, children who are not the biological offspring of the adults. When allocating resources within the household, parents often give priority to their own children over other children whom they have accepted into their own house (Christiansen 2005b; Ntozi and others 1999; Nyambedha and Aagaard-Hansen 2003). Moreover, the distribution of resources to these extra children tends to be unequal. The rationale behind such differentiation among fostered children is that children are seen as links between adults, so that resource allocations to children become barom-eters of adult relations (Bledsoe 1995). Caring for others' children shows that one cares about their parents; conversely, mistreating others' children is likely if relations between a parent and the caretaker are poor. Mothers sometimes avoid placing their offspring in the care of a co-wife because of the competition and inevitable jealousy between co-wives or women who produce children with the same man. It is in the context of female competition for the man's affection and material resources that one can grasp why stepmothers are notorious for mistreating the children of their husband's previous unions (Christiansen 2003; Ministry of Gender, Labour, and Social Development 2004b; Whyte and Whyte 2004).[11]

When children and adults in Uganda refer to someone being mistreated, this mistreatment usually involves denial or stinginess with food, excessive domestic work, delayed health care, and occasionally physical discipline (see Ntozi and others 1999). From an early age, children are expected to help in domestic chores: girls generally do child care, laundry, cleaning, and cooking, whereas boys fetch water, cut grass around the compound, and look after goats and cattle. It is not unusual for the children who are the first to be assigned domestic chores to also be the last in line when food is distributed. However, children may also be rewarded through these contributions to the household for socially valued competences such as being quick, hard working and well behaved toward the adult caretaker (Meinert 2001; Whyte 1998). Children, even at an early age, are recognized for their personal characteristics and engagement in work. In other words, they may actively negotiate their own position by contributing to the maintenance of the household.

Children are expensive to raise nowadays, because they require school expenses, clothes, medicine, and food, but schooling prevents them from performing many hours of household chores. In Uganda, orphaning, birth out of wedlock, divorce, polygamy, and work migration are everyday phenomena that cause children not to live with their biological parents and depend profoundly on care provided by the extended family. The ethnographic data show that, in a context of widespread poverty and complex family patterns of childrearing, multiple factors can include or exclude children from care and access to resources with the relatives with whom they are staying (often grandparents). These factors include the child's gender and positioning within the household, the child's relation with the head of the house (or the female in charge), and the resource availability within the household and close social networks.

This section has shown that it is important to consider both the resource availability and the internal distribution when attempting to understand the dynamics that include or exclude children from basic needs in the family-based social security networks. "Domestic citizenship" involves belonging to a network of kinfolk where entitlements and obligations are provided and expected in relation to the child's social positioning rather than in relation to the child as an individual. This kind of citizenship produces differentiation between children and, in this sense, is fundamentally different from the ideal of equal rights among citizens as expressed in the CRC. As the following two sections illuminate, these different notions of children's "citizenships" may clash and lead to unintended consequences for children's long-term social security.

Targeted Interventions and Kinship Networks

The following section provides examples from programs targeting two categories of children who have received immense policy attention: orphans and child domestic workers. These examples will be used to examine the differences in concepts of citizenship between the family and the state-NGO arenas.

When an intervention offers education for an out-of-school child living in a very poor household, the adult caretaker often prioritizes his or her own offspring over that of a relative. This tendency points to the intergenerational bargain (Barnett and Whiteside 2003; Cattell 1997) whereby adults care for their offspring partly in anticipation that their children will later in life provide for them. From this perspective, it makes sense to argue that a son (or a son's son) should benefit from the intervention, as he is expected to stay on the land and provide for the parent (or grandparent). A daughter may marry at a distance and bring bridewealth to the home. Though she is not present on a daily basis, she is expected to visit and send gifts to her parents. A young orphaned relative still "belongs" elsewhere and is not expected to assist the present caretaker later.

The practice of everyday family life is not so neatly organized, nor is it determined only by such structures of intergenerational care patterns. For example, a mother may recognize that a bright daughter could bring more benefit than a son. But, in general, scarcity of resources forces adults to make priorities among the children in their care. In this sense, an intervention may provide a life chance not only to the child obtaining education, but also to the adult caretaker, because education is considered the path to social security and mobility of the family as a whole (Meinert 2003; Whyte and Whyte 1998). Such a rationale conflicts with the rationale behind the intervention, which targets the most vulnerable on the basis of a fixed set of criteria.

This dilemma could be resolved by supporting the household as a unit and by targeting individual children. As box 12.1 shows, the parish development committees select impoverished households, within which the program picks one child as a beneficiary. It would be more reasonable from

BOX 12.1

Interfaces of Programs and Parents

An externally funded program granted funding for 250 orphans' education in rural eastern Uganda. The publicly recognized parish development committees in two subcounties were asked to identify the most vulnerable orphans for enrollment in the program. Only one child per home could be enrolled. The parish development committee identified households that they perceived as very poor: those with a female or elderly caregiver or head of household, with a chronically ill adult, or with several "extra" children and few resources.

When the program managers went to each of the identified homes to select a child, they often discussed at length with the caretaking adults which child should benefit from the project. Because many homes consisted of widows, their children, and orphaned relatives, several children met the enrollment criteria: being orphaned, poor, and out-of-school. However, the project had further criteria: to enroll children, preferably girls, who did not live with either of their parents.

According to the project managers, many widows wanted one of their own children to be enrolled rather than an orphaned relative, because their own (orphaned) children were equally poor. Moreover, many adults preferred a boy rather than a girl to be enrolled. In some cases, the project managers had to threaten that no children at all would be enrolled from that home if the orphaned relative, preferably a girl, was not enrolled. Then, the project-identified child would be enrolled.

a local perspective to recognize the interdependency of the household members (in the immediate and long term) and select two children living in that household—a child of the parent and an "extra" child. Such an approach would reduce the risk of straining relations between the guardian and the program-selected extra child. The method of providing for the household and a targeted member is appreciated locally by programs providing food aid to people living with AIDS or disabilities, because the resources benefit both the vulnerable person and the household's common kitchen.

From a local point of view, the policy focus on orphans, as children who have lost one or both parents, may seem peculiar as a first criterion for entitlement to assistance. Increasing numbers of children have lost a parent through death, so the category partly corresponds with local reality. However, many other children are in the de facto situation of having only one parent because of illness, neglect, or unstable parental relations (estrangement, divorce, and children born outside wedlock). If the father did not recognize the child as his offspring, the child has no clan identity and, in the case of a boy, no rights to land. A divorce often leads to children living with their maternal grandmother, because parents remarry and the children of a previous union are not always welcomed by a stepfather or stepmother. These children do not qualify for entitlement, because no parent has died, yet their situations may be just as difficult as those of orphans.

The following case illustrates how disparate understandings of children's obligations to contribute to family well-being and children's rights to education lead to different understandings of another category of child beneficiaries of a target program: so-called child domestic workers.

The cultural conception of childhood as a period in which children are given the skills, knowledge, and social competences that they need to become socially responsible people implies that they must engage in household chores, farming, and other kinds of work. In the CRC, by contrast, childhood is perceived as a time of learning through formal education, relaxing, and playing in safe environments, preferably at home where parents protect the children from harm (Boyden 1997). The gap between global (Western) and local notions of children as, respectively, individual beings or socially embedded actors is immense.

According to key actors in Ugandan civil society organizations, the past 15 years of implementing the CRC has simply turned child rights into a parallel universe to local reality. An example is the issue of child labor and interventions, such as that in box 12.2. Besides the local expectations that children perform duties around the home, adults (or the children themselves) may value chances for the children to produce money, food, or educational opportunities through working for other people (kin as well as nonkin). As Kyaddondo (2004) has argued on the basis of data from the rice fields in eastern Uganda, children engaged in agricultural activities learn to earn and to spend as they contribute money to the household or buy food, snacks, and scholastic material for themselves.

In the semiurban context, several of the adolescents selected were earning small salaries from doing household chores at nonkin homes or working in the informal sector as hawkers, bar workers, and unskilled laborers. Most of them had left school when the home they stayed in had become so poor that they had to make some money. It is notable that

BOX 12.2

Gap between Global Category and Local Reality

In 1999, the International Labour Organization implemented a project against child domestic labor in 14 districts in Uganda. The project aimed to reduce the number of child domestic workers by providing education to about 300 such workers in each district. At the national level, the project was implemented through the National Council for Children; at the district level, it was implemented through the probation and welfare officer and the parish development committees.

In Busia district, children were identified in the semiurban district center and in a rural parish. It was also announced over the radio that children could register themselves with project managers. In the semiurban area, the project identified many children working in homes of nonkin or in the informal sector. In the rural area, most identified children were very poor and out of school. Some had both parents but were so poor that they could not afford school expenses; some lived with only their grandmother, so they performed most of the domestic work. A few were working in small businesses.

According to program managers, the project was an eye-opener to adults in the district who were not aware that children's rights restricted their labor to light house-hold work. According to 35 adolescents interviewed, they were identified because they were among those "most in need," which they associated with living in poverty, being out of school, working for money, being orphaned and living with relatives, or living with only a grandparent. The concept of child domestic workers was not part of the youngsters' view of their situations or their vocabulary. Their views were shared by most local adults, including several who had been sensitized about the CRC.

such youngsters underlined that it was their decision to go "looking for money," a decision that mirrored their own image of being responsible youngsters who contributed to the home of an aging grandmother, an ill mother, and often several younger siblings.

The capacity of such children should not be romanticized, and there must be recognition of their common desire for education rather than current income-generating opportunities. In the rural setting, most selected beneficiaries were out of school and living in very poor households—at least, that is how they and other adults explained enrollment in the education program. It is notable that the local adults trained in the CRC pointed out that there were no clear lines between when children were "helping out" at home, doing chores at other relatives' homes, or "working." While some mention salary or being outside the domestic space or networks as relevant criteria, there was no local consensus. For the children themselves, there was a potential conflict between their right to schooling as state citizens and their obligation as "domestic citizens" to help support their kin.

It seems to simplify implementation and contribute to transparency and accountability to have fixed criteria for a target group, such as experiencing the death of a parent, living on the street, or being engaged in employment. However, these criteria of inclusion and exclusion may not appear legitimate in local eyes, because they do not reflect the actual, far broader, needs of children and caretakers. In a context of widespread poverty and complex family patterns of childrearing, multiple factors can include or exclude children from care and access to basic needs within the family-based social security networks. These factors include the child's gender, positioning within the household, and relation with the head of the house (or the female in charge), as well as the resources available within the household and close social networks.

In summary, it is fundamentally important to recognize that children are embedded in family relationships where "domestic citizenship" is at stake, as well as to focus on the state-NGO individual rights–based approach enshrined in instruments such as the CRC. In practice, such a change of attitude should lead to interventions that approach and support the household, as well as a targeted child within that home. Such an approach would have a greater immediate effect on the child's situation and would reduce the risk of straining relations between the guardian and the program-selected "extra" child within the home. As social actors, children actively seek to attain competencies to become socially responsible people and to engage in diverse kinds of work and income-generating activities. To sustain both the child and the home, policies need to empower children to fulfill these values, for example, by allowing them to contribute to the household at the same time as protecting them from excessive work.

Universal Policies and Gendered Positions

This section focuses on the incorporation of gender differences into the work of diverse institutions (the family, civil society organizations, and public institutions) and the possibilities and implications of a national law that seeks to ensure gender equality.

Within the web of family relations, girls are cared for as cherished daughters, granddaughters, nieces, sisters, and cousins, who in time are supposed to join another family through marriage. Boys, however, are cared for as sons, grandsons, nephews, brothers, and cousins, who in time will settle down and later inherit land from their father. When a girl marries, an alliance is formed with another family, to whom the girl's children will belong, although they may come to stay for prolonged periods of time as visitors (Whyte and Whyte 2004). It is through the exchange of bridewealth that the family of the husband-to-be acknowledges the girl's paternal relatives as the "owners" of the girl's competence, fertility, and labor. Also through the exchange of bridewealth, the girl's qualities come to "belong" to the husband and his family. This section will therefore focus on access to female bodies and other resources, considering children, respectively, as citizens of a state and of a family.

Patterns of marriage are changing in eastern Uganda, as in much of eastern and southern Africa. Although the ideal still exists of formal marriage after a couple have studied each other's behavior and the families have been properly introduced, many relationships are not formalized for some years. Girls develop relationships with unmarried or married men with whom, in time, they will have a recognized marriage.[12] Such relationships usually involve sexual intimacy and the possibility of pregnancy and childbirth. Sometimes the partners regularize their relationship before or soon after the birth of the child. When they do not, responsibility to support the new mother and baby usually falls on the girl's relatives.

In Uganda, it is obvious from national statistics that childbearing begins early: 30 percent of girls ages 15 to 19 are already mothers or pregnant with their first child (Uganda Bureau of Statistics 2001). Teenage childbearing is closely related to girls' education in two ways. First, it interrupts education. When girls discover the pregnancy, they tend to drop out of school because of embarrassment; when the teachers discover the pregnancy, the girls are usually expelled. From the teachers' point of view, such a girl (regardless of whether she is in UPE or secondary school) has wasted her chance and may influence other girls to engage in "man-hunting instead of concentrating on the homework" (interview with a primary schoolteacher by C. Christiansen, Busia district, April 18, 2004). Second, education seems to protect against early childbearing: 60 percent of teenage girls with no education have become mothers or are pregnant with their first child, compared with 33 percent of those with some primary education and 17 percent of those who attend secondary school (Uganda Bureau of Statistics 2001).[13]

According to a 2003 study conducted with 388 adolescent girls in Busia district, a range of socioeconomic and cultural factors, combined with limited access to adolescent health services and relevant information, is behind the local high rates of teenage pregnancies (Ssekiwunga and Mulimba 2003). The adolescents pointed specifically to lack of parental care, high levels of poverty associated with parental failure to provide daughters with basic necessities, and strong desire by parents to obtain bridewealth. Others reported that parents and guardians were not giving them proper advice on how to behave in order to avoid getting pregnant. Some girls also expressed interest in "booking a man," that is, establishing a marriage on the basis of a pregnancy (Ssekiwunga and Mulimba 2003).

The government is concerned with the high rate of teenage pregnancies not only because they interrupt education, but also because they endanger health. There is also a moral component, in that girls are thought to need protection from male harassment and possible HIV infection. Females ages 15 to 24 make up a substantial proportion of new HIV infections (UN-AIDS 2004). In the late 1990s, the government endorsed a law that defined sexual intimacy with a girl below the age of 18 as defilement. Defilement is a capital offense, and the offender faces up to lifetime in prison (Parry-Williams 2005).

When fathers and brothers use the threat of police action and litigation to settle a defilement case privately, it can be said that "defilement is commercialized" (Parry-Williams 2005) or, more frankly, that "defilement can produce bridewealth" (see box 12.3). In practice, the "defiler" acknowledges that he has violated the father's rights over his daughter's sexuality (or fertility) and compensates him. While the law was intended to protect the young girl, neither she nor the child of the pregnancy benefits from this situation. When the case is settled out of court, the offense is treated as an infringement of the rights of her patri-kin. When the case is tried and the defiler is punished, the offense is against the state, and no compensation is paid to the girl.

While the defilement law has not had much effect on the protection of girls' sexuality, it has had grave consequences in terms of the large numbers of boys who are imprisoned on capital offense charges for having sex with their girlfriends. In 2000, a study of police, court, and local council records documented that defilement was the second most common offense in juvenile justice. For children committed to the High Court in eight districts across the country, defilement made up 90 to 100 percent of the cases (Parry-Williams 2005). Save the Children Alliance and other actors working on juvenile justice suggest that defilement should not

---

BOX 12.3

Does the Law Ensure Bridewealth or Social Protection?

A 13-year-old primary school girl was living with her mother in a small trading center. The mother initiated a relationship with one of the daughter's schoolteachers. After the girl had become familiar with the teacher, he told her at the school to come to his place alone in the afternoon so that he could help her with homework. The girl did not tell her mother but went to the teacher's home. The teacher had a television and gave the girl a soda, which she enjoyed while watching the television. She started to spend more time at the teacher's place, and he treated her nicely, so she began to care for him. One day he wanted to be sexually intimate, and she did not mind. After some months, she became pregnant. When her mother discovered the pregnancy, she contacted her husband in a nearby town. The father arrived a few days later, and together the parents pressured the girl to reveal who was responsible for the pregnancy. When the girl told the father, he went straight to the teacher with demands of U Sh 400,000 (US$230), threatening otherwise to report him to the police.

After some time, the teacher produced the money, which was equivalent to four months' salary. The father of the girl started bragging about how he got the money from the teacher, and the local police heard about the situation. The police then arrested the father of the girl on the grounds that he should have reported the case to the police so they could deal with the offender. After several days, the father was bailed out of jail. The mother of the girl did not want to press charges against the teacher, although she was angry with him. Instead, she reasoned that, if the teacher kept his job, he would be able to provide for the newborn child, whereas if he went to jail, he would not be able to contribute anything—so who would benefit from the teacher's imprisonment?

---

be regarded as a capital offense (which substantially prolongs the boys' imprisonment) and push for a test case concerning defilement where the boy and the girl are within two or three years of each other in age and having sex by mutual consent.

This suggestion recognizes that girls below age 18 may consent to sexual intimacy and, as individuals, should be held responsible for their own actions. From this perspective, girls have a right to their own sexuality, and the government rationale in criminalizing their sexual relations can be questioned, at least for those in their later teenage years. Rather, legal measures should be taken to assist the girls and their children through paternity support.

The high rate of teenage pregnancies is partly related to poverty. As ethnographic studies from eastern Africa have shown, sexual favors are often rewarded with gifts and money (for example, Cole 2004; Haram 1995; Ringsted 2004; Silberschmidt and Rasch 2001). Whether or not they are in school, poor girls appreciate and need the extra resources, however small, that lovers provide. Alternative sources of income are scarce. As these girls themselves point out, poor girls often live in poor households (Ssekiwunga and Mulimba 2003). Supporting them might also involve supporting the household as a unit—for example, by facilitating income generation for the girl and her guardian. Particularly for young girls out of school, such measures could reduce the motivation to seek small resources through sexual relations.

In sum, the protection of girls from sexual harassment and teenage pregnancies is a central concern in both the family and CRC policy arenas. The two arenas are, however, based on two different rationales of providing social security. In the case of teenage pregnancy, the local rationale is concerned with the consequences that punishing the offender (the father of the child) might have for the young mother, her father, and the unborn baby. The legal measures taken so far to incorporate gender issues into social policies have failed to recognize these dynamics of family networks and social security, which are intertwined with customary law. This lack of correspondence between family and policy rationales has meant limited influence and severe side effects, especially the prolonged imprisonment of boys for having consensual sex with their girlfriends.

Children as Citizens of State and Family

This chapter's focus on children has provided an apt example of how citizens participate in several arenas with different patterns of social relations, rights, and obligations. In a low-income country such as Uganda, where the state has only partially emerged and citizens cannot rely on legally guaranteed rights of citizenship, other kinds of networks, in which claims and obligations rest on norms and moral economy, continue to be central for matters of social security (Kabeer and Cook 2000). Given the difficulty of conceptualizing what citizenship entails (in the sense of a social contract between individual citizens and the state) in a context where the state cannot be presumed to be neutral and effective, it is all the more important to understand what notions of entitlements and obligations prevail in other spheres of society.

This chapter has illuminated how children's lives unfold within a framework of kinship relations where children are ascribed positions, obligations, and entitlement. Within this network, children realize "domestic citizenship" more or less fully. Multiple factors include or exclude children from care and access to resources within this kin-based arena of child support. As the chapter has stressed, these factors include the child's gender and positioning within the household, the child's relation with the head of the house, and the availability of resources within the household and close social networks. In the interfaces of family and targeted child support provided by the state and NGOs, having fixed criteria for a target group, such as experiencing the death of a parent, living on the street, or being engaged in employment, appears to simplify implementation and contribute to transparency and accountability. In local terms, however, such criteria of inclusion and exclusion may seem illegitimate, because they do not reflect the actual needs of children and caretakers, which are far broader.

In the long term, children's social security must be achieved within the everyday contexts of household and kin networks. Hence, interventions cannot focus solely on individual human rights as set out in the CRC. They must also support the vulnerable households of which children are a part, just as they must secure the rights of widowed mothers as well as orphans. Support for out-of-school children might take the form of income-generating projects or training that includes guardians and caretakers. Gender issues, such as teenage pregnancy, must be approached within the relevant local contexts of social relationships. CRC and other human rights issues are important forces for change within local contexts, but attention must be given to ways of implementing them in specific settings that attend to children's various kinds of citizenship.

Notes

1. NGOs are organizations formed on a voluntary basis (but operating with paid staff), either for the benefit of members or to provide services to or on behalf of others (Semboja and Therkildsen 1995: 1).
2. On the basis of the CRC, the government developed the Uganda National Programme of Actions for Children (UNPAC) in 1992/93. The main goal

of UNPAC was to establish survival, protection, and development goals related to children and women through a multisectoral effort (Ministry of Gender, Labour, and Social Development 2001) In 1996, the Uganda Children Statute was formulated and ratified to provide a comprehensive legal and institutional framework for the protection of children and a legal instrument to address the rights of children and the obligations of children to society. The National Council for Children was established within the Ministry of Gender, Labour, and Social Development in 1996 to ensure the implementation of UNPAC and the Uganda Children Statute at the national level, and actions were taken to establish similar institutions at district levels (see also Wakhweya and others 2002).

3. The strong links between social protection and the human rights framework are obvious within, as well as beyond the field of child welfare (Norton, Conway, and Foster 2002: 542).

4. Because rights and relationships within the domestic sphere are so different from those within the state-NGO sphere, "domestic citizenship" is in quotation marks in this chapter.

5. The 644 projects had a total value of about US$800,000, with 33 projects accounting for 46 percent of the financial resources (Christiansen 2005a). The great majority of the projects were implemented by people's organizations in the sense of groups formed on the basis of locality, kinship, gender, or religion engaged in activities aimed at improving the livelihoods of members and controlled by them (Semboja and Therkildsen 1995).

6. This section draws heavily on two reports: "The Social Development Sector Strategic Investment Plan, 2003–2008" (Ministry of Gender, Labour, and Social Development 2003) and "Social Protection in Uganda: Facilitating the Process of Mainstreaming Social Protection into the PEAP Provision" (Devereux and Sabates-Wheeler 2003).

7. The Ministry of Gender, Labour, and Social Development coordinated the elaboration of the NSSPI, which has been developed in collaboration with institutions both in and outside Uganda, such as the U.S. Agency for International Development, the United Nations Children's Fund, World Vision, and Save the Children USA.

8. Since the 1980s, the private parent–teacher associations had become the major funding organs of primary education in Uganda (Passi 1995). The main source of funds for the UPE program came from a concerted donor effort and the use of Heavily Indebted Poor Countries Initiative funds. The program was supplemented with strong advocacy campaigns for girls' education, a decentralized mode of implementation, and a far-reaching restructuring of public spending in the sector to the benefit of basic education (Deininger 2003: 294).

9. For similar findings in neighboring Kenya, see Cattell 1997; Nyambedha and Aagaard-Hansen 2003.

10. In the African context, foster parents are most often kin, particularly grandparents, aunts, and uncles.
11. An interesting exception occurs in Busia district, where stepmothers are thought to be softer toward stepchildren whose mothers have died. Hence, maternal orphans may have a more favorable position in their father's home than children of divorce (Christiansen 2005b).
12. One in three married women in Uganda is in a polygymous relationship (Uganda Bureau of Statistics 2001).
13. The level of education continues to influence childbearing, because women with no education have a fertility rate of 7.8 children per woman, whereas women who have attended secondary education on average give birth to 3.9 children (Uganda Bureau of Statistics 2001).

References

Barnett, T., and A. Whiteside. 2003. *AIDS in the Twenty-First Century: Disease and Globalization*. New York: Palgrave Macmillan.

Bledsoe, C. 1995. "Marginal Members: Children of Previous Unions in Mende Households in Sierra Leone." In *Situating Fertility: Anthropology and Demographic Inquiry*, ed. S. Greenhalgh, 130–53. Cambridge, U.K.: Cambridge University Press.

Boyden, J. 1997. "Childhood and the Policy Makers: A Comparative Perspective on the Globalization of Childhood." In *Constructing and Reconstructing Childhood*, ed. A. James and A. Prout, 190–230. London: Falmer.

Cattell, M. 1997. "The Discourse of Neglect: Family Support for the Elderly in Samia." In *African Families and the Crisis of Social Change*, eds. T. S. Weisner, C. Bradley, and P. Kilbride, 157–83. Westport, CT: Bergin & Garvey.

Christiansen, C. 2003. "Reflections on the Changing Patterns of Care for Orphans." *CODESRIA Bulletin* 2, 3, and 4: 94–97.

———. 2004. "Befriending Relatives and Making Relative Friendships: Social Networking among Samia Youth in Uganda." Paper presented at the Nordic Workshop on Researching Children and Youth in Africa held at the Nordic Africa Institute, Uppsala, Sweden.

———. 2005a. "Developing Busia District." Results from a mapping of community-based projects in 2004. Nordic Africa Institute, Sweden.

———. 2005b. "Positioning Children and Childcare Institutions in Uganda." *African Journal of AIDS Research* 4 (3): 173–82.

———. Forthcoming. "When AIDS Becomes Part of the (Christian) Family: Dynamics between Kinship and Religious Networks in Uganda." In *Creating Social (In)Security through Religious Networks: Ethnographic Perspectives*, eds. T. Thelen, C. Leutloff-Grandits, and A. Peleikis. London: Berghahn.

Cole, J. 2004. "Fresh Contact in Tamtave, Madagascar: Sex, Money, and Intergenerational Transformation." *American Ethnologist* 31 (4): 573–88.

Das, V., and R. Addlakha. 2001. "Disability and Domestic Citizenship: Voice, Gender, and the Making of the Subject." *Public Culture* 13 (3): 511–32.

Deininger, K. 2003. "Does the Cost of Schooling Affect Enrollment by the Poor? Universal Primary Education in Uganda." *Economics of Education Review* 22 (3): 291–305.

Devereux, S., and R. Sabates-Wheeler. 2003. "Social Protection in Uganda: Facilitating the Process of Mainstreaming Social Protection into the PEAP Provision." Ministry of Gender, Labour, and Social Development, Kampala.

Goody, E. N. 1982. *Parenthood and Social Reproduction: Fostering and Occupational Roles in West Africa*. Cambridge, U.K.: Cambridge University Press.

Haram, L. 1995. "Negotiating Sexuality in Times of Economic Want: The Young and Modern Meru Women." In *Young People at Risk: Fighting AIDS in Northern Tanzania*, eds. K. I. Klepp, P. M. Biswalo, and A. Talle, 31–48. Oslo: Scandinavian University Press.

Hunter, S. 1990. "Orphans as a Window on the AIDS Epidemic in Sub-Saharan Africa: Initial Results and Implications of a Study in Uganda." *Social Science and Medicine* 31 (6): 681–90.

Kabeer, N., and S. Cook. 2000. "Re-visioning Social Policy in the South: Challenges and Concepts." *IDS Bulletin* 31 (4): 1–10.

Kilbride, P. L., and J. C. Kilbride. 1990. *Changing Family Life in East Africa: Women and Children at Risk*. University Park: Pennsylvania State University Press.

Kyaddondo, D. 2004. "Rice Is a Jealous Crop: Subsistence, Markets, and Morality in a Changing Economy in Eastern Uganda." Doctoral thesis, Institute of Anthropology, University of Copenhagen, Copenhagen.

Meinert, L. 2001. "The Quest for a Good Life: Health and Education among Children in Eastern Uganda." Doctoral thesis, Institute of Anthropology, University of Copenhagen, Copenhagen.

———. 2003. "Sweet and Bitter Places: The Politics of Schoolchildren's Orientation in Rural Uganda." In *Children's Places: Cross-Cultural Perspectives*, eds. K. F. Olwig and E. Gulløv, 179–96. London: Routledge.

Ministry of Finance, Planning, and Economic Development. 2002. "Background to the Budget 2001/02." Uganda Poverty Reduction Strategy Paper Progress Report 2002, Ministry of Finance, Planning, and Economic Development, Kampala.

Ministry of Gender, Labour, and Social Development 2001. "Assessment of Progress and Performance of the Uganda National Programme of Action for Children (UNPAC), 1992–2000." National Council for Children.

———. 2003. "The Social Development Sector Strategic Investment Plan (SDIP) 2003–2008." Ministry of Gender, Labour, and Social Development, Kampala.

———. 2004a. "National Strategic Programme Plan of Interventions for Orphans and Other Vulnerable Children, 2006–2010." Ministry of Gender, Labour, and Social Development, Kampala.

———. 2004b. "Children in Need of Special Protection Measures (CNSPM) Study in Busia District, 2004." Ministry of Gender, Labour, and Social Development, Kampala.

Mkandawire, T. 2006. "Targeting and Universalism in Poverty Reduction." Social Policy and Development Programme Paper 23. Geneva: United Nations Research Institute for Social Development.

Norton, A., T. Conway, and M. Foster. 2002. "Social Protection: Defining the Field of Action and Policy." *Development Policy Review* 20 (5): 541–67.

Ntozi, J. P. M., F. E. Ahimbisibwe, J. O. Odwee, N. Ayiga, and F. N. Okurut. 1999. "Orphan Care: The Role of the Extended Family in Northern Uganda." In *The Continuing African HIV/AIDS Epidemic*, eds. J. C. Caldwell, I. O. Orubuloye, and J. P. M. Ntozi, 225–36. Canberra: Health Transition Centre, Australian National University.

Nyambedha, E., and J. Aagaard-Hansen. 2003. "Changing Place, Changing Position: Orphans' Movements in a Community with High HIV/AIDS Prevalence in Western Kenya." In *Children's Places: Cross-Cultural Perspectives*, ed. K. F. Olwig and E. Gulløv, 162–76. London: Routledge.

Odongkara, F. 1999. "Situational Analysis of District Authorities in Relation to Child Care and Protection Issues." Ministry of Gender, Labour, and Social Development, Kampala.

Okuonzi, S. A. 2004. "Dying for Economic Growth? Evidence of a Flawed Economic Policy in Uganda." *Lancet* 364: 1632–37.

Parry-Williams, J. 2005. "Comparative Study and Evaluation of the Impact of the Children's Act in Relation to Children in Conflict with the Law in Eight Districts of Uganda." Compiled for the Ministry of Gender, Labour, and Social Development, Kampala.

Passi F. O. 1995. "The Rise of People's Organizations in Primary Education in Uganda." In *Service Provision under Stress in East Africa: The State, NGOs, and People's Organizations in Kenya, Tanzania, and Uganda*, ed. J. Semboja and O. Therkildsen, 209–22. London: James Currey.

Ringsted, M. 2004. "Growing Up Pregnant: Events of Kinship in Everyday Life." *African Sociological Review* 8 (1): 100–17.

Semboja, J., and O. Therkildsen, eds. 1995. *Service Provision under Stress in East Africa: The State, NGOs, and People's Organizations in Kenya, Tanzania, and Uganda*. London: James Currey.

Silberschmidt, M., and V. Rasch. 2001. "Adolescent Girls, Illegal Abortions, and 'Sugar-Daddies' in Dar es Salaam: Vulnerable Victims and Active Social Agents." *Social Science and Medicine* 52: 1815–26.

Ssekiwunga, R., and R. Mulimba. 2003. "'She Will Grow with Her Husband': A Study of Factors Contributing to Early Pregnancies and Marriages among

Adolescent Girls in Busia District." Child Health and Development Centre, Makerere University, Kampala.

Townsend, P. 2004. "From Universalism to Safety Nets: The Rise and Fall of Keynesian Influence on Social Development." In *Social Policy in a Development Context*, ed. T. Mkandawire, 37–62. Hampshire, U.K.: Palgrave.

Uganda Bureau of Statistics. 2001. "Demographic and Health Survey: Uganda 2000–2001." Uganda Bureau of Statistics, Kampala.

UNAIDS (Joint United Nations Programme on HIV/AIDS). 2004. *Report on the Global AIDS Epidemic: 4th Global Report*. Geneva: UNAIDS.

UNICEF (United Nations Children's Fund) and UNAIDS (Joint United Nations Programme on HIV/AIDS). 2004. "The Framework for the Protection, Care, and Support of Orphans and Vulnerable Children Living in a World with HIV/AIDS." UNICEF and UNAIDS, Geneva.

Wakhweya, A., C. Kateregga, J. Konde-Lule, R. Mukyala, L. Sabin, M. Williams, and H. K. Heggenhougen. 2002. "Situational Analysis of Orphans in Uganda: Orphans and Their Households: Caring for Their Future—Today." Government of Uganda and Uganda AIDS Commission, Kampala.

Weisner, T. S. 1995. "Support for Children and the African Family Crisis." In *African Families and the Crisis of Social Change*, ed. T. S. Weisner, C. Bradley, and P. L. Kilbride, 20–45. Westport, CT: Bergin & Garvey.

Whyte, S. R. 1997. *Questioning Misfortune: The Pragmatics of Uncertainty in Eastern Uganda*. Cambridge, U.K.: Cambridge University Press.

——— 1998. "Slow Cookers and Madmen: Competence of Heart and Head in Rural Uganda." In *Questions of Competence: Culture, Classification, and Intellectual Disability*, ed. R. Jenkins, 153–75. Cambridge, U.K.: Cambridge University Press.

Whyte, M. A., and S. R. Whyte. 1998. "The Values of Development: Conceiving Growth and Progress in Bunyole." In *Developing Uganda*, eds. H. B. Hansen and M. Twaddle, 227–44. London: James Currey.

Whyte, S. R., and M. A. Whyte. 2004. "Children's Children: Time and Relatedness in Eastern Uganda." *Africa* 74 (1): 76–94.

CHAPTER 13

Monitoring Social Policy Outcomes in Jamaica: Democratic Evaluation and Institutional Change

Ann-Marie Bonner, Jeremy Holland, Andy Norton, and Ken Sigrist

This chapter documents the methodology that was developed during the past five years to monitor and improve social policy in Jamaica. Designed as a key component of the Jamaica Social Policy Evaluation (Jaspev)[1] process, the methodology seeks to embed a combination of methods within a participatory process of institutional change at different levels of governance.

Postindependence social policy in Jamaica produced strong social outcomes, particularly in the health and education sectors. Recently, however, there has been increasing concern as to whether social policy delivery has been effective in a present-day context of scarce public resources. A perception also exists within and beyond government that, with high levels of unemployment, violence, and social exclusion, there is an urgent need for joined-up social policy that goes beyond narrow and separated concerns with social sectors. The Jaspev process was designed to address a range of specific concerns about the management and implementation of social policy. These concerns included a perceived lack of ways to achieve policy coherence, a lack of mechanisms for establishing and updating strategic priorities, a continued reduction in public resources for social policy, and a perceived lack of a culture of evaluation and responsiveness to users in the delivery of public services.

In its first phase, the two key outputs of the Jaspev process were a social policy framework titled "Jamaica 2015" (Government of Jamaica

2002) and a five-year Action Plan (2002–07). Together, these documents seek to provide:

- A vision for the kind of society Jamaica aspires to be
- A set of seven key policy outcome goals that sum up a range of concrete outcomes representing progress toward realization of the vision
- A set of goals and objectives for changes in institutional systems and relationships supporting the achievement of the policy goals
- A framework for assessing progress over time toward the goals
- An action plan outlining a five-year program of measures to strengthen the design and implementation of social policy and to drive progress toward the outcome and process goals outlined.

The key goals identified in "Jamaica 2015" (Government of Jamaica 2002) are grouped into outcome and process goals, each with accompanying frameworks of benchmark indicators. The relevant parts of the document are listed in summary form in box 13.1. The first phase of Jaspev involved a yearlong process of analysis, consultation, reflection, and design. It also built relationships among communities, local governments, the administration, the political directorate, civil society, and the research community, thereby providing the platform for the second phase—implementation.

BOX 13.1

Jamaica 2015: Social Policy Goals

To realize the vision of a better Jamaica, the government commits itself to achieving progress toward the following key goals, constantly assessing our progress, reformulating our policies and strategies according to the best analysis and information available, and reporting back to the Jamaican people on the progress that has been achieved.

Key Outcome Goals

1. *Human security*. A peaceful and mutually respectful society with increased safety, security, and freedom from fear in the home and in public spaces
2. *Social integration*. An inclusive and nondiscriminatory society that respects group and individual rights, promotes social justice, accepts diversity, and builds trust and communication between all groups

(continued)

BOX 13.1

Jamaica 2015: Social Policy Goals (*continued*)

3. *Governance.* More effective, complementary, accountable, and transparent government structures, seeking to move decision making closer to the people
4. *Secure and sustainable livelihoods.* Widened, higher-quality livelihood and employment opportunities for all Jamaicans, with particular reference to those disadvantaged in the labor market
5. *Environment.* Improved environment for quality of life, for Jamaicans living and as yet unborn
6. *Education and skills.* An education that facilitates lifelong learning and acquisition of social and life skills for all
7. *Health and physical well-being.* Enhancement of the broadly defined health status of the population.

Key Process Goals

1. *The policy process.* Strengthening coherence, timeliness, ownership, participation, and quality in the formulation of social policy
2. *Strategic planning and resource allocation.* Strengthening the integration and effectiveness of planning and budget processes through enhanced prioritization, collaboration across ministerial and other boundaries, realism about available resources, reliability of delivery of budget allocations, and flexibility of resource allocation
3. *Responsiveness and institutional learning.* Promotion of the development of a more responsive, people-oriented, and innovative culture in Jamaican social policy institutions
4. *Monitoring of social trends and outcomes.* Promotion of enhanced effectiveness of social information systems in shaping the development of policy through improved timeliness, relevance, richness, presentation, and participation.

Source: Government of Jamaica 2002.

Part of a broader emerging paradigm of democratizing research, the Jaspev process was based on the proposition that broad ownership of the generation and analysis of evidence will lead to a more effective and sustainable policy process. The process was influenced by methodological traditions with contrasting ideological roots but complementary objectives and methods, including new public management approaches, emphasizing outcome-based diagnosis and demand-led institutional transformation, and participatory monitoring and evaluation, rooted in project and community development. Under Jaspev, the Jamaican Cabinet Office promoted a system of locally generated but nationally comparable benchmark indicators designed to encourage mutual learning and institutional change.

Policy, Power, and Institutional Change: The Inheritance

Monitoring at national and local levels can be key to achieving social policy goals. In some contexts, this function can be undertaken by third parties, such as public sector auditing bodies. Yet in many countries, independent public sector watchdogs do not exist and have little chance of being established and accepted by civil society in the short term. In these cases, nongovernmental organizations (NGOs) can play an effective monitoring and social auditing role (Zadek, Pruzan, and Evans 1997) by developing a consensus on what should be monitored and establishing a process for placing information in the public domain. Methods have been designed and adapted for this purpose, with report cards (Gopakumar and Balakrishnan 1999) a good example of a tool used successfully to audit service providers.

An alternative to using third-party monitoring is to have community actors themselves benchmark outcomes and use the data to evaluate social policy design and implementation. For example, community actors could identify a more peaceful community or the frequency of public telephone vandalism as outcome indicators and, from there, design social policy and other interventions. Importantly, this process prompts local diagnosis and action, often involving new forms of institutional alignment and forcing a higher level of accountability among participating agencies or duty bearers. It also develops a revisable model of effects that permits longer-term outcomes to be tracked in the shorter term.

Local government initiatives in the United States (the Oregon Shines program[2]) and Australia (Tasmania Together[3]) have demonstrated this powerful process, in which local information generation drives institutional change. The Oregon initiative reflects a tradition of thinking about institutional learning and change that can be traced through management models. It builds on familiar elements of new public management approaches, including an emphasis on improved coordination, joined-up government, and innovative partnerships between the public, private, and voluntary sectors, as well as flexibility and orientation to outcomes in the management of public policy. The Oregon model adds to this mix a strong emphasis on local-level engagement in defining benchmarks and the organization of appropriate local-level action to tackle identified issues and problems.

A quite separate but latterly converging stream of thinking about change is rooted in participatory development. Francis (2002) notes the convergence of ideological strands of thinking on participation and highlights the radical tradition of participation in Latin America, with its emphasis on empowering process (Fals Borda 1988; Freire 1972), and the participatory rural appraisal tradition emerging from agricultural research in the South (summarized by Chambers 1994). Francis (2002) links these traditions and the more functional management and organizational thinking of the United States, with its emphasis on improving efficiency and outcomes.

Participatory monitoring and evaluation approaches challenge the instrumental use of quantitative input-output indicators to measure project progress. They reflect the principles of participatory development by stressing processes of assessment, reflection, and action that override the concerns of extractive data collection by project outsiders (see Crawford 2005; Estrella with others 2000; Guijt and Gaventa 1998).

It is the emphasis on process, however, that connects the institutional learning approach of new public management with participatory research's interpretation of reflection and action. The convergence provides new opportunities to democratize the process of public policy management through institutional change. Institutional change occurs when parties perceive that, in order to renegotiate a contract, they need to restructure a higher set of rules or violate some norm of behavior (North 1990). The incentives that influence those contractual decisions can be either price based or norm based. Fundamental changes in relative prices are an important source of institutional change in a market-based economy because of their effect on the economic incentives that shape contracts (North 1990: 84). Critical here is that sociocultural norms evolve and change over time and are often transmitted from generation to generation or from administration to administration. So, while formal rules can be changed or introduced reasonably quickly, informal constraints, embodied in tradition and social norms, change slowly and are relatively impervious to formal rule changes.

When reflecting on historical or contemporary contexts in which "good" institutional change happened, one can see that Foucault's (1980) concept of "positive" power in the construction of new subjective truths provides the key to these considerations. The changes in norm-based discourse that gave rise to institutional change—in the shape of the abolition of slavery in the United States, for example—emerged not from utilitarian price-based rationality (slavery remained profitable), but from a process of norm-based deliberation in the context of a functioning electoral system. The concept of deliberative democracy, or decision making by free and equal citizens, can be traced from Pericles to Habermas (Elster 1998; see also Fung and Wright 2003), and is evident in Sen's (1999) plea for democratic freedom as a critical component of individual capabilities. In the context of policy, monitoring institutional improvement requires changes in the incentives and sanctions operating on the actors involved at the same time that deliberative spaces are created for the voices of those previously excluded from the policy process. This concept moves us toward what Evans (2004: 32) describes as an emerging "theory of institutional change"—a theory that informs much of the case study discussion in this chapter.

An institutional perspective on the sanctions and incentives governing policy change demands an operational focus on enhancing the transparency and accountability of political decision making. The World Bank, for instance, has sharpened its operational focus on governance and social accountability in the wake of its three-pillared strategy outlined in *World Development Report 2000/2001: Attacking Poverty* (World Bank 2000). The accountability triangle (see figure 13.1) presented in the *World Development Report 2004: Making Services Work for the Poor* (World Bank 2004) provides a clear analytical framework for identifying operational entry points for generating transparency and accountability in practice.

The short route to accountability (Route A in the figure) brings citizens and providers together through participatory mechanisms that include health sector committees, community-based school management, and participation in the delivery of social protection instruments, such as social funds. Here, much good work is being done by the World Bank and its country partners to identify mechanisms for strengthening social accountability in service delivery.

Figure 13.1. A The Accountability Triangle: A Framework of Accountability Relationships

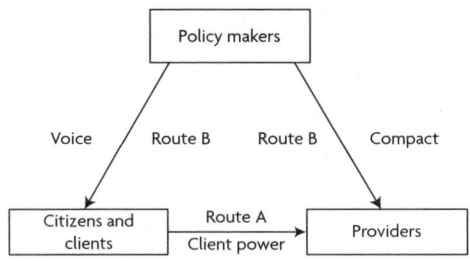

Source: World Bank 2003.

This short route can bring quick wins, but it can also be captured or compromised relatively easily in the absence of interventions that tackle the longer route to accountability through voice in policy making and the compact between policy makers and service providers. One of the most powerful ways of increasing voice and accountability in policy making is information (World Bank 2004: 7). National and local public policy monitoring has provided a great deal of knowledge about ways to transform the institutional structures that govern the policy process, including creating new channels of information and spaces to evaluate information at the macrolevel, mesolevel, and microlevel, thus encouraging institutional realignments of policy makers, bureaucrats, and citizens. The following section considers one innovative example of this approach being developed and implemented for social policy monitoring in Jamaica.

Monitoring Social Policy in Jamaica

The methodological challenge for those seeking to improve social policy outcomes in Jamaica was threefold:

- To establish more effective institutional links between the providers and users of policy-relevant information, so that the information generated is timely and relevant, resulting in powerful, evidence-based policy analysis
- To combine more effectively data sources and methods for social policy analysis, allied to an increased appreciation of the comparative advantages of different methods

- To embed policy research into a continuing process of institutional transformation and empowerment at different levels of governance so that the policy process is demand led by local society, as well as supply driven by technocratic expertise (Holland and others 2005).

Recognizing these challenges, the Jaspev taskforce developed an organizational arrangement allied to a social policy information system that aimed to stimulate the institutional connections necessary for improved social policy design, delivery, and outcomes. The driving force behind the system was the process of benchmarking indicators of change at the local level (see figure 13.2). Community members across different localities identified their own benchmarks, and teams of volunteers measured and monitored progress against these benchmarks in comparison with other localities.

For the monitoring instrument to be useful for analysis and action, it needed to possess three types of measures: diagnostic, process, and outcome. *Diagnostic measures* refer primarily to questions that elicit information and provide a context for understanding the existing reality, while driving debate, discussion, and diagnosis about the outcome. Table 13.1 provides an example of an indicator of youth inclusion in employment that identifies and codes the factors that prevent youth in a community from taking a job.

Process measures refer primarily to questions that help local people take immediate action to advance toward the desired benchmarked outcomes. These measures tend to be intermediate, and they assist the community in developing a plan of action. Such measures reveal aspects of attitudes, perceptions, behaviors, relationships, and resources that, if reordered,

Figure 13.2. Evaluating Social Policy at the Local Level in Jamaica

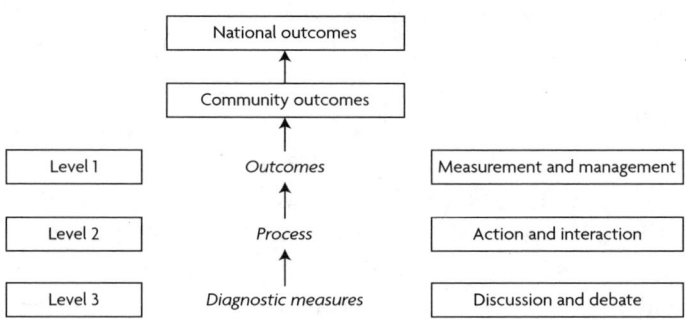

Source: Holland and others 2005.

Table 13.1. Example of a Diagnostic Measure of Youth Inclusion

What would be the main reason preventing you from taking a job if one were available now?								
Nothing [would accept]	Awaiting promised job	Pregnancy	Amount of pay	Have to stay with children or other relatives	Home duties	Do not need a job	Illness	Other (specify)
1 o	2 o	3 o	4 o	5 o	6 o	7 o	8 o	9 o

Source: Holland and others 2005.

Table 13.2. Example of a Process Measure (Individual Action) of Youth Inclusion

What efforts have you made to get a job? (multiple responses allowed)						
Applied in writing	Applied in person	Registered at an employment agency	Advertised on the radio or in a newspaper	Asked friends	Tried to get a loan	Other (specify)
1 o	2 o	3 o	4 o	5 o	6 o	7 o

Source: Holland and others 2005.

could lead to significant progress toward the outcome. At best, they are measures that reflect a mutually agreed theory of change that will drive local action and reorder how people relate and interact with each other with a view to achieving outcomes. Table 13.2 illustrates the range of measures that out-of-work youth might take to get a job.

In addition to measuring individual actions, process measures can also be applied to the performance of service providers in their relationship with users. In the case of employment status, table 13.3 illustrates the use of perception scores to track and compare the performance of continuing education service providers as perceived by users.

Outcome measures, as illustrated in table 13.4, arise from asking the local community questions about what will indicate progress toward achieving the stated outcomes. These measures tend to be more long term and are relatively crude. If measurement of the outcomes shows that progress is not being made, then the assumptions, diagnosis, theory of change, and identified actions will have to be revisited.

Outcome measures are not likely to see any change in the short term. It is best to use process measures in the interim and check outcome measures at a time when data are more likely to be available. For example, level of educational attainment data are not likely to be generated until the end of an academic year; however, the desire for further studies or the level

Table 13.3. Example of a Process Measure (Performance) of Youth Inclusion: Jaspev Community Scorecard on Continuing Education Service Standards

Name of community: _____ Code: ☐☐ Name of parish _____ Code ☐☐

Level of satisfaction with services: 1 = very satisfied; 2 = satisfied; 3 = OK; 4 = dissatisfied; 5 = very dissatisfied; 6 = not applicable

Service standard indicators	Jamaica Movement for the Advancement of Literacy	Human Employment and Resource Training	Social Development Commission	Jamaica Business Development Centre	National Youth Service	National Council on Drug Abuse	Parenting Partners	Comments
Length of time it takes for the telephone to be answered								
Level of respect and courtesy displayed by administrative staff members								
Level of respect displayed by facilitators and trainers								

Length of time it takes for response to applications, letters, and queries

Length of time spent in lines waiting for services at the agency

Quality of communication and information given by staff about services

Source: Jaspev 2005.

Table 13.4. Example of an Outcome Measure of Youth Inclusion

What were you doing for most of the time over the past month?							
Working	Have job but on leave	Looking for work	At home	Trying to start a business	In a formal or informal training program	At school full time	Other (specify) 1Ð
1 o	2 o	3 o	4 o	5 o	6 o	7 o	8 o

Source: Holland and others 2005.

of enrollment in education and training programs could be intermediate proxies of the outcome that could register change.

The data generated by participants served different purposes. A core of indicators needed to be quantifiable and, for benchmarking purposes, comparable across time and locations. A further set of indicators could be more contextual and qualitative, allowing research participants and the consultative network to generate their own local narratives, analysis, and action for change. This mix was necessary because of the intent to bring together in one discussion a combination of tacit local knowledge and centrally available expert knowledge.

The institutional context for this data generation and diagnostic work was key to the performance of the model. The institutional design of Jaspev drew on the relational concepts underpinning social networks for understanding and influencing social roles and responsibilities (Burt 2000; Wasserman and Faust 1994). Burt's analysis of networks invites a focus on the role of independent or lightly connected third parties and the power they can exert, in part, through the unique information possibilities open to them. The third party creates tension and uncertainty by his or her presence, and—importantly for institutional designers—that tension has potential for providing automatic or built-in governance. Not that such automatic governance is necessarily a free good—costs can be added to transactions by the involvement of a third party. Nonetheless, the idea of built-in or automatic governance has some appeal, given the obvious costs and uncertainties of institutional arrangements for supporting hierarchical governance. These arrangements include detailed reporting regulations for purposes of accountability, boards of appeal, elaborate systems of rules, lengthy due process, audit arrangements, ombudsmen, and anticorruption agencies.

What was of interest to the Jaspev designers was precisely the generalization of the automatic governance potential of third-party arrangements and the scope for designing systems in which an empowering third-party role might be deliberately assigned, not to a political patron or his or her client, but to an oppressed class or socially excluded group. This possibility was one of the key ideas behind the mechanism called *thematic prototype*, a prototype designed for implementing social policy goals from the bottom up, as well as from the top down. This effort in institutionalizing action research was intended to provide lessons for the design of future institutional reforms in the public sector.

The Jaspev institutional model was therefore based on a third-party arrangement. It had a policy leadership node, a strategic management (or technical) node, and an operational node or nodes. Assessment of outcomes and process against a particular social policy theme or prototype by the operational nodes was shared with a group of technical specialists (chosen on the basis of their expertise and their institutional capacity as change agents) in that thematic area and with a group of three policy makers (cross-party members of Parliament and junior ministers)—a policy troika with its own third-party function—whose departments linked to that theme.

This setup was deliberately unstable; each node scrutinized the relations between the other two nodes and had some means to influence those relations. The kind of unaccountable complicity that can develop between reporting levels and that arises in any organizational hierarchy, creating what economists refer to as "the agency problem," was, therefore, largely designed out of this system. The prototype mechanism was designed to have both the incentive and the capacity to inspect and judge its own ongoing performance. Hence, the external accountability that had to be imposed to keep the prototype on track was residual and limited. It applied largely to ensuring that the prototype as a whole remained moderately unstable (that is, that it did not "freeze") and that the overall focus on an overarching policy goal was maintained.

This triangular institutional arrangement formed the basis for a continuing loop of assessment, diagnosis, design, and delivery of social policy. In this arrangement, the local actors were not merely observer-participants with a voice, but they were granted a degree of leverage; they could become a load-bearing element in the process of evidence-based policy adjustment. In this way, the process also created an institutional space at the local level for new alliances of civil society and state actors to mobilize local and private resources toward increased public accountability and improved policy outcomes.

To achieve this result, the Jaspev taskforce was faced with significant questions and challenges:

- What is the correct balance between local actors' and policy makers' demand for information?
- What are the right questions that communities need to ask that will lead to institutional and policy action?
- How much information do communities need to collect in order to influence institutional and policy processes?
- What measures for ongoing monitoring will inform the taskforce about how overall efforts are taking it closer to its outcomes?

In grappling with these questions, the Jaspev taskforce viewed its work as a large-scale project of action research, but to be acceptable politically at all levels, the emphasis had to remain predominantly on action.

Progress and Lessons Learned to Date

The Jaspev process was operational for seven years, with project funding now ended and much significant and groundbreaking progress made during that period. The challenge was to simultaneously change the incentives and sanctions operating on the political directorate, while opening up local space for deliberation and improving the flow of evidence to support policy discussions. A social policy information system was established that fed policy debates among stakeholders in the policy process. Indicator review meetings to monitor progress against the seven social policy outcome goals (see box 13.1) were highly successful and proved an effective way to organize technical specialists to debate and provide inputs to the Jaspev national progress reports.

At the technical node level of policy deliberation, organizational learning through thematic networks took hold. At least two networks were established during the life of the project. More groupings took place around common functions for the purposes of exchanging information, honing skills, and learning more about internal processes and international best practices. Some of these arrangements were loose, with sharing occurring occasionally; others met formally every month or quarter. Members of networks cited better understanding of processes and access to information as key benefits of membership. Individual development was the main benefit of network participation. However, it was less effective in supporting teamwork in the ministries. Many people still work in silos and rarely seek the advice or support of colleagues in working through issues or solving problems. Monitoring as a motivational tool for performance is difficult to assess. Ministries are inundated with requests for reports. In many cases, such reports are routine and are not as effective as intended. Tools such as community scorecards, which are simple, not time consuming, and show how ministries stack against each other, seem to be most promising for generating incentives for action.

The strongest support for the Jaspev process came from the operational node of the Jaspev triangle: the communities that wanted some connection with the process so that they could articulate their concerns and play their part. The democratization of data and evidence gathering was an important step in the development of the project. It engaged the youth in the community and gave them tools they could apply to empower themselves. In partnership with the Social Development Commission,[4] the Jaspev team cultivated deliberative space at the local level for measurement, reflection, and action on the theme of youth inclusion. The use of community scorecards (see table 13.5), for example, sparked interest and demand from within the Ministry of National Security regarding the theme of police–youth relations. A number of other public agencies expressed interest in developing scorecards for their services. The long-term effect of this process on community-level action needs to be explored further to determine how well communities have applied their skills and exploited their deliberative spaces to seek their own objectives.

However, the greatest hurdle to the successful shift of Jaspev to a transformed system of social policy governance was the challenge of effectively engaging policy makers in a new policy dialogue. The triangular relationship described in the Jaspev model was designed to create new channels of communication and new modes of behavior in addressing both short and long routes of accountability for social policy delivery. Yet this system is vulnerable if one or more of the nodes does not function as predicted. During the life of the project, this problem was most evident at the political directorate node for the Jaspev process.

Change in political culture requires political leadership that is prepared to take the risks involved in challenging the system. With the challenge of cultural change in mind, at first glance, the fact that all members of the troika of politicians were relatively young seemed to be positive. They represented the future direction and new arrangement for public policy

Table 13.5. Jaspev Community Scorecard on Police–Youth Relations

Name of community: Sex: ☐ M ☐ F	Code: ☐☐ Name of parish Code ☐☐ Age: ☐15–19 ☐20–24 ☐25–29	
	Level of satisfaction with services: 1 = very satisfied; 2 = satisfied; 3 = OK; 4 = dissatisfied; 5 = very dissatisfied; 6 = not applicable	
Service standard indicators	Score	Comments
Level of trust the youth have in the police		
Level of trust police have in the youth		
Level of respect and courtesy displayed by the police		
Level of courtesy and respect displayed by the youth		
Level of fairness displayed by the police		
Level of fairness displayed by the youth with the police		

Level of effort made by
  the police to interact with
  the youth		

Level of effort made by
  the youth to interact with
  the police		

Source: Jaspev 2005.

governance and were predisposed to exploring new notions of political culture. However, their youth and accompanying need to earn their political stripes also created disincentives to behavioral and institutional change. Furthermore, in the absence of a clear mechanism governing how they would bring the information and evaluation generated to bear on the policy process, the process was actually hampered by their inexperience and lack of influence with more senior ministers in government. More experienced and committed practitioners can initiate policy dialogues and change in a more structured and effective way.

Over and above appeals to leadership and behavioral change, the context of institutional reform can fundamentally determine the pace at which such changes take place. In Jamaica's case, the political culture (a highly clientelistic form of the inherited Westminster two-party system) is a major constraint to reform. Changes in the governance culture and structural arrangements are constrained by electoral concerns. The joint leadership approach, exemplified by Jaspev's cross-party experiment of a troika of politicians to lead each of the thematic initiatives, was limited by this political culture. Although it sent out a strong symbolic signal that both political parties were prepared to work together on issues, in reality, it functioned in the same vein of narrow party interest. Both sets of political representatives saw Jaspev as a way to promote their particular interests without refocusing on the aspect of joint leadership around the issues in the national interest. One representative, for example, used the information and insight gathered through his involvement to push through an initiative on youth unemployment. However, it was a missed opportunity at the level of the political directorate to show a unified political position on the first prototype theme of youth inclusion.

The distorting effects of these entrenched sets of political incentives on the Jaspev process was strengthened by the lack of incentives among politicians to consistently engage in and support the process. The Jaspev objective competed with other policy objectives that brought more tangible outputs. Process issues often are relegated to a secondary position or are deemed esoteric. Despite many efforts, the ministerial leadership remained lukewarm to the possibilities Jaspev could offer to the overall policy- and decision-making process. This factor led to the perception that the reform was being led by the administration without the full support of the political leadership. In part, the loss of momentum at the political directorate level between the design and implementation stages could be attributed to changes in the position of key stakeholders. It must be acknowledged, therefore, that the element of Jaspev that sought to produce changes in incentives for political actors through a participatory process of policy design, implementation, and evaluation was only a partial success.

The incentives for pursuing joined-up government are no less elusive. The challenge has been how to effect these changes in the context of an administrative system that does not reward these efforts. Jaspev's issues-based approach to promoting cooperation and teamwork across administrative boundaries produced some encouraging results. In the leading reform cells of the administration, the Policy Analysis and Review Unit and the Public Sector Reform Unit, a strong effort was made to take joint approaches to work around the deliverables of the Jaspev initiative. On the whole, the results have been positive, and the outputs of these efforts have been more effective. The work was made easier because a common commitment existed to meet project goals and achieve the overall reform objectives. This common vision was what drove the team to seek concrete results in the face of difficulties. In the absence of this joined-up approach, change is difficult. The efforts with the ministries were most successful where the shared vision was consistent with the objectives of the ministry itself and where results, however incremental, could be demonstrated. Work on police–youth relations, for example, addressed a priority concern of the Ministry of National Security, and, when it succeeded, it could be mapped onto broader objectives. Furthermore, the range of players who need to be joined up in this instance were fewer and included stakeholders with whom the ministry had often worked.[5] "Joining up" is fairly easy to achieve in this situation, but it would be far more problematic for a Ministry of Finance, for example, which does not work directly with its stakeholders and would find joining with new stakeholders challenging.

There are signs that policy makers became more receptive to getting citizen feedback and securing evidence as a basis for planning and policy development. The Jaspev team sought to capitalize on this growing receptiveness, while challenging from below the entrenched nature of national policy-making behavior. For instance, it scheduled a decentralized series of regional cross-party constituency council sessions with workers from both parties and planning regional executive cross-party sessions with members of Parliament to discuss the design, implementation, and outcomes of social policy and social service delivery at regional level. If the political node of the social policy triangle was decentralized, there was a good chance that the well-functioning technical and operational nodes would at last find a more willing and accessible political audience for deliberative policy making.

Conclusion

The recent convergence of varied strands of thinking about monitoring and evaluation provides new opportunities to democratize the process of public policy management. This chapter has briefly outlined an innovative approach to community-based monitoring that seeks to inform and provoke change in the design and implementation of social policy in Jamaica. The approach adopted in the Jaspev process was highly ambitious in its attempt to combine technical innovation in the collection and flow of information with institutional transformation at different levels of governance. The explicit objective of including the political directorate in the change process was a key innovation—but also the level of the Jaspev design that proved hardest to make work in practice.

The institutional challenge proved serious and poses a continuing risk to the success of Jaspev as a process beyond the completion of international donor support through project funding, a reminder that evidence-based policy management is far from being a technical and technocratic exercise. The politicized nature of institutions in Jamaica, the role of hierarchy and patronage, and the tendency for political parties to be territorial are widely recognized and criticized by a cynical and weary civil society. The challenge faced should not be understated, yet Jaspev, though managerialist in tone and influence, has created political space for institutional change through an emphasis on the interaction of nodes of local and national process. A twin-track approach is needed to challenge this political culture. The first track is to shift incentives and sanctions to encourage joined-up thinking and political commitment to more inclusive governance of the policy process. The second is to strengthen external accountability mechanisms by liberating and connecting local actors who are ready to take responsibility for policy results and are willing to hold political actors publicly accountable for results. Ultimately, it is on the democratic generation and ownership of information that emerging systems of accountability and delineation of responsibility for the delivery of social policy will stand or fall.

Notes

1. The Jaspev process was funded for seven years through two phases of the U.K. Department for International Development (DFID) project funding. The second phase ended in 1997.
2. The experience of the Oregon Progress Board and the Oregon Shines program in the United States is documented in various reports on a regularly updated Web site: http://www.oregon.gov/DAS/OPB/os.shtml.
3. For further information about Tasmania Together, see http://www.tasmania together.tas.gov.au/.
4. The Social Development Commission is a Jamaican government agency that works through outreach activities on community development activities. For more information, see http://www.sdc.gov.jm/about/.
5. An example of successful collaborative work in this area was the adoption by the Ministry of National Security of the police–youth relations indicator as a tool for deepening citizen involvement in the fight against crime (Jaspev 2005).

References

Burt, R. 2000. "The Network Structure of Social Capital." In *Research in Organizational Behavior*, ed. B. Staw and R. Sutton. New York: JAI Press.

Chambers, R. 1994. "The Origins and Practice of Participatory Rural Appraisal." *World Development* 22 (7): 953–69.

Crawford, G. 2005. "Evaluating Democracy Assistance: The Inadequacy of Numbers and the Promise of Participation." In *Methods in Development Research: Combining Quantitative and Qualitative Approaches*, ed. J. Holland and J. Campbell, 205–18. London: ITDG.

Elster, J., ed. 1998. *Deliberative Democracy*. Cambridge, U.K.: Cambridge University Press.

Estrella, M., with J. Blauert, D. Campilan, J. Gaventa, J. Gonsalves, I. Guijt, D. Johnson, and R. Ricafort, eds. 2000. *Learning from Change: Issues and Experience in Participatory Monitoring and Evaluation*. Ottawa: International Development Research Centre.

Evans, P. 2004. "Development as Institutional Change: The Pitfalls of Monocropping and the Potentials of Deliberation." *Studies in Comparative International Development* 38 (4): 30–52.

Fals Borda, O. 1988. *Knowledge and People's Power: Lessons with Peasants in Nicaragua, Mexico, and Colombia*. Geneva: International Labour Organization.

Foucault, M. 1980. *Power/Knowledge: Selected Interviews and Other Writings 1972–1977*. London: Harvester Press.

Francis, P. 2002. "Community Participation and Decision-Making." In *Handbook on Development Policy and Management,* ed. C. Kirkpatrick, R. Clarke, and C. Polidano, 400–10. Cheltenham, U.K.: Edward Elgar.

Freire, P. 1972. *Pedagogy of the Oppressed*. London: Penguin Books.

Fung, A., and E. Wright. 2003. *Deepening Democracy: Institutional Innovations in Empowered Participatory Governance*. London: Verso.

Gopakumar, K., and S. Balakrishnan, eds. 1999. "Citizen Feedback and State Accountability: Report Cards as an Aid to Improve Local Governance." In *Working from Below: Techniques to Strengthen Local Governance in India*, ed. S. Lingayah, A. MacGillivray, and M. Helqvist. London: New Economics Foundation.

Government of Jamaica. 2002. "Jamaica 2015: A Framework and Action Plan for Improving Effectiveness, Collaboration, and Accountability in the Delivery of Social Policy." Planning Institute of Jamaica, Kingston. http://www.jaspev.org/documents/docs/General/socialpolicyframework2015.pdf.

Guijt, I., and J. Gaventa. 1998. "Participatory Monitoring and Evaluation: Learning from Change." Brighton, U.K.: Institute of Development Studies.

Holland, J., S. Noble, A. Norton, and K. Sigrist. 2005. "Monitoring Social Policy Outcomes in Jamaica: Combined Methods, Democratic Research, and Institutional Change." In *Methods in Development Research: Combining Quantitative and Qualitative Approaches*, ed. J. Holland and J. Campbell, 219–26. London: ITDG.

Jaspev. 2005. *Quarterly Progress Report*. Kingston: Jaspev. May

North, D. C. 1990. *Institutions, Institutional Change, and Economic Performance*. Cambridge, U.K.: Cambridge University Press.

Sen, A. 1999. *Development as Freedom*. New York: Alfred A. Knopf.

Wasserman, S., and K. Faust. 1994. *Social Network Analysis*. Cambridge, U.K.: Cambridge University Press.

World Bank. 2000. *World Development Report 2000/2001: Attacking Poverty*. Washington, DC: World Bank.

———. 2004. *World Development Report 2004: Making Services Work for the Poor*. Washington, DC: World Bank.

Zadek, S., P. Pruzan, and R. Evans. 1997. *Building Corporate Accountability: Emerging Practices in Social and Ethical Accounting, Auditing, and Reporting*. London: Earthscan.

CHAPTER 14

Public Interest Litigation, Social Rights, and Social Policy

Siri Gloppen

Can social rights litigation contribute to more equitable and socially sustainable development outcomes? This chapter investigates the potential of public interest litigation to advance social rights and channel the voices of marginalized people into social policy processes. In doing so, it identifies factors that condition the various stages of the litigation process, accounting for its failure or success.

Why is this topic of interest? Increasingly, public interest litigation is used and proposed as a strategy to influence social policy in fields such as health, environment, housing, land, education, and gender. Activists see it as a channel through which the voices of the poor can be articulated into the legal-political system and as a mechanism to make the state more responsive and accountable to their rights. International nongovernmental organizations (NGOs) and networks specialize in particular areas of cause lawyering, and donors support and encourage public interest litigation, providing incentives for local NGOs and activists to take up test cases.[1]

The move to litigation can be seen as part of a broader trend toward legalization or judicialization of politics, to some extent driven by ideological factors, the international human rights movement, and a liberal reform agenda. Academic research, in contrast, does not generally

This chapter draws on Domingo, Gargarella, and Roux (2006), which includes an earlier version of the framework presented here (Gloppen 2006). It also builds on collaborative work in the Courts in Transition group of the Chr. Michelsen Institute (Gargarella and others 2004).

advocate litigation as a means to effect social change, warning that the law—shaped by power—favors those with more resources and that "the haves" tend to come out ahead in court even in countries with reasonably strong and well-functioning legal systems.[2]

Still, public interest litigation is taken up by, or on behalf of, marginalized groups also in developing and transitioning countries where social inequalities are stark and judicial systems are weak—sometimes with success. Given that poor people often lack institutional channels to voice their concerns, systematically exploring the potential of social rights litigation and looking for comparative sensibilities are worthwhile.[3]

Litigating to Advance Social Rights

Public interest litigation here refers to various legal actions taken to establish a legal principle or right that is of public importance and is aimed at social change.[4] It relates to the protection of economic and social rights in various ways. In some cases, social rights (international human rights norms or domestic rights) are the explicit basis for litigation. In other cases, civil and political rights are used to indirectly establish social rights,[5] or social benefits have been extended to new groups by relying on the right to equality. In addition, auxiliary litigation (ranging from test cases securing freedom of speech and assembly to ad hoc measures to keep activists out of jail when they are arrested for breaking the law) may provide political and social space, enabling groups and individuals to voice claims and struggle for social rights in other arenas (Cavallaro and Schaffer 2004). This chapter focuses on social rights litigation in the narrow sense, but that is only one aspect of public interest litigation.

The aim of public interest litigation is to transform the situation not only for the litigants but also for all those similarly situated: that is, to alter structured inequalities and power relations in society in ways that reduce the weight of morally irrelevant circumstances, such as socioeconomic status, gender, race, religion, or sexual orientation.[6] Thus, the success of litigation should be judged not only in terms of how a case fares in court but also on whether the terms of the judgment are complied with. Even more important is the systemic impact—the broader effects on social policy, public discourses on social rights, and the development of jurisprudence.

Although this chapter shows that the litigation process itself may have an independent influence on public discourse and policy regardless of the outcome of the case, winning court cases is at the core. The chapter starts by examining what it takes to win.

Factors Affecting Success in Court

To illustrate how various factors affect the likelihood of a favorable court judgment, one must disaggregate the litigation process to show its main structural components. As figure 14.1 shows, several stages or hurdles need to be overcome for litigation to succeed:

- Poor people must be able to identify and articulate their rights claims and voice them in the legal system or have their rights asserted on their behalf.
- Judicial bodies must be responsive to these social rights claims and accept them as matters belonging within their domain.
- Judges must be capable of finding legal means to address the social rights claims and find effective remedies.
- For judgments to have a social impact, they must also be accepted, complied with, implemented, and translated into systemic change through social policy and political practice.

Legal systems differ, but generally—and particularly in the common law tradition—courts respond to cases brought before them rather than to individuals acting on their own initiative. Therefore, understanding the circumstances under which poor people's grievances are transformed into effective voice in the form of social rights claims is important.

Figure 14.1. The Main Components of the Litigation Process

Marginalized groups' **a**	Courts' **b**	Judges' **c**	Authorities' **d**	Social policy **d**
voice	responsiveness	capability	compliance and implementation	systemic change

Source: An earlier version of this figure appeared in Gloppen (2006: 43). See also Gloppen (2005).
a. Social rights cases brought to court.
b. Cases accepted by the courts.
c. Judgments giving effect to social rights.
d. Transformation effect (effect on social rights and inclusion of marginalized groups).

What Determines the Legal Voice of the Poor?

As figure 14.2 illustrates, a crucial parameter of poor people's ability to voice rights claims is their opportunity situation: the formal (or systemic) and informal barriers that define them as litigants in the legal process (Moore 1987). Whose claims are voiced—as well as how—depends on the affected people's resources to articulate and mobilize and on the interaction between marginalized groups and public interest litigators.

Sometimes marginalized people bring their own cases, but usually legal professionals are involved, such as lawyers acting pro bono or on a contingency fee basis; local, national, or international legal services organizations (see Manning 1999, 2001; World Bank 2005); university legal clinics; or public institutions.[7]

The decision to litigate may come from either set of actors, but who is in the driver's seat has implications for the nature of the process. For litigation to emerge from marginalized groups, several hurdles have to be overcome, each involving significant challenges and requiring resources. Such groups must understand the situation they experience as violating their rights and be aware that legal remedies exist, identify their grievance in a way that is sufficiently explicit to provide the basis for litigation, and identify who bears the moral and legal responsibility. In addition, they must be able to mobilize the legal resources to transform their grievances into legal claims that the system will accept.[8]

Figure 14.2. Factors Affecting Litigants' Voice

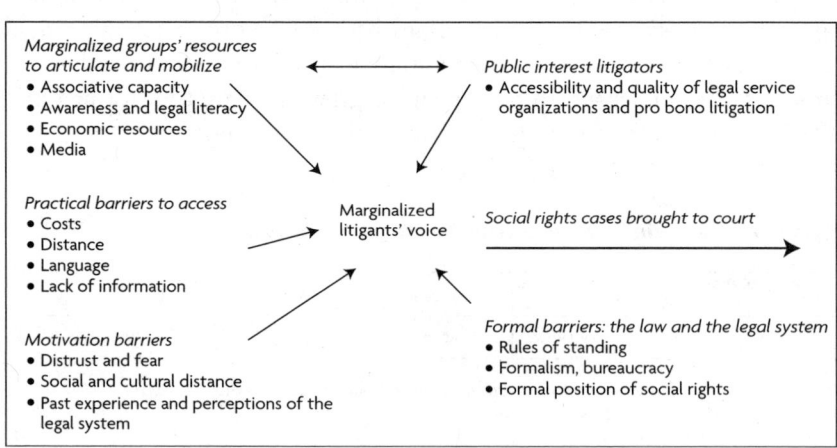

Source: An earlier version of this figure appeared in Gloppen (2006: 45). See also Gloppen (2005).

Barriers exist at each stage. Some are practical: lack of basic legal literacy and rights awareness prevents people from seeing their problems and grievances as rights violations. Insufficient information about who is to blame, how they can be held responsible, and where claims can be addressed are also common obstacles. For the most marginalized, such as poor, rural people in developing countries, legal expertise is often out of reach, or they lack the resources necessary to make use of such expertise (Gargarella 2002).

Equally important are motivational barriers. Poor people often view the legal system with distrust and fear—and not without reason. The law reflects power relations in society and often has an antipoor bias (see, for example, Decker, Sage, and Stefanova 2005). Many poor people live their lives in conditions of illegality—as illegal immigrants, squatters, or employees in the informal sector. This status, in turn, subjects them to insecurity and vulnerability, thereby contributing to their poverty.[9] The law offers them little protection, and they encounter the justice system mainly in a punitive capacity, often in ways perceived as arbitrary and corrupt. Moreover, in many developing countries, legal systems are weak, plagued by corruption, and subject to elite capture.[10] When the law and the legal system lack legitimacy (because they are perceived as a tool of domination or they are at odds with socially entrenched customary law[11]), the motivation for turning to the state for support is affected.

The nature of the law and the formal barriers of the legal system also affect marginalized groups' motivation and ability to voice social rights claims. A clear legal basis for social rights is conducive to seeking redress, as are possibilities for class action, but what has emerged from comparative evidence as most important are the criteria for *standing*, or the right to bring a case before the court (see Gargarella, Domingo, and Roux 2006). A striking feature of countries where courts have become an important arena for the pursuit of social rights (such as Colombia, Costa Rica, Hungary, India, and South Africa) is that they have lenient criteria for standing and allow organizations and individuals to litigate on behalf of others. Reduction in legal formalities is also important, including simplified procedures for lodging cases. In countries where the court aids litigants in investigating their cases, as in Costa Rica and India (Wilson 2005), poor litigants depend less on legal expertise than they do in countries where they must provide all the evidence and present argument in a prescribed format.[12] Nevertheless, also where barriers are low, the poorest risk being crowded out by the not so poor, who are in a better position to litigate. This, to some extent, has been the case in India.

The motivation to pursue legal action depends on whether other realistic alternatives are available, such as electoral mobilization; lobbyig of political bodies; strikes; demonstrations or media campaigns; or alternative courtlike institutions, such as ombudsman institutions, human rights commissions, or traditional courts and tribunals.[13] Even where potentially more effective alternative avenues exist, litigation may form part of a broader strategy that is valued for its mobilization potential and for the official recognition that the court can give of the grievance as a rights violation.

Despite the obstacles, marginalized groups lodge social rights cases (see Domingo, Gargarella, and Roux 2006; Epp 1998), but what are the resources and strategies enabling them to overcome the barriers? A key factor is *associative capacity*—that is, the ability to join forces, link up with legal expertise, form associations with the capacity to mobilize around social rights issues, and generate resources and sustain collective action (Epp 1998). The strategies used are important—the ways in which claims and grievances are publicized (for example, through protest marches and public rallies) and turned into a mainstream legal process (Heywood 2005). This factor, in turn, points to the importance of personal agency. Personalities and leadership are central to understanding why some marginal groups are able to articulate their concerns well enough to pave the way for a judicial process or inquiry and sustain it.

Public interest litigators may also initiate litigation, either as an ad hoc effort to assist in a concrete situation or as part of a long-term strategy to build jurisprudence.[14] Litigation from outside bypasses many of the barriers, but the aims of professional public interest litigators do not always converge fully with the interests of their clients. Fear or rejection of the formal legal system may prevent marginalized people from cooperating with litigators offering to act on their behalf. Constructive collaboration with people whose social rights are most at risk may be difficult. These people include those who are very poor, socially outcast, located in remote rural areas, without a permanent home, or without a functioning social structure (COHRE 2003). Although externally initiated cases can be voiced with minimal input from the victims, experienced litigators emphasize the importance of interaction with those affected.

This connection adds strength and concreteness to the claims that are presented, which, in turn, add momentum to the process (see COHRE 2003; Heywood 2005).

The voicing of claims is only the first phase of the litigation process. The next hurdle is entry into the legal system—whether the court is responsive to the social rights claims and accepts the case as a matter belonging within its proper jurisdiction.

Responsiveness of the Courts

Legal systems vary in their responsiveness or in their willingness to accept social rights cases and public interest litigation. The formal criteria of standing and admissibility, as well as the judges' practicing of those criteria, cause differences.

As figure 14.3 indicates, courts' responsiveness to social rights claims is partly a function of voice—both content and form. Whether a case is accepted depends on its merits, the skill with which the case is articulated and framed, and the legal strategies used. Again, this factor makes access to high-quality legal services central, and more so the less open a system is to social rights claims. The legal system's responsiveness depends on two sets of factors: (a) formal characteristics of the law and the legal system and (b) the nature of the judiciary.

Figure 14.3. Factors Conditioning Courts' Responsiveness to Social Rights

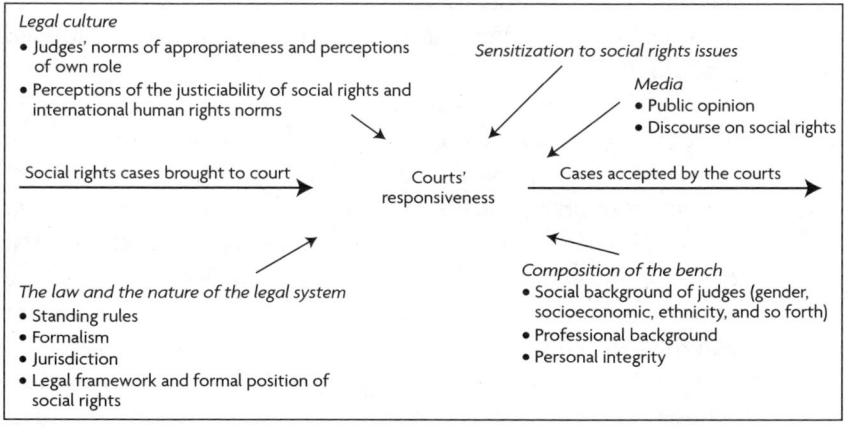

Source: An earlier version of this figure appeared in Gloppen (2006: 49). See also Gloppen (2005).

The formal features of the legal system that influence prospective litigants' decisions concerning whether to invest in legal strategies are also relevant for courts' responsiveness (which is what accounts for their motivational force): the rules of standing, the legal procedure and evidence, and the legal basis for litigating in the public interest. Whether a court accepts a social rights claim also depends on the legal basis for the claim, including whether social rights are protected in the constitution and domestic legislation, whether the country has signed and ratified international social rights conventions, and whether social rights are explicitly justiciable or defined as "directive principles" outside the scope of the court's jurisdiction. Inequalities built into the law, such as discrimination against women or indigenous people, may also influence the admissibility of a case (see Decker, Sage, and Stefanova 2005: 8–11).

How judges interpret the rules on standing and admissibility of social rights claims is as important as the legal formalities. This point is vividly illustrated by Indian judges' relaxation of standing rules and procedures and by their inference of social rights from the constitutional right to life and dignity. In contrast, the South African Constitutional Court, operating on the basis of a constitution that on paper is much more conducive to accessibility and social rights litigation than the Indian constitution, has severely limited the possibility for direct access (Dugard 2005). In many African and Latin American countries with a relatively solid constitutional basis for social rights, judges have interpreted the constitution and the law very restrictively, maintaining limited criteria for standing, dismissing public interest litigation, and declining jurisdiction on social rights (Domingo, Gargarella, and Roux 2006; Gloppen and Kanyongolo 2007).

Few disagree that judicial interpretation is important, but little agreement exists regarding which factors are most decisive in shaping it.[15] In some cases, political pressure and corruption influence judges' decisions, disadvantaging poor and politically marginal litigants. In developing and transitional contexts with weak legal systems, few effective sanctions exist against judges submitting to extralegal influences, particularly where the society tolerates corruption and notions of judicial independence are not embedded in the legal culture.

How legal norms are interpreted in a particular case is also linked to the individual judge's personal, ideological, and professional values. These values combine with the legal culture to shape the judge's perception of his or her role, the understanding of what is the appropriate way to deal with social rights, and the extent to which social rights are within the proper domain of the courts. The judges' sensitivity—individually and collectively—to the concerns of marginalized people is crucial to their interpretation of the law.[16] Training and experience shape this consciousness, but the composition of the bench (the judges' social, cultural, and ideological background; their legal education and professional qualities; and their integrity and commitment) has the most profound influence. Studies conducted in Argentina, Colombia, and India conclude that appointment of judges who are sensitive to the suffering of disadvantaged groups significantly favors courts' responsiveness to social rights (Gargarella, Domingo, and Roux 2006). Institutionally, the composition of the bench is a function of the system and criteria for appointment of judges. Inclusive and transparent appointment systems may create more diverse and socially sensitive courts, but formal procedures do not necessarily change courts' responsiveness to the concerns of the poor—and more responsive courts have come about without changes in the appointment procedures.

Judges' Capability to Give Effect to Social Rights Claims

Whether judges, faced with claims concerning the social rights of marginalized people, endorse them and are able to create effective remedies depends on a number of factors that combine to constitute the judges' professional capabilities and the political-legal context in which they operate. Judges' capability to make progressive social rights judgments is influenced by external incentives and constraints, as well as by internal resources and professional craftsmanship. (For a visualization of the factors affecting judges' capability, see figure 5 in Gloppen 2006: 51.)

Rules regulating the courts' jurisdiction, review powers, and competences define the area—and reach—of courts' decisions. Other aspects of the legal framework (notably the status of social rights within the domestic legal system) set important parameters for judges' ability to devise effective remedies. Within this space, judicial procedure—the status of precedent, international and comparative jurisprudence, and judges' authority to investigate and appoint research commissions and experts—defines the tools judges have to develop social rights jurisprudence.

Although legal norms constrain, there is scope for interpretation, and judges' interpretation of the law is as important as the law itself. External pressure, the legal culture, judges' conception of their own role, and what their peers recognize as sound jurisprudence may influence judges' interpretation of the law. Judges' sensitivity to the concerns raised also depends on their social and professional background. Judges are usually drawn from the elite, and their life experiences and values often render them insensitive to the plight and socioeconomic rights of the marginalized. Additionally, the education and training of judges has traditionally done little to sensitize them to equality and social rights concerns. Increasingly, sensitization to equality issues and social rights is included in curricula for legal education and on-the-job training of judges, and this trend is likely to make a difference to interpretation of social rights and how these rights are given legal effect. Similarly, where judges are drawn from a broader range of backgrounds (academic lawyers, activists, private practice), courts appear to be more active in terms of giving effect to social rights.[17]

In many cases, political pressure influences judicial decisions—pressure from the state, higher judicial officers, or extrainstitutional actors (economic elite, pressure groups, lobbies, demonstrations) (Helmke 2005). From the perspective of advancing social rights, this permeability of the judicial process to external pressure is ambiguous. It is conducive to the success of social rights litigation when judges respond to social mobilization and media attention accompanying the litigation, whereas other forms of pressure from powerful social interests may effectively bar social rights judgments, unless the judges have sufficient independence to withstand it.

Judicial independence from the other political branches is never absolute—and should not be. A reasonably well-functioning legal-political system requires two-way accountability relationships.[18] At the core of the concept of judicial independence lies the notion that judges, in reaching their decisions, should rely only on their understanding of the law and the case at hand (Larkins 1996). Guarantees and procedures that make judges less dependent on the government for their appointment, tenure, and salaries facilitate their independence by insulating them from political pressure. Norms of legalism and appropriateness in the political and legal culture may provide incentives for independent behavior, and professional forums may strengthen professional standards. Neither, however, can guarantee independent judges. Ultimately, individual judges' personal values, integrity, and sense of security and support are decisive.

Collectively and individually, judges have to carefully manage their relationships with other power holders to maintain legitimacy and space for action. Progressive social rights judgments may help build social legitimacy for courts, as the cases of Colombia, Costa Rica, and India demonstrate. However, bold judgments that challenge those in power also run the risk of political backlash. Progressive social rights judgments are more likely when they represent a limited political challenge because they only marginally change the prior situation and resource allocation or because they are not fundamentally at odds with the government's political orientation and ideology. Judges find affirming social rights claims and devising remedies easier where the matter involves including new groups in existing schemes and where the court can rely on legal arguments that are relatively uncontroversial from a professional point of view.[19]

Even where judges are motivated to remedy social rights violations and have sufficient independence to do so, the question is whether they have the means. Again, the quality of the voice is important. To develop sophisticated social rights jurisprudence requires considerable legal skills, research capacity, and access to a range of legal materials. Besides providing judges with the facts, litigants often bring forth norms, precedents, and legal arguments that the judges can draw on to develop legal remedies. For adversarial judicial processes, arguments by litigants (and sometimes amicus curiae[20]) are fundamental to their operation, and the importance of such arguments can hardly be overstated. Yet judges' ability to independently assess the claims made—and thus offset inequalities in legal representation—is key to a fair hearing.[21] In developing countries, judges often lack the necessary resources to do so. Poor access to legal materials and lack of research capacity, in addition to poor training and service conditions militating against recruitment of the brightest legal minds to the bench, detract from the professional capabilities of courts to develop sound social rights jurisprudence. The lack of capacity on the part of judges is particularly consequential where courts also have an investigative function or where marginalized litigants lack adequate legal representation.

The quality of jurisprudence is also affected by courts' caseload and control over the docket. In Argentina, where the Supreme Court decides approximately 15,000 cases per year, and in India, where the Supreme Court decides more than 30,000 cases annually, judges spread their time and resources extremely thinly. Although the large number of cases may enhance legitimacy, it detracts from courts' ability to "focus sustained attention on particular issues" (Epp 1998: 109) and develop particular areas of jurisprudence. In contrast, the U.S. Supreme Court selects which cases to take on and hears only between 70 and 90 cases per year. The South African Constitutional Court hears even fewer cases, but although its small caseload has provided excellent conditions for well-reasoned judgments, it has also limited the court's ability to select cases strategically to develop its jurisprudence (Gargarella, Domingo, and Roux 2006).

Resources matter, but they are not decisive. Gargarella, Domingo, and Roux (2006) conclude that many of the cases they have looked at show that judges who are willing to take an active role regarding social rights manage to create new instruments or to find solutions even in the midst of poverty, inequality, and social tension. Indian judges developed a series of new mechanisms to better address what they held to be socially relevant cases: epistolary jurisdiction was introduced to provide easy access to the court; special commissions of inquiry were created to overcome problems related to establishing facts; and traditional legal remedies were supplemented with monitoring agencies in charge of enforcing court orders (Hunt 1996). South Africa's *Grootboom* case on the right to housing[22] is an example of how a creative court can decide social rights claims. Here, the court ordered the state to "devise a comprehensive and workable plan" to meet the needs of people in desperate need (see Gloppen 2005; Roux 2004). Examples from Colombia and Costa Rica similarly demonstrate the creativity of constitutional courts in finding new legal remedies to be applied in social rights cases (Gargarella, Domingo, and Roux 2006; Wilson 2005).[23]

The choice of legal remedy depends in part on what the law says, but it is also a function of judges' and litigators' ability, individually and as a professional community, to develop effective remedies to repair social rights violations (Epp 1998; Jacob 1996). Although some courts restrict themselves to a short list of judicial remedies, others introduce unorthodox remedies to ensure rights protection. Legal culture and theories of judicial interpretation are also important in this respect.

Beyond the Courtroom: The Broader Effects of Social Rights Litigation

A progressive social rights judgment does not in itself mean that the situation will change on the ground or that the judgment will be complied with—or reflected in legislation or social policy. To understand the effect of social rights litigation in a particular context, one must look beyond the chances of winning in court. As figure 14.4 indicates, what takes place in court is only one aspect of the litigation process. Social and political

Figure 14.4. A New Look at Litigation: Broader Avenues of Potential Influence

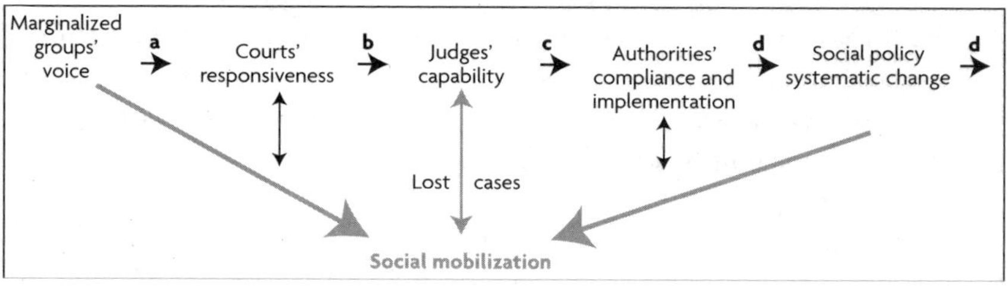

Source: Author's representation.
a. Social rights cases brought to court.
b. Cases accepted by the courts.
c. Judgments giving effect to social rights.
d. Transformation effect (effect on social rights and inclusion of marginalized groups).

implications of winning or losing a case depend as much on out-of-court mobilization as on the judgment itself; the processes are not separate. At every stage of the litigation process, legal strategies and outcomes may influence mobilization efforts and public debate. The process of researching a case may provide the impetus for social mobilization and tools for advocacy and training. Moreover, if a case is "won in the streets," in the sense of having strong public support, judges have an easier time ruling favorably.[24] Even litigation that is unsuccessful provides a platform for voicing social rights concerns, which may generate public debate and political momentum and may induce authorities to act (settle out of court or introduce new legislation or policies). These indirect political effects are represented in figure 14.4 by the downward pointing arrows. In many cases, implementation also depends on social movements to monitor and follow up when compliance is lacking (COHRE 2003; Heywood 2005).[25]

Two avenues of social effect are distinguished. The first is the litigation process proper, which considers the implementation of the judgment in the sense of compliance with its terms. The second concerns the systemic influence on social policy of litigation broadly conceived.

Compliance and Implementation of Judgments

Court judgments are not self-enforcing; they rely on other branches for execution and implementation. To improve the rights situation on the ground, they must be accepted, and political action must be taken to implement the ruling. Whether judgments are implemented or not influences factors in the legal chain as previously laid out, such as the strength of litigant's voice and the terms on which cases are accepted into the system. Compliance also depends on the judges themselves—the extent to which they are able to devise acceptable remedies, make their rulings authoritative, balance political forces, and secure their independence and legitimacy in various sections of society. (For a visualization of the factors affecting the compliance with and implementation of judgments, see figure 6 in Gloppen 2006: 54.)

Judges can increase the likelihood of compliance with the terms of their judgments in a number of ways, such as by setting time frames, by requiring the responsible parties to report back to the court on progress in implementation, and by instigating contempt of court proceedings if they fail to comply.

Compliance also depends on factors outside the legal system. Factors beyond judges' control, such as the government's capacity to implement rulings and its political will to do so, may undermine pro-transformation judgments. The balance of power between the competing political forces is important, such as whether a dominant party can afford to ignore court decisions or a balance of social forces exists where the courts have protective constituencies, rendering it potentially costly to overrule or ignore decisions (Widner 1999). Political culture—whether a tradition of legalism prevails and courts have a basic legitimacy in society—also influences the cost of ignoring court orders.

Political elites are more likely to ignore or overrule social rights decisions that are at cross-purposes with their ideology, whereas rulings that are in line with and articulate the broader policy direction of the government may harness the political will to follow up and give priority to social rights issues. Political will is crucial, but implementation of court rulings also depends on the state's capacity (financial, institutional, and administrative).

Finally, voice is also important for implementation by providing an apparatus to follow up on implementation of judgments and, if necessary, take the case back to court for lack of compliance (COHRE 2003; Heywood 2005).

Litigation and Social Policy

This discussion brings us to the broader role of litigation in the shaping of social policy. As illustrated in figure 14.5, judgments may influence social policy directly when public policies are (re)formulated as part of the

Figure 14.5. Litigation and Social Policy Formation

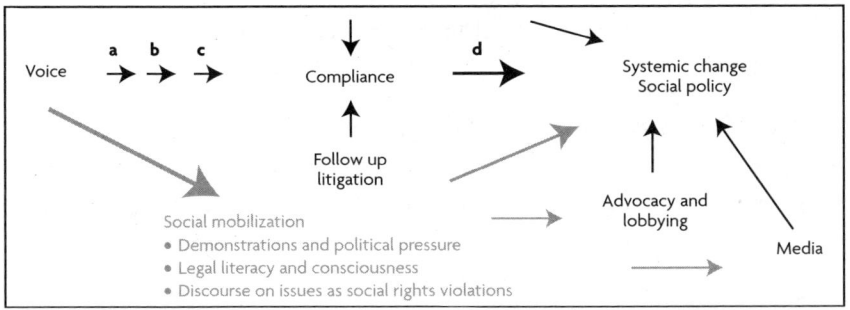

Source: Author's representation.
a. Social rights cases brought to court.
b. Cases accepted by the courts.
c. Judgments giving effect to social rights.
d. Transformation effect or policy impact (social rights and inclusion of marginalized groups).

implementation process. Where courts order the implementation or extension of an existing policy or development of a new policy, policy effect becomes an aspect of compliance (see Gloppen 2005 for the example of the South African *Grootboom* case). The government may also develop new policies in response to declaratory judgments.

Litigation processes may influence social policy formation in ways that are more indirect too. For example, they may influence policy by stimulating social mobilization around social rights issues, by creating awareness and media attention, by feeding advocacy, by bringing social rights issues into social and political discourse, and by framing marginalized peoples' grievances in terms of social rights violations.

Courts as Constrained Actors

In his analysis of the political influence of U.S. courts, Rosenberg (1991) concludes that courts are constrained and are generally unable to influence policy on their own. Other actors must provide incentives for compliance or use the decision as a "leverage or a shield, cover, or excuse" to implement social reforms (Rosenberg 1991: 35; Schultz and Gottlieb 1996). Analyses of courts elsewhere and activists' experiences confirm this conclusion,[26] but it does not mean that litigation is powerless as a policy-shaping instrument.

Three dynamics are particularly important: (a) judgments' direct influence on political actors, (b) the relationship between litigation and social mobilization, and (c) the role of litigation in shaping public discourse on social rights.

Direct Effects of Judgments on Policy Makers

The most direct way social rights litigation affects public policy is when a judgment is implemented in a way that produces a policy change.[27] However, according to Schultz and Gottlieb (1996: 66), "the most important aspect of judicial influence [is] the power of courts to redefine structures and expectations." Court judgments can profoundly affect political actors, redefining priorities and providing leverage and arguments for actors (whether in government or the opposition) supporting policy reform. Having a judgment backing a policy may also depoliticize the issue, thereby making it easier to draw support from across the political spectrum.

Litigation, Social Mobilization, and Political Discourse

The effect of litigation on social policy formation also goes through social mobilization and political discourse. The relationship between litigation and social mobilization is multifaceted. In some cases, litigation enhances the ability of marginalized people to organize around their grievances and contribute toward broader mobilization and the building of community spirit. From the perspective of litigation, community involvement increases the chances of success. Also, the more involved the affected communities are in driving the litigation process, the more likely they are to profit in terms of mobilization and consolidation around the cause. However, although links between marginalized people and resourceful legal service organizations may provide important tools for mobilization, a level of initial association seems necessary for a positive cycle to be set in motion. The poorest or most marginalized often lack the resources to voice claims, as well as the ability to contribute significantly to, or benefit from, the voicing of claims on their behalf (COHRE 2003).

Litigation that forms part of a broader mobilization strategy is more likely to cause policy changes. Although a single case may significantly affect jurisprudence and lead to a change in social policy, a systemic effect is more likely when a comprehensive strategy exists to build jurisprudence in the field and when an organizational apparatus exists to capitalize on the momentum and sustain political pressure. For example, the fact that the Indian Supreme Court has not yet developed a sustained agenda on individual rights, despite being very active and supportive of egalitarian and procedural rights, seems to arise from the weak and fragmented support structure for legal mobilization in India and the inadequate funding to finance continuing litigation campaigns (Epp 1998). The importance of a long-term strategy, gradually building up jurisprudence, is widely recognized among experienced social rights activists. Over the past decade, international networks and NGOs have built expertise in various areas of law. When forming part of a broader campaign, supplemented by effective out-of-court voice, litigation can provide a focal point for media attention and social mobilization, thereby creating awareness and political pressure. The research, compilation, and structuring of data for legal arguments are useful for advocacy purposes and as input in policy formation processes and the wider discourses on social rights.[28] Similarly, progressive social rights judgments that are not conformed with and implemented may influence jurisprudence and discourses, both nationally and internationally.[29] Social rights litigation may also "domesticate" international human rights discourse and stimulate engagement with international legal norms and jurisprudence.

Thus, litigation may be worthwhile—even where it is unlikely to succeed in the narrow sense—but is not necessarily so. Positive effects are unlikely where litigation efforts are ad hoc and disconnected from broader strategies for social change. Risks are also involved. Not all lost (or even won) cases are productive, and poorly argued or restrictively decided cases may create damaging setbacks. Given that much of the policy effect goes through social mobilization and political discourse, the transformative potential of social rights litigation is linked to the political space for social movements, freedom of expression, and the media.

Conclusion

This chapter shows that litigation has been useful for some marginalized groups, in some contexts; however, one should be cautious about embracing social rights litigation as an institutional voice of the poor. Questions remain with regard to its efficacy and appropriateness—not least with regard to "success for whom?" Is it the concerns and grievances of the poorest that come through as social rights claims?

Litigation is generally market led. Judges respond to cases that are brought before them, and the danger is that stronger litigants may eclipse the most marginalized, as has been happening in India, where public interest litigation has become a means for advancing middle-class concerns. This co-optation may lead to a situation where the elite and the not so poor capture the legal system entirely, using it to advance their rights and interests—not those of the poorest.

Legal service organizations may be a partial answer, providing institutional support for people who lack the resources to effectively voice claims on their own. However, professional litigators do not always reach—or target—the poorest. One effect of the increasing specialization and professionalism of public interest litigators is that, in many cases, they have become the most important drivers of social rights litigation. This accentuates the question of whose interests drive the litigation. As noted earlier, the interests and motivations of marginalized groups and public interest litigators do not necessarily converge. For people who are marginalized and whose social rights are violated, the goal is to alter an intolerable condition, and litigation is just one possible means to achieve this end. In contrast, for public interest litigators, finding cases that will bring social rights jurisprudence forward generally or in their field of specialization is important. Equally important is the need for professional recognition and continued funding for their organization. These factors may make litigators more concerned with taking cases that are winnable and fit their long-term strategy than with solving a concrete problem for particular people. So, although they share a social rights concern, professional litigators may have a less grounded commitment to specific violations. However, where litigation is driven by organizations with a long-term involvement with a particular community or cause and where litigation forms part of a broader strategy of advocacy and social mobilization, winnability may be less of a premium, and even cases that are not likely to succeed may be worth taking to court. In these cases, the litigation "voice" is more likely to reflect the concerns of the marginalized group—although not necessarily the poorest or most marginalized sections of society.

Another worry is that social rights litigation may fuel a judicialization of politics and politicization of the judiciary by bringing to court distributive matters that lie at the heart of politics and that judges are not institutionally equipped to deal with (Fuller 1978). Social rights decisions are feared to produce conflict between judiciaries and political institutions, thereby undermining their institutional capital. Although this possibility presents dilemmas at the theoretical level, in reality, distributive matters do not seem particularly prone to lead to politicization of the courts.

Where governments have sought to limit courts' jurisdiction or independence or to rein in the judiciary by packing the courts, it is generally not because of conflicts over social rights jurisprudence. Although reason exists to dismiss a general distinction between social rights and other rights in this respect, whether courts, in all cases, are the best forums for grievances regarding social and economic rights is still questionable.

From the perspective of social policy, a structural problem with social rights litigation is its casuistic nature. Cases emerge in an uncoordinated fashion, and each claim is judged on its own terms against a set of rights acting as trumps. The result of successful litigation is thus a decentralized, ad hoc pattern of resource allocation that does not necessarily channel resources to where the needs are greatest. This result conflicts with the need for rational priority setting, which is particularly important in contexts where resources are scarce. However, the tension is less clear in practice, because resources seldom are allocated on the basis of fairness and rational principles; rather, resource allocation usually results from interest group politics where the voice of the poorest rarely wins through. In this context, social rights litigation may shift resource distribution in a more just and rational direction, despite the weaknesses and limitations inherent in this approach.

The importance of litigation compared with other ways of shaping social policy should not be overemphasized. Several barriers exist, and often the effects on the ground are limited. In some contexts, however, litigation has had a significant influence. Moreover, given the lack of opportunity for poor people to have their voice heard in other institutional channels, the potential of litigation to channel the voices of the poor (although not always the poorest) should not be dismissed. Litigation could play a significant role, at least where the context is—or can be made—reasonably conducive and where the judiciary is not fully reined in by the government or captured by the social and economic elite.

Notes

1. External encouragement to shift toward test-case litigation was communicated in the author's interviews with NGOs in Malawi, Tanzania, and Zanzibar but was also expressed as the NGOs' own ambition. On international cause lawyering, see Sarat and Scheingold (2001).
2. See Bell (2004), Rosenberg (1991), and Schultz and Gottlieb (1996) for a critical analysis of the potential of law and courts to effect social change.

See Gloppen (2005) for the theoretical debate on whether social rights belong in the courtroom, questioning the justifiability of social rights on normative and methodological grounds.

3. Sources include findings from the Chr. Michelsen Institute's Courts in Transition research program, bringing together research on Africa, Asia, Eastern Europe, and Latin America (Domingo, Gargarella, and Roux 2006); the author's own interviews with judges, lawyers, and activists in South Africa, Malawi, Zambia, Tanzania, and Uganda; and published material, including an informative study by the Centre on Housing Rights and Evictions on litigating social economic and cultural rights, covering 21 case studies (COHRE 2003).

4. The term is used synonymously with *public impact litigation*, *social impact litigation*, and *test-case litigation*. The modalities of bringing such cases vary between legal systems, and *public interest litigation*, as the term is used here, covers a range of different legal actions—class actions as well as individual cases, directed against the state or private companies. The public interest litigation framework developed by the Indian Supreme Court is thus one form of the broader term.

5. The Indian Supreme Court relied on the right to life and human dignity to develop its social rights jurisprudence (Mohapatra 2003; Sudarshan 2006).

6. This definition of *social transformation* is attributed to Roberto Gargarella (see Gloppen 2006).

7. In some countries, public interest litigation is undertaken by public institutions such as ombudsmen, human rights commissions, or public prosecutors, such as Brazil's Ministério Público.

8. See Anderson (2003: 30) and Felstiner, Abel, and Sarat (1981) for a summary of the stages in the voicing of claims.

9. The poverty-lawlessness dynamic is laid out by Anderson (2003). Gloppen and Kanyongolo (2007) describe how it plays out in the Malawian context.

10. See Decker, Sage, and Stefanova (2005) for the notion of elite capture. See also Skaar and Van-Dúnem's (2006) analysis of Angola.

11. See Chirayath, Sage, and Woolcock (2005) for the relative importance of traditional legal institutions.

12. When the Indian Supreme Court made direct access simple, cheap, and unbureaucratic by introducing so-called epistolary jurisdiction (which allowed every person or group to "activate" the court by simply writing a letter on behalf of the poor), a nonadversarial process, and lenient criteria of legal standing, a surge of public litigation resulted. A landmark case is *People's Union for Democratic Right v. Union of India* [1982 (2) SCC 253], where the Indian Supreme Court held that a third party could directly petition the court, through a letter or other means, and seek its intervention in a matter in which another party's fundamental rights were being violated (Baxi 1987; Bhagwati 1985).

13. Pilar Domingo and colleagues show how poor people in Bolivia voice their grievances to the human rights ombudsman rather than in the formal courts, which lack legitimacy (Domingo, Gargarella, and Roux 2006; see also Gargarella and others 2004).

14. These litigators constitute an increasingly internationalized set of actors. Inspiration, legal strategies, and resources flow across borders, and many organizations and networks have a long-term commitment to a particular cause or to the development of jurisprudence in a particular field (Sarat and Scheingold 2001).

15. The literature has a strong U.S. focus, but some efforts are made to investigate this issue in developing and transitional countries (see, for example, Helmke 2005; VonDoepp 2005).

16. Public interest litigators often emphasize the importance of judges' identifying with the situation of the victims (COHRE 2003; author interviews). This observation argues for diversity on the bench and supports the rationale behind the sensitivity training in equality matters provided to judges in South Africa (Gloppen 2001).

17. For example, the constitutional courts of Colombia and South Africa include former academic lawyers and activists, as well as people drawn from the judicial hierarchy.

18. See Gloppen (2001) and Gloppen, Gargarella, and Skaar (2004) on the accountability function of courts and strategies to build and maintain judicial independence.

19. See Roux (2004) for discussion on how the South African Constitutional Court's social rights jurisprudence can be seen as both a partial critique and partial support strategy in relation to political authorities.

20. An *amicus curiae* is a friend of the court with relevant expertise who is accepted (and, in some cases, invited) by the court to present an argument without being a party to the case.

21. Investigations into whether and why "the haves" come out ahead shows that this result depends, to a large extent, on differentials in legal representation (the well-off, such as rich corporations, can afford better lawyers) and on the experience of "repeat players." Frequent litigants, such as large state institutions, build expertise in engaging with the courts (Galanter 1974; Galanter and Krishnan 2004; Kritzer and Silbey 2003; Wheeler and others 1987).

22. *Government of the Republic of South Africa and Ors v. Grootboom and Ors* [2000] ICHRL 72 (October 4, 2000).

23. Remedies in social rights cases range from minimal affirmation (requiring the state to respect a social right in the negative sense of noninterference), via rulings requiring the state to protect social rights against encroachment by others, to judgments ordering the state actively to promote particular social rights by developing policy or concrete orders for state agencies to fulfill

the individual claimant's social rights. Court orders are often declaratory, stating that laws or actions are in breach of a social rights obligation but leaving the state to devise a remedy. In other cases, they are mandatory, requiring specific actions to be taken. In some cases, courts have also taken on a supervisory role, requiring the relevant agency to report back within a set timeframe (Roux 2004).

24. Roux (2004) shows how the South African Constitutional Court—which initiated its social rights jurisprudence from a low base in *Grootboom*, issuing a declaratory order that many commentators felt was weak—handed down a more intrusive order in the *Treatment Action Campaign* case (*Treatment Action Campaign and Ors v. Minister of Health and Ors* [2002] (4) BCLR 356 (T)), which occurred in the context of a mass mobilization campaign that insulated the court from the repercussions of its decision.

25. Effects of court decisions—and of the litigation process—are difficult to isolate, and consequences for the situation on the ground can rarely be measured directly. A more realistic methodology for assessing the transformative effect of particular judgments or litigation efforts is to look qualitatively at their ripple effects. That is, one must investigate what steps were taken to comply with and implement the judgment; whether it has led to changes in laws, regulations, and policies or has changed the pattern of administrative and lower court decisions; and what norms are applied by other institutions (for example, in the monitoring standards of human rights commissions).

26. See discussion of this literature in Gargarella, Domingo, and Roux (2006) and perceptions of activists confirming this conclusion in COHRE (2003).

27. In some cases, however, progressive judgments have adverse policy effects. Judgments recognizing marginalized groups' equal rights to social benefits have resulted in "equalizing downward"—that is, creating equality by taking away from existing beneficiaries (COHRE 2003). Court decisions to protect against forcible evictions have backfired, as procedural protections erected to protect vulnerable groups have been turned into a recipe for how to effectively evict people.

28. An example is the Treatment Action Campaign, where South African aid activists have used litigation as part of their broader campaign for HIV/AIDS treatment.

29. The South African Constitutional Court's *Grootboom* judgment has been poorly implemented but central in shaping housing jurisprudence.

References

Anderson, M. R. 2003. "Access to Justice and Legal Process: Making Legal Institutions Responsive to Poor People in LDCs." IDS Working Paper 178, Institute of Development Studies, Sussex, U.K.

Baxi, U. 1987. "Taking Suffering Seriously: Social Action Litigation in the Supreme Court of India." In *The Role of the Judiciary in Plural Societies*, eds. N. Tiruchelvam and R. Coomaraswamy, 3–60. New York: St. Martin's Press: 3–60.

Bell, D. A. 2004. *Silent Covenants: Brown v. Board of Education and the Unfulfilled Hopes for Racial Reform*. Oxford, U.K.: Oxford University Press.

Bhagwati, P. N. 1985. "Judicial Activism and Public Interest Litigation." *Columbia Journal of Transnational Law* 23 (3): 561–77.

Cavallaro, J. L., and E. J. Schaffer. 2004. "Less as More: Rethinking Supranational Litigation of Economic and Social Rights in the Americas." *Hastings Law Journal* 56 (2): 217–81.

Chirayath, L., C. Sage, and M. Woolcock. 2005. "Customary Law and Policy Reform." Background paper for *World Development Report 2006: Equity and Development*. Washington, DC: World Bank. http://siteresources.worldbank.org/INTWDR2006/Resources/477383-1118673432908/Customary_Law_and_Policy_Reform.pdf.

COHRE (Centre on Housing Rights and Evictions). 2003. *Litigating Economic, Social, and Cultural Rights: Achievements, Challenges, and Strategies*. Geneva: COHRE.

Decker, K., C. Sage, and M. Stefanova. 2005. "Law or Justice: Building Equitable Legal Institutions." Background paper for *World Development Report 2006: Equity and Development*. Washington, DC: World Bank. http://siteresources.worldbank.org/INTWDR2006/Resources/477383-1118673432908/Law_or_Justice_Building_Equitable_Legal_Institutions.pdf.

Domingo, P., R. Gargarella, and T. Roux, eds. 2006. *Courts and Social Transformation in New Democracies: An Institutional Voice for the Poor?* Burlington, VT: Ashgate.

Dugard, J. 2005. "The Court of Last Instance? Analyzing Direct Access to South Africa's Constitutional Court by the Poor." Paper presented to a workshop on Courts and the Marginalized, Diego Portales University, Santiago, Chile, December 1–3.

Epp, C. R. 1998. *The Rights Revolution: Lawyers, Activists, and Supreme Courts in Comparative Perspective*. Chicago: University of Chicago Press.

Felstiner, W. L. S., R. L. Abel, and A. Sarat. 1981. "The Emergence and Transformation of Disputes: Naming, Blaming, Claiming …" *Law and Society Review* 15 (3–4): 631–54.

Fuller, L. L. 1978. "The Forms and Limits of Adjudication." *Harvard Law Review* 92 (2): 356–409.

Galanter, M. 1974. "Why Haves Come Out Ahead: Speculations on the Limits of Social Change." *Law and Society Review* 9 (1): 95–160.

Galanter, M., and J. K. Krishnan. 2004. "Bread for the Poor: Access to Justice and the Rights of the Needy in India." *Hastings Law Journal* 55 (4): 789–834.

Gargarella, R. 2002. "'Too Far Removed from the People': Access to Justice for the Poor—The Case of Latin America." United Nations Development Programme, Geneva. http://www.undp.org/oslocentre/PAR_Bergen_2002/latin-america.pdf

Gargarella, R., P. Domingo, and T. Roux. 2006. "Conclusion." In *Courts and Social Transformation in New Democracies: An Institutional Voice for the Poor?*, eds. P. Domingo, R. Gargarella, and T. Roux, 256–81. Burlington, VT: Ashgate.

Gargarella, R., S. Gloppen, A. Knudsen, E. Jul-Larsen, H. Stokke, and K. Ask. 2004. "The Poor and the Judiciary." Application to the Norwegian Research Council, Chr. Michelsen Institute, Bergen, Norway.

Gloppen, S. 2001. "South African Constitutionalism 1994–2000: The Difficult Balancing Act of the Constitutional Court." Doctoral dissertation, University of Bergen, Bergen, Norway.

———. 2005. "Social Rights Litigation as Transformation: South African Perspectives." In *Democratising Development: The Politics of Socio-Economic Rights in South Africa*, eds. P. Jones and K. Stokke, 153–79. Leiden, Netherlands: Martinus Nijhoff.

———. 2006. "Courts and Social Transformation: An Analytical Framework." In *Courts and Social Transformation in New Democracies: An Institutional Voice for the Poor?*, eds. P. Domingo, R. Gargarella, and T. Roux, 35–49. Burlington, VT: Ashgate.

Gloppen, S., R. Gargarella, and E. Skaar, eds. 2004. *Democratization and the Judiciary: The Accountability Function of Courts in New Democracies*. London: Frank Cass.

Gloppen, S., and F. E. Kanyongolo. 2007. "Courts and the Poor in Malawi: Marginalization, Vulnerability, and the Law." *International Journal of Constitutional Law* 5 (2): 258–93.

Helmke, G. 2005. *Courts under Constraints: Judges, Generals, and Presidents in Argentina*. New York: Cambridge University Press.

Heywood, M. 2005. "Shaping, Making, and Breaking the Law in the Campaign for a National HIV/AIDS Treatment Plan." In *Democratising Development: The Politics of Socio-Economic Rights in South Africa*, eds. P. Jones and K. Stokke, 181–212. Leiden, Netherlands: Martinus Nijhoff.

Hunt, P. 1996. *Reclaiming Social Rights*. Aldershot, U.K.: Dartmouth.

Jacob, H. 1996. *Courts, Law, and Politics in Comparative Perspective*. New Haven, CT: Yale University Press.

Kritzer, H. M., and S. S. Silbey. 2003. *In Litigation: Do the "Haves" Still Come Out Ahead?* Stanford, CA: Stanford University Press.

Larkins, C. 1996. "Judicial Independence and Democratization: A Theoretical and Conceptual Analysis." *American Journal of Comparative Law* 44 (4): 605–26.

Manning, D. S. 1999. *The Role of Legal Services Organizations in Attacking Poverty*. Washington, DC: World Bank. http://siteresources.worldbank.org/EXTAFRREGTOPGENDER/Resources/RoleLegal_en.pdf.

————. 2001. "The Role of Legal Services Organizations in Attacking Poverty." Paper presented at a conference on "Empowerment, Security, and Opportunity through Law and Justice," St. Petersburg, Russia, July 8–12.

Mohapatra, A. R. 2003. *Public Interest Litigation and Human Rights in India.* New Delhi: Radha.

Moore, S. F. 1987. *Law as Process: An Anthropological Approach.* London: Routledge & Kegan Paul.

Rosenberg, G. N. 1991. *The Hollow Hope: Can Courts Bring about Social Change?* Chicago: University of Chicago Press.

Roux, T. 2004. "Legitimating Transformation: Political Resource Allocation in the South African Constitutional Court." In *Democratization and the Judiciary: The Accountability Function of Courts in New Democracies,* eds. S. Gloppen, R. Gargarella, and E. Skaar. London: Frank Cass

Sarat, A., and S. A. Scheingold, eds. 2001. *Cause Lawyering and the State in a Global Era.* Oxford, U.K.: Oxford University Press.

Schultz, D., and S. E. Gottlieb. 1996. "Legal Functionalism and Social Change: A Reassessment of Rosenberg's *The Hollow Hope: Can Courts Bring about Social Change.*" *Journal of Law and Politics* 12 (1): 63.

Skaar, E., and J. O. Serra Van-Dúnem. 2006. "Courts under Construction in Angola: What Can They Do for the Poor?" In *Courts and Social Transformation in New Democracies: An Institutional Voice for the Poor?,* eds. P. Domingo, R. Gargarella, and T. Roux. Burlington, VT: Ashgate.

Sudarshan, R. 2006. "Courts and Social Transformation in India." In *Courts and Social Transformation in New Democracies: An Institutional Voice for the Poor?,* eds. P. Domingo, R. Gargarella, and T. Roux. Burlington, VT: Ashgate.

VonDoepp, P. 2005. "The Problem of Judicial Control in Africa's Neopatrimonial Democracies: Malawi and Zambia in Comparative View." *Political Science Quarterly* 120 (2): 275–301.

Wheeler, S., B. Cartwright, R. Kagan, and L. M. Friedman. 1987. "Do the 'Haves' Come Out Ahead? Winning and Losing in State Supreme Courts, 1870–1970." *Law and Society Review* 21 (3): 403–46.

Widner, J. 1999. "Building Judicial Independence in Common Law Africa." In *The Self-Restraining State: Power and Accountability in New Democracies,* eds. A. Schedler, L. Diamond, and M. F. Plattner, 177–94. Boulder, CO: Lynne Rienner.

Wilson, B. M. 2005. "What Happens When Marginalized Groups Win Constitutional Decisions? Evidence from Costa Rica." Paper presented to a workshop on Courts and the Marginalized, Diego Portales University, Santiago, Chile, December 1–3.

World Bank. 2005. "New Frontiers of Social Policy." Concept note, World Bank, Washington, DC. http://web.worldbank.org/WBSITE/EXTERNAL/TOPICS/ EXTSOCIALDEVELOPMENT/ 0,,contentMDK:20692151~pagePK:210058~ piPK:210062~theSitePK:244363,00.html.

CHAPTER 15

Breaking Legal Inequality Traps: New Approaches to Building Justice Systems for the Poor in Developing Countries

Caroline Sage and Michael Woolcock

Development scholars and practitioners now widely accept the importance of an effectively functioning legal and regulatory system for achieving equitable and sustainable development outcomes. Strengthening the rule of law is explicitly identified both as a priority development goal in recent international declarations[1] and as one of the four pillars of development in the World Bank's Comprehensive Development Framework. The World Bank currently finances more than 600 projects relating to legal and judicial reform, including 30 freestanding projects in five regions, and has recently committed to scaling up these efforts through the new Legal Modernization Initiative. Other bilateral development agencies and multilateral donors have committed hundreds of millions of dollars to reforming judicial systems, with the majority of developing countries and former socialist states now receiving assistance for some kind of justice sector reform (Messick 1999).

This commitment is based on the ongoing belief that effective legal and regulatory institutions are essential for sustaining economic growth and crafting equitable development strategies.[2] For example, effective economic institutions have historically required (a) enforcement of property rights for a broad section of society and (b) equality of opportunity (including equality before the law) so that individuals have both the incentive and the opportunity to take part in economic activity.[3] Well-functioning legal systems have served to reduce transaction costs and increase the predictability of behavior and certainty of process (Matsuo 2004). The creation of formal property rights has been shown to reduce the time and costs of transacting by standardizing a transferable title system. Also, countries that have succeeded in removing the fear of expropriation through enforceable rule systems have been associated with faster levels of economic growth.[4]

A well-functioning justice system has also been crucial for the effective delivery of public services and the distribution of socioeconomic and political rights. In many countries, the "rule of law" provides the fundamental constraint on executive power. A rule-of-law system is generally characterized by multiple arms of government (executive, legislature, and judiciary), with each branch holding the others accountable through differing "checks and balances."[5] The judicial branch, in particular, exists to protect citizens against the arbitrary use of political or economic power. Furthermore, predictable and fair "rules of the game" and secure legal rights are regarded as the basis for an effectively functioning society where people's basic rights are protected and conflicts within and between communities are mediated.

Unfortunately, this ideal bears little resemblance to reality in many countries around the world, where legal systems in fact serve to perpetuate inequitable power relations and discrimination, producing "legal inequality traps." In many more countries, the formal legal rules are reflected in neither policy nor practice, or they have no relationship to local rule-based systems and the social norms that underpin such systems. Formal rules that appear to protect the interests of the broader community are undermined by institutional practices, informal strategies, or conflicting rule-based systems and social norms. Structures of inequality affect both the creation of institutions in the justice sector and the context within which they operate; they are embedded in the rules, practice, and norms that perpetuate these institutions. Legal and regulatory institutions, in turn, affect the distribution of opportunities and the processes by which these opportunities can be leveraged to enhance well-being.

If a consensus is emerging on the general importance of these issues, however, it has not yet translated into a successful program of action for building "rule-of-law" systems in low-income countries. Indeed, attempts by development practitioners and policy makers to undertake judicial reform to build the rule of law and thereby enhance good governance have a long and rather unhappy history. This chapter outlines an explanation for this problematic history that builds on and refines previous approaches, while offering an alternative research-based policy agenda. First, it provides a summary of the literature that has assessed and attempted to explain the record of judicial reform initiatives over the past four decades. Then, it documents three central elements that have largely been absent from both these explanations and the models underpinning the judicial reform initiatives themselves. These elements can be summarized, loosely, as the missing law in policy, the missing rules in law, and the missing norms in rules. The concluding section shows how correcting these missteps has led—and might plausibly continue to lead—to strategies with (one hopes) a higher probability of success.

Assessing and Explaining Judicial Reform Initiatives since the 1960s: A Brief Survey

The insight that law is essential to development stems from a long history of jurisprudential and economic thought (Tamanaha 2004), but it was first clearly articulated in the law and development movement of the 1960s. More than a decade of legal reform projects and initiatives, funded primarily by the Ford Foundation and private U.S. donors, involved academics from leading universities in the United States in helping countries to reform their substantive laws and legal frameworks. The movement rested on the belief that law could be used to change society, "that law itself was an engine for change," and that "lawyers and judges could serve as social engineers" for change (Messick 1999: 12). The primary goal was to transform "legal culture" through legal education and the transplantation of select "modern" laws and institutions, with an emphasis on economic (commercial) law and the training of pragmatic business lawyers (Trubek 2003).

A decade later, the movement was declared a failure, and those involved in the process attempted to understand its demise.[6] Arguably, the most significant criticism was of the underlying assumption—that American-style "legal liberalism" could be transplanted wholesale to developing countries—which was accused of bringing about the movement's failure. Reformers found that local legal cultures were highly resistant to change and that, even when laws were changed, they often had little influence in practice. Of still greater concern to those involved, in some cases new laws actually served to enhance the power of local elites, presenting "the frightening possibility that legalism, instrumentalism, and authoritarianism might form a stable amalgam so that their efforts to improve economic law and lawyering could strengthen authoritarian rule" (Trubek 2003: 6). Critics argued that the movement lacked the theoretical understanding of law, the role of justice systems, or the effect of law on development that could have informed this engagement with other types of justice systems. Local contexts and the systems of justice operating within them were largely ignored. Thus, the movement failed to acknowledge the systems by which many people (if not most poor people) in developing countries order their lives (Trubek and Galanter 1974).

The current legal and judicial reform (LJR) movement emerged in the late 1980s, with an understanding that the problems the law and development movement had attempted to address were still relevant—in other words, that legal and regulatory frameworks were crucial for effective development. Armed with the lessons of the previous movement, the new initiatives focused more on strengthening key legal and judicial institutions than on the laws themselves, with a number of predetermined institutions (courts, ministries of justice, bar associations, and law schools) accepted by convention as the essential building blocks of a rule-of-law system.[7]

In general, initiatives have aimed to make the judicial branch independent, speed up the processing of cases through the courts, increase access to dispute resolution mechanisms, and professionalize the bench and the bar (Messick 1999). Activities to accomplish these goals have ranged from reforming law school curricula, to training judges and legal professionals, to setting up specialized courts and introducing comprehensive case management systems into the courts. Accordingly, they have generally been designed as top-down technocratic solutions to (what are seen as) institutional gaps or weaknesses. In some instances, reform activities have included establishing legal aid clinics and legal information, awareness, and literacy programs.

Unfortunately, however, the latest spate of LJR projects, programs, and strategies has failed to report any significant increase in success over the previous law and development movement. Although little consensus exists on what a successful project entails, examples of significant, positive, and sustained impacts are few. At the same time, numerous surveys and evaluations have brought accepted approaches to reform into question again (see, for example, Faundez 1997; Gardner 1980; Gupta, Kleinfeld, and Salinas 2002; Hammergren 1998; Lawyers Committee for Human Rights 1996; Rose 1998; see also Chopra and Hohe 2004). As Thomas Carothers (1999: 170) notes, LJR projects "have fallen far short of their goals." Regrettably, some of the explanations given for these disappointing results mirror the lessons of the 1960s: elite capture of the formal system and the reform process, lack of attention to local contexts and informal institutions, and an ongoing tendency to interpret the "rule of law" and the role of law and the judiciary on only a U.S. (or Western) model (Garth 2001). Other explanations of failure have included such related issues as the lack of political will within countries and pervasive corruption (for example, see Hammergren 1998).

Reforms continue to lack a sound theoretical or empirical basis. Although more than 40 years have passed since the law and development movement[8] and well over a decade since the revived interest in justice sector reform, there remains a dearth of systematic empirical research on the efficacy of justice sector reform.[9] Again, approaches have been criticized for their lack of engagement with local-level contexts, circumstances, and value systems; systematic research on the interface between informal or customary legal systems and the state regime is particularly limited.[10] Critics argue that a centralized, top-down approach to law making and judicial reform has caused "social rejection of the formal legal system among marginalized segments of the populations in developing countries who perceive themselves as 'divorced' from the formal frameworks of public institutions" (Buscaglia 2001: 2). Moreover, state law is often at odds with informal or customary institutions, which frequently operate independently. At the same time, reforms that undermine existing informal institutions without providing viable alternatives can lead to power grabbing, lawlessness, or even violent conflict.

The framing of justice sector reform as technical assistance or infrastructure reform has created a contrasting problem. Justice sector reform entails social and political change and, as such, often involves realignments of the distribution of power and control over rights and responsibilities. Frank Upham (2002: 7) argues that the "new conventional wisdom," or "new rule of law orthodoxy," within development circles is based on a belief in "regimes defined by their absolute adherence to established legal rules and completely free of the corrupting influences of politics" (see also Golub 2003). Policy and project design often neglects the distributional effects of reform and thus the fact that such processes will often be contested (Pistor 1999; Pistor and Wellons 1999). Although these possible tradeoffs may only be short term and may in fact even be necessary for the long-term prosperity of a country, they can still present difficulties in terms of gathering (and sustaining) the political support necessary for effective reform. Upham (2002) argues that much of the rule-of-law orthodoxy is based on myths; not only do such systems not exist anywhere in the industrial world, but also attempts to transplant a template of rules and institutions into a developing country often undermine preexisting systems of regulation and conflict resolution.[11]

It should be clear from the preceding passages that a major reason behind the consistently disappointing record of judicial reform initiatives by the international development community is the inadequate theory underpinning them. Given this, it would be reasonable to suggest that an alternative theory would give rise to alternative (and, at least potentially, superior) approaches. The next sections provide a companion analytical critique of the judicial reform initiatives, regarding them as emblematic of broader faults with development policy in general. This critique is organized around three central themes: the missing law in policy, the missing rules in law, and the missing norms in rules.

Toward an Alternative Approach: Three Levels of Understanding

In the modern state, law permeates every aspect of our lives, from everyday transactions such as catching a bus to actions as "natural" or "personal" as having children. Yet social interactions are so embedded within dominant norm-based institutions that these guiding and controlling structures are barely recognized in their everyday functions, unless, of course, the rules are transgressed or broken. Only in these transgressions is the reach and inherent power of the system laid bare, as is the interdependence of law and what is called "policy." Moreover, only in these transgressions is the need for a basic compatibility between social norms and laws highlighted. That is, through such transgressions, the law's dependence on broad, mutually agreed social norms (which, in turn, are shaped by legal institutions) for its legitimacy and authority becomes evident.

These concerns can be articulated more formally as follows. Cultural norms and social context crucially determine the content, legitimacy, and enforceability of rules systems. These rules systems, in all their heterogeneity, both underpin and are a constituent element of the prevailing legal system, and it is the legal system that underpins (and makes actionable) government policies. Therefore, any attempt to enact or change development policies (including social development policies) must engage with the legal system. Engaging with the legal system, in turn, means understanding the constituent rules systems, which, in turn, means understanding the social norms on which they rest. All three steps of this sequence are missing (or are mostly missing). This observation applies not only in most graphically (for present purposes) with respect to judicial reform initiatives but also more broadly in development discourse and practice. This chapter explores these steps by drawing on three simple examples from countries with arguably similar legal traditions based on the British common-law system: the United Kingdom, Australia, and South Africa.

The Missing Law in Policy

Consider a law student at a London university who is caught plagiarizing on an assignment. It may seem obvious to many people that plagiarism attracts tough sanctions within a law school. It may be less immediately obvious, if not thought through in detail, how and why such sanctions play out in practice and what this response tells us about the source of their legitimacy.

When faced with such a student suspected of plagiarism, a lecturer has a number of sanctions at his or her disposal. Both possible sanctions and possible responses to these sanctions by an accused student are set out in law school policy. However, such a policy gains its authority and legitimacy from two areas of crosscheck, which are of equal importance: the broader university regulations and the normative understanding that makes such sanctions broadly acceptable to the university community.

The broader university regulations allow (in fact, often require) each faculty and school within the university to establish a set of policies consistent with (and gaining their authority from) the broader set of regulations. The university regulations, in turn, are given their authority by the act that established the university, which was most probably made possible by delegated powers outlined in the government's higher-education legislation. Finally, the parliament is given authority to pass higher-education legislation by constitutional principles, which set out the division of powers between each arm of government.[12]

It might thus be said that a lecturer's actions within his or her law class are indirectly governed by the highest law of the land. Moreover, this broader legal framework provides a pathway along which the student can challenge such behavior; the vertical layers of authority legitimating a lecturer's actions, down to the law school lecture hall, provide corresponding mechanisms to challenge or appeal those actions upward. In this way, the overarching legal system provides for the distribution and articulation of corresponding rights and responsibilities, providing mediating institutions for human interactions and relationships and the inherent distribution of power in those relationships. If an appeal has failed at the level of the law school, the student has a number of other avenues of redress within the university, often ending with an internal academic tribunal. If this avenue fails, the student may then appeal to the external court system and, in principle, work his or her way all the way up the system to the House of Lords.

Hence, the rules governing interactions with the law school (as outlined in law school policy) and the adjudication processes that resolve disputes around these actions are governed by an integrated, multilayered system that stems up to and reaches down from the highest law of the land. At the same time, all levels of this system depend on the system itself being broadly understood and accepted by the wider community.

Although law is clearly embedded in both policy and practice in such an industrial world context, development practitioners (arguably recognizing the importance of law) tend to take it for granted, ignore it, or focus on isolated laws taken out of their institutional context (Decker, Sage, and Stefanova 2005). As previously indicated, those who do focus on the role of law in development have tended to focus on institutions seen as making up the justice sector in an isolated and disconnected way; thus, reforms of the justice sector are often disconnected from the broader policy environment that is, on the one hand, crucial to the translation of law into practice and, on the other hand, dependent on a legal framework and institutional system for legitimacy, authority, and ultimately enforcement. Understanding the interdependence of laws, policies, and norms is even more crucial when multiple normative and rule-based systems are at play, as is the case in most developing countries. The examples later in this chapter show that people's abilities to order their lives and resolve their disputes are often complicated by the existence of competing rule systems. In situations where an overarching legal framework conflicts with local rule-based systems, local systems tend to be either regulated (and thus generally suppressed) by the dominant system or left unmediated, often creating either a void of interaction or potential conflict. Understanding the nature of these dynamics is key to understanding and supporting processes of change.

The Missing Rules in Law

If the efficacy of policies turns, ultimately, on their grounding in the law, the efficacy of the law is influenced by its compatibility with the broader rules systems of which it is a part. Consider, for example, human rights law in postapartheid South Africa. South Africa's 1996 constitution has been touted as one of the developing world's most progressive national constitutions. In an attempt to combat years of oppression and dispossession, the government of South Africa made legal reform and the commitment to human rights and nondiscrimination a national priority. At the same time, in an effort to recognize the country's cultural heritage and respect the right to cultural self-determination, the government has maintained a dual system of law that explicitly recognizes traditional systems of governance and customary law. Although an admirable approach to a complex history and a diverse set of interests, this approach is not without its difficulties for some of the most vulnerable in the community.

Colonial rule has arguably had a large (distorting) impact on the customary law systems of many African countries today (Mamdani 1996). As early as 1830, in a process now labeled "indirect rule," chiefs in the U.K.-administered Cape Colony were granted authority to enforce indigenous law, subject to colonial review. By 1927, the evolved dual system of law was formalized under the Black Administration Act, which formed the basis of the apartheid system. About 1,500 chiefs' and headmen's courts continue to operate in rural parts of the country and remain governed by the 1927 act (Bennett 1991).

Since 1994, South Africa has worked on bringing traditional systems into the state framework. Traditional institutions and laws are all officially recognized in the 1996 constitution and, after a long political process, the National Traditional Leadership and Governance Framework Act was promulgated in 2004. This act set out the roles and responsibilities of different levels of traditional leaders and institutions and described their relationships to the different levels of government. Many celebrated the constitutional and administrative recognition of customary law, but difficulties remain. For example, although the principles of equality and nondiscrimination are enshrined in the constitution and the right to culture is deemed secondary to the right to equal treatment, the dualistic system of laws still has the potential to discriminate against marginalized groups.

Historically, women have been discriminated against under customary law, which has denied them the right to own land, leaving them under the guardianship of their husband or male relative. In almost all tribes in South Africa, succession is based on the principle of primogeniture, whereby the estate is essentially passed down to the next male kin. Although the male heir is generally responsible for caring for the estate, which includes the widow and children, this responsibility is, in practice, often very difficult for the widow to enforce.

The formal protection of women's rights under the constitution meets numerous obstacles in practice. In general, women lack access to the formal court system to claim or enforce their rights. Any attempts to override the customary system may lead to further ostracism from the community. Furthermore, the formal system is often inconsistent in its attitude to discriminatory customary practices. It is often unclear to magistrates and judicial officers when they are bound to follow customary law and when they might consider such customs discriminatory.[13] For example, in the 1997 case *Mthembu v. Letsela*, the court ruled that the principle of primogeniture is not discriminatory given that women are entitled to maintenance out of the estate. However, in 2003, the High Court in the landmark *Bhe* case held that two girls, who were minors, had the right to inherit their deceased father's estate. In this case, the court held that not only is primogeniture discriminatory, but also that any legislation allowing such discriminatory laws to be applied is unconstitutional. The case goes some way, arguably, to furthering the protection of women's constitutional rights, but it does not address the dominant pressures and constrictions that women face in terms of social norms and practices, nor the limitations they have in terms of access to justice.

Clearly, designing or reforming legal frameworks that are disconnected from (or in contradiction with) local rule systems is unlikely in practice to produce the types of changes that one might hope for. To be effective, law must be socially embedded. Yet for communities to gain access to broader political decision-making processes, economic markets, or public services, or if they need to resolve a conflict with a government official or another community or entity, a common, agreed-on set of "meta-rules" must exist within which people can operate.[14] The question for development practitioners then becomes how such "compatible" or more widely accepted legal systems are developed.

The Missing Norms in Rules

If policies need to be grounded in the law, and the law, in turn, in an understanding of constituent rules systems, then rules systems themselves also need to be considered in the context of the political structures, social relations, and cultural norms from whence they arise and in which they are necessarily embedded. The failure (or perhaps, given the organizational logic and imperatives within which they operate, the inability) of the policy community to understand the importance of social norms for effective rules systems is graphically exemplified by the case of indigenous communities in Arnhem Land, in northern Australia.

Many Aboriginal communities in Australia live in "fourth-world" conditions (see Altman 2004; Halloran 2004). The encroaching modern world prompted the construction of towns such as Maningrida, where a variety of different clan groups are brought together to live and to benefit (arguably) from the provision of aid and modern services such as education and health care. These groups formerly maintained a subsistence lifestyle by moving across different parts of the country, now closed off by "modern" property rights. The importation of modern diseases, coupled with the breakdown of traditional social practices that may have provided alternative health care (or at least more healthy diets), has left these towns a melting pot of diseases, many of which are unheard of in the rest of Australia. In response, the Australian government has attempted to provide myriad health-related services, from vaccinations, to general health care clinics, to care facilities for the elderly.

Because the town is relatively isolated, most specialist medical needs are serviced from Darwin, a two-hour flight from Maningrida. In particular, prenatal care, birthing, and postnatal care are all provided in Darwin; expectant mothers are flown there for up to four months. Given the prevalence of disease and serious health problems, low life expectancies, and high levels of neonatal deaths among Arnhem Land communities (and the criticism faced by the Australian government in relation to these problems), the Australian health authorities see the provision of specialist services in Darwin as a serious attempt to provide high-level medical care and to increase the chances of healthy births. Growing criticism and declining health statistics have resulted in an extremely regulated health care regime: these natal services are not just provided; they are required. All pregnant women in the community are referred to Darwin. If a woman does not want to go, local health care authorities persuade or cajole her and, ultimately, provide no alternative. Traditional midwives, where they still exist, are not recognized by law and are considered "dangerous" by local health care authorities. If, in the last instance, a woman refuses to go (as happened in a recent case), the local health care authorities present her with a suite of legal disclaimer documents, denying any legal responsibility or liability to the government.

In the face of the serious health care situation in Maningrida, this response may seem reasonable (and correspondingly serious) on the part of the Australian government. In fact, given that all these services are freely provided and that the level of care provided in Darwin is in line with world standards, the program may seem extremely generous, progressive, and rights based (because it fulfills and protects people's right to health). In addition to possible issues with the general level of social control highlighted by this situation, however, this picture has another overwhelming problem: under indigenous law in Arnhem Land communities, the place of birth is a key cultural determinant of clan lines, rights, and authority.

Differing systems of law obtain among the different clan groups now residing in Maningrida, but birthplace is accorded some significance by all of them. Women who are expecting a child are obliged, under traditional law, to return to their "country" to ensure the ongoing connection of their children to the land and to the laws that are seen to emanate from it. This physical connection to the land provides the basis for a child's clan lineage and rights and responsibilities as an ongoing custodian of that land. For Australian health care authorities, however, these birthing practices are too difficult to regulate or to service. Also, servicing health care needs in some areas would actually transgress private property rights, where traditional lands have been transformed into private farms.

In practice, however, many women continue to travel back to their traditional lands to birth their children. Their actions are outlawed (or at least are outside the law), and so they are given no assistance by local health care providers, who are, in fact, obliged by law not to help them. Thanks to the breakdown of local communities and the movement of most communities into constructed towns such as Maningrida, even when traditional health care practitioners and midwives do exist, they tend not to be found in outlying areas. There, women continue to experience high levels of birth-related health problems and high levels of maternal and infant mortality. Conversely, although those women who agree to travel to Darwin do experience better health outcomes, the birth of many children "off country" serves to undermine traditional norms and increases the conflict between local communities and government services, or between local communities.

The conflict between these local cultural norms and the dominant regulatory framework tends to play out (and so reinforce inequitable social relations or influence social change) in a number of ways. First, to frame processes of birthing as a technical problem with a corresponding technical regulatory solution is to ignore—and thus to undermine—prevailing social norms within the community. The primacy of modern Australian law in these circumstances "outlaws" traditional practices. As a result, traditional laws are either eroded or forced underground. The breakdown of such practices at birth has cascading ripple effects through all other areas of traditional law.

Second, the conflicts that already existed between the laws of different clans, now forced to coexist in a newly constructed social space, are exacerbated. Rather than supporting the development of mediating institutions to assist communities in shaping new shared normative institutions, these practices serve only to construct a distinction between "authentic" indigenous people and those who have "broken" with traditional law. This distinction leads to conflicts between different evolving notions of traditional rules at the local level. Yet those who have, arguably, broken with traditional law do not have clear pathways into an alternative system. The space for them to enter into modern Australian life is limited by their socioeconomic situations and their isolation, not to mention the ongoing racism faced by indigenous people in broader Australian society. Somewhat ironically, one of the few pathways into modern socioeconomic relations is through the exchange of traditional knowledge and artifacts, which themselves are highly dependent on notions of authenticity and "traditional" culture.

In short, given the conflicting legal norms faced by a pregnant woman in Maningrida, what may seem as simple and as natural as giving birth to a child has far-reaching consequences for her, her child, and the wider local community, as well as the relationship between this community and broader Australian society. Because of these conflicts, what might have been designed as a sensible, progressive, and well-funded development initiative may actually undermine the overall well-being of these women and children and decrease broader development aims despite (indeed, because of) the primacy of the dominant legal framework. Moreover, the problem occurs despite the plentiful resources that exist to support development activities in these communities. In fact, both government resources and aid workers are in oversupply in a town like Maningrida, which boasts a service provider or aid worker for every 12 indigenous people, a state-of-the-art school and health care clinic, and even a newly constructed outreach center from Charles Darwin University (with a single indigenous student). Resources and intentions are not the problem. Rather, the problem is a misunderstanding of the nature and power of law.

Three Questions

Three questions relevant to development practice arise from the preceding examples. First, what can such a modern system of regulation tell us about the constituent elements and functions of a rule-of-law system and the role of "policy" within the overall framework? Second, what are the consequences of conflicting rule-based systems within a modern legal framework, and how are (or might be) these incompatibilities managed? Third, what can the modern manifestation of social regulation tell us about the types of interventions that might or might not be useful in communities (or even countries) where such a mutually accepted and embedded system does not exist?

The Contemporary "Justice Sector Reform" Challenge

It is important to consider the nature and scope of the problems to be addressed. As already highlighted, the vast majority of human behavior is shaped and influenced by rule-based and normative frameworks. Even in those societies with the most developed legal systems, only about 5 percent of legal disputes end up in court. (That is, 5 percent of situations are understood as "legal.") At the same time, nearly all aspects of our everyday lives are mediated by formal and informal legal systems, as well as normative frameworks.[15]

Where state and nonstate or normative rule-based systems have developed in relation to each other, however, they often complement and reinforce socially accepted codes and rules. It is well documented that, in countries with more developed legal systems, the formal law acts as a "backdrop" (or shadow) for normative behavior and interactions (see, for example, Ellickson 1991; Posner 2002). In contrast, in communities where the state systems lack legitimacy, political reach, or both, local-level rule-based systems often act completely independently from the state legal system, which may be rejected, ignored, or not understood. In many developing countries, rule-based systems operating outside the state regime are the dominant form of regulation and dispute resolution, with forms of customary law covering up to 90 percent of the population in parts of Africa.[16] Real difficulties arise when the normative understandings embedded in local-level systems are at odds with the rights and responsibilities articulated by state law. In many communities, not only do traditional systems reflect prevailing community norms and values, but also the state systems lack legitimacy; they are seen as mechanisms of control and coercion for oppressive regimes.

Some Sub-Saharan states have tried to integrate traditional systems into wider legal and regulatory frameworks, often with little success. For example, the constitution of Ethiopia permits the adjudication of personal and family matters by religious or customary laws,[17] and, as previously outlined, South Africa's 1996 democratic constitution recognizes customary law explicitly (Bush 1979). Efforts to recognize customary rights have also been made in Latin America and Southeast Asia.[18] In practice, these systems generally continue to operate independently of the state system (and sometimes in uneasy tensions with prevailing religious and legal traditions).

Imposing formal mechanisms on communities without regard for the local-level processes and informal legal systems not only is potentially ineffectual, but also can actually create major problems, for several reasons. First, the failure to recognize different systems of understanding may in itself be discriminatory or exclusionary and, hence, inequitable. Second, many people have very good reasons for choosing to use informal or customary systems (for example, because they are readily accessible, are understood, and are believed to have a legitimate jurisdictional mandate). Third, ample evidence shows that ignoring or trying to stamp out customary practices does not work and, in some cases, has serious negative implications.[19] Fourth, ignoring traditional systems and believing that top-down reform strategies will eventually change practice at the local level may mean that ongoing discriminatory practices and the oppression of marginalized groups in the local context will go unchallenged. Finally, focusing purely on state regimes and access to formal systems involves implicitly assuming that such systems can be made accessible to all. This assumption, clearly, is not the case, even in the most industrial countries, and state institutions in many developing countries lack basic infrastructure or the capacity to turn "law in books" into "law in action" (see Buscaglia 1997).

Reimagining Judicial Reform Initiatives: A Different Theory, a Different Strategy

Given the nature and scale of the problems outlined, what do they mean for contemporary justice sector reform and for policy initiatives that aim to enhance access to justice? Despite the accepted failures of past legal and judicial reform initiatives, effective legal and regulatory frameworks are still widely recognized as essential for sustainable economic development and poverty reduction. The question, therefore, is not whether justice sector reform interventions can or should occur, but rather what does experience tell us about how best to approach, design, implement, and assess policy and project initiatives that attempt to build more equitable justice systems for the poor?

A coherently integrated, theoretically grounded, iteratively sequenced reform package is needed to inform supportable strategies for designing, implementing, and assessing all development projects, especially those that entail trying to improve the quality of justice systems for the poor. One of the main problems with the justice sector reform movement has been its focus on a predetermined ideal articulated in terms of its form, rather than based on an understanding of the socioeconomic and political functions played by rule-based systems in any given society.[20] Institutional myths surrounding the rule-of-law model are embodied in justice reform programs. This approach reflects a theoretical model that starts with a perfect rule-of-law system, from which dysfunctional systems are deemed to have deviated.[21]

Perfect systems are regarded as useful starting points in orthodox economic models because they are considered reasonable approximations of reality that give practitioners a useful common point of departure and a shared language and understanding.[22] Furthermore, such models give us a basis for empirical work, providing categories, theorems, and proofs that can be measured and tested. For Rajan (2004), however, the complete market model used by many economists is too far distanced from reality to be useful. Rajan (2004: 56) argues that relying on orthodox economic models makes solutions to development problems seem far simpler than they actually are, with particular policy reform problems being addressed as if they occur in a world where everything else works. Ultimately, he contends, we might be better served by starting with an assumption that nothing works, "assuming anarchy as a starting point rather than a pristine world of complete contracts" (Rajan 2004: 57).

Current approaches to justice sector reform have been shaped by their starting point of a perfect rule-of-law system, from which countries deviate. This starting point helps support a technocratic approach to reform, in which technical experts try to fill "gaps" by replicating or importing the laws and legal institutions of industrial countries into the developing context. As with the approaches to economic reforms described by Rajan, this approach makes solutions seem easier than they are and leads to compartmentalized reforms that assume (and often, in fact, require) a working broader system. Not only does the broader system not work in many contexts, but also there is often no such system, or the one that exists is at odds with the assumptions underpinning the reform design.

This is not to say that the actual justice sector is not central to the overall institutional framework of a given society or to deny that it plays an important role in designing, maintaining, and enforcing the different rights and responsibilities necessary for other institutions to function effectively. Clearly, it is and does. However, the justice sector relies on powerful normative and political institutions for its legitimacy, authority, and accountability. Although political, economic, and social rights for disadvantaged people may be introduced with legal reforms, real change is unlikely to occur without attention to broader social dynamics and the effects of reforms on those dynamics.

Intracountry differences in legal systems, much like cultural diversity, are part of most societies and do not always result in conflict. When a clear and enforceable system of meta-rules is in place, it can serve as a guiding principle by which parties can agree to disagree in a peaceful manner. This meta-rules system is defined as an overarching system of rules and processes designed to mediate differences (generally provided by the formal system) (Barron, Smith, and Woolcock 2004). In cases where the meta-rules do not cohere with local-level traditional laws, however, negative outcomes are averted with difficulty. This problem of incompatibility is prevalent between the formal and informal system, as well as between different customary systems operating in a shared geographic space, a process only intensified by contemporary globalization and associated factors, such as transport and communications, which lower the barriers to both intra- and intergroup interaction.

Engaging with a multiplicity of systems operating in a particular context is extremely difficult, given the ever-changing nature of such systems and their complexity. The central difficulty for both state- and local-level systems is dealing with their potential or actual incompatibilities. Working with local institutions to create change has proved to be a more viable way of establishing and supporting the constituencies needed to make reforms sustainable. Furthermore, without engaging with these constituencies, local-level customary institutions continue to undermine the effectiveness of state-level reforms.

The Justice for the Poor programs in Cambodia and Indonesia provide an alternative model for studying informal dispute resolution at the community level, as well as a fruitful strategy for assessing interactions between customary and state legal systems.[23] In Indonesia, the initial research project was set up in 41 villages across four districts, within two very distinct provinces in Indonesia (East Java and East Nusa Tenggara), as a means to understand the trajectories followed by local-level conflict. Part of the objective was to evaluate the evolution of conflict by tracking it from beginning to end. The approach mixes qualitative with quantitative methods, combining hundreds of interviews of village leaders and stakeholders with key informant surveys, newspaper databases, and national surveys to inform a rigorous sampling framework.

The idea was to discern information on and perceptions of conflict at multiple units of analysis. Local village characteristics,[24] obtained mostly from surveys, were included in the analysis. The methods applied were also designed purposely to address a complementary concern: whether existing development efforts (through the Kecamatan Development Project) had affected the management of conflicts. The approach, in two environments with very different socioeconomic characteristics, allowed for comparison of the trajectories taken in dealing with conflict. Perhaps the study's most significant contribution derives from the possibility of replication. Conflict associated with economic and political transitions is a global phenomenon, and studies like this one help dissect its dynamics, provide operational value, and set the groundwork for future complementary research that can guide legal reform efforts on the basis of context-specific knowledge.

One consequence of this research on local conflict trajectories and companion operational work on "justice for the poor" in Indonesia has been the design of a new project, Support to Poor and Disadvantaged Areas (SPADA), for regions experiencing conflict. This project will include a specific component on access to justice (SPADA+). In SPADA+, judicial reform does not involve importing institutions from outside. Rather, it consists of using trained paralegal facilitators, with their extensive knowledge of local cultures and contexts, to help the poor (and other marginalized groups) to navigate their way more effectively and equitably between *adat* ("customary") law, religious law, and state law. Moreover, experience from Indonesia is being used to inform a spate of initiatives in a number of countries in East Asia and Africa, as part of a broader Justice for the Poor research and development program. A similar initiative has been under way in Cambodia for more than two years. Primary research on collective disputes between villagers and the state about land and labor is being used to inform the design of new social development projects. With support from the Australian government, similar operational research is being considered for other countries in the Pacific. Related operational research is being undertaken in Kenya and Sierra Leone. The overarching objective of this research will be to assess how prevailing customary legal systems interact with the state, how the poor navigate through these systems, and how development projects could facilitate more equitable processes and outcomes for the poor and marginalized.

Conclusions

The central call of this chapter is for a reexamination of the theoretical assumptions underpinning issues at the intersection of social development, policy, and judicial reform. The largely unhappy policy record of attempts to "build the rule of law" and undertake effective judicial reform is a function of a flawed ontological understanding of what norms, rules, and laws "are" and how their inherent interdependence renders problematic any attempt to focus solely on enhancing "the law" (property rights, contracts) and its associated institutions (courts, law schools) as part of a development strategy, no matter how well intentioned. Moreover, inadequate theory and prior social research—rather than misguided intentions, a surfeit of "political will," or insufficient resources—have undermined the capacity of practitioners to implement legitimate and sustainable legal reforms in low-income countries. These inadequacies become manifest in three specific analytical domains: the missing law in policy, the missing rules in law, and the missing normative and cultural understandings in rules. Put more formally, discussions of "policy" routinely overlook the fact that these are instruments whose content and enforceability is largely grounded in law; discussions of law tend to focus exclusively on formal manifestations and codifications of rules, rather than on the much broader array of rules systems of which "the law" is a (small) part; and discussions of rules too often ignore the fact that they are social constructions—that is, cultural and normative understandings that establish and legitimize appropriate behavior.

Although serious criticism is important to make sense of past failures and create space for new approaches, one would be remiss to enter that space without a coherent, supportable, and implementable alternative. The alternative this chapter proposes is self-consciously (but confidently) grounded in a social theory of local-level transformations and the modernization of social relations, combined with an anthropological sensibility regarding the social construction of rules systems (both formal and informal). This approach has informed, is informing, and will continue to inform a new generation of in-depth mixed-method (qualitative and quantitative) empirical studies in Africa and East Asia. The goal is to generate a rigorous, context-specific evidence base to boost understanding of prevailing local rule and dispute resolution systems; the nature and extent of their articulation with the state; and the efficacy of local interventions designed to improve the coherence, accessibility, legitimacy, and accountability of both.

As the word itself implies, *development* is a deliberate attempt to initiate or facilitate modernization. Moreover, social relations and rules (formal and informal) underpin the basis of exchange in even the most advanced economies. Thus, attempts to "modernize" the legal systems of low-income countries must necessarily be undertaken as part of a broader strategy—that is, one that explicitly recognizes that the judiciary is only one (very) small part of the broader set of decision-making, priority-setting, and dispute resolution mechanisms in society. Put most starkly, judicial reform is bound to fail if it focuses only on the formal, codified aspects of those mechanisms, ignoring (by design or default) the broader system of rules that gives them legitimacy. Finally, "modernizing" rules systems is an uncertain and messy (even dangerous) business, not least because it entails shifting a prevailing equilibrium—one in which certain powerful groups have a vested interest or role that they are unlikely to relinquish without a struggle. As such, and because no development professional (from any disciplinary background) is formally trained to do any of this,[25] project designers and researchers alike should undertake such ventures iteratively, with their own feedback and accountability mechanisms, and, not least, with a circumspection borne of direct personal engagement with the political economy and cultural challenges at hand.

Notes

1. These include the Millennium Declaration (September 2000), the Monterrey Consensus (March 2002), and the World Summit on Sustainable Development (September 2002).
2. This topic is explored in some detail in *World Development Report 2006: Equity and Development* (World Bank 2005).

3. These characteristics of and requirements for good economic institutions are discussed in detail in *World Development Report 2006: Equity and Development* (World Bank 2005).

4. See, for example, the large literature inspired by Knack and Keefer (1995).

5. This system also arguably maintains competition within political institutions by establishing mechanisms for vetoes on power and sanctions for the misuse of power (see, for example, Haber 2003).

6. For a discussion of the law and development movement by those involved, see Gardner (1980), Merryman (1977), Trubek (2003), and Trubek and Galanter (1974).

7. World Bank (2003) provides a nice discussion of the different institutions that make up a rule-of-law system.

8. Further discussions about the "failure" of the law and development movement are provided in Burg (1975), Merryman (1977), and Trubek and Galanter (1974).

9. For a discussion of the problem of knowledge in rule-of-law programs, see Carothers (2004).

10. For a survey of literature on the interplay between formal and informal dispute resolution mechanisms, see Messick (1999).

11. For a discussion of institutional myth making in other public sector development contexts, see Pritchett and Woolcock (2004).

12. The U.K. constitution is unwritten, unlike the constitutions of many other common-law countries. Instead, this uncodified constitution is found in a variety of documents and constitutional conventions. The supremacy of Parliament and the rule of law are the two basic principles of the constitution.

13. See Centre for Housing Rights and Evictions (2004) for discussion of the arbitrary nature of magistrate's decision making in relation to customary law.

14. The concept of "meta-rules" comes from Barron, Smith, and Woolcock (2004).

15. It is important to note that a vast array of practices, systems, and traditions have been defined as informal, traditional, or customary law, all existing within vastly differing contexts. The term *informal* is used in contrast to formal state systems and is not meant to imply that such institutions are procedurally informal.

16. In Sierra Leone, for example, approximately 85 percent of the population falls under the jurisdiction of customary law, which is defined under chapter XII, article 170(3) of the constitution as "the rules of law which, by custom, are applicable to particular communities in Sierra Leone."

17. Under article 34 of the Ethiopian constitution, both parties must consent to have the case heard in a traditional forum. In practice, however, there are no formal links between the traditional and the formal system and no mechanisms to monitor the consent of parties.

18. On Indonesia, for example, see Bowen (2003).
19. For example, numerous studies have shown that when neither formal nor informal mechanisms are functioning, human rights abuses and serious conflict are more likely to occur.
20. See Pritchett and Woolcock (2004) for a more detailed discussion of this broader point beyond judicial reform initiatives.
21. This argument draws on Raghuram Rajan's (2004) critique of orthodox economic models.
22. Rajan (2004) provides a most useful discussion of this issue; see also Dixit (2004).
23. The information presented regarding the Indonesia case is based on Barron, Smith, and Woolcock (2004) and Barron, Diprose, and Woolcock (2007).
24. These factors included economic, psychological, social, political, institutional, cultural, and many other potentially influential characteristics specific to the village where the case takes place.
25. Development professionals have, at best, a driver's license, their training primarily preparing them to operate (or at most tinker with) an existing, well-functioning system rather than design one from scratch.

References

Altman, J. 2004. "Economic Development and Indigenous Australia: Contestations over Property, Institutions, and Ideology." *Australian Journal of Agricultural and Resource Economics* 18 (3): 513–34.

Barron, P., R. Diprose, and M. Woolcock. 2007. "Local Conflict and Community Development in Indonesia: Assessing the Impact of the Kecamatan Development Program." Indonesian Social Development Paper 10, World Bank, Jakarta. http://www.conflictanddevelopment.org/page.php?id=60.

Barron, P., C. Smith, and M. Woolcock. 2004. "Understanding Local Level Conflict in Developing Countries: Theory, Evidence, and Implications from Indonesia." Social Development Paper 19, Conflict Prevention and Reconstruction Unit, World Bank, Washington, DC.

Bennett, T. W. 1991. *A Sourcebook of African Customary Law for Southern Africa*. Cape Town, South Africa: Juta.

Bowen, J. 2003. *Islam, Law, and Equality in Indonesia: An Anthropology of Public Reasoning*. New York: Cambridge University Press.

Burg, E. M. 1975. "Law and Development: A Review of the Literature and a Critique of 'Scholars in Self- Estrangement.'" *American Journal of International Law* 25 (3): 492–530.

Buscaglia, E. 1997. *The Law and Economics of Development*. Greenwich: JAI Press.

Buscaglia, E. 2001. "Justice and the Poor, Formal vs. Informal Dispute Resolution Mechanisms: A Governance-Based Approach." Paper delivered at the World Bank Conference on Empowerment, Security and Opportunity through Law and Justice, St. Petersburg, FL, July 8–12.

Bush, R. 1979. "Access to Justice and Societal Pluralism." In *Access to Justice*, vol. 3, ed. M. Cappelletti and B. Garth. Milan, Italy: Guiffre Editore.

Carothers, T. 1999. *Aiding Democracy: The Learning Curve*. Washington, DC: Carnegie Endowment for International Peace.

———. 2004. "Promoting the Rule of Law Abroad: The Problem of Knowledge." In *Critical Mission: Essays on Democracy Promotion*. Washington, DC: Carnegie Endowment for International Peace.

Centre for Housing Rights and Evictions. 2004. *Bringing Equality Home: Promoting and Protecting the Inheritance Rights of Women*. Geneva: Centre for Housing Rights and Evictions.

Chopra, J., and T. Hohe. 2004. "Participatory Intervention." *Global Governance* 10 (3): 289–305.

Decker, K., C. Sage, and M. Stefanova. 2005. "Law or Justice: Building Equitable Legal Institutions." Background Paper for *World Development Report 2006: Equity and Development*. Washington, DC: World Bank. http://siteresources. worldbank.org/INTWDR2006/Resources/477383-1118673432908/Law_or_ Justice_Building_Equitable_Legal_Institutions.pdf.

Dixit, A. 2004. *Lawlessness and Economics: Alternative Modes of Governance*. Princeton, NJ: Princeton University Press.

Ellickson, R. 1991. *Order without Law: How Neighbors Settle Disputes*. Cambridge, MA: Harvard University Press.

Faundez, J. 1997. *Good Governance and Law: Legal and Institutional Reform in Developing Countries*. New York: St. Martin's Press.

Gardner, J. 1980. *Legal Imperialism: American Lawyers and Foreign Aid in Latin America*. Madison: University of Wisconsin Press.

Garth, B. 2001. "What Makes a Successful Legal and Judicial Reform System? Rethinking the Processes and the Criteria for Success." Paper presented at the World Bank Conference on Comprehensive Legal and Judicial Development: Towards an Agenda for a Just and Equitable Society in the 21st Century, Washington, DC, June 5–7.

Golub, S. 2003. "Beyond the Rule of Law Orthodoxy: The Legal Empowerment Alternative." Rule of Law Working Paper 41, Carnegie Endowment for International Peace, Washington, DC.

Gupta, P., R. Kleinfeld, and G. Salinas. 2002. *Legal and Judicial Reform in Europe and Central Asia*. Washington, DC: World Bank, Operations Evaluation Department.

Haber, S. 2003. "Political Institutions and Banking Systems: Lessons from the Economic Histories of Mexico and the United States, 1790–1914." Working

Paper 123, Center for Research on Economic Development and Reform, Stanford University, Stanford, CA.

Halloran, M. 2004. "Cultural Maintenance and Trauma in Indigenous Australia." Paper presented at the 23rd Annual Australia and New Zealand Law and History Society Conference, Murdoch University, Perth, Australia, July 2–4.

Hammergren, L. 1998. *The Politics of Justice and Justice Reform in Latin America: The Peruvian Case in Comparative Perspective*. Boulder, CO: Westview Press.

Knack, S., and P. Keefer. 1995. "Institutions and Economic Performance: Cross-Country Tests Using Alternative Institutional Measures." *Economics and Politics* 7 (3): 207–27.

Lawyers Committee for Human Rights. 1996. *Halfway to Reform: The World Bank and the Venezuelan Justice System*. New York: Lawyers Committee for Human Rights.

Mamdani, M. 1996. *Citizen and Subject: Contemporary Africa and the Legacy of Late Colonialism*. Princeton, NJ: Princeton University Press.

Matsuo, H. 2004. "The Rule of Law and Economic Development: A Cause or a Result?" Keio Law School, Tokyo.

Merryman, J. H. 1977. "Comparative Law and Social Change: On the Origins, Style, Decline, and Revival of the Law and Development Movement." *American Journal of Comparative Law* 25 (3): 457–91.

Messick, R. 1999. "Judicial Reform and Economic Development: A Review of the Issues." *World Bank Research Observer* 14 (1): 117–36.

Pistor, K. 1999. "The Evolution of Legal Institutions and Economic Regime Change." Paper Presented at the Annual World Bank Conference on Development Economics: Governance, Equity, and Global Markets, Paris, June 21–23.

Pistor, K., and P. Wellons. 1999. *The Role of Law and Legal Institutions in Asian Economic Development*. New York: Oxford University Press.

Posner, E. 2002. *Law and Social Norms*. Cambridge, MA: Harvard University Press.

Pritchett, L., and M. Woolcock. 2004. "Solutions When the Solution Is the Problem: Arraying the Disarray in Development." *World Development* 32 (2): 191–212.

Rajan, R. 2004. "Assume Anarchy? Why an Orthodox Economic Model Might Not Be the Best Guide for Policy." *Finance and Development* 41 (3): 56–57.

Rose, C. V. 1998. "The 'New' Law and Development Movement in the Post–Cold War Era: A Vietnam Case Study." *Law and Society Review* 32 (1): 93–140.

Tamanaha, B. 2004. *On the Rule of Law: History, Politics, Theory*. Cambridge, U.K.: Cambridge University Press.

Trubek, D. 2003. "The 'Rule of Law' in Development Assistance: Past, Present, and Future." Paper given at Conference on Law and Economic Development: Critiques and Beyond. Harvard Law School, Cambridge, MA, April 12–13.

Trubek, D., and M. Galanter. 1974. "Scholars in Self-Estrangement: Some Reflections on the Crisis in Law and Development Studies in the United States." *Wisconsin Law Review* 4: 1062–1101.

Upham, F. 2002. "Myth Making in the Rule of Law Orthodoxy." Rule of Law Working Paper 30, Carnegie Endowment for International Peace, Washington, DC.

World Bank. 2003. *Legal and Judicial Reform: Strategic Directions*. Washington, DC: Legal Vice Presidency, World Bank.

———. 2005. *World Development Report 2006: Equity and Development*. New York: Oxford University Press.

Boxes, figures, notes, and tables are indicated by b, f, n, and t.